TROUBLE
IN THE
TRIBE

TROUBLE
IN THE
TRIBE

THE
AMERICAN JEWISH
CONFLICT
OVER ISRAEL

DOV WAXMAN

PRINCETON UNIVERSITY PRESS
PRINCETON AND OXFORD

Library of Congress Cataloging-in-Publication Data

Names: Waxman, Dov, author.

Title: Trouble in the tribe : the American Jewish conflict over Israel /
Dov Waxman.
Description: Princeton, New Jersey : Princeton University Press,
[2016] | ?2016 | Includes bibliographical references and index.
Identifiers: LCCN 2015038764 | ISBN 9780691168999 (hardback)
Subjects: LCSH: Israel and the diaspora. | Jews—United States—
Attitudes toward Israel.
Classification: LCC DS132 .W39 2016 | DDC
303.48/256940089924073—dc23 LC record available at
http://lccn.loc.gov/2015038764

British Library Cataloging-in-Publication Data is available

This book has been composed in Adobe Caslon Pro
and Trade Gothic LT Std

Printed on acid-free paper. ∞

Printed in the United States of America

1 3 5 7 9 10 8 6 4 2

CONTENTS

PREFACE AND ACKNOWLEDGMENTS

I first started thinking about writing this book in the summer of 2009 while I was doing research in Israel for a book about the Palestinian minority in Israel and Jewish-Arab relations in the country (*Israel's Palestinians: The Conflict Within*, co-authored with Ilan Peleg). President Barack Obama had just begun his first term in office, promising a vigorous new effort at making peace between Israel and the Palestinians, and J Street, a new liberal American Jewish advocacy group, had recently been established to help him do just that. Hope and change, as the slogan went, was in the air in the United States, but thousands of miles away in Israel there seemed to be little change and no hope. Benjamin Netanyahu had become prime minister in February 2009, for the second time, and he headed an unwieldy national unity government that seemed unlikely to significantly change Israel's policies toward the Palestinians, let alone end the conflict with them. The bloody and bitter stalemate between Israelis and Palestinians looked set to continue for more years to come. Many of my Israeli friends, most of them liberals, felt utterly despondent by the situation, but some were buoyed by President Obama's election and J Street's founding and hoped that somehow the United States, and American Jews in particular, would come to the rescue, and save Israel from itself. Was this possible, they asked me? Would Obama pressure the Netanyahu government to make peace? Would American Jews support him in doing so? Had they grown tired of uncritically backing Israel? I could not answer their questions, but I suspected that President Obama and American Jewry would not be the deus ex machina that my Israeli friends wished for (a suspicion that turned out to be correct). Nevertheless, I was intrigued by the possibility that American

Jews, steadfast supporters of Israel for so long, might be changing their attitude toward Israel and its conflict with the Palestinians, and that this might help to finally break the Israeli-Palestinian deadlock. It was with this possibility in mind that I began my research on American Jewry's relationship with Israel.

Learning about American Jewish politics and the organized American Jewish community was also a way for me to learn more about a community in which I was both an insider and an outsider, as a British Jew who had become a naturalized American citizen. Having spent almost half my life living in the United States, I've become an American Jew, but I retain somewhat of an outsider's perspective. I believe that this vantage point has allowed me to observe and understand the American Jewish community's relationship with Israel in ways that Jews who are born into it seldom can—in particular, it gives me the ability to stand back from the acrimonious communal conflict over Israel and not take sides in it, as many American Jewish writers on this subject tend to do. To be sure, I do not, and cannot, claim impartiality. I am not simply an outside observer of the current conflict over Israel among American Jews. I am, sometimes voluntarily and sometimes not, a participant in it. In writing this book, I have tried to be as objective as possible in my research and analysis and avoid being one-sided, but my own politics surely come through at times. I do not expect everyone who reads this book to fully agree with me, but I do hope that everyone, whatever their politics, will at least learn something important and valuable about the American Jewish community today and its changing and contentious relationship with Israel.

In many ways, the American Jewish relationship with Israel—complicated, and often conflicted—mirrors my own personal relationship with Israel. Just as the American Jewish relationship with Israel has evolved over the years, so too has my own relationship with Israel, from one of uncritical support to a more critical engagement with the country. This shift has not always been easy or comfortable for me, nor has it been for many American Jews whose attitude to Israel has undergone a similar change. In trying to better understand what is driving this change and what its consequences are, writing this book has in this respect been deeply personal for me. There is, I believe, an autobiographical element in many books, and this one is no exception.

I have been working on this book for more than four years, during which time I have attended and observed numerous conferences and meetings held by American Jewish organizations, and interviewed dozens of American Jewish communal leaders, activists, journalists, and scholars. I am grateful to the following individuals for generously giving me their time and sharing their insights and observations: Eric Alterman, Yonatan Ariel, Sharon Ashley, Steven Bayme, Peter Beinart, Jeremy Ben-Ami, Kenneth Bob, Steven M. Cohen, Lisa Colton, Stosh Cotler, David Dabscheck, Ethan Felson, Dan Fleshler, Rabbi Steve Gutow, David Harris, Malcolm Hoenlein, Rabbi Jill Jacobs, Kenneth Jacobson, Deborah Kaufman, Nancy Kaufman, Shawn Landres, Rachel Lerner, Peter Medding, Ruth Messinger, Martin Raffel, Rabbi Ed Rettig, Mark Rosenblum, John Ruskay, Nigel Savage, Yona Shem-Tov, Gideon Shimoni, Barry Shrage, Alan Snitow, Rebecca Vilkomerson, Chaim Waxman, Rabbi Melissa Weintraub, Rabbi Ari Weiss, and Rabbi Alissa Wise. I would also like to express my gratitude to Jonathan Rynhold, Brent Sasley, and Sarah-Anne Minkin for providing me with helpful feedback on parts of this manuscript, and a special thanks to Lori Lefkovitz, Kenneth Wald, and Theodore Sasson, who kindly provided detailed comments on the whole manuscript. I would also like to thank Mairav Zonszein and Ari Young for their excellent research assistance, Philip Turner for his careful editing of the manuscript, and Gili Getz for freely providing the outstanding photographs in this book. I am very grateful to my agent, Don Fehr of Trident Media Group, and to Eric Crahan, my editor at Princeton University Press, for their encouragement and guidance, and to Leslie Grundfest, my production editor at Princeton, and Jennifer Harris, my copy editor, for their meticulous work preparing the manuscript for publication. Finally, I would like to acknowledge the research institutes and universities that have hosted me and financially supported the research for this book: St. John's College, University of Oxford; the Oxford Center for Hebrew and

Jewish Studies at the University of Oxford; the Avraham Harman Institute for Contemporary Jewry at the Hebrew University, Baruch College of the City University of New York; the Professional Staff Congress of the City University of New York; and, my home institution, Northeastern University. Since moving there in 2014, its faculty, staff, and students have made me feel very much at home.

TROUBLE
IN THE
TRIBE

INTRODUCTION

On January 3, 2011, within hours of his government's latest announcement that, despite American and Palestinian objections, it would move ahead with the construction of more Jewish housing in East Jerusalem, Israeli Prime Minister Benjamin Netanyahu gave a stirring speech at the Jewish Federations of North America's General Assembly in New Orleans.[1] Speaking to a cavernous room filled with Jewish communal leaders, professionals, and grassroots activists—the core membership of the organized American Jewish community—Netanyahu solemnly warned of the many dangers facing the Jewish state. One of these dangers, he claimed, was "the assault on Israel's legitimacy." Linking this to previous threats against the Jewish people, Netanyahu declared in his American-accented English: "We know from our history that attacks on the Jews were often preceded by attempts to delegitimize the Jewish people; to paint them as vile criminals, as the scourge of humanity. And this is why the attempts by our enemies, and their misguided fellow travelers, to delegitimize the Jewish state must be countered."[2]

While his adoring audience clapped in approval, a young woman suddenly stood up and shouted amid the din of applause: "Young Jews say the Loyalty Oath delegitimizes Israel! The Loyalty Oath delegitimizes Israel!" She continued shouting this as police officers quickly surrounded her, grabbed her, and dragged her out of the room, while the crowd started hissing and booing. Unruffled, Netanyahu told the crowd, "I'm going to talk about delegitimizing Israel, but they really have the wrong address." His off-the-cuff remark was greeted with loud cheers and a standing ovation.

1

"For too many, Israel is guilty until proven guilty," Netanyahu continued, "and the greatest success of our detractors is when Jews start believing that themselves. We are seeing that today." As the audience enthusiastically applauded again, a young man got up on a chair and repeatedly yelled out: "The Occupation delegitimizes Israel!" He was quickly pulled down from the chair and bundled away by police officers as the crowd became irritated and people shouted obscenities at him.

Netanyahu resumed his speech, until a few minutes later he was interrupted yet again by another heckler, a young woman shouting, "The settlements delegitimize Israel!" By now, the audience was really irate, and they immediately began to drown out her protest with loud, angry jeers. Before the police could get to her to usher her away, she was physically assaulted by some of the people around her. "I was instantly attacked from all sides," the young woman later recounted. "A man in the row in front of me pulled the El Al seat cover off his chair and tried to gag me with it. Another man came up from the side and grabbed me by the throat. I fell into a pile of chairs until two female sheriffs buoyed me up and hustled me out of the room. The police later confided that they were trying to protect me from the angry mob and get me out of there in one piece."[3]

This protest by some young American Jews, who were members of a left-wing group called Jewish Voice for Peace (JVP), and the angry, aggressive reaction of other American Jews to it, is not a one-off, isolated incident. It is just the most dramatic manifestation of a wider conflict over Israel that is now raging within the American Jewish community.[4] It is a conflict that has become increasingly bitter and polarizing. It is also very public, much to the consternation of American Jewish communal leaders who have long sought to keep intra-Jewish conflicts behind closed doors. In its intensity and visibility, it is a conflict unlike any other the American Jewish community has ever had. And it is a conflict with profound consequences not only for American Jews, but also potentially for Israel and the United States. It threatens to divide the American Jewish community, weaken American Jewish political support for Israel, and impact U.S. government policy toward Israel and the Israeli-Palestinian conflict. For all these reasons, the current American Jewish conflict over Israel matters not only to American Jews, but also to Americans in general, Israelis, Palestinians, and indeed anyone concerned about the future of Israel and the Israeli-Palestinian conflict.

This book offers an in-depth look at the internecine battle over Israel among American Jews, a battle that is growing ever more intense as Israel faces mounting international condemnation, its domestic politics shifts further to the right, the Israeli-Palestinian peace process remains in deep freeze, and the two-state solution appears increasingly remote, if not altogether unlikely. The book's central thesis is that a historic change has been taking place in the American Jewish relationship with Israel. The age of unquestioning and unstinting support for Israel is over. The pro-Israel consensus that once united American Jews is eroding, and Israel is fast becoming a source of division rather than unity for American Jewry. As the consensus concerning Israel within the American Jewish community is slowly coming apart, a new era of American Jewish conflict over Israel is replacing the old era of solidarity. In short, Israel used to bring American Jews together. Now it is driving them apart.

In this book, I examine the causes and consequences of the American Jewish conflict over Israel. I explore the sources of this conflict, emphasizing that it is driven not only by changes in Israel and in the Israeli-Palestinian conflict (as media reports often suggest), but also by changes within the American Jewish community itself. In doing so, I highlight the deeper, structural reasons for the growing tension among American Jews over Israel, and between American Jews and Israel. I also explore the impact that the growing conflict over Israel is having on local Jewish communities, on the pro-Israel lobby in Washington, DC, and on the American Jewish communal establishment.

For decades, especially after the Six-Day War in 1967, the American Jewish relationship with Israel was largely characterized by unwavering support for Israel by most American Jews. Supporting Israel was an important part of American Jewish life and a central element in the "civil religion" of American Jewry. It was also a central component in American Jewish identity, especially among secular Jews for whom supporting Israel effectively became a kind of substitute religion and a new way of being Jewish. Although relatively few American Jews chose to live in Israel, many saw the Jewish state as a potential place of refuge, and a powerful symbol of Jewish rebirth after the Holocaust.

The mythic Israel that many American Jews idealized was a source of pride and unity. At a time when the religious and cultural ties that once united them were steadily diminishing, support for Israel became the glue that held the American Jewish community together.[5] Although there were always small pockets of critics, for the most part there was an overwhelming consensus within the American Jewish community in support of Israel. As two experts on the American Jewish community wrote in 1990: "Support for Israel dominates [American Jewish] public life, is part and parcel of the American Jewish consensus on what it means to be a Jew, and is voiced by a large majority of American Jews."[6] This support for Israel was expressed politically through advocacy for Israel, and financially through charitable donations to Israel. Politically, American Jews became vocal and highly effective proponents for U.S. economic, military, and diplomatic support for Israel. The pro-Israel lobby in Washington, DC, especially the American Israel Public Affairs Committee (AIPAC), emerged as an influential actor in U.S.-Israeli relations. Financially, as annual campaigns to raise money for Israel and fundraising dinners for Israeli causes became staples of American Jewish life, American Jews donated huge sums of money to Israel and played a crucial role in the country's economic development.

However, the era of uncritical American Jewish support for Israel —of "Israel, right or wrong"—is now long past. For the past two decades, a fundamental shift has occurred in the American Jewish relationship with Israel, as growing numbers of American Jews have become less willing to unquestioningly support Israel and more willing to publicly criticize its governments. Today, amid a widespread sense of disillusionment with Israel, many American Jews have a more critical and contentious relationship with the country. Although the vast majority of them still care about Israel, there is now much more ambivalence toward it and much less agreement about its policies. Many American Jews, especially younger ones, are becoming increasingly uncomfortable with Israel's policies in its conflict with the Palestinians and skeptical of its governments' proclaimed desire for peace. As the political consensus about Israel within the American Jewish community has steadily eroded, divisions over Israel are growing among American Jews, and discussions about Israel have become increasingly antagonistic. American Jewish discourse about Israel now regularly degenerates into vitriol, hostile accusations, and ad hominem attacks. Indeed, the subject of Israel has become so highly charged and controversial among American Jews that some now completely avoid talking about it lest the discussion degenerate into an angry argument, as it often will.

While there have always been some disagreements about Israel among American Jews—and well before the state was even established there were intense debates about Zionism among American Jews—these disagreements have become more frequent, more ferocious, and more open than ever before. Whereas American Jews once generally presented a united front in public in support of Israel, there is now much more public criticism of Israeli government policies and actions, especially with regard to the Palestinians. More than ever before, American Jews are publicly arguing about Israeli policies and what it means to be pro-Israel—whether one can be a supporter of Israel and publicly criticize its governments. Growing numbers of American Jews who are critical of Israeli government policies are now speaking up and mobilizing politically.

The changing attitude toward Israel among American Jews is leading to significant changes in American Jewish politics. Major American Jewish organizations—the so-called Jewish establishment—are now accused of trying to stifle the growing debate about Israel among Jews and attacked for being unrepresentative and out of touch. The pro-Israel lobby—long regarded by admirers and critics alike as a model of an effective political pressure group—is splintering as new advocacy groups (such as J Street) have emerged to challenge AIPAC's influence. American Jewish philanthropy toward Israel is also changing as more money goes to support specific political causes and agendas in Israel (such as Israeli human rights organizations or settlement groups).

These developments have far-reaching repercussions. To dismiss the American Jewish conflict over Israel as merely an intra-Jewish

5

affair is to ignore the importance of the American Jewish community, both domestically within the United States, and internationally, especially for Israel. Put simply, American Jewish politics directly affects American politics in general, particularly when it comes to Israel. For Israel itself, American Jewish politics is of even greater significance. Indeed, it is perhaps no exaggeration to say that Israel's very future depends in part on whether, and how, American Jews support it.

In a classic text on the American Jewish community first published in 1976, the late Daniel Elazar described American Jews as "the world's most powerful Jewry in the world's most powerful nation."[7] This remains true today, although the United States may not be quite as powerful as it was back then. Numbering roughly six to seven million,[8] American Jews constitute about 40 percent of world Jewry and almost 70 percent of Diaspora Jewry.[9] While they are just 2 percent of the U.S. population and about 4 percent of the voting population, American Jews undoubtedly exercise a disproportionate influence in American politics—a fact that is both widely admired and resented. Although it is often overstated, sometimes ludicrously and sometimes maliciously, American Jewish political power cannot be denied.[10] The so-called Jewish vote is prized in presidential elections because of the concentration of Jews in states with a lot of electoral college votes (California, Florida, New York, and Pennsylvania), and particularly in key battleground states (such as Florida and Pennsylvania). Jews are also disproportionately represented among major campaign donors and fundraisers for politicians and for both political parties.[11] American Jews are also very well represented in the U.S. government and in think tanks, journalism, and academia.

As a result of this access and influence (the extent of which is perhaps unprecedented in Jewish history), "Jewish issues have become interwoven into America's routine political agenda. Jewish concerns have become Americanized. They are adopted, promoted, shaped and responded to by leading American political figures, including the president, cabinet members, key administration officials and congressional leaders, and not just by Jews."[12] Of all the Jewish issues and concerns on the American political agenda, none has received nearly as much attention as Israel has. Although it is by no means the only issue that American Jews care about, for decades American Jewish political power has been directed largely on behalf of Israel. Consequently, support for Israel has become part and parcel of American domestic politics—so much so, in fact, that both political parties routinely compete over which one is more pro-Israel, and politicians proudly tout their support for Israel whenever they can.

Nor is it only American politicians and policymakers who pay attention to the American Jewish community. Governments across the world do too, as the journalist J. J. Goldberg writes in his book *Jewish Power: Inside the American Jewish Establishment*: "From the Vatican to the Kremlin, from the White House to Capitol Hill, the world's movers and shakers view American Jewry as a force to be reckoned with."[13] The belief in many capitals around the world (perhaps fueled by latent or overt anti-Semitism or even philo-Semitism) that American Jews exercise a powerful sway over the American government has led some foreign governments to court the American Jewish community, sometimes by adopting foreign policies supportive of Israel, or merely by establishing diplomatic relations with Israel.[14] American Jewish leaders travel the world like ambassadors, often meeting with foreign presidents and prime ministers, and foreign diplomats in the United States regularly consult with American Jewish groups.

No foreign government pays such close attention to the American Jewish community as the Israeli government—which is not to say that they listen carefully to, let alone heed, American Jewish concerns and wishes. Although American Jews often complain of being ignored by Israeli governments, in reality Israeli officials, especially diplomats, give a lot of attention to the American Jewish community, certainly vastly more attention than they give to any other Diaspora Jewish community. The reason for this is simple—American Jewry is a "strategic asset" for Israel.[15] Whether they like it or not, Israeli policymakers recognize that Israel depends upon American Jewish support. While Israel is probably less dependent upon this support today than it once was when its economy was much smaller and more reliant upon American Jewish largesse, the American Jewish community is still a crucial, perhaps indispensable, source of economic, political, and psychological support to Israel.

Since Israel's establishment in 1948, and even before then, American Jews have made an incalculable contribution to the country's development, if not its very survival. Indeed, one scholar writes that "no citizens of one country have ever been so committed to the success of another as American Jews have been to Israel."[16] Over the years, they have donated vast sums of money to Israeli governments,[17] and to a multitude of Israeli charities, hospitals, universities, schools, and other Israeli institutions. Although American Jews give to a host of causes, to this day more money from American Jewish donors goes to Israel than to any other cause.[18] Indeed, it is estimated that American Jews give more than a billion dollars every year to organizations and charities in Israel.[19] For many years, American Jews have also channeled large sums of money to their own elected officials in order to encourage them to support Israel, and they have energetically lobbied American policymakers on Israel's behalf. In the public arena, American Jews have vigorously defended and justified Israel's policies and actions to the American public at large. They have also done this in the international community, as major American Jewish organizations frequently act as unofficial emissaries and interlocutors for Israel to foreign governments and groups.

Arguably no less important for Israel is the psychological reassurance that American Jewish support provides. The belief among Israeli Jews that American Jews are backing them, thereby helping to ensure the support of the most powerful country in the world, is a source of great comfort and assurance. The Israeli-Jewish sense of isolation in the world is eased, but not alleviated entirely, by the feeling that American Jews are deeply committed to their security and well-being. If, as David Ben-Gurion, Israel's founder and first prime minister once said, "Israel's only absolutely reliable ally is world Jewry," then American Jewry—by far, the largest, richest, and most powerful Diaspora Jewish community in the world—is surely Israel's most important ally.[20] Indeed, Ben-Gurion himself once described American Jewry as "a link and a bridge between Israel and America."[21] As such, Israel cannot afford to ignore the views of American Jews, even if Israeli leaders might wish they could. Israelis themselves are well aware of this. In a 2013 survey, for example, two-thirds of them said that the American Jewish community had a positive influence on Israel's national security, and two-thirds also thought that the Israeli government should take into account the views of American Jews about the peace process with the Palestinians.[22]

There is also another reason why Israeli policymakers must pay attention to American Jews—they are increasingly involved in Israeli domestic politics. No longer content to simply support Israel from afar, American Jews now directly lobby Israeli governments, fund the primary election campaigns of Israeli politicians, and give money to Israeli pressure groups. American Jews are no longer just passive outside spectators to Israeli politics; they have become active participants in it.[23]

In addition to their involvement in Israeli politics, American Jews are also participants in the Israeli-Palestinian conflict. Some have volunteered to join the Israeli army and have fought in the conflict, some have moved to Jewish settlements in the West Bank,[24] and many more have lobbied their senators and representatives to vote in favor of American arms sales and military aid to Israel. The formidable pro-Israel lobby that American Jews have established has undoubtedly helped secure vital U.S. government support for Israel in its long-running conflict with the Palestinians and Arab states.

American Jews have also been heavily involved in efforts to make peace between Israel and the Palestinians, both actively supporting and opposing these efforts. During the Oslo peace process, for instance, American Jewish groups lined up for and against it. Some pushed for U.S. aid to the fledgling Palestinian Authority; others tried to block it. In the mid-1990s, American Jewish opponents of the Oslo Accords even financed a campaign in Israel against them.[25] And for many years, right-wing American Jews have funneled hundreds of millions of dollars to Jewish settlements in the West Bank and East Jerusalem (and benefited from U.S. tax breaks in the process).[26] Indeed, Israel's controversial settlement enterprise—one of the biggest obstacles in the way of an Israeli-Palestinian peace agreement—has been partially subsidized (as well as populated) by American Jews. But it is not only right-wing American Jews who are players in the Israeli-Palestinian conflict, so too are left-wing and liberal American Jews. They have persistently prodded U.S. administrations to get involved and stay involved in making peace between Israel and the Palestinians, and they have enthusiastically supported diplomatic initiatives by American presidents, such as those by Clinton, George W. Bush, and Obama. In fact, some prominent American Jews, both inside and outside the U.S. government, have been closely involved in these peace initiatives.

American Jewish politics, therefore, has an impact well beyond the American Jewish community. But, despite its wide significance, it remains remarkably poorly understood. In particular, when it comes to the much discussed issue of Israel and its conflict with the Palestinians, there is still a common tendency to regard almost all American Jews simply as steadfast supporters of Israel, and to ignore their internal political divisions and debates. All too often, American Jews are depicted in newspaper articles and popular books as a monolithic lobby or voting bloc passionately committed to promoting Israel's cause. While this is certainly true of some American Jews, for others Israel may be a distant concern, or an object of sharp criticism. The consensus about Israel that prevailed within the American Jewish community in the 1960s and 1970s has long since disappeared. Instead, there is now a rancorous and divisive debate pitting left against right, critics against defenders of Israeli government policies, Jews against Jews.

At the center of this debate are burning questions about Israel's future as a Jewish state, and about whether and how it can make peace with the Palestinians and become secure in a region now racked with violent turmoil and upheaval. But underlying this debate is an even deeper, more fundamental set of questions: What kind of relationship should American Jews have with Israel? Must they support it? Should American Jews support Israel unconditionally, even when it acts in ways that they believe are self-defeating or morally problematic? What kinds of opinions and attitudes toward Israel are acceptable, and what should be permitted within the American Jewish community? Can Jews publicly criticize Israel? Can they support boycotts against Israel? Can they even oppose the existence of the Jewish state itself? In short, what loyalty, if any, do Jews owe the Jewish state?

It is not only American Jews who have been publicly wrestling with these difficult questions in recent years. So too, have Jews elsewhere, particularly in other liberal democracies in Western Europe, Canada, and Australia. While Jews in these places tend to be even more attached to Israel (unlike most American Jews, the vast majority of British, French, Canadian, and Australian Jews, for instance, have visited Israel at least once), there has also been growing Jewish criticism of Israeli policies and an increasing number of Jewish groups publicly opposing many of these policies.[27] Within the Jewish communities in all of these countries, Israel is becoming a major source of tension and controversy (linked in some cases to rising concerns over a resurgent anti-Semitism).[28] All across the Jewish world, Jews are increasingly divided in their attitudes to Israel as the once automatic support for Israel is declining. What is happening within the American Jewish community, therefore, is not entirely unique, although I believe its consequences are more far-reaching.

Nor is the contemporary debate about Israel among American Jews entirely without precedent. Although it has some significant novel features, it echoes earlier debates about Zionism that occurred before 1948. Then, as now, there were fierce disagreements among American Jews, and the American Jewish establishment was frequently criticized, especially by younger generations. It was only after Israel's founding that the communal consensus in support of Israel emerged, and it was only after 1967 that this consensus came to dominate American Jewish politics. Thus, from a historical perspective, the pro-Israel consensus that once reigned within the American Jewish community is the aberration, rather than the rule. Jewish debate and division on Israel is historically the norm.

It is also not at all surprising that Israel and its policies have become a topic of such vituperative debate among American Jews, as well as Diaspora Jews in general. After all, the existence of a Jewish state compels Jews everywhere to confront the question of what Israel means to them and what responsibility, if any, they have toward it. Since Israel claims to speak and act in their name, not only on behalf of its own citizens, it is almost impossible for Diaspora Jews to ignore Israel, even if they wanted to. Very few can remain apathetic about what is happening there, and they are almost obligated to have an opinion about Israel and the Israeli-Palestinian conflict, especially now that it has become such a big, almost obsessive, issue for Western public opinion. For better or worse, many Diaspora Jews often feel somehow implicated in Israel's actions. What Israel does, what happens to Israel, and what happens in Israel, therefore, affects Jews worldwide. That is why the subject of Israel is at the center of Jewish political debate. Indeed, it has become the new "Jewish question." Whereas the old Jewish question that dominated Jewish politics in the nineteenth century fundamentally revolved around the issue of Jewish statelessness, the new Jewish question that has dominated Jewish politics in the twentieth and twenty-first century revolves around the issue of Jewish statehood. For the first time in two thousand years, Jews have a state of their own. This inevitably raises tough questions and poses new challenges for a people unaccustomed to statehood. And since this state has also been locked in a protracted violent conflict, the questions and challenges it presents to Jews are even more difficult and unavoidable.

In the chapters that follow, I show how American Jewish attitudes and behavior toward Israel have changed over time, and I explore some of the major consequences of these changes. Chapter 1 gives a broad overview of the evolving American Jewish relationship with Israel and the factors that shape this relationship. I begin by challenging the idea that Jewish support for Israel is natural and inevitable, and explain what really motivates this support, identifying what I term the "five pillars of pro-Israelism." I then provide some historical perspective, charting a gradual shift that has taken place in attitudes toward Israel among American Jews—from initial indifference and even hostility to Zionism in the pre–World War II period, to acceptance of Zionism and lukewarm support for Israel after the Holocaust and the founding of the State of Israel, to passionate devotion after the 1967 war, to today's growing disillusionment and ambivalence as American Jews have a less idealized image of Israel and become more aware of its problems and flaws. I argue that while most American Jews remain strongly attached to Israel, what is changing is the way in which this attachment is expressed—American Jews are becoming more critical of Israeli government policies and more willing to express this criticism.

Chapter 2 focuses on the shift that is currently occurring in the American Jewish relationship with Israel from unconditional support to critical engagement. I argue that the traditional norm against Jews publicly criticizing Israel has gradually eroded, and that it is now becoming increasingly acceptable, if still controversial, for Jews to openly question, debate, and challenge Israeli government policies and practices. While some American Jews welcome this development, others vociferously oppose it and even try to suppress it. In the chapter, I discuss the growth of Jewish dissent about Israel and the underlying reasons for it. I then describe the right-wing backlash against dissent and the growing debate among American Jews about the legitimacy of dissent. Finally, I look at how various dissident Jewish groups from the 1970s to the present day have been treated by the organized American Jewish community in order to answer the question of whether it is becoming more open and tolerant toward dissent about Israel. I contend that, contrary to the common claim that the American Jewish community is intolerant of dissent and tries to silence all criticism of Israel, there is, in fact, increasing acceptance of the legitimacy of public criticism of Israel, although this acceptance goes only so far: there are still communal "red lines" and dissident Jewish groups still get blacklisted.

Chapter 3 surveys the fractious debate—more accurately, the argument—about Israel that is now raging within the American Jewish community. I begin by mapping out the different American Jewish camps in the debate over Israel, and particularly over the Israeli-Palestinian conflict—the heart of the debate. I then emphasize what is significantly different about the debate today from the way American Jews discussed and debated Israel in the past. In doing so, I explain why the American Jewish debate has become so acrimonious in recent years. The chapter ends by discussing the impact this vitriol is having upon many Jewish communities throughout the United States, describing how Israel has become a fraught topic of discussion in local Jewish communities, leading Jewish communal organizations to introduce "civility" initiatives in an effort to encourage more productive conversations about Israel. These initiatives are a clear acknowledgment that the growing conflict over Israel is threatening to tear Jewish communities apart.

Chapter 4 analyzes American Jewish public opinion on the Israeli-Palestinian conflict. Drawing upon numerous opinion polls conducted over the past three decades, I dissect the views of American Jews about the conflict and outline the major trends in American Jewish opinion, asking whether American Jews are becoming more "dovish" or "hawkish" in their views and whether they are becoming more polarized. I argue that the broad political consensus that once existed is slowly eroding, although it has not entirely disappeared. After summarizing the views of most American Jews—whom I characterize as "ambivalent centrists"—I discuss the impact that religiosity, general political orientation, and age have upon shaping American Jewish attitudes toward the Israeli-Palestinian conflict, underlining the fact that more secular, more liberal, and younger American Jews are much more likely to hold "dovish" views about the conflict than more religious, more conservative, and older Jews.

Chapter 5 examines the American Jewish pro-Israel lobby, widely considered to be one of the most effective lobbies in Washington, DC. After describing its historical development, focusing on the rise of AIPAC and the Conference of Presidents of Major American Jewish Organizations (the two preeminent groups in the pro-Israel lobby), I discuss the big changes that have taken place in pro-Israel advocacy in recent years, particularly the growth of left-wing and right-wing pro-Israel groups. This has resulted in the splintering of the pro-Israel lobby. It has also challenged the ability of centrist groups to speak authoritatively on behalf of American Jews. I argue that pro-Israel lobbying in the United States is becoming increasingly partisan and contentious as there is no longer a single, widely accepted meaning of the term "pro-Israel." This development may weaken the political influence of the pro-Israel lobby in the future.

Chapter 6 discusses the current critique of the American Jewish establishment and the challenges that it faces today. Critics accuse it of being unrepresentative and out of touch with the views of American Jews, especially on the issue of Israel. I evaluate this critique and argue that the real problem with the American Jewish establishment is not that it is entirely unrepresentative, but that it only represents a small and shrinking segment of American Jewry. Most American Jews simply have little, if anything, do with it. This is not, however, primarily due to the Jewish establishment's politics concerning Israel. For a variety of reasons, long-established Jewish organizations are less attractive and less relevant to American Jews today, especially to younger Jews who prefer new types of Jewish organizations championing different issues (most notably, social justice and the environment). As a result, the old Jewish organizations that have long dominated American Jewish politics are steadily losing ground to newer, niche organizations.

Chapter 7 places the American Jewish conflict over Israel in the context of a broader process of polarization between non-Orthodox and Orthodox Jews. I argue that the divide between non-Orthodox and Orthodox Jews in their views concerning the Israeli-Palestinian conflict is actually part of a wider political and cultural divide between the two groups. Moreover, current sociocultural and demographic trends within the American Jewish community suggest that this divide is likely to grow as non-Orthodox Jews become more secular, less "tribal," and less emotionally attached to Israel over time. While this might not lessen overall American Jewish support for Israel in the future—because Orthodox Jews, who remain staunchly attached to Israel, are growing in number and strength—it does threaten the future cohesion of the American Jewish community. Ultimately, however, the rapid demographic growth of Orthodox Jewry in the United States, and the decline of the non-Orthodox, points to a potential long-term future in which the American Jewish community is increasingly Orthodox, and more right-wing.

Finally, in the conclusion, I briefly summarize the book, and present its implications for American Jews, for Israeli governments, and for U.S. policymakers. I emphasize that American Jewish debate and division concerning Israel is unlikely to disappear, and that Israeli and American policymakers, American Jewish leaders, and American Jews themselves must come to terms with this.

As I write these words, in August 2015, this debate and division is strikingly apparent in the strong and opposing reactions among

American Jews to the recently announced agreement by the United States and other world powers to lift international sanctions on Iran in exchange for restrictions on its nuclear program. The nuclear deal with Iran has become the centerpiece of President Barack Obama's foreign policy, and the target of a fierce, largely partisan, domestic battle in the United States as Congress is set to vote on whether to approve or reject the deal. The American Jewish community has become a prominent player in this major political drama, as competing pro-Israel lobby groups campaign furiously for and against the agreement (mostly the latter), and many American Jewish communal organizations—urged on by Prime Minister Netanyahu in Israel[29]—desperately try to mobilize the masses of American Jews to oppose the nuclear accord,[30] although initial polling showed that most Jews actually supported it.[31]

Approaching what has been widely described as one of the most consequential and controversial American foreign policy decisions of our time, American Jews are being explicitly called upon by their communal leadership, by the Israeli government, and even by the president of the United States himself,[32] to take a clear stand—a stand that will put them directly at odds with either President Obama or Prime Minister Netanyahu. Never before has American Jewry found itself in such an uncomfortable predicament, the object of an open tug-of-war between an American president and an Israeli prime minister, and never before have American Jews been as sharply, and as publicly, divided as they are now. "Nowhere has the nuclear accord been more divisive than among American Jews," a reporter for the *New York Times* noted.[33] The disagreement among American Jews over the nuclear deal with Iran has provoked a vituperative debate within the American Jewish community. "Within families and across the American Jewish community, discussion of the Iran deal is fiery," the *New York Times* columnist Roger Cohen observed.[34] Another commentator writing for Israel's *Ha'aretz* newspaper went further, describing the debate among American Jews over the Iran nuclear deal as:

> a battle royal that is taking place in the boardrooms of Jewish organizations from coast to coast, in synagogues, community

centers and social gatherings, behind closed doors or out in the open, in polite debate or, increasingly, in heated emotional dispute. It pits Jews against Jews, conservatives vs. liberals, hawks and doves, Republicans and Democrats, donors against professionals, rabbis against their flock and, in recent days, against one another. . . . Whether the deal is as good as the Obama administration claims or as bad as Netanyahu says, it has already claimed its first victim: a fractured American Jewish community.[35]

In fact, as I will argue in this book, the American Jewish community has been fracturing for some time over Israel. The divisions over the Iran nuclear deal are just the latest manifestation of this, but they have put the lack of American Jewish unity under the spotlight. As Gary Rosenblatt, the editor and publisher of the largest Jewish newspaper in the United States, wrote: "One of the lessons learned from the intense debate over the Iran nuclear deal is that there is a serious and growing divide within American Jewry."[36] The lack of unity among American Jews on the nuclear deal was even the subject of a classified telegram sent to the Israeli government by its consul general in Philadelphia, Yaron Sideman, in which he warned: "At this crucial point of the Iranian issue—which for years has been at the core of Israeli foreign policy and was described countless times by the Israeli leadership as an existential threat—the Jewish community in the United States is not standing as a united front behind Israel and important parts of it are on the fence."[37] This warning, however, did not stop the Israeli government from trying its hardest to persuade American Jews to help it torpedo the nuclear deal through a vote in the Republican-controlled Congress (a vote that President Obama promised to veto if it went against him). Whatever the outcome of the congressional vote (due to take place after the time of this writing), and whatever the fate of the Iran nuclear deal, it is already abundantly clear that the divisions among American Jews that this book describes and analyzes are of great importance not only for American Jews, but also for Israel, for the United States, and even for the future of the Middle East, if not the world.

1.

THE CHANGING AMERICAN JEWISH
RELATIONSHIP WITH ISRAEL

Supporting and loving Israel should be more than a simply yes-or-no proposition. It should be a meaningful relationship filled with hugging and wrestling, questioning and arguing.

—Jeremy Ben-Ami, President of J Street[1]

To any passer-by, the sight of thousands of American Jews marching along Manhattan's Fifth Avenue proudly waving blue and white Israeli flags and carrying banners with Hebrew slogans in New York City's annual Celebrate Israel Parade is a hugely impressive demonstration of American Jewish support for Israel. That is, of course, the parade's purpose—to publicly display the passionate commitment of American Jews to Israel. In this sense, it is undoubtedly a great success. Since it was first held in 1964, the parade (formerly known as the Salute to Israel Parade) has grown in size to become, according to its organizers, "the largest yearly gathering of support for Israel in the world,"[2] with more than 30,000 participants in recent years. But the parade has changed in other ways too. It has become much more religiously Orthodox in composition, and also much more contentious. These changes point to the profound shifts occurring in the nature of American Jewish support for Israel.

Although aimed at gathering Jews from across the religious spectrum, over the years the Celebrate Israel Parade has attracted fewer and fewer secular Jews. Instead, it has become an event mostly for Orthodox Jews, as the majority of the marchers—mainly children who attend Orthodox day schools and Hebrew schools—and many of the spectators lining Fifth Avenue are Orthodox. Without this large contingent of Orthodox Jews, the parade would be a much smaller and quieter affair. The possible implications of this have alarmed some commentators in the American Jewish community. The editor of a local Jewish newspaper in New York, for example, has ruefully observed:

> The naked fact is that the great majority of New York Jewry is nowhere to be found on the one day of the year we celebrate Israel together. . . . Perhaps it tells us more than we care to know about the engaged pro-Israel community of New York when we look up and down Fifth Avenue and note the disproportionate involvement of Modern Orthodox Jewry and core activists, and wonder about the level of participation—or lack thereof—of the great majority of New York Jews. Is this a microcosm of the American Jewish relationship with Israel going forward?[3]

If attracting Jews from across the religious spectrum is one problem that the parade has faced in recent years, another problem has been trying to include Jews from across the political spectrum. Although the parade's organizers have emphasized its political inclusiveness, right-wing Jewish activists have challenged this inclusivity and tried to prevent the participation of left-wing Jewish groups. In the run-up to the 2012 parade, for instance, a campaign was launched by a group calling itself the "Committee for a Pro-Israel Parade" to pressure the parade organizers, the Jewish Community Relations Council of New York and the UJA-Federation of New York, into not allowing a host of American Jewish organizations that they accused of being anti-Israel to march in the parade.[4] During the parade itself, some spectators even booed the members of these left-wing organizations as they passed by—hardly the kind of demonstration of American Jewish unity in support of Israel that the parade's organizers touted it to be.[5]

Instead of simply being a festive showcase of wall-to-wall American Jewish support for Israel, the Celebrate Israel Parade also reveals the cracks in this façade of unity. Support for Israel among American Jews, though still strong, is not as broad and deep as many, inside and outside the American Jewish community, believe it to be. Nor is it as unconditional and uncritical as it is often depicted in the media. Rather, the nature of American Jewish support for Israel is more complex, more fluid, and—increasingly—more ambivalent than the popular image of a passionately pro-Israel American Jewish community.

This chapter explores the nature of American Jewish support for Israel. I examine how strong and extensive it is, the underlying factors motivating this support, and how American Jewish attitudes to Israel have changed over time. I argue that while most American Jews still care about Israel, growing numbers of them are becoming disillusioned with the country and more critical of its governments. Disillusionment does not engender indifference. Contrary to the predictions of many scholars and the fears of many officials and activists in the Jewish community, American Jews have not become emotionally disconnected and detached from Israel; but they have become more critical of Israeli government actions and policies, especially concerning the Israeli-Palestinian conflict. Thus, the majority of American Jews still support Israel, but not necessarily the policies of its governments. This split between emotional attachment to Israel and political support for its governments is fundamentally reshaping the relationship between American Jews and Israel. As such, the American Jewish relationship with Israel is evolving, but not eroding (at least not yet).

Before discussing how the collective attitudes, beliefs, and perceptions of American Jews concerning Israel have changed over time, it is first necessary to immediately dispel a popular misconception about American Jewish support for Israel, and then explain what really motivates this support.

DEMYSTIFYING AMERICAN JEWISH SUPPORT FOR ISRAEL

The notion that all Jews wholeheartedly support Israel, except for perhaps a few renegades and outcasts, is widely held, not just in the United States, but around the world. Indeed, this popular belief has been a boon to Israel over the years as it has encouraged numerous countries to improve their relations with the Jewish state in the hopes of gaining favor with world, and especially American, Jewry.[6] In public discourse and the mass media in the United States, American Jewish support for Israel is generally taken for granted. American Jews are frequently depicted in the media as being obsessed with Israel and single-minded in their devotion to it, as if Israel's security and well-being was their chief concern. In the run-up to local and national elections, for example, journalists routinely describe how politicians try to win the "Jewish vote" by emphasizing their staunch support for Israel and how Jewish voters try to decide who to vote for based upon who they consider to be the most "pro-Israel." The implicit assumption is that American Jews are so committed to Israel that its interests will be uppermost in their minds in the voting booth, rather than other interests of theirs, or priorities held by many Americans.

This is not, in fact, the case. Israel is not at the top of the list of American Jews' political concerns. It is not even close.[7] Nor is it only when they vote that American Jews are not quite as devoted to Israel as they are often depicted to be. Many American Jews rarely even talk about Israel and probably don't think about it all that much.[8] Most have never been to Israel,[9] and most don't know much about it.[10] To be sure, according to surveys, the majority of American Jews *do* care about Israel, but observers should not exaggerate the importance of Israel to American Jews, or the extent and depth of American Jewish support for Israel, as so often happens. In a major landmark survey of American Jews conducted by the Pew Research Center in 2013, just 43 percent of respondents said that caring about Israel is an essential part of what being Jewish meant to them—strikingly, this was almost the same number as those who said that having a good sense of humor was essential to their Jewish identity![11] By comparison, almost three-quarters of American Jews said that remembering the Holocaust was essential to their sense of Jewishness, and more than half, 56 percent, said that working for justice and equality was essential to what being Jewish meant to them.[12] The Pew survey also revealed a large generational divide in the importance attached to caring about Israel,[13] and significant differences among Orthodox, Conservative, and Reform Jews in the importance they attach to Israel.[14]

There is, therefore, much more diversity in American Jewish attitudes toward Israel than is commonly acknowledged in the media (and by most American Jewish organizations). The level of concern for and commitment to Israel varies considerably among American Jews.[15] Contrary to the popular stereotype and sweeping generalizations made about American Jews, surveys show that only a minority—around 30 percent or so—feel very strongly attached to Israel, while a similar number feel distant. The rest are just moderately attached to Israel.[16] In their emotional connection to Israel, therefore, the American Jewish population can be roughly divided into thirds: a third are very connected, a third are somewhat connected, and a third are disconnected.[17] Unsurprisingly, it is those American Jews who are most strongly attached to Israel, not the majority who are not, that tend to dominate the discussion of Israel within the American Jewish community, shaping the community's public stance concerning Israel, as well as American Jewry's relationship with Israel. They are the American Jews whose voices are heard most often, both in the United States and in Israel.

American Jewish support for Israel is neither universal nor automatic. The fact that not all American Jews really care about Israel requires us to explain what motivates those Jews who do. This analysis is seldom done. All too often, American Jewish support for Israel is simply assumed, rather than explained, as if supporting Israel was somehow intrinsic or essential to being Jewish. But, clearly, being Jewish and supporting Israel are not the same, and there is no necessary, inevitable connection between them (despite repeated proclamations by Israeli governments and major American Jewish organizations). Although attachment to Israel is positively associated with attachment to Jewishness—generally speaking, the more Jewish one feels, the more attached to Israel one is—quite a few American Jews are not attached to Israel, despite their attachment to their Jewish identities.[18] In the words of Judith Butler, a prominent American Jewish academic who has been outspoken in her criticism of Israel and Zionism:

The argument that all Jews have a heartfelt investment in the state of Israel is untrue. Some have a heartfelt investment in corned beef sandwiches or in certain Talmudic tales, religious rituals and liturgy, in memories of their grandmother, the taste of borscht or the sounds of the old Yiddish theatre. Others have an investment in historical and cultural archives from Eastern Europe or from the Holocaust, or in forms of labor activism, civil rights struggles and social justice that are thoroughly secular, and exist in relative independence from the question of Israel.[19]

If supporting Israel is not intrinsic to Jewishness, then why do so many American Jews support Israel?

THE FIVE PILLARS OF PRO-ISRAELISM: FAMILISM, FEAR, FUNCTIONALITY, FAITH, AND FANTASY

At the heart of American Jewish support for Israel lays a deep familial sentiment, "a sense of familial solidarity" in the words of Gideon Shimoni.[20] Many American Jews have traditionally felt a strong sense of kinship—seeing themselves as "part of an extended family"—and this "familism" promotes a sense of mutual responsibility among them.[21] The belief that Jews, as members of a kind of extended family, have a responsibility toward one another is, according to Charles Liebman and Steven Cohen, "an axiomatic principle of public Jewish life."[22] It has motivated much of the charitable activities of the organized American Jewish community directed toward poor, hungry, and destitute Jews, in the United States and elsewhere, and it has also motivated American Jewish support for Israel—more specifically, for Jews in Israel.[23] Helping Israeli Jews, whether financially or politically, is, in this respect, essentially equivalent to helping other Jews in need, wherever they may be. It is an act of charity, driven by feelings of kinship, not by ideological beliefs or political sentiments. Just as many American Jews have traditionally felt obliged to help other less fortunate American Jews (or, in the past, Soviet Jews, for example), they have also felt obliged to help Jews in Israel, and thus, by extension, the State of Israel.

While familism is perhaps the most fundamental force motivating American Jewish support for Israel, it is not the only one. Fear is another powerful motive. As Steven Cohen writes: "American Jewish

23

feelings about Israel are dominated by fear far more than hope, by nightmares more than dreams."[24] There is a combination of fears at work here: a fear for the safety of Israeli Jews who are believed to be threatened by a hostile Arab world (and, more recently, by Iran); a fear for the safety of Jews in other countries who are believed to be threatened by anti-Semitism in their societies; and a fear for their own safety and that of their children and grandchildren who, despite living in a seemingly safe American environment largely free of anti-Semitism, are nevertheless believed to be always at risk from a resurgence of this age-old hatred.

Harboring a deep sense of victimhood and an abiding fear of persecution, anti-Semitism, real or imagined—whether in Europe, the Middle East, the United States, or elsewhere—is a continual source of anxiety for American Jews, and a constant motivation behind their support for Israel. Since the establishment of the State, American Jews have regarded Israel as a safe haven for persecuted and endangered Jews (especially following the Holocaust). Indeed, Israel has served as a refuge for Holocaust survivors, North African and Middle Eastern Jews, Ethiopian Jews, and Soviet Jews, as well as other endangered Jews. Although Israel's role as a place of refuge for Jews at risk is, in the minds of most American Jews, primarily for the sake of Jews around the world who face the greatest risk of persecution, for many American Jews fearful of the possibility of anti-Semitism in the United States, Israel's vital role as a potential safe haven applies to them as well. Despite a steady decrease in anti-Semitism in American society since the end of World War II, many American Jews are still concerned about anti-Semitism. Although they are well aware of the unprecedented freedom and acceptance that Jews enjoy in the United States, they are nevertheless vigilant to the ever-present potential for a resurgence of anti-Semitism (mindful of the tragic example of German Jews in the 1920s and 1930s who also felt secure). In so far as Israel is regarded as an available refuge, then, supporting it is a kind of "insurance policy" for those American Jews who continue to fear anti-Semitism and, even, another Holocaust.[25]

The perception of Israel as a potential place of refuge, however, is only a small part of why American Jews support Israel. Despite lingering fears of anti-Semitism, by and large, American Jews feel secure in the United States (probably more secure than Jews anywhere else in the world, including Israel). They are more worried about losing their collective identity than their lives. Assimilation is a bigger problem than anti-Semitism. It is the open embrace of gentile American society, not its hostility, that poses by far the greatest challenge to the American Jewish community. Supporting Israel helps in this respect, as it has become a crucial means of sustaining and expressing Jewish identity. Support for Israel has become a constitutive element of American Jewish identity, especially since the 1967 war. In the words of Charles Liebman, one of the preeminent scholars of American Jewry: "Israel has become instrumental to one's American Jewish identity. Israel, and concern for Israel, are preeminently a symbol of Jewish identity."[26] Thus, supporting Israel is functional for the maintenance of American Jewish identity, and the need for identity may be an even more powerful motivation behind American Jewish support for Israel than the need for security.

Nothing better illustrates the functional value of Israel for American Jewish identity than the "Taglit-Birthright Israel" program that provides free tours to Israel for young American Jews (as well as other Diaspora Jews).[27] Initiated in the mid-1990s, largely in response to the alarm within the American Jewish community provoked by the 1990 National Jewish Population Survey (NJPS) that revealed high rates of intermarriage, decreasing involvement in the Jewish community, and weakening attachment to Israel among young Jews, the goal of "Birthright Israel" is to counter Jewish assimilation by strengthening participants' Jewish identity and their attachment to Israel. Rather than being aimed at encouraging young Diaspora Jews to make *aliyah* (settle in Israel), the fundamental purpose of these tours is to foster Diaspora Jewish attachment to Israel and bolster Diaspora Jewish identity, thereby preserving Jewish life in the Diaspora. As sociologist Shaul Kelner puts it: "Birthright Israel's raison d'être is to ensure the continued existence of vibrant, Israel-oriented Jewish communities abroad."[28] Since the Birthright trips began in 1999, approximately 500,000 Diaspora Jews aged 18 to 26, from over sixty-six countries—two-thirds of them from the United States—have been on these ten-day tours, and they have become almost a rite of passage for young Jews.[29] Almost 50 percent of young American Jews who have visited Israel have done so on a Birthright tour.[30]

Youth trips to Israel are just one of the many ways in which Israel has become central to sustaining American Jewish identity. Even if they have never been to Israel and have no intention of going, supporting Israel is an important element of the Jewish identity of many American Jews, albeit not necessarily the most important.[31] For most American Jews, supporting Israel is part of what it means to be a good Jew.[32] This is especially true for more secular American Jews who rarely observe Jewish religious practices or perform traditional Jewish customs. Supporting Israel serves a particularly important psychological function for nonreligious American Jews as it enables them to still identify themselves as Jewish, without having to observe religious laws or subscribe to religious beliefs. For many secular Jews, then, supporting Israel has become a way of being Jewish without having to be religious—amounting to what Arthur Hertzberg once called a "substitute religion."[33] This "substitute religion" is also a lot less taxing than traditional Judaism with all its prohibitions and demands.[34] While supporting Israel might involve occasionally giving money to Israel or lobbying on its behalf, practicing Judaism requires constant devotion. As such, supporting Israel is a comfortable and convenient outlet for Jews assimilating into American society, but still wanting to maintain and express their Jewish identity.

Not only does their attachment to Israel help secular American Jews actively identify as Jews, it also gives them a vicarious feeling of pride in Israel's accomplishments. For decades, especially during the 1960s and 1970s, Israel had a heroic image in the eyes of American Jews. Its lightning victory against Arab states in the Six-Day War of 1967, its daring rescue of Israeli and Jewish hostages in the Entebbe raid in 1976, and its massive airlifts to safety of Ethiopian Jews in 1984 and 1991, for instance, have thrilled American Jews and filled many of them with pride. Although these kinds of dramatic Israeli exploits have become much rarer in recent years, Israel still has the ability to instill collective pride in American Jews, as well as Jews elsewhere. Nowadays, however, it is more likely to be due to the country's impressive economic and technological achievements—leading it to be acclaimed the "Start-up Nation."[35] Thus, Jack Wertheimer writes, "American Jews once were most proud of Israel's pioneering spirit and its creation of a haven of refuge for downtrodden coreligionists; later they most admired Israel's military might and its kibbutzim; and more recently they have focused on its technological prowess and scientific research."[36]

Israel's role in reinforcing American Jewish identity and boosting Jewish pride does not mean, however, that it is primarily of value to more assimilated, secular Jews. On the contrary, Israel is generally of even greater significance to religious Jews. There is a strong correlation between religious belief and attachment to Israel, with surveys over the years consistently showing that attachment to Israel varies according to a person's denominational affiliation (Orthodox Jews are the most attached to Israel, followed by Conservative Jews, while Reform Jews are the least attached).[37] The connection between religious faith and attachment to Israel is understandable given the fact that the Land of Israel (*Eretz Yisrael*) is a core element in Jewish theology, and the notion of an eventual return to the "Promised Land" is deeply embedded in Jewish ritual and belief. Indeed, 40 percent of American Jews say they believe that God gave the Land of Israel to the Jewish people.[38] Nevertheless, while all of the major Jewish denominations in the United States (Reconstructionist, Reform, Conservative, and Modern Orthodox) have embraced Israel, according it a religious significance[39] and including references to it in their liturgy,[40] Israel does not have much religious significance for the majority of American Jews. It is the minority of Modern Orthodox Jews—roughly 2 to 3 percent of the total American Jewish population—for whom Israel has the most religious significance. Even if they do not subscribe to messianic religious Zionism and believe that Israel represents the "beginning of the flowering of Jewish redemption" (as described in contemporary Jewish liturgy), Modern Orthodox Jews still tend to regard Israel's creation as a modern-day miracle.[41] Moreover, the religious leaders of Modern Orthodoxy in the United States, particularly the late Rabbi Joseph B. Soloveitchik, have always stressed the crucial importance of the State of Israel and the need for Orthodox Jews to wholeheartedly support it.[42]

Israel, then, is a source of security, identity, pride, and faith for American Jews, and supporting it serves their psychological, emotional, and spiritual needs. American Jewish support for Israel, then, is primarily driven by American Jewish needs and desires.[43] In short, it is more about American Jews than it is about Israel. What makes this possible is the fact that Israel is an "imaginary homeland"[44] for American Jews—"imaginary" not just because it is not their actual home, but also because it exists primarily in their imagination. American Jewish attachment to Israel is based upon an imaginary, not real Israel. Few of them know much about, let alone experience, the real Israel, even if they do visit the country (which most have not). For most American Jews, Israel has been more of a mythic land than an actual place. It functions, therefore, as a kind of screen on which American Jews may project their hopes, fantasies, and fears.

Many observers have commented on the superficial image of Israel held by American Jews. They "perceived the Jewish state as a collection of clichés," writes Steven Rosenthal.[45] Jack Wertheimer noted that: "Until now, American Jews have peered at Israel through a metaphorical kaleidoscope. Looking into the view-finder from the literal and psychological distance of America's shores, they have selectively seen shards of Israeli life. The colorful pieces of Israel they have noticed are far from the total reality; at best, they reflect only a partial set of images."[46] It is not just that most American Jews do not actually know Israel very well; they also tend to idealize and romanticize the country and its people.[47] As Charles Liebman wrote twenty years ago:

> Many American Jews . . . have created their own conception of Israel. This is the chunk of Israel that they see and/or they imagine they see or they are shown when they visit Israel. . . . It is not an Israel of self-serving and inept leaders, of a rude populace, and, . . . an increasingly xenophobic culture. Rather, it is a society that exudes universalist sentiment wrapped in the symbols of Jewish particularism. It is an Israel where Jerusalem looms

more centrally than in the Israel which its citizens know. . . . It
is an Israel of universities, youth seminars, Jewish Agency tours
and kibbutzim. Above all else, it is an Israel filled with spirit and
spirituality.[48]

The highly romanticized image of Israel and Israelis long held by
many American Jews was due in no small part to the massive popularity of Leon Uris's best-selling novel *Exodus* published in 1958 and
later made into a blockbuster Hollywood movie starring Paul New-
man as the brave and dashing Israeli hero Ari Ben Canaan. More
than any other popular book or film about Israel, *Exodus* captured
the imagination of American Jews, becoming what Arthur Hertzberg called "the contemporary 'bible' of much of the American Jewish community."[49] Despite its fictional nature, *Exodus* played a major
role in shaping American Jews' image of the *Sabra* (the native Israeli
Jew).[50]

American Jews, however, had been fantasizing about Israel long before *Exodus* appeared. The tendency to romanticize and idealize Israel
is deeply rooted in American Jewish history. Describing the historic
images that American Jews had of the Land of Israel (*Eretz Yisrael*)
before 1948, Jonathan Sarna, a historian of American Jewry, writes
that: "The Zion of the American Jewish imagination . . . became
something of a fantasy land: a seductive heaven-on-earth, where enemies were vanquished, guilt assuaged, hopes realized, and deeply felt
longings satisfied."[51] According to Sarna, "American Jewish images of
Zion . . . developed from—and addressed—the needs of American
Jewry and were, as a result, increasingly out of touch with reality back
in Eretz Israel. Over time, this 'Israel of American Jews' became more
and more of an idealized dream world."[52] From the outset, therefore,
American Jews fell in love with a mythical Israel.

Clearly, a potent mix of beliefs and emotions drives American Jewish support for Israel. What is significantly missing from this mix is
ideology, specifically Zionist ideology. Most American Jews do not
support Israel out of ideological conviction. Their connection with
Israel is largely emotional, not ideological. Hence, American Jewish support for Israel is more accurately described as "pro-Israelism"

29

rather than Zionism. Although many, perhaps most, American Jews today would describe themselves as Zionists, their "Zionism" is generally shallow and facile. As Shaul Magid writes: "many American Jews who identify as "Zionist" today actually know little about Zionism. That is, they know little about the complex, self-critical, and often messy history of Zionism, an ideology that has been at war with itself for most of its history. Their 'Zionism' is arguably 'pro-Israelism,' the advocacy of a nation-state and its polices against its critics."[53]

Zionism plays a surprisingly small role in American Jewish support for Israel. Part of the reason for this is the fact that since Israel's founding, Zionist leaders and activists within the American Jewish community have not been in charge of mobilizing the community's support for Israel. Although American Zionist organizations (most notably, the Zionist Organization of America, or ZOA, and Hadassah, the women's Zionist organization) were instrumental in mobilizing American Jewish support for the Zionist movement before 1948, afterward, Israeli policymakers, chiefly Prime Minister David Ben-Gurion, decided to transfer the tasks of fundraising and political lobbying for Israel from Zionist organizations (specifically, the ZOA) to non-Zionist ones.[54] Ben-Gurion did this because he objected to the attempts by some American Zionist leaders (especially ZOA leader Abba Hillel Silver) to become directly involved in shaping the new state. Ben-Gurion, along with other members of the Israeli political establishment in the 1950s, wanted to limit the role of American Jews to only providing financial and political support from afar,[55] something that the less politicized leadership of local Jewish Federations, well-established non-Zionist groups like the American Jewish Committee (AJC), and the newly created organizations the American Zionist Council of Public Affairs (renamed the American Israel Public Affairs Committee [AIPAC] in 1959) and the Conference of Presidents of Major American Jewish Organizations (CoP) were happy to oblige with. Consequently, as the role of American Jews in the Israeli state-building project was restricted to catering to the fledgling state's desperate need for financial and political support, and fundraising and lobbying became the designated means by which

American Jews could actively support Israel, this support was increasingly solicited, and generally given, on nonideological grounds.[56]

The biggest reason, however, for the marginal role that Zionist ideology plays in motivating American Jewish support for Israel is simply that most American Jews are not really Zionists, at least not in the classical (or Israeli) sense of the term. As Ben-Gurion once stated: "most of the people in the diaspora who now call themselves 'Zionists' do not mean in all respects exactly the same thing that was meant by those who coined the term Zionism and by the majority who used the word during the first fifty years of the Zionist movement."[57] Classical Zionism—which was a response to the conditions facing European Jewry, particularly Eastern European Jewry, in the late nineteenth century—has never had much relevance or appeal to American Jewry.[58] Indeed, the vast majority of American Jews reject the basic tenets of classical Zionism—that Diaspora Jews live in exile from their homeland, that all Jews should live in Israel, that Jewish life in Israel is superior to life in the Diaspora, and that Diaspora Jewish life is doomed to eventually disappear.[59] American Jews do not think that they live in exile and they do not regard Israel as their homeland (except in so far as they might believe that it is the place from which their distant ancestors originated). As Jacob Blaustein, the president of the American Jewish Committee, wrote in a famous "exchange of views" with Ben-Gurion in 1950: "American Jews vigorously repudiate any suggestion or implication that they are in exile. American Jews—young and old alike, Zionists and non-Zionists alike—are profoundly attached to America. . . . To American Jews, America is home."[60] In fact, for many American Jews, America is more than just home; it is itself a kind of Zion, an "almost promised land."[61] The United States is not just an alternative *to* Zion, but in many respects an alternative Zion.[62]

Zionism has never succeeded in winning over the majority of American Jews. From its establishment in 1898 right up until World War II,[63] the American Zionist movement failed to gain mass support among American Jews and encountered a lot of resistance from the (mostly German-Jewish) leadership of American Jewry who were concerned that Zionism might jeopardize the position of American Jews by calling their national allegiance into question.[64] Throughout this period, anti-Zionism was a widely held and respectable opinion within the American Jewish community (a fact that has been largely erased from the collective memory of American Jewry[65]). Although American Jews became the main financial backers of the Zionist project, relatively few actually joined the Zionist movement.[66] Even among those who did, their Zionism was very different from that of their European Jewish counterparts. In order for Zionism to gain support in the United States, it had to be fundamentally reformulated. Louis Brandeis (then a Boston attorney, later a Supreme Court judge), the leader of the Federation of American Zionists from 1914–1921, did this by arguing that Zionism was the solution for European Jews who faced persecution and homelessness (not for American Jews who were at home in the United States). Instead of urging American Jews to move to Palestine, therefore, Brandeis merely encouraged them to philanthropically support the efforts of Jewish pioneers there.

This "philanthropic Zionism" became the typical way that American Jews supported the Zionist project. Unlike European Zionism, which called for the "return" of all Jews to the Jewish homeland,[67] American Zionism was aimed only at helping persecuted European Jews settle in Palestine, and did not call for American Jews themselves to make *aliyah*.[68] In fact, American Zionism stressed that support for Jewish settlement in Palestine was entirely compatible with loyalty to America. As Brandeis himself put it: "Every American Jew who aids in advancing Jewish settlement in Palestine, though he feels that neither he nor his descendants will ever live there, will likewise be a better man and a better American for doing so."[69] Brandeis's fusion of Zionism with American patriotism—encapsulated in his statement: "To be good Americans, we must become better Jews, and to be better Jews we must become Zionists"[70]—was crucial to the success, albeit limited, of the American Zionist movement in gaining popular Jewish support.[71] As Steven Rosenthal observes: "It was not until Zionism was able to demonstrate its compatibility with the American patriotism that was the primary identification of American Jews that it was able to gain broad appeal in the United States."[72]

To this day, American Jewish support for Israel is publicly legitimized to Jews and non-Jews alike in terms of its compatibility with American patriotism. Supporting Israel is not disloyal or "un-American," it is often argued, because Israel is an important American ally, and an outpost of democracy in the Middle East, and most Americans support Israel. American Jews, therefore, can be pro-Israel and pro-American at the same time, which makes it much easier for them to support Israel. In this respect, American Jewish pro-Israelism is reinforced by the wider American political culture.

THE RISE AND FALL OF "ISRAELOLATRY"

The preceding section discussed the roles that familism, fear, functionality, faith, and fantasy play in motivating American Jews to support Israel. Although these factors have consistently driven American Jewish support for Israel, this support has never been static and unchanging. The American Jewish relationship with Israel has always been in flux. Contrary to the common belief that American Jews have always been strong supporters of Israel, in fact, the extent and intensity of American Jewish support for Israel has significantly fluctuated over time. Not only has American Jewish interest in Israel waxed and waned, but also American Jewish attitudes toward Israel have evolved, broadly speaking, from disinterest, to devotion, to disillusionment. This evolution has occurred over the course of three different periods: (1) from Israel's establishment in 1948 until the Six-Day War of June 1967; (2) from the 1967 war until the coming to power in Israel of Menachem Begin and his Likud Party in 1977; and (3) from the 1977 Israeli election until the present day.

DISINTEREST (1948–1967)

Although American Jewry, for the most part, did not embrace Zionism and relatively few American Jews joined the Zionist movement, by the end of World War II, the vast majority of American Jews had come to wholeheartedly support the establishment of a Jewish state in Palestine, largely in reaction to the mass murder of European Jewry in the Holocaust. As a result, American Jews became a vital source of economic and political support for the *Yishuv* (the prestate Jewish community in Palestine) as it sought to achieve sovereignty and prepared for war with the Palestinians and surrounding Arab states. American Jewish lobbying (including the personal lobbying of President Truman's friend and former business partner, Eddie Jacobson) helped convince Truman to support the United Nations' partition plan of 1947 and then to officially recognize the State of Israel, against the advice of his own State Department, when it declared independence in May 1948. As Truman himself later acknowledged in his memoirs: "I do not think I ever had as much pressure and propaganda aimed at the White House as I had in this instance."[73] In addition to energetically lobbying the Truman administration, American Jews also provided the *Yishuv* with large amounts of money and arms (the latter illegally smuggled into Palestine because the United States maintained an arms embargo during the 1948 war).[74] The money and munitions provided by American Jews were crucial to ensuring Israel's victory in the 1948 war.[75]

But while American Jews played an important—and often overlooked—part in Israel's creation, they quickly lost interest afterward. After the initial euphoria that American Jews, like Jews everywhere, felt when the Jewish state was born, American Jewish excitement and enthusiasm for Israel soon died down and was followed by a long period of indifference. Israel was of little interest and concern to most American Jews during the early years of Israeli statehood from 1948 to 1967. This was a time of upward mobility, suburbanization, and assimilation for American Jews, and the needs of a foreign country thousands of miles away were a lot less pressing to them than their own needs for prosperity, security, and belonging—especially as American Jews still frequently faced domestic discrimination and anti-Semitism. Most American Jews were simply preoccupied with their own immediate concerns and did not think about Israel very much. They were also concerned about being accused of having "dual loyalties," a concern that was heightened by the prevailing anti-Communist sentiment in the early Cold War period.[76]

American Jewish disinterest in Israel in the 1950s and early 1960s was evident in many ways. Only about 10,000 American Jews emigrated to Israel between 1948 and 1967,[77] the amount of money American Jews gave to Israel through the North American Federations' United Jewish Appeal (UJA) steadily declined (from $150 million in 1948 to $60 million in 1955[78]), and membership in American Zionist organizations shrank. Sociological studies of local Jewish communities at the time also revealed how surprisingly little Israel figured in American Jewish life.[79] Thus, in 1957 sociologist Nathan Glazer commented that Israel's founding has "had remarkably slight effects on the inner life of American Jewry."[80] Nor was supporting Israel the most important item on the political agenda of the American Jewish community during this period. Although raising money for the fledgling state (through the sale of "Israel Bonds" and annual UJA fundraising campaigns) was a communal priority,[81] and pro-Israel advocacy in Washington, DC (led by AIPAC and the Conference of Presidents), became an ongoing activity, the organized American Jewish community was generally more concerned with advancing Jewish rights and security in the United States than supporting Israel. It was only after 1967 that supporting Israel came to dominate the Jewish communal agenda.

DEVOTION (1967–1977)

More than any other event in Israeli history, the Six-Day War of June 1967 transformed the American Jewish relationship with Israel.[82] Having been largely absent from the consciousness of most American Jews up until 1967, Israel suddenly consumed the thoughts and feelings of American Jewry in the weeks of mounting tension and dread preceding the war and in its euphoric aftermath. The widespread fear of a second Holocaust prior to the war, followed by the relief and jubilation felt after Israel's swift and stunning victory, led to a spontaneous outpouring of support for Israel from American Jews. Lucy Dawidowicz's description at the time captures the collective mood of American Jewry in the wake of the 1967 war: "Israel's military victory brought elation and pride, but, even more, release from tension, gratitude, a sense of deliverance. Of course the pride was one of being victorious, a new kind of pride in being Jewish, in the aura that radiated from General Moshe Dayan, his ruggedness, vigor, determination. Many Jews took pride in the changed image of the Jew, no longer seen as victim or the historic typification of a persecuted people."[83]

Ironically, although Israel dramatically displayed its military might in the 1967 war and emerged as arguably the dominant regional power in the Middle East, American Jews became much more concerned with Israel's survival after the war than they were before. As J. J. Goldberg notes: "Objectively, the Six-Day War demonstrated that Israel was more secure than anyone had dreamed. . . . What the American Jewish community learned from the war was the reverse: that Israel might be destroyed at any moment."[84] This heightened concern with Israel's survival, coupled with the newfound pride of American Jews in the Jewish state's military prowess, propelled Israel to the top of the American Jewish communal agenda.[85] After the 1967 war, Steven Rosenthal writes, "Israel became the primary focus of Jewish emotion and activity, and its actions became almost sacrosanct in the eyes of most American Jews."[86]

In retrospect, the decade from 1967 to 1977 was the golden era in American Jewish support for Israel. Not only was there a huge surge in fundraising and political advocacy for Israel (and a brief surge in emigration to Israel), but Israel also became an "object of secular veneration" for many American Jews,[87] the centerpiece of what Jonathan Woocher termed "the new civil religion of American Jews."[88] So intense was the devotion to Israel among American Jews during this time that it was characterized by Daniel Elazar as "Israelolatry," implying that it was a kind of idolatry.[89] This Israelolatry was marked by unequivocal popular support for Israel, near total unanimity of opinion concerning the Arab-Israeli conflict (according to which Israel was the innocent victim of Arab animosity and aggression), and a massive grassroots mobilization on Israel's behalf.

The outpouring of American Jewish emotional, political, and financial support for Israel in the decade from 1967 to 1977 was exceptional. Although it had a profound and lasting impact on the relationship between the American Jewish community and Israel, this period of devotion to Israel—Israelolatry—was comparatively brief and unusual. It has certainly not been the norm—a fact worth emphasizing given the tendency of many Jews and non-Jews alike to assume that the American Jewish community has always been so fervently devoted to Israel. It was partly the result of a series of dramatic events involving Israel that occurred over the course of the decade, including three wars (the 1967 war, the War of Attrition with Egypt from 1969 to 1971, and the Yom Kippur War in October 1973); numerous high-profile terrorist attacks (most famously, the seizure and subsequent murder of Israeli athletes at the Munich Olympic games in 1972 and the Entebbe hijacking and rescue in 1976); and the passage of a resolution in the United Nations in 1975 describing Zionism as racism. But the surge of American Jewish support for Israel after 1967 was also the result of a confluence of longer-term processes and developments within the American Jewish community and in American society at large, particularly the growing consciousness of the Holocaust and the rise of identity politics. It was the convergence of Holocaust consciousness and identity politics in the United States, as much as events directly concerning Israel, that turned the American Jewish community from being largely disinterested in Israel to passionately devoted to it.

The Holocaust had always affected American Jewish attitudes toward Israel. As early as May 1942, even before news of the Nazis' "Final Solution to the Jewish Question in Europe" was widely known (it became official Nazi policy at the Wannsee Conference on January 20, 1942, but had begun in practice before then), the systematic persecution, enslavement, and killing of European Jews galvanized American Jewish support for the establishment of a Jewish state and led to the "Biltmore Program," in which the world Zionist movement, including American Zionist organizations, for the first time declared statehood to be its goal.[90] After World War II, American Jews' support for Israel's establishment was also driven partly by a desire to assuage their guilt over their inability to help European Jews during the Holocaust.[91] The Holocaust, however, had an even greater impact upon American Jewish support for Israel from the late 1960s onward as the collective memory of the Holocaust, and the specific lessons attached to it, came to dominate American Jewish identity and politics.[92]

As the Holocaust became increasingly significant for American Jews, Israel became increasingly important to them. Although there was never a pervasive silence about the Holocaust within the American Jewish community in the 1950s, as many believe,[93] in the 1960s the Holocaust began to assume a much greater place in American Jewish consciousness (the Eichmann Trial in 1961 and the publication in 1968 of Arthur D. Morse's book *While Six Million Died: A Chronicle of American Apathy* were instrumental in this respect[94]). Indeed, it gradually became the central element in the collective memory and Jewish identity of American Jewry. Moreover, the collective meaning that American Jews attributed to the Holocaust significantly changed—it was seen less in universalistic terms as a tragic lesson of what humans can do to each other as a result of hate, prejudice, and dehumanization, and more in particularistic terms as a terrible lesson of what gentiles can do to Jews as a result of anti-Semitism and Jewish powerlessness. Instead of underlining the importance of fighting against prejudice and discrimination, the Holocaust was increasingly seen as demonstrating the need for Jewish power, vigilance, even violence.[95] Thus, whereas previously the Holocaust was often invoked in American Jewish discussions about racism in the United States and the civil rights movement,[96] from the late 1960s onward the Holocaust was constantly invoked in relation to Israel. The Jewish state became a symbol of "Jewish power and self-defense," in sharp contrast to the Holocaust, which symbolized Jewish powerlessness and vulnerability.[97]

As the Holocaust was interpreted as providing incontestable proof of the need for a Jewish state, it became Israel's fundamental raison d'être for many, if not most, American Jews (as well as for other Jews in the Diaspora and, indeed, Jews in Israel). Without a state of their own to protect them, European Jewry had been powerless in the face of Hitler's genocidal anti-Semitism. With a state of their own, however, Jews would never again be so weak and defenseless. This became (and still is) the major, and certainly most important, rationale for

Israel's existence in the minds of American Jews. Hence, the Holocaust became the definitive reason for American Jews to support Israel (something that American Jewish organizations have frequently made use of in their efforts to mobilize support for Israel).

The Holocaust also became discursively linked to Israel in the "Holocaust to rebirth" narrative that became increasingly popular among American Jews. This narrative links the Holocaust and the creation of the State of Israel, depicting the latter as representing the revival (or redemption, in more religious terms) of the Jewish people after its near destruction.[98] The Jewish state thus comes to symbolize the Jewish people, and as such, its survival is implicitly equated with Jewish survival. Concern for Jewish survival, then, is expressed through supporting Israel; and in so far as Jewish survival is believed to be perpetually at risk, supporting Israel becomes a constant necessity. In short, since Israel symbolizes and secures Jewish survival, all Jews should support it.

American Jewish support for Israel intensified, therefore, as consciousness of the Holocaust grew, and it became increasingly symbolically and psychologically associated with Israel. Whether to make amends for their inability to save European Jews, to banish their feeling of impotence during the Holocaust, or to prevent another Holocaust, the ardent pro-Israel activism of many American Jews in the late 1960s and 1970s was motivated in large part by their growing Holocaust consciousness.

Another important development that promoted American Jewish pro-Israel activism in the 1970s was the rise of identity politics in the United States.[99] During an era when women, African Americans, Native Americans, gays and lesbians, and a host of other social groups publicly affirmed and celebrated their difference, it also became acceptable, even fashionable, for Jews to be openly Jewish and publicly affirm their support for Israel. Unlike in the past when American Jews were worried that overt displays of support for Israel might provoke accusations of "dual loyalty," by the 1970s more and more of them felt comfortable and confident about expressing their support for Israel, and doing so became a manifestation of their ethnic pride. In this sense, pro-Israel activism became for many American Jews, especially younger ones, what feminism was for women, or the Black

Power movement was for African Americans—a proud, even defiant, assertion of identity (the increasingly popular campaign to free Soviet Jewry also fulfilled this purpose for many American Jews during this time). Moreover, as with the feminist and Black Power movements, supporting Israel gave American Jews a sense of empowerment as well as pride. This new feeling of Jewish pride and power, which arose after 1967, was also a repudiation of the "victim mentality" that Diaspora Jews had long been accused of (especially by Zionists) and that allegedly reached its apogee during the Holocaust.[100] Jews would no longer be passive, weak, and helpless victims; instead they would actively and loudly stand up for themselves and for the Jewish state. The Jewish Defense League (JDL), the radical right-wing group founded by Rabbi Meir Kahane in New York City in 1968, exemplified this newly assertive attitude. Although the JDL had only a small number of members, its slogan "Never Again" and its ethos of Jewish self-defense and "toughness" resonated with many American Jews (one in four supported the group, according to a poll taken in the late 1960s).[101]

For many young American Jews in this period, supporting Israel was also wholly in accordance with liberal and left-wing political values and ideals they held. From afar, they saw Israel as an egalitarian, progressive, and secular society, ruled by Labor governments, with female soldiers, and socialist kibbutzim. It appeared to be a country committed to social democracy, to economic and gender equality, and, above all, to peace. As such, it was easy to support, even idolize. Indeed, the popular image of Israel as a progressive's utopia was so alluring to some idealistic young American Jews (and other young Jews in the Diaspora) that they went there to work on kibbutzim, join the army, and even live in new Jewish settlements that were being established in the West Bank.[102]

DISILLUSIONMENT (1977–PRESENT)

If American Jews fell in love with Israel during the 1960s and early 1970s, by the end of the 1970s and throughout the 1980s, the romance was wearing off. "The American Jewish love affair with Israel" was short-lived, lasting only about ten years.[103] What followed it was not so much disaffection, but disillusionment and dissent over Israeli government policies (especially those of Likud-led governments). This period of disillusionment has lasted much longer than the brief period of intense and uncritical devotion to Israel between 1967 and 1977. For more than three decades, the American Jewish relationship with Israel has been marked more by ambivalence, unease, and an almost constant chorus of criticism than unequivocal support. This state of affairs, often lamented by some American Jewish and Israeli commentators, is therefore the most normal state, and perhaps the most lasting one.

Why have growing numbers of American Jews become disenchanted with Israel and more critical of it since the late 1970s? Undoubtedly, part of the reason for this shift in American Jewish attitudes is that Israel has changed in ways that have disappointed, disturbed, and even angered many secular, liberal American Jews. Instead of being the secular, social-democratic, egalitarian, idealistic, and peace-seeking country that American Jews once perceived from afar (whether accurately or not), a different, altogether less attractive, Israel appeared from the late 1970s onward. It was more right wing, more religious, more intolerant, more unequal, and more aggressive and expansionist than the Israel that American Jews had fallen in love with.

This "new" Israel first emerged with the surprise victory of the right-wing Likud Party led by Menachem Begin in the May 1977 general election, an event known as the *mahapach* ("upheaval") in Israel. Likud's rise to power, after almost three decades of uninterrupted Mapai/Labor Party rule, resulted in significant changes in Israeli government policies toward the Palestinians and the territories that Israel had occupied since the 1967 war. Having long been accustomed to Labor-led governments in Israel with whom they felt a greater affinity, American Jews became increasingly uncomfortable with the hawkish, hard-line approach to Israel's conflict with the Palestinians and Arab states taken by the governments of Menachem Begin and his Likud successor Yitzhak Shamir.[104] Of particular concern to American Jews was Likud's settlement policy in the West Bank and

Gaza Strip, which seemed aimed at preventing the possibility of any kind of territorial compromise in the future.[105] On July 2, 1980, for instance, fifty-six prominent American Jews (including three former chairmen of the Conference of Presidents) issued a public statement titled "Our Way Is Not Theirs," which criticized the Begin government's settlement policy and called for a territorial compromise.[106]

A turning point in American Jewish attitudes to Israel came following Israel's invasion of Lebanon in June 1982. At first, most American Jews supported the war in Lebanon,[107] much as they had supported Israel's previous wars. But this quickly changed in the wake of the massacre of hundreds of Palestinian civilians in the Sabra and Shatila refugee camps in Beirut by Israel's Lebanese Christian Phalangist allies on September 16–17, 1982.[108] Although Israeli soldiers did not carry out the massacre, most American Jews considered Israel to be at least partially responsible for it (as did most Israelis).[109] The Sabra and Shatila massacre was a watershed in American Jewish attitudes to Israel, as it undermined their idealized image of the country, and their long-standing belief that Israel's wars were always just and its wartime conduct morally pure. In response, American Jewish criticism of Israel grew, and with it support for Israeli and American-Jewish groups (such as Peace Now and its newly established American offshoot, American Friends of Peace Now) that advocated for major changes in Israeli policies in the Arab-Israeli conflict.[110]

While there was a public outcry from American Jews in reaction to the Sabra and Shatila massacre, the first Palestinian Intifada, which began in December 1987 and lasted until 1991, generated an unprecedented amount of American Jewish criticism of Israel, as well as international condemnation. The largely nonviolent mass uprising of Palestinian civilians in the Occupied Territories against Israeli rule, and the Israeli army's harsh crackdown in response to it (in line with then Israeli Defense Minister Yitzhak Rabin's proclaimed policy of "force, might, beatings"), were deeply unsettling for American Jews accustomed to regarding Israel as the innocent victim in the Arab-Israeli conflict. Now that they were being regularly confronted with shocking images of Israeli soldiers shooting and beating Palestinian protestors (including women and children), many American Jews were reluctantly forced to recognize that their view of the conflict and their perception of Israel were inaccurate at best—Israel was not entirely blameless. The Israel that regularly appeared on American television screens during the first Intifada was certainly not the mythic Israel of the American Jewish collective imagination. Thus, the first Intifada further undermined the idealized image of Israel held by American Jews and led to growing disillusionment with Israel among more liberal and progressive Jews. Writing in the *New York Times Magazine* a few months after the beginning of the Intifada, Albert Vorspan, one of the lay leaders of the Reform Movement, forcefully expressed the disillusionment with Israel that many American Jews were experiencing at the time:

> Beyond any issue in recent years, American Jews are traumatized by events in Israel. This is the downside of the euphoric mood after the Six Day War, when we felt 10 feet tall. Now, suffering under the shame and stress of pictures of Israeli brutality televised nightly, we want to crawl into a hole. This is the price we pay for having made of Israel an icon—a surrogate faith, surrogate synagogue, surrogate God. Israel could not withstand our romantic idealization. . . . Now Israel reveals itself, a nation like all the others.[111]

There was a continuous stream of American Jewish criticism of Israel during the first Intifada. Previously, such criticism was sporadic and a mostly marginal phenomenon—restricted to fringe groups and a few outspoken individuals—but American Jewish criticism of Israel went mainstream during the first Intifada. As Steven Rosenthal writes: "The Palestinian Intifada . . . converted American Jewish disagreement with Israeli policy into a mass phenomenon."[112] Not only were more American Jews criticizing Israel than ever before, but also they were no longer just criticizing specific Israeli government actions. Criticism was now being leveled against Israel's policy toward the Palestinians and the Occupied Territories in general. A majority of American Jews were critical of the Shamir government's response to the Intifada,[113] and a growing number felt that Israel's occupation of the West Bank and Gaza would "erode Israel's democratic and humanitarian character"—by 1990, half of American Jews believed this, up from 30 percent in the spring of 1988, and just 11 percent who felt this way before the first Intifada.[114] Dissatisfaction with Israeli government policy toward the territories was also manifested in American Jewish approval of the Reagan administration's initiation of talks with Israel's archenemy, the Palestinian Liberation Organization (PLO), against Israel's wishes, and in growing calls for Israel itself to negotiate with the PLO. In 1990, about three-quarters of American Jews disagreed with Israeli policy at the time and wanted Israel to negotiate with the PLO.[115] Even Jewish communal leaders were becoming less supportive of Israeli policy. In a national survey of American Jewish leaders (including professionals and volunteers in local Jewish Federations, heads of Jewish organizations, and rabbis) conducted in 1990, for instance, 73 percent wanted Israel to negotiate with the PLO, if the latter renounced terrorism.[116]

By the end of the 1980s, Israel's settlement policy, its handling of the first Intifada, and its refusal to negotiate with the PLO had all became increasingly controversial within the American Jewish community. "For the first time a substantial portion of the American Jewish community had begun to attack not specific Israeli actions but the whole thrust of Israeli foreign policy."[117] Widespread criticism of Israeli government policies, both from the grassroots and from the leadership of the American Jewish community, clearly testified to the growing disillusionment with Israel that American Jews experienced in the 1980s. It is easy to place all the blame for this, as many have previously done,[118] on Israeli policies and actions in the 1980s, but they should not be held solely responsible for American Jewish disillusionment with Israel. Israeli governments were certainly insensitive at times to American Jewish concerns (most notably during the uproar over the 1985 arrest and subsequent conviction of U.S. navy analyst Jonathan Pollard on charges of spying for Israel[119]), and while some Israeli policies were highly unpopular among American Jews, to focus solely on Israeli government policies and actions overlooks an important change that occurred in the nature of the Arab-Israeli conflict itself, which also contributed to the process of American Jewish disillusionment with Israel.

After Israel's landmark peace treaty with Egypt in 1979, the conflict became largely an Israeli-Palestinian one and less of a conflict between Israel and the Arab states surrounding it (since, without Egypt, the Arab states no longer had a credible military option against Israel). As the Arab-Israeli conflict subsided and the Israeli-Palestinian conflict took center-stage, popular perceptions of Israel changed. It was no longer David against the Arab Goliath; instead, in a role reversal, Israel became Goliath and the Palestinians became David—widely perceived as the weaker, more vulnerable party in the conflict. In stark contrast to the way in which Israel was once perceived as embattled and heroic, from the 1980s onward Israel was widely perceived as a dominant military power, an oppressor of Palestinians, and an illegal occupier of their territories. This new, negative image of Israel gained international prominence during the first Intifada, and profoundly affected how many American Jews thought of Israel, especially younger ones who had no "generational memory" of the country before the 1980s.[120]

Another major development in the Arab-Israeli conflict that has gradually impacted upon American Jewish attitudes toward Israel has been the shift from interstate warfare between the Israel Defense Forces (IDF) and the armies of Arab states to asymmetrical warfare pitting the IDF against nonstate actors often operating in densely populated civilian areas (such as the PLO in Beirut during the first Lebanon War, or more recently Hezbollah in southern Lebanon, and Hamas in the Gaza Strip). This has led to many noncombatant casualties and extensive destruction of civilian infrastructure, for which Israel generally gets blamed (whether fairly or not). Beginning with the first Lebanon War against the PLO in 1982 and continuing through to the second Lebanon war against Hezbollah in 2006 and Israel's "Operation Cast Lead" and "Operation Protective Edge" against Hamas in 2008–2009 and 2014, respectively, Israel's recent wars have all been mired in controversy as the IDF has been repeatedly accused of "disportionate" use of force and disregard for Lebanese and Palestinian civilians. These accusations have tainted the IDF's image in the eyes of many American Jews, who once fondly regarded it as the most moral army in the world. Even if they staunchly supported Israel's right to defend itself against terrorist attacks, large numbers of American Jews have been uncomfortable with the apparently heavy-handed manner with which Israel has fought its enemies.[121]

The IDF, however, was never as morally pure as American Jews once believed it to be. Historians of the Arab-Israeli conflict such as Benny Morris, for instance, have thoroughly documented various atrocities and war crimes committed by Jewish and Israeli forces in the 1948 war and in cross-border "reprisal raids" carried out in the early 1950s.[122] Nor was Israel the paragon of democracy and egalitarianism in its early decades that American Jews imagined it to be (for one thing, it maintained military rule over its own Arab citizens until 1966). It was always much more flawed in reality than the vast majority of American Jews realized. Why, then, was it not until the 1980s and 1990s that many American Jews became disillusioned with Israel?

In order to fully explain this timing, the impact of a third set of changes, in addition to changes in Israel and changes in the Arab-Israeli conflict, needs to be understood. These changes involve American Jews themselves, specifically their level of engagement with Israel and their level of knowledge about it. Put simply, more American Jews are visiting Israel, learning about Israel, and paying closer attention to what's happening there than in the past. As a result, there is now greater familiarity with Israel and knowledge about it among American Jews than ever before. The net effect of this familiarity is, unavoidably, a certain amount of disillusionment because the more "real" Israel becomes to American Jews, the less idealized it is.[123] In the words of Steven Cohen, an expert on American Jewry: "Blind romance and unfounded idealization can last only so long."[124]

In the past, American Jews knew very little about Israeli history, politics, society, and culture.[125] As Steven Rosenthal wrote: "the vast majority of American Jews have remained astonishingly ignorant of the object of their devotion [Israel]."[126] This widespread ignorance was partly due to the fact that it was prohibitively expensive to visit Israel, and very few American Jews knew enough Hebrew to read Israeli newspapers or books (which were, in any case, hard to obtain), but it was also due to sheer lack of interest. However much they admired Israel, even idolized it, American Jews were, for the most, not particularly interested in knowing much about it. "The fact . . . that American Jews are concerned about Israel," Charles Liebman observed in the 1970s, "does not mean that they are very interested in or informed about Israel itself, much less its policies."[127]

The fundamental reason for this lack of interest, according to Liebman, was because Israel was more of an abstract symbol to American Jews than an actual place. "Israel is the preeminent Jewish symbol," he wrote. "Israel, therefore, is recognized as important less for what it *does* than for what it *is*."[128] As the "preeminent Jewish symbol," Israel represented a variety of Jewish aspirations and ideals: as Theodore Sasson notes: "Israel represented the revival of the Jewish people following the Holocaust. . . . As a young democracy with a strong welfare state, moreover, Israel represented the Jewish commitment to social justice and progressive values. And as a regional military power whose prowess was evidenced most dramatically in the Six-Day War, Israel represented the emergence of a new kind of Jew, tough and resourceful—the antithesis of Diaspora bookishness."[129] In a similar vein, Jack Wertheimer, another scholar of American Jewry, writes that: "At different times, Israel symbolized very different aspects of Jewish civilization—liberation from exile, David fighting Goliath, Jewish cultural renaissance, concern for fellow Jews, and religious renewal."[130]

Since Israel was primarily a symbol of Jewishness to American Jews, their support for Israel was fundamentally an expression of support for Jewishness and for the Jewish people.[131] As such, Israel's actual behavior and policies were of no great concern to American Jews.[132] What mattered to them was what Israel represented, not what it did. Thus, Israel's immense symbolic significance to American Jews meant that it could safely rely upon their support. "Mesmerized by the state's symbolic power," Steven Rosenthal writes, "most American Jews were content to support Israel without question and to enthusiastically provide whatever financial and political aid the Israeli government deemed appropriate."[133]

Although Israel is still symbolically important to American Jews— which is why its flag adorns the walls of many Jewish schools, stands inside many synagogues, and is often waved at Jewish rallies[134]—it is no longer just a symbol to growing numbers of them. Over time, it has steadily become less abstract, and more real—an actual country with its problems and flaws.[135] To be sure, many American Jews remain quite ignorant about Israel, but more and more of them are gaining some knowledge of Israeli politics and society due to extensive foreign news reporting about Israel and the easy accessibility of English-language versions of major Israeli newspapers on the Internet (notably *Ha'aretz, Yedioth Ahronot, Israel Hayom, Jerusalem Post,* and *Times of Israel*);[136] and because Israeli media tend to be highly partisan, American Jews are also getting exposed to sharply different views in Israeli politics. Hence, as American Jews have become more able to regularly read about social issues, economic problems, and political debates in Israel, they have gradually become better informed; in a national survey conducted in 2000–2001, 86 percent of American Jews said that they were very or somewhat familiar with the "social and political situation in Israel."[137] American Jews are also learning more about Israel by actually going there. There has been a significant increase in travel to Israel, with the number of American Jews who have visited the country at least once rising from just 14 percent in 1970, to 27 percent in 1990, to 35 percent in 2000, to 42 percent in 2013.[138] Finally, the emergence and rapid growth of Jewish Studies and Israel Studies programs in American universities over the past two decades has enabled some younger American Jews to learn in depth about Israeli history, politics, and culture.[139] Thus, instead of relying upon Leon Uris's novel *Exodus* for their understanding of Israel's early history as many of their parents once did, these young, well-educated American Jews are more likely to read the work of Israel's "New Historians," which presents this history in a much less favorable light.[140]

As American Jews read about Israel more often, travel there more, and learn more about it, their views of the country inevitably change—becoming less idealistic, and more realistic.[141] According to sociologist Theodore Sasson, the "new realism" that increasingly characterizes American Jewish perspectives about Israel is the outcome of a major change in the way in which American Jews relate to Israel. From the

1950s until the 1980s, the vast majority of American Jewry had a very distant and indirect relationship with Israel. Sasson writes that: "For most American Jews, Israel was in fact quite remote. They related to Israel through their local institutions, especially their synagogues. . . . They identified with the Jewish state by attending Israel day festivals and parades, dancing the hora, and decorating their homes with Israel-related art and artifacts. If they traveled to Israel, they likely did so as part of a tightly scheduled synagogue mission or denominationally sponsored youth tour."[142] This has been changing since the late 1980s as American Jews, or at least a significant minority of them, have begun to develop a more direct and personal relationship with Israel through travel and study there, and through regular consumption of Israeli news and culture (such as Israeli books, movies, and music which have become more readily available in the United States).[143]

Increasing "direct engagement" with Israel by American Jews has, therefore, led to a less rosy-eyed view of the country and a more critical attitude toward it. As American Jews have gotten to know Israel better, they have become more critical of those aspects of Israel that conflict with their own values and beliefs. This is especially true for younger American Jews (those between the ages of 18 and 35), who make up about a quarter of the total American Jewish population. Born long after the Holocaust and Israel's founding, they have no nostalgic memory of Israel's early years and no experience of the emotional highs and lows of the Six-Day War. Instead, they have grown up during the years of the first Intifada, the failed Oslo peace process, the assassination of Prime Minister Yitzhak Rabin, the second Intifada, and Israel's wars with Hezbollah and Hamas, and consequently their "generational memory" significantly differs from those of older American Jews.[144] They look at Israel, therefore, through a very different lens. They do not idealize Israel the way their parents or grandparents might have done.[145] To them, Israel is not the mythic land that American Jews once fantasized about. It is a real country with real problems; a country that many of them have been to, not a symbol that they worship from afar.

Growing up with Israel as a military power and an occupier has given younger generations of American Jews a very different image of the country and its people. While baby boomers may fondly recall images of young, smiling, suntanned *kibbutznikim* dancing the *hora*, many younger Jews have images in their minds of young, stern-faced soldiers manning military checkpoints in the West Bank. Indeed, for many young American Jews, Israel, so often mired in controversy, is a source of shame, rather than pride—in a 2007 survey, 40 percent believed that "Israel occupies land belonging to someone else," and over 30 percent reported sometimes feeling "ashamed" of Israel's actions.[146] Young American Jews are also more inclined to see Israel as powerful, not weak and endangered, and thus less in need of their absolute support. Their attitude toward Israel tends to be more skeptical,[147] and often more critical (especially of Israel's behavior toward the Palestinians).[148] Their support for Israel, therefore, is more tentative and less automatic.[149] The notion of always supporting the policies of the Israeli government is altogether alien to them. They will support Israel only if it acts in accordance with their values and beliefs. In fact, many young American Jews today believe that Israel deserves their criticism, not their unquestioning support.[150] A significant number are even critical of their own government's support for Israel—with a quarter of American Jews aged 18 to 29 in the Pew survey saying that the United States supports Israel too much (by way of comparison, only 5 percent of American Jews over 50 thought this).[151]

CONCLUSION: AN ENDURING ATTACHMENT

In this chapter, I challenged a popular myth that all American Jews are diehard supporters of Israel by arguing that American Jewish support for Israel is neither universal nor automatic. American Jewish attitudes toward Israel are not monolithic—while some American Jews are indeed passionate supporters, others are ambivalent, some quite apathetic about Israel, and some quite critical of the state. Not only are there significant differences among American Jews in their attitudes toward Israel, but also these attitudes have changed considerably over time. Israel has not always been as important to the American Jewish community as it is today. In its first two decades, Israel was actually of marginal interest to American Jewry, and it was only after the

1967 war that it became central to American Jewish life and politics. Since then, although Israel has dominated American Jewish politics, its image in the eyes of American Jews has gradually changed. It has slowly lost its aura of innocence and heroism, and steadily come to be seen as a more normal and more flawed country. From the beginning of the 1980s onward, a sometimes-painful process of disillusionment with Israel has occurred within the American Jewish community, and with it has come growing criticism of the state's actions and policies. While it is common to place most, if not all, of the blame for this on Israeli governments, especially Likud-led governments,[152] American Jewish disillusionment with Israel was not just a consequence of changes in Israel, but also of changes in the Arab-Israeli conflict and changes among American Jews themselves. Ultimately, some degree of disillusionment was probably inevitable because Israel could never remain the idealized place that American Jews had imagined it to be.

Contrary to the predictions of many experts, however, while disillusionment with Israel among American Jews has grown, it has not yet led to growing alienation from the country. Since the 1980s, it has often been claimed that American Jews, especially younger ones, were becoming less attached to Israel, and that the American Jewish community and Israel were slowly "drifting apart," becoming ever more distant and estranged from each other.[153] This claim has provoked a lot of anxiety and agonizing within the organized Jewish community.[154] Dozens of seminars, symposia, surveys, and studies have been sponsored by American Jewish organizations addressing the "problem" of American Jewish "distancing" from Israel and trying to answer the questions of whether this is happening and if so why, and what can possibly be done to stop it.[155] The purportedly weak commitment of young American Jews to Israel has been the focus of particular concern.[156]

The persistent worry within the American Jewish community for more than two decades about distancing from Israel has, so far at least, been completely unfounded.[157] In regular surveys conducted by the AJC between 1986 and 2010, between three-fifths and three-quarters of American Jews have consistently reported feeling "close to Israel."[158] Although levels of American Jewish attachment to Israel have fluctuated slightly from year to year, overall, attachment to Israel has been remarkably stable throughout this long period of time. It was not affected by all the negative events involving Israel in the 1980s (the 1982 invasion of Lebanon and subsequent Sabra and Shatila massacre, the imprisonment of Jonathan Pollard for spying on behalf of Israel in 1986, the first Intifada, and the "who is a Jew?" controversy in 1988).[159] However many American Jews may have been dismayed by the policies of Israeli governments in the 1980s and disturbed by some of their actions, they did not distance themselves from Israel. Nor did American Jews grow more distant from Israel in the 1990s despite the organized Jewish community's insular focus during this decade as it became preoccupied with "Jewish continuity" in the United States (which was believed to be threatened by rising rates of intermarriage and ongoing assimilation).[160] More recently, since the year 2000, American Jews have remained steadfastly attached to Israel, even as they have become more widely critical of its policies.[161]

Over the course of three tumultuous decades in relations between American Jews and Israel, therefore, there has been no general decline in attachment to Israel, despite a rise in critical views among many Jews.[162] Notwithstanding their disillusionment with Israel and their disagreements with Israeli governments (particularly Likud-led governments), American Jews have not turned from away Israel and become indifferent toward it. This is because caring about Israel does not necessarily mean agreeing with Israeli policies or liking particular Israeli governments. As Steven Cohen notes: "ill feelings about Israeli leaders or policy cannot be seen as signs of distancing or disengagement. We must recall that the people (or institutions) whom we love most dearly are those that disturb us most readily. In our personal lives, distress is a sign of engagement, not a sign of distancing. Accordingly, few Jews who are disturbed by Israel can properly be seen as distant from Israel, let alone anti-Israel."[163] It is thus important to distinguish between emotional attachment to Israel and political support for Israeli governments. Being emotionally distant from Israel entails being apathetic about it—not thinking about it and not caring about it. This is very different from being opposed to Israeli government policies, which involves thinking about Israel and, at least for most Jewish critics of Israel's policies, caring about Israel and its future. One can be strongly opposed to Israel's policies and actions, therefore, but still feel strongly attached to the country.[164]

Rather than growing more disconnected from Israel, as many have claimed, American Jews have actually become more actively involved with Israel over the past two decades.[165] More American Jews are reading about Israel, learning about Israel, and going to Israel than ever before. They are more engaged with Israel than previous generations whose connection with Israel was largely limited to donating money every year to local Jewish Federations to pass on to Israel. The big change that is taking place in the American Jewish relationship with Israel is not that American Jews are disengaging from it, but that they are critically engaging with Israel—they are, as many now put it, "hugging and wrestling" with Israel. There is much more public questioning and heated debate about Israel in the American Jewish community today than in the past. This is a manifestation of critical engagement with Israel, not alienation from it. Jack Wertheimer puts it well: "Debate over Israeli policies is a form of engagement and participation, if only from afar. Public silence or conformity in regard to Israel may signal indifference and apathy."[166] As American Jews' critical engagement with Israel has increased, so too has their willingness to challenge those aspects of Israel they find objectionable (such as its settlement building in the West Bank, its treatment of its Arab citizens, and its ultra Orthodox-dominated religious establishment). Thus, while American Jews remain emotionally invested in Israel, growing numbers of them have become more critical of its policies and more outspoken in their criticism.

American Jews' relationship with Israel is changing profoundly, therefore, but not in the way many people believe. Most American Jews still fundamentally support Israel in the sense of wanting it to exist and caring about its welfare and safety. What is different today is not the level of American Jewish support for Israel, but rather its mode of expression—it has become more critical than it was in the past, and it is no longer expressed politically simply through knee-jerk support for whatever Israeli governments do. While supporting Israel continues to be at the top of the American Jewish political agenda, there is growing disagreement about how to support Israel. Fewer American Jews are now willing to provide blanket support for Israeli policies and actions, and many now express their support for Israel by opposing, and even lobbying against, the policies of Israeli governments. In short, American Jewish support for Israel is no longer unquestioning and uncritical.

In the next chapter, I discuss the consequences of this development—specifically, the growing public criticism of Israel by American Jews, the backlash against this, and the organized American Jewish community's response to dissident groups.

2.
THE END OF "ISRAEL, RIGHT OR WRONG"

There is more tolerance for dissent in Israel than in the Jewish community.

—Abraham Foxman, former head of the
Anti-Defamation League[1]

In May 2013, when Naftali Bennett, Israel's minister for economics and Diaspora affairs, one of the rising stars of Israeli politics, went to the podium to give the keynote speech at a ceremony in Jerusalem for young Diaspora Jews participating on an Israeli government–sponsored program called "Masa Israel Journey," he must have expected to receive a warm welcome and rousing applause. After all, his young audience was supposed to be the next generation of Zionists, future advocates for Israel, and maybe even future immigrants. Bennett must have been shocked, therefore, when members of the audience started heckling him and chanting in English and Hebrew, "Diaspora Jews say 'end the occupation,' Diaspora Jews say 'no to annexation.'" Later that evening, the hecklers—mostly 18- and 19-year-old American Jews spending their gap year in Israel—issued a press release on the Facebook page of their newly formed group All That's Left, describing themselves as a "collective unequivocally committed to ending the occupation and focused on building the diaspora angle of resistance."[2]

What is remarkable about this incident is not that a senior Israeli official's speech was interrupted by protesters—this is a frequent occurrence nowadays—but that the protesters were young Diaspora Jews who had chosen to spend an extended amount of time studying, working, and volunteering in Israel. They were obviously attached to Israel and very engaged with it, yet at the same time, they were strongly critical of its policies and practices in the Occupied Territories. They were also willing to publicly voice this criticism, and unafraid to openly denounce the views of one of Israel's leading politicians—in front of him no less! Such an open and assertive display of dissent would surely have been unthinkable in the past. But it is only the tip of the iceberg. Beneath it lays a much broader shift occurring in the American Jewish relationship with Israel—a shift from unconditional support to critical engagement.

This chapter explores this shift, examining its causes and consequences for the American Jewish community. I argue that while American Jews remain strongly attached to Israel, they are now less inclined to blindly support its governments. It is no longer axiomatic among American Jews that to be "pro-Israel" requires supporting Israeli governments or that criticizing them is necessarily "anti-Israel." As the traditional norm against Jews publicly criticizing Israel has gradually eroded, it is becoming increasingly acceptable, if still controversial, for Jews to openly question, debate, and challenge Israeli government policies and practices. In particular, there is now frequent American Jewish criticism of Israel's occupation of the West Bank, its settlement building, and its treatment of Palestinians. Some have welcomed this development in the belief that a lively debate about Israel is a sign of a healthy, vibrant American Jewish community and a more accurate expression of the multiple perspectives and diverse opinions regarding Israel that exist within it. Others view it more warily, concerned that it undermines American Jewish unity and could eventually jeopardize American government support for Israel (upon which many believe Israel sorely depends). A right-wing minority vociferously opposes this criticism of Israel and tries to actively suppress it.

THE PROLIFERATION OF JEWISH DISSENT

In the past, particularly during the 1960s and 1970s, American Jewish support for Israel was generally unconditional and unequivocal. After the 1967 war, as pro-Israelism came to be seen as an essential component of American Jewish identity and unwavering support for Israel came to occupy a central place in organized Jewish communal life, being a "good Jew" entailed "uncritically supporting, promoting, and defending the Israeli government."[3] Questioning the actions and policies of Israeli governments was generally frowned upon, and criticizing them, especially in public, was forbidden. For a Jew to criticize Israel, especially before a gentile audience, was widely considered to be an act of disloyalty, even heresy. As Rabbi Arthur Hertzberg, a Conservative rabbi, prolific scholar, and outspoken activist, wrote in 1979: "One can no longer be excommunicated in Modern America for not believing in God, for living totally outside of the tradition, or even for marrying out. Instead, a new heresy had now emerged to mark the boundaries of legitimate Jewish identity, the heresy of opposition to Israel and Zionism."[4] Jews who spoke out against Israel's behavior could find themselves ostracized and stigmatized as "self-hating" Jews (a charge that is tantamount to calling them anti-Semitic). Thus, while there were always some critical voices within the Jewish community, dissent was largely stifled. The vast majority of American Jews abided by the communal prohibition and refrained from any public criticism of Israel, even if they privately harbored doubts and misgivings about the actions and policies of Israeli governments.

It was not only the prevailing communal norm governing Jewish public discourse regarding Israel that limited the willingness of American Jews to publicly question and challenge Israel's policies and actions. Most American Jews also adopted—with the encouragement of mainstream American Jewish organizations and institutions—a deferential, even subservient, attitude toward Israeli governments, uncritically accepting and endorsing whatever they did. Instead of questioning or challenging Israeli government policies and actions, American Jews "saw their roles as providing automatic financial and political support for whatever goals or policies the Jewish state chose to pursue."[5] The uncritical and deferential attitude to Israel held by most American Jews allowed Israeli governments to take American Jewish support for granted, confident in the knowledge that American Jews would overwhelmingly give their backing to whatever they did. "Whatever the issue, Israel could count on the enthusiastic, unified support of American Jews almost without exception."[6]

Since the 1980s, however, as American Jews have become steadily more disenchanted with Israel, their support for it has been changing. It has not fundamentally declined—American Jews still care about Israel just as much as they once did—but their support for it has become more qualified and more contingent than it was in the past. American Jews are now less willing to give Israel their full, unconditional, and unquestioning support. Instead of automatically issuing blanket expressions of support for Israel, growing numbers of American Jews will only support Israel if it acts in accordance with their own (generally liberal) values and beliefs.[7] As Jeremy Ben-Ami, founder and president of J Street (a liberal American Jewish advocacy organization), puts it: "the Israel we support is one that values human rights, one that promotes equality for all regardless of religion or ethnic background, and one that practices a vibrant form of democracy."[8] Thus, if Israeli governments engage in human rights violations, discriminatory practices, or undemocratic behavior, they are liable to lose the support of many American Jews and instead become the target of their condemnation and criticism. This means that Israeli governments can no longer count on the uncritical support of American Jews in the way that they used to.

The era of "Israel, right or wrong" is over. Nowadays, American Jewish support for Israel is much more complicated. American Jews are no longer sure how they should support Israel. Can they support Israel and also be critical of it? While the vast majority of American Jews (89 percent in the Pew Survey of 2013) now think that you can be Jewish and "strongly critical of Israel,"[9] many agonize over whether they should criticize Israel, especially in public. Many feel deeply conflicted between their emotional attachment to Israel and their disapproval of the actions and policies of its governments. As Rabbi Arthur Hertzberg wrote during the second Intifada: "The American Jewish community is torn right now between its love of Israel and its distaste for Israel's policies."[10] While undoubtedly heightened during the bloody years of the second Intifada, such ambivalence has now become a constant state of affairs for many American Jews. An editorial in the *Jewish Week* (the largest circulation Jewish newspaper in the United States) in March 2011, for instance, described the discomfort felt by many American Jews about recent political developments in Israel: "Most American Jews want to feel proud of the Jewish State, not frustrated or ashamed. It doesn't help when they read of settlement growth, the flotilla debacle, Foreign Minister Lieberman's hard-line comments about Israeli Arabs and other issues, or that the Knesset conducted inquiries into the funding sources of NGOs, or that the Chief Rabbinate is increasingly rigid on matters of marriage, divorce and conversion."[11]

Feeling deeply troubled by developments in Israel, more and more American Jews are starting to believe that you can indeed support Israel and also be critical of its governments. Writing in Israel's *Ha'aretz* newspaper in July 2013, Uri Misgav observes that: "American Jews are increasingly coming to realize that support for Israel does not mean automatic support for the Israeli government, whatever its policies. American Jews are increasingly coming to realize that genuine support for Israel means supporting Israelis—and that there are many Israelis to support, of all different types and streams."[12] Hence, for liberal American Jews supporting Israel might involve donating money to Israeli civil rights and human rights organizations (such as the New Israel Fund and B'Tselem) or joining American Jewish groups that try to promote peace between Israel and the Palestinians (such as J Street and Americans for Peace Now), while right-wing American Jews might give money to Jewish settlements in the West Bank (through the One Israel Fund, for example) or to right-wing political parties in Israel (the Likud Party, for instance, receives American Jewish financial support through American Friends of Likud and Likud USA).[13] A liberal American Jewish billionaire (Daniel Abraham) has even financed a public campaign prior to the 2015 Israeli election to unseat the right-wing Israeli government under Prime Minister Netanyahu,[14] and a right-wing American Jewish billionaire (Sheldon

Adelson) has purchased Israeli media outlets (most notably, *Israel Hayom*, a free newspaper that has become the most widely read in Israel) to support the Likud Party, and Netanyahu in particular.

Whatever their political orientations, therefore, for increasing numbers of American Jews supporting Israel no longer means automatically supporting its government's policies. In fact, it may even involve actively and vocally opposing those policies. Publicly criticizing Israeli governments, once almost taboo within the American Jewish community, has now become for many American Jews a way of supporting Israel. Their criticism is not driven by hostility to Israel, as it is sometimes depicted to be, but rather by genuine concern for Israel. As Steven Bayme notes: "Frequently, those who are most outspokenly critical of one or another aspect of Israeli policy are those most committed and attached to Israel as a Jewish state."[15] For these people, criticizing Israel is intended to "save it from itself." This kind of sentiment is clearly apparent in the words of Rabbi Jill Jacobs, the executive director of T'ruah: The Rabbinic Call for Human Rights: "We believe that Israel must continue to exist as a safe and secure Jewish state. But we're not willing to stand by as the current Israeli government destroys the chances for peace, isolates itself from the world, and angers the United States—its closest ally."[16]

In recent years, as American Jews have become increasingly alarmed about the direction in which Israel is heading and worried for the country's future, they have spoken out in public with greater urgency and frequency. The continued expansion of Jewish settlements, the treatment of Palestinians under Israeli military control in the West Bank, racist speech and violent attacks against Arab citizens of Israel, ultra-Orthodox attempts to exclude women from public spaces in Israel, the deportation and detention of African migrants and asylum seekers, laws aimed at restricting the activities and funding of Israeli nongovernmental organizations, and legislation enshrining and elevating Israel's status as a Jewish state—to name just a few examples— have all elicited a lot of vocal criticism from American Jews. But it is not only liberal and left-wing American Jews who publicly criticize Israel. Right-wing American Jews have been equally vociferous in their criticisms of Israeli governments, albeit generally for very differ-

ent reasons.[17] They fiercely denounced the Rabin government for signing the Oslo Accords with the PLO in the early 1990s, for example,
and they assailed the governments of Ehud Barak and Ehud Olmert
for their willingness to make concessions to the Palestinians in order
to reach a peace agreement (Prime Minister Barak's and Prime Minister Olmert's reported offers to the Palestinians, in 2000–2001 and
2008, respectively, to divide Jerusalem and give up much of the West
Bank were particularly criticized by those on the right). Even Israeli
Prime Minister Ariel Sharon—a longtime hero to many right-wing
Jews—was strongly criticized for his government's unilateral disengagement from the Gaza Strip in August 2005. Thus, left-wing and
right-wing, secular and religious, American Jews now openly challenge
the policies of Israeli governments and publicly voice their criticisms.

While there has always been some criticism of Israel from American
Jews, it has slowly spread over time. At first, in the years immediately
following the 1967 war, it was made mostly behind closed doors—in
the conference rooms of American Jewish organizations and maybe
around family dinner tables—or on college campuses.[18] Then some small
radical left-wing groups started doing it publicly,[19] and sometimes even a
few outspoken mainstream communal leaders.[20] Today, however, many
individuals and organizations almost incessantly publicly criticize Israel. What is different now, therefore, is the extent and frequency of
American Jewish criticism of Israel. It has gone from being a largely
elite and fringe phenomenon to a mass phenomenon; as many more
American Jews are now willing to publicly criticize Israeli policies and
actions. Indeed, criticism of Israel has not merely gone mainstream,
it has "gone viral." It has also gone from being a sporadic occurrence
to an almost daily one. There is now a constant chorus of criticism of
Israel by American Jews, especially of Israel's occupation of the West
Bank and its treatment of Palestinians there.

What accounts for this proliferation of dissent is not merely greater
opposition among American Jews (on both the left and the right)
to Israeli government policies, but also a growing sense of assertiveness vis-à-vis Israel. American Jews today are less deferential toward
Israeli governments, and more inclined to form their own opinions
about what Israel should or shouldn't do. They are also more willing

to loudly voice these opinions, believing that they have the right and even the obligation to do so. As Albert Vorspan, a longtime leader of the Reform Movement in the United States, declared during the first Intifada: "We owe Israel our support, yes, but we also owe to it our best judgment, our honest disagreement, and our conscience."[21] Another liberal American Jewish leader, Rabbi Arthur Hertzberg, made the same point in an article written during the second Intifada, stating: "We who love Israel have an obligation to say what we believe. We have for a century or more helped and supported the Zionist endeavor in the state of Israel. We have long lived with the notion that Israeli governments, from right to left, have tried to inculcate in us —that they determine policy, and we are privileged to say amen on cue. This nonsense is now bankrupt."[22] More recently, William Daroff, the Washington director of the Jewish Federations of North America (the national umbrella organization for Jewish Federations), expressed this perspective when he stated: "There are things that Israel can and should do to make it a better country. Diaspora Jewry has an obligation to stand up."[23]

In line with this more assertive attitude, American Jews are no longer prepared to quiescently accept whatever Israeli governments do, and to simply send their money to Israel and lobby on its behalf. Instead, they now want to have a bigger say in Israel's future. Having long been "silent partners" in the Israeli-Zionist project, American Jews increasingly want to be active participants, if only from afar. In the words of Jeremy Ben-Ami: "For too long, the relationship between Israel and the Diaspora has been defined by Israel's requests for assistance from friends abroad. We've been asked to send money. To move to Israel. To lobby. To send our children to visit. . . . [I]t is now time for friends of Israel to perform the ultimate act of Zionism—to tell Israel the truth."[24] In a similar vein, Rabbi Jill Jacobs writes that:

Since long before the creation of the state, the relationship between Israel and Diaspora Jews has been an unequal one. For too long, we have accepted the assumption that Diaspora Jews will send money and keep our mouths shut. . . . Increasingly, few of us are willing to accept this paradigm. . . . We are engaged global citizens who protest when the United States, Canada, Sudan, China, Syria, or any other country violates international human rights laws. We are increasingly unwilling to give the Israeli government a pass on the standards to which we hold the rest of the world. And we believe that the relationship between Israel and Diaspora Jews should be a two-way street, in which we each acknowledge that we have much to learn from the other.[25]

Greater assertiveness toward Israel is ultimately the product of deeper changes in the collective psychology of American Jews. American Jewry's economic success, political power, and cultural vitality has imbued American Jews with confidence and pride. As such, they are not in the least ashamed of or apologetic about living in the Diaspora (if, in fact, they see themselves as living in diaspora at all),[26] and they feel that they are completely equal, not inferior, to Jews in Israel. It is from this vantage point that many American Jews now feel entitled to criticize Israel, whereas previous generations did not. American Jews are also more secure about their place in society, and less fearful than they were in the past, due to the decline of anti-Semitism in the United States and their successful integration into American society. The diminished sense of threat means that they feel less of a need for solidarity with each other or with Israel. Hence, they are quicker to "break ranks" and voice dissent. This is particularly true for younger American Jews who do not feel at all vulnerable in the United States, and see no reason not to freely voice their own opinions about Israel. As noted in the previous chapter, younger American Jews are also less likely to perceive Israel as vulnerable and embattled. Instead, to many of them Israel appears to be a strong and militarily powerful state, hence they also feel that it is perfectly safe to criticize it.

THE RIGHT-WING BACKLASH

As American Jewish criticism of Israel has become more frequent and more widespread, the American Jewish community has struggled to come to terms with it. It has been difficult for many American Jews to accept such criticism of Israel, especially at a time when Israel is being widely condemned in the international community. Nostalgic for the period when Israel received uncritical support from American Jews, and convinced that such support is more necessary than ever in the face of (what they see as) mounting "delegitimization" of the Jewish state, many American Jews are deeply disturbed by what they see as the willingness of Jewish critics of Israel to lend their voices to the "anti-Israel" choir. In their minds, Jewish criticism of Israel is, at best, misguided and naïve, if not downright disloyal. Rather than reluctantly accepting such criticism, some have sought to silence it altogether or at least restrict its expression in Jewish communal settings. Thus, there has been a furious backlash against Jewish criticism of Israel in the United States (as well as in Israel itself).[27]

The most common form this backlash has taken has been the demonization of prominent outspoken Jewish critics of Israel such as Judith Butler, Norman Finkelstein, and the late Tony Judt, who have all been publicly assailed as "Israel bashers," "self-hating Jews," terrorist sympathizers, and anti-Semites.[28] Judith Butler's anti-Zionism and advocacy of Boycott, Divestment, and Sanctions (BDS) has led not only to her being denounced as an anti-Semite and accused of supporting Hamas and Hezbollah, but also to her being prevented from appearing in Jewish venues. According to Shaul Magid, the attempt to exclude Judith Butler from the "Jewish public sphere"—including an outcry from some Jews who objected to an invitation extended to her by the Jewish Museum of New York to speak at a February 2014 event on Franz Kafka, from which she ultimately withdrew[29]— represents more than an act of censorship. It amounts to an effort to excommunicate her from the Jewish community, much like the Dutch Jewish community excommunicated Baruch Spinoza in the seventeenth century because of his heretical views.[30]

Even well-known supporters of Israel, like author Peter Beinart and the *New York Times* columnist Thomas Friedman, have been subject to vituperative criticism for their much milder critiques of Israel.[31] The vitriolic and ad hominem attacks leveled against these individuals (and many others), however, is only the most public manifestation of intolerance of left-wing and liberal American Jewish criticism of Israel. Intolerance is also often expressed privately, in behind-the-scenes efforts to prevent critics of Israel from speaking in Jewish venues, such as synagogues, Jewish Community Centers (JCCs), university Hillel clubs, and even museums.[32] These efforts sometimes succeed in making Jewish critics of Israel personae non gratae. In November 2010, for example, J Street President Jeremy Ben-Ami's scheduled speaking appearance at a Reform synagogue in Newton, Massachusetts, was cancelled because of pressure from some right-wing members of the congregation.[33] Similarly, in November 2012, Peter Beinart was disinvited by the organizers of a Jewish book festival held in the Jewish Community Center of Atlanta, reportedly after complaints from some of its members.[34] Even individuals who have been invited to speak or perform in Jewish venues and whose opinions about Israel have nothing do with their talks or performances have had their invitations rescinded because of critical statements they have made about Israel and Zionism. In January 2014, David Harris-Gershon, author of a memoir about his response to his wife's injury in a Palestinian terrorist attack in Israel, was disinvited by the Jewish Community Center in Washington, DC, because of comments he had made in a blog post that were deemed to be supportive of boycotting Israel. The performance of a Jewish feminist punk rock group at a music festival organized by the Washington, DC, JCC was also cancelled because its lead singer was critical of Zionism.[35]

While effectively blacklisting certain individuals, this kind of behind-the-scenes pressure (often conducted by e-mail and in closed-door meetings) can also have a wider "chilling effect"—whether intended or not—on public criticism of Israel in local Jewish communities because Jewish community officials and rabbis may prefer not to invite potentially controversial speakers to their institutions and congregations in order to avoid offending anyone and creating strife. "All across the country," Jeremy Ben-Ami writes, "rabbis, Hillel directors and other organizational leaders are forced to consider whether they can or want to deal with the headaches, slander and vitriol from conservative voices in their community before they think of giving a platform to views outside the party line."[36]

It is not just the desire to avoid headaches and controversy that can prevent synagogues, JCCs, and other Jewish venues from hosting critics of Israel or sponsoring events critical of the country. Their funding may also be at stake, as they run the risk of alienating major donors if they disapprove of their activities.[37] They might even be faced with direct threats that donations will be cut back or cease altogether. In a period when many Jewish organizations are struggling financially, such threats are hard to ignore. The threat to funding was most apparent in the aftermath of the huge controversy that erupted in July 2009 over the San Francisco Jewish Film Festival's screening of the film *Rachel*, about the life and death of Rachel Corrie,[38] and the invitation to her mother, Cindy Corrie, to speak after the screening.[39] In protest, five members of the film festival's board resigned and several of its major funders withdrew their support. The local Jewish Federation (the Jewish Community Federation of San Francisco) was one of the main funders of the film festival, and in the wake of the controversy it drew up guidelines limiting the kinds of "Israel-Related Programming" it would fund in the future. These guidelines stipulated that the San Francisco Jewish Federation would not provide funding to any organization that has programs about Israel which "undermine the legitimacy of the State of Israel" or to any organization that co-sponsors programs with groups that are considered to undermine Israel's legitimacy (what exactly constituted undermining Israel's legitimacy was left undefined).[40] In response to these guidelines, critics charged that they would have a "chilling effect on the San Francisco Bay Area's Jewish community."[41]

Since the San Francisco Jewish Federation issued its guidelines on Israel programming in February 2010, there have been concerted attempts—involving threats to cut funding—made to get other local Jewish Federations and JCCs to adopt similar guidelines restricting them from funding activities or groups that allegedly undermine Israel's legitimacy.[42] A group calling itself "JCCWatch" has waged an aggressive campaign in New York City against the JCC in Manhattan and the UJA-Federation of New York opposing the JCC's sponsorship of the Other Israel Film Festival (which screens films by and about Arab citizens of Israel), and the fact that it allowed groups like the New Israel Fund and B'Tselem to use its facilities.[43] The JCC in Washington, DC, and the Jewish Federation of Greater Washington,

which partially funds it, have come under persistent attack for providing the performance space for a local Jewish theater company, Theater
J, to stage plays that right-wing critics have accused of delegitimizing
Israel.[44] In the fall of 2013, for example, a group of activists calling
themselves "Citizens Opposed to Propaganda Masquerading as Art"
waged a public campaign to stop the JCC from allowing Theater J to
perform the controversial play "The Admission" by the Israeli play-
wright Motti Lerner (the play deals with claims that Israeli soldiers
carried out a massacre of Arab civilians in the village of Tantura during
the 1948 war). The group targeted donors to the Jewish Federation,
calling on them to withhold their donations unless it ceased its support for the Washington JCC. Eventually, the scheduled performance
of the play was cancelled and replaced with a workshop about it.[45] The
next year, the JCC cancelled Theater J's annual Voices from a Changing Middle East Festival, which had previously staged plays that were
critical of Israel. In an internal document describing the pressure it
has faced, Ari Roth, Theater J's longtime artistic director complained:
"Increasingly, Theater J is being kept from programming as freely, as
fiercely, and expressing itself as fully as it needs. We find the culture of
open discourse and dissent within our Jewish Community Center to
be evaporating." He went on to note that: "The [Jewish Community]
Center wants to stand united with Federation in support of Israel, at
war and at peace; aligned with the Government of Israel. The theater
wants to shine a light on trouble-spots as part of a comprehensive
engagement with Israel."[46] Shortly after making this complaint and
publicly criticizing the DC JCC's censorship of Theater J, Ari Roth
was fired for insubordination.[47]

Right-wing protests against Jewish cultural events and speakers
accused of being "anti-Israel" have led many left-wing American Jewish critics of Israel to claim that they are being "muzzled" and that
an intolerant "McCarthyite" atmosphere prevails within the American Jewish community.[48] In reality, such claims seem exaggerated. Of
course, it is impossible to really know how much potential dissent has
been silenced. Right-wing efforts to suppress Jewish dissent about
Israel are undoubtedly effective at times. Noisy public campaigns
or quiet private pressure from a few wealthy donors can sometimes

succeed in curtailing the expression of dissenting views about Israel within the American Jewish community.[49] Some Jewish institutions and congregations have surely refrained from hosting critics of Israel or staging critical events about it in order to avoid controversy or cuts in their funding, and some left-wing Jewish critics of Israel may well be intimidated into silence, rather than risk becoming the object of character assassination and vilification by those on the right. Nevertheless, the fact is that there is more public criticism of Israel and debate about it in the American Jewish community today than ever before. Lively, and often ill-tempered, discussions about Israel are now a common feature of American Jewish life, and Jewish critics of Israel, once communal outcasts who were rarely heard from, now regularly appear before Jewish audiences (although when they do, they must often be "balanced" with right-wing speakers, whereas the converse seldom occurs).[50] Far from being silenced, American Jewish criticism of Israel has only gotten louder. Thus, although there is certainly strong disapproval, if not active suppression, of dissent about Israel within some parts of the American Jewish community, overall the efforts to silence dissent have largely failed.[51]

THE DEBATE ABOUT DISSENT

Left-wing Jewish criticism of Israel and the right-wing backlash against it have fueled an ongoing debate within the American Jewish community over dissent about Israel.[52] This debate is not simply about whether Israeli government policies and actions deserve to be criticized, but more fundamentally about the legitimacy of Diaspora Jews publicly criticizing Israel. At the heart of the debate over dissent are the questions of whether American Jews, and Diaspora Jews more generally, are entitled to criticize Israel, and whether or not they should do so in public. These questions have been the subject of a long-running, and sometimes bitter disagreement, dating back to the mid-1970s. As the journalist J. J. Goldberg observed in his 1996 book about American Jewish politics: "The right of Jews to dissent from Israeli policy is the most sordidly painful issue to arise in Jewish community life in the last generation."[53] The issue has continued to be a salient one in the American Jewish community because there is no consensus among American Jews about the "norms of dissent."[54]

According to the traditional norm within the American Jewish community that prevailed until the 1980s, public dissent about Israel was basically forbidden, or at least strongly discouraged and frowned upon. This norm held that all Jews should support and defend Israel (through *Hasbara* [public relations], political lobbying, and donating money to Israeli causes), and never criticize it in public, especially in non-Jewish settings. As Abraham Foxman, the longtime head of the Anti-Defamation League (ADL) once put it: "Israeli democracy should decide; American Jews should support."[55] The prohibition on criticism was generally justified on the grounds that Jews in the Diaspora are not entitled to criticize Israeli government policies because they do not live in Israel and therefore do not have to live with the consequences of their political opinions and preferred policies. Since their lives are not at risk, and their children do not have to serve in the IDF, they do not have the right to criticize Israel. In other words, Diaspora Jews have no business telling Israeli Jews what to do when it comes to their security and their lives.[56]

Even if it is conceded that, in principle, Diaspora Jews can criticize Israel, it is often argued that, in practice, because the (international and/or domestic) climate of opinion is already so unsympathetic and even hostile to Israel, Diaspora Jews should not criticize Israel publicly because Israel's enemies can always exploit this. Well-intended Jewish criticism of Israel can be used to promote the "delegitimization" of the Jewish state, for instance, or provide a "cover" for anti-Semitism. In addition, it is also argued that public Jewish dissent about Israel conveys Jewish disunity and thus weakness. Hence, if at all necessary, Jewish criticism of Israeli policies and actions should only be conveyed in private to Israeli diplomats and policymakers. Publicly, Diaspora Jews must always present a united front in support of Israel, whatever their personal qualms or misgivings might be. This view was clearly conveyed by Rabbi Alexander Schindler, a longtime leader of the Reform movement and the chairman of the Conference of Presidents in the late 1970s, when he told a journalist: "Dissent ought not and should not be made public because . . . when Jewish dissent is made public in the daily press or in the halls of government, the result is to give aid and comfort to the enemy and to weaken that Jewish unity which is essential for the security of Israel."[57]

The power of the traditional norm against Jewish public criticism of Israel has gradually diminished in the American Jewish community over time, as it has been repeatedly challenged. Some have argued that Diaspora Jews have the right to criticize Israel because it is the state of the Jewish people, which claims to act in their name and on their behalf, and not just on behalf of Israeli citizens.[58] Others argue that since Israel's policies and actions can sometimes have adverse effects upon Jews living outside Israel, Diaspora Jews are entitled to voice their opinions about these policies and actions. Another common argument is that because Diaspora Jews care so much about Israel, it is only natural for them to express their concerns and criticisms about what it does. In the words of J. J. Goldberg: "Jews have been urged continually to speak out and protest the policies of the French, Soviet, Swedish, Sudanese and Iranian governments. The one country about which we are expected to keep silent is the one to which we have the deepest spiritual connection. It makes no sense."[59] An extension of this argument is that "honest," "friendly" Diaspora Jewish criticism of Israel is particularly appropriate when Israel is acting in ways that are contrary to its long-term interests and jeopardizing its future (for instance, by expanding settlements in the West Bank), just as you should tell a member of your own family if they were behaving self-destructively. Thus, J Street's Jeremy Ben-Ami has argued that: "The American Jewish community would serve Israel best at this moment not by circling the wagons in unquestioning support but with a friendly reminder to Israel that its long-term survival and security depends on reaching a viable peace with its enemies."[60] It is also sometimes argued that public Jewish criticism of Israel is often necessary because it is the only way to really get the attention of Israeli governments and the Israeli public. Finally, some contend that American Jews have a special obligation to speak out because of the political clout they possess and because their taxes indirectly help to support the Israeli Occupation through American aid to Israel.

In general, most American Jews think that it is legitimate, at least in principle, for Jews to publicly criticize Israel (except perhaps when Israel is at war). When asked in surveys over a number of years, they have regularly rejected the view that American Jews should not publicly criticize Israeli government policies.[61] Although a majority of American Jews consistently supports the right of American Jews to criticize Israeli government policies, a majority (ranging from 53 to 66 percent in the AJC annual surveys) also consistently says that American Jews should support the policies of Israeli governments regardless of one's personal views. Thus, it seems that most American Jews believe in supporting Israeli governments, while also insisting upon their freedom of speech. Although there is a consensus that it is acceptable for American Jews to publicly criticize Israel, there is no agreement among American Jews about whether it is desirable to do so. A plurality of American Jews think that it is better for both Israel and for American Jewry when the American Jewish community "speaks with a unified voice regarding Israeli government policy," but a significant minority disagrees with this on both counts.[62] American Jews, in other words, are divided over whether or not public criticism of Israel can be a good thing for Israel or for American Jews themselves.

As far as most American Jews are concerned, therefore, it is not completely taboo to publicly criticize Israel, even if many believe it is undesirable and some find it bothersome.[63] It is not just rank-and-file American Jews who accept criticism of Israel, so too do American Jewish leaders—at least up to a point—despite the fact that they are frequently accused of trying to repress all criticism of Israel. Perhaps the most powerful American Jewish leader, Malcolm Hoenlein, the executive vice chairman of the Conference of Presidents (who is widely believed to be politically right wing) has said in an interview that:

I'm not troubled when people criticize or differ with Israeli policy. I don't think it makes them anti-Semites or anti-Israel if it's on a policy basis. I do think it's unacceptable when it's about

Israel's right to exist and to defend its citizens, and when people here are determining what security over there should be rather than leaving it to Israel which is free and democratic. It doesn't mean they can't express their points of view, but they have to do it in responsible ways—by that I mean, thinking about the consequences of your words—do they do damage to the security and interests of Israel?[64]

In this statement, Hoenlein accepts Jewish criticism of Israel, except when it concerns Israel's security and legitimacy (a potentially broad exception). According to him, criticism of Israeli military actions, counter-terrorism and security policies, and so on are off-limits to criticism, as is questioning its right to exist (which, presumably, means its right to exist as a Jewish state). The distinction that Hoenlein draws between permissible and impermissible subjects of criticism is a common one within the organized American Jewish community.[65] Generally speaking, public criticism of internal Israeli issues—especially those directly concerning Jews and Judaism, such as the Orthodox Rabbinate's control of conversion and marriage in Israel—is widely regarded as being acceptable, whereas public criticism of Israeli foreign and security policies or the conduct of the IDF is deemed to be absolutely unacceptable.[66]

Mainstream American Jewish organizations like the ADL and AJC, therefore, are willing to publicly criticize Israeli governments on issues concerning religious pluralism in Israel (a subject of great concern to many non-Orthodox American Jews),[67] and increasingly on issues affecting the quality of Israeli democracy and civil society (such as Israeli government attempts to limit the funding of human rights and civil rights NGOs in Israel, or Knesset bills that prioritize Israel's Jewish identity over its democratic character).[68] In recent years, the ADL and many other groups within the organized American Jewish community have also become more vocal in complaining about discrimination against Israel's Arab minority, racist attacks against Arab citizens, and politically motivated vandalism of Arab property and desecration of mosques (all of which have been on the rise in Israel). A broad coalition of mainstream American Jewish organizations have even established an "Inter-Agency Taskforce on Israeli Arab Issues" to raise awareness within the American Jewish community about the challenges and problems of Israel's Arab minority and help promote civic equality and Arab-Jewish coexistence in Israel.[69] The treatment of foreign migrants and asylum-seekers in Israel has also recently attracted stinging public rebukes from some mainstream communal leaders and organizations.[70]

Major Jewish organizations are no longer just defending Israel as they once did; they are now also increasingly criticizing it,[71] albeit in a highly circumscribed manner. Barely a week goes by nowadays when an American Jewish organization does not publicly weigh in on some domestic Israeli issue. Thus, like American Jewry in general, the organized American Jewish community has become much more willing to publicly express criticism of Israel, although it continues to largely refrain from speaking out on most issues concerning Israeli security and foreign policy (the notable exception to this concerns the future of Jerusalem, which is widely regarded as an issue that all Jews have a right to voice an opinion about[72]). Israel's occupation of Palestinian territories and the actions of the IDF, especially during wartime, remain immune from criticism for much of the organized American Jewish community. This only really applies, however, to liberal and left-wing criticism. When right-wing Jewish groups like the Zionist Organization of America (ZOA) assail Israeli governments for failing to be "tougher" in their dealings with the Palestinians and other enemies of Israel (such as Hezbollah and Iran)—which they have done—they are rarely, if ever, rebuked for doing so by other American Jewish organizations. This is evidence of a double standard within the organized American Jewish community when it comes to criticism of Israel, with right-wing criticism of Israel treated much more leniently than left-wing criticism of Israel.[73] As J. J. Goldberg points out:

There is a taboo against Jews urging Israel to adopt more liberal policies toward the Palestinians and the neighboring Arab states. There is no taboo against urging more hardline policies. The unstated logic behind this one-sided stricture is readily apparent.

Advocating a more conciliatory policy can be depicted, fairly or not (usually not) as siding with the enemy. By contrast, no one argues seriously that urging greater inflexibility is meant to weaken Israel and strengthen its foes, even though that may well be the practical result.[74]

"HOW BIG IS THE TENT?" THE EXCLUSION AND INCLUSION OF DISSIDENT GROUPS

The most hotly debated question in the organized American Jewish community today is not whether public Jewish criticism of Israel is allowed—most accept that it is—but rather how far can this criticism go and still be acceptable? Can critics challenge Israel's legitimacy as a Jewish state? Can they criticize Zionism? Can they call for Israel to become a binational state or for a "one-state" solution to the Israeli-Palestinian conflict? Closely related to this is the question of what kinds of political activities and tactics can critics engage in or endorse? Specifically, can they support pressure, sanctions, or boycotts against Israel? At issue, therefore, is whether certain political views and activities vis-à-vis Israel are simply beyond the pale. Are communal "red lines" on Israel necessary? If so, where should they be drawn? And how should groups that cross these red lines be treated? Should they be excluded from the organized Jewish community? In short, as the question is widely phrased within the community, "how big is the tent?"[75]

This is by no means a new question for the organized American Jewish community. In fact, it has been grappling with the issue of how to manage dissenting opinions and groups, and whether to accommodate them, since the formation of "Breira: A Project of Concern in Diaspora-Israel Relations" in the aftermath of the 1973 war. Breira (meaning "alternative" in Hebrew, a play on the then popular Israeli slogan *Ain Breira*—"There is no choice") was a completely new phenomenon—a Jewish, and explicitly Zionist, organization that claimed to support Israel but was also strongly critical of its policies.[76] Going against the prevailing consensus within Israel and the American Jewish community, Breira called for the establishment of a Palestinian state in the Occupied Territories (both major political parties in Israel at the time opposed this),[77] and even more controversially, it called for Israel to negotiate with the PLO, which was then widely regarded by American Jews (and Israeli Jews) as a terrorist organization implacably dedicated to Israel's destruction. Breira's advocacy of these then-radical views was controversial enough for the mainstream Jewish community, but the fact that it did so publicly, and attracted a lot of media attention in the process (it received coverage, for instance, in the *New York Times* and *Washington Post*), made it even more controversial since it broke the taboo on public criticism of Israel within the American Jewish community.[78] This was very deliberate on Breira's part, as one of its declared aims when it was established was "to legitimize public dissent within the American Jewish community . . . ."[79] Not only did Breira publicly criticize Israeli policies toward the Palestinians and the Occupied Territories, it also openly and directly challenged the organized American Jewish community, accusing its leadership of muzzling communal debate over Israeli policies, and calling for "the creation of a grass-roots based democratic structure for American Jewry."[80]

While Breira's views about the Israeli-Palestinian conflict, its criticisms of Israeli government policies, and its critique of the American Jewish establishment were highly provocative and controversial within the organized American Jewish community at the time, Breira was initially grudgingly tolerated during its first three years in existence. It was not until a newspaper article revealed that two of its members had been part of an American Jewish delegation (which also included individuals from the AJC and B'nai B'rith) that had secretly met in November 1976 with two Palestinians who had close ties to the PLO (this was when the Israeli and American governments refused to speak with the PLO) that Breira became the target of a "vicious campaign" against it by right-wing groups (notably the ZOA and American Friends for a Safe Israel).[81] It was accused of being anti-Israel, and depicted as a group of Israel-bashing, PLO-supporting Jews. The president of the ZOA at the time went so far as to denounce Breira's leaders as "the Jewish spokesmen of the PLO,"[82] and called for Breira to be "scoured from the community."[83]

75

Along with harsh ad hominem attacks against Breira's leaders, the group's members were denounced as traitors and shunned.[84] Breira members were removed from the boards of local Jewish Federations, rabbis identified with Breira were fired, and Breira members working for Jewish organizations like B'nai B'rith were pressured by their employers and faced with the threat that they could lose their jobs if they continued their activities.[85] Faced with this extremely hostile reaction, the group was eventually forced to disband shortly after its first and only national conference in March 1977 (the meeting itself was violently disrupted by members of the Jewish Defense League).

Judging from the sustained campaign against Breira within the organized American Jewish community, one might think that the group posed a real challenge to American Jewry's support for Israel or to the power of the community's existing leadership. In reality, this was far from being the case. For all the attention and controversy it generated, Breira was just a small organization—at its peak, it had only three paid staff, about 1,500 members, and a budget of less than $200,000.[86] It was hardly in a position to challenge the major, established, Jewish organizations that shaped and channeled American Jewish support for Israel, nor could it possibly undermine this support at the time (nor did it actually want to). Thus, Steven Rosenthal observes that: "In retrospect what was most significant about Breira was that the reaction it elicited was all out of proportion to its power and influence."[87]

Why, then, did Breira provoke such a disproportionate, almost hysterical reaction within the organized American Jewish community? What makes this even more puzzling was the fact that Breira's membership was largely drawn from the ranks of the organized Jewish community—hardly people who could be branded as traitors.[88] They were mostly young rabbinical students, Jewish educators, Hillel directors, and Jewish professionals working in mainstream organizations like the AJC and B'nai B'rith. Breira also had nearly one hundred Reform and Conservative rabbis on its Advisory Council (which was chaired by Rabbi Arnold Jacob Wolf, the director of Yale University's Hillel Society, and included some well-known rabbis like Rabbi Everett Gendler, Rabbi Eugene Borowitz, and Rabbi Balfour Brickner), and it had the support of some famous Jewish intellectuals (like Irving Howe and Nathan Glazer).[89]

The very fact, however, that Breira drew support from people working inside the organized Jewish community and from leading rabbis and Jewish intellectuals helps account for the potential threat that it was perceived to pose (it was also the group's vulnerability, since many of its members depended upon the organized Jewish community for their livelihoods, and they could therefore be more easily pressured to stop their activities). Although Breira was small, it was not a marginal, fringe organization. It came from the heart of the American Jewish community and, as such, it threatened to overturn the status quo and legitimize public Jewish dissent about Israel at a time when such dissent was still forbidden in mainstream Jewish circles. Breira's members could not easily be dismissed as "self-hating Jews," and their active roles and prominent positions in the organized Jewish community meant that they were well placed to spread their dissenting opinions to other American Jews. The attack against Breira, therefore, was aimed at silencing public Jewish dissent before it could spread. As Marla Brettschneider writes: "The story of Breira unfortunately demonstrates that the American Jewish community of the 1970s, in terms of its relationship to Israel, was plagued by efforts to keep the public discourse of the community closed through a politics of silencing."[90]

This changed in the 1980s, however, as a host of left-wing Jewish groups emerged (such as New Jewish Agenda, Americans for Peace Now, Project Nishma, and the Jewish Peace Lobby), spurred on by the rise of the Israeli peace movement, particularly the activities of *Shalom Acshav* ("Peace Now," formed in 1978).[91] These groups were also openly critical of Israeli government policies and advocated views about the Israeli-Palestinian conflict similar to those of Breira. But while they generally encountered a lot of hostility at first, these groups fared much better than Breira. Indeed, in some cases, they were even accepted into important Jewish umbrella organizations (most notably, Americans for Peace Now, which was admitted into the Conference of Presidents in 1993 despite objections that it was pro-Arab and supported the PLO).[92] The contrast between the organized Jewish community's ostracism of Breira and its acceptance of the group New Jewish Agenda is particularly telling in this respect. Established in 1980 (and disbanded in 1992), New Jewish Agenda was in many respects Breira's successor.[93] The organization included many former Breira members, and like Breira, it called for Israel to stop its settlement activities in the West Bank and Gaza Strip, recognize the PLO, and allow for the establishment of a Palestinian state (it actually went further than Breira, calling for peace talks between Israel and the PLO, without insisting that the PLO first renounce terrorism or recognize Israel's right to exist).[94] Echoing Breira, New Jewish Agenda also insisted upon "the right and necessity of Jews everywhere to engage in democratic debate and open discussion regarding Israeli policies,"[95] and it called for greater democracy within the organized American Jewish community, advocating "the transformation of Jewish institutions and the creation of new ones to represent the whole spectrum of views of U.S. Jewry."[96]

Despite New Jewish Agenda's similarities with Breira, and the fact that it had many more members that Breira ever did (at its peak in the mid-1980s it had over 5,000 members in fifty chapters across the United States and Canada),[97] its members were not ostracized, nor were their jobs threatened. Instead of being intimidated, pressured, and shunned by the organized Jewish community, New Jewish Agenda members were allowed to make presentations to mainstream Jewish organizations, and some of them joined local Jewish Community Relations Councils (JCRCs).[98] In 1983, the group even managed to introduce a motion for debate at the General Assembly of Jewish Federations calling for a settlement freeze in the West Bank (the motion was heard and tabled).[99] While there are many reasons why New Jewish Agenda received much better treatment from the organized Jewish community than Breira did (having to do with its strategy, messaging, and support base),[100] the biggest reason is simply because the American Jewish community in general became more tolerant of dissent about Israel —if not more receptive to it—during the course of the 1980s (especially as a result of the Lebanon War and the first Intifada).[101]

The differences between Breira's experience and those of New Jewish Agenda and Americans for Peace Now demonstrate that dissenting groups are not necessarily excluded from the organized Jewish community. They can, in fact, sometimes be accommodated and given "a seat at the table." But getting a seat at the Jewish communal table is by no means easy, as the experience of J Street since its establishment in 2008 demonstrates. J Street's stated purpose is to provide "a political voice for friends of Israel who care deeply about its long-term survival and security and who are willing, when appropriate, to break with Israeli government policy. Who are ready to say that the United States may need to press not only the Palestinians and Arabs to make peace, but the Israelis, too."[102] Regardless of its effort to present itself as solidly pro-Israel, J Street, like other groups before it that are critical of Israeli government policies, has been denounced as "anti-Israel" and vilified for some of the public stances it has taken on the Israeli-Palestinian conflict, especially during its early years.[103] Its refusal to endorse Israel's "Operation Cast Lead" in Gaza in December 2008, for instance, was particularly galling to some within the American Jewish community, and led to a lot of opprobrium for the fledgling group.[104] J Street has also been attacked for its donors, specifically the liberal philanthropist George Soros, and supposedly some Muslim Arabs.[105] Much of the American Jewish establishment initially shunned J Street and tried to marginalize it—the leaders of the AJC, ADL, and AIPAC allegedly refused to speak in public alongside Jeremy Ben-Ami[106]—while some right-wing organizations went further, actively trying to discredit the group (as did some right-wing members of Israel's Parliament[107]). The Zionist Organization of America, for instance, accused J Street of "siding with Israel's enemies."[108] An organization called Americans for Peace and Tolerance even produced a scathing documentary film called the *J Street Challenge* that was screened in JCCs and synagogues across the United States.[109] In the film, a variety of prominent critics of J Street (such as Alan Dershowitz and Ruth Wisse) accuse the group of "dividing the Jewish community," and of being naïve, arrogant, and "imperialistic" in its views about Israel and the peace process.

Yet, despite being ostracized and relentlessly criticized, J Street has attracted growing support among American Jews, especially younger ones. Within a year of its founding, it had 115,000 online supporters and 7,000 donors (most of whom were Jewish). By 2013, it had around 180,000 registered supporters, 20,000 donors, and over forty-five local chapters across the United States.[110] It also had a Rabbinic Cabinet, composed of hundreds of rabbis, and a national student organization (J Street U) with over 7,500 student members and more than fifty campus chapters. J Street's popular appeal among American Jews stems in part from the frustration that many American Jews feel over what they perceive as the reluctance of Israel's government, led by Benjamin Netanyahu, to seriously advance the peace process with the Palestinians.[111] But it went deeper than this. J Street also tapped into a widespread desire among liberal American Jews to connect with Israel and criticize it at the same time, while also connecting with other like-minded Jews. As the journalist and author Peter Beinart, who himself became something of an icon among liberal American Jews, puts it: "Until J Street came along, liberal American Jews often felt forced to choose between progressive activism that allowed no room for their Jewish identity and a Jewish establishment that offered no room for their progressive ideals, at least not on Israel. J Street has changed that. Its supporters love it—even if it has not brought peace closer—because it has created a space that does not require them to check one half of themselves at the door."[112]

As J Street's support within the Jewish community has steadily increased, mainstream Jewish organizations have gradually begun to accept the upstart organization (as has the Israeli government[113]), albeit perhaps only grudgingly. J Street representatives are now frequently invited to speak in JCCs and synagogues across the country,[114] J Street chapters have won battles for admission into some local JCRCs,[115] and J Street U has been accepted as a partner organization of Hillel, the largest Jewish campus organization in the United States.[116] Rachel Lerner, who leads J Street's work in the Jewish community, claims that although it is still controversial, the overall trend is clearly toward a growing communal acceptance and inclusion of J Street.[117]

Undoubtedly, part of the reason for J Street's increasing legitimacy in the organized Jewish community (and in Israel) are deliberate changes in the organization's tone and strategy. According to Lerner, after initially taking a "confrontational" and "aggressive" approach to the organized Jewish community out of a desire to challenge it and gain attention, J Street has become less adversarial and its "messaging has changed."[118] J Street takes pains to emphasize its pro-Israel credentials and tries to present itself as a moderate group—in Jeremy Ben-Ami's words, J Street seeks to "rally moderate Jewish Americans who care deeply about Israel to express themselves politically."[119] J Street has also burnished its moderate image by opposing the Palestinian bid for full UN membership in 2011, and opposing all forms of boycotting Israel and Israeli products, including a limited boycott of Israeli goods produced in the West Bank. J Street's opposition to the global Boycott, Divestment, and Sanctions (BDS) campaign targeting Israel (first launched in 2005 by the Palestinian Boycott National Committee), especially its active lobbying against divestment initiatives on college campuses, has been particularly important in positioning it as a more centrist, rather than leftist, organization.[120]

J Street's growing acceptance within the Jewish community is more than just a result of its effective public relations and its moderate— some might say cautious—stances on some controversial issues. Fundamentally, it reflects the fact that its basic message, as Ben-Ami puts it, "You don't have to be noncritical. You don't have to adopt the party line. It's not, 'Israel, right or wrong,'" resonates widely within the American Jewish community today.[121] J Street has capitalized on the Jewish community's increasing acceptance of public criticism of Israel. While J Street has benefited from the critical space that has opened up within the Jewish community concerning Israel, it has also enlarged this space, helping to further legitimize criticism of Israeli policies within the mainstream of the American Jewish community. In the words of one J Street official: "We have changed the conversation [about Israel] within the organized Jewish community."[122]

To be sure, J Street is not welcome everywhere in the organized Jewish community, and there is still fierce resistance in some quarters to its message of both supporting and criticizing Israel. This resistance was most apparent in April 2014, when the members of the Conference of Presidents rejected J Street's application to join the umbrella organization.[123] The contentious vote against J Street, which reportedly broke down largely along political and religious lines with left-wing and non-Orthodox groups supporting J Street's membership and right-wing and Orthodox groups opposing it,[124] was welcomed by J Street's detractors and denounced by its sympathizers.[125] But while the vote was widely perceived as a repudiation of J Street and what it stood for, and a serious setback to its bid for mainstream acceptance, the vote also demonstrated that there was significant, even majority, support for J Street within the wider American Jewish community, since it received the backing of some of the largest and most important communal organizations (the Reform movement, the Conservative movement, the Jewish Council for Public Affairs, and the ADL).[126] While these major establishment organizations did not necessarily vote to accept J Street into the Conference of Presidents because they agreed with its views about Israel and the peace process with the Palestinians, the fact that they voted to accept J Street testifies, at the very least, to the recognition of its status as a major Jewish organization.

The experiences of groups like J Street and Americans for Peace Now show that a lot has changed since the late 1970s, when Breira was hounded out of existence. American Jewish criticism of Israel has become much more common, and there is greater tolerance of it within the Jewish community. It is now broadly—but by no means universally—accepted that criticizing Israeli government policies does not necessarily make one anti-Israel. Opinions about Israel and its conflict with the Palestinians that were considered radical when Breira advocated them are now mainstream (most notably, support for the establishment of a Palestinian state). There has also been a growing recognition within the organized Jewish community that it is necessary to allow for some criticism of Israel to be voiced or else people may simply leave the community altogether (since participation is entirely voluntary). The need to prevent young liberal Jews in particular from opting out of the organized Jewish community because they feel unable to voice their views and concerns about Israel has been cited by some communal leaders as a reason to provide a "big tent" in which different political opinions about Israel are permitted.[127] This was probably the reason why, for example, a large delegation of student activists from J Street U was allowed to attend the 2014 General Assembly of the Jewish Federation of North America—the biggest annual get-together of the organized Jewish community. In the words of Sarah Turbow, the director of J Street U: "Jewish communal institutions are very concerned about young people. That's why we are now able to engage with Federation officials who have been reluctant to talk to us in the past. It is very difficult for them to decline invitations to speak to students."[128]

Nevertheless, although the communal "tent" has become larger over the last three decades, accommodating more opinions about Israel and more criticism of it, it is still not an "open tent." Only those groups and individuals that endorse Israel as a Jewish and democratic state are allowed within the communal tent—something that senior officials within the organized Jewish community have publicly stated.[129] Not all opinions concerning Israel are tolerated, and the willingness to accept criticism of Israel only goes so far. When it comes to Israel, there is a limit to the kind of dissent that is allowed within the organized Jewish community. Dissent that violates certain communal "red lines" is not tolerated, and those whose views or activities cross these red lines are still excluded and shunned.

The biggest red line for the organized Jewish community is challenging Israel's basic legitimacy. Although it is unclear what exactly constitutes "delegitimizing" Israel,[130] it is generally agreed within the organized Jewish community that it is unacceptable to reject the justness of Zionism (by characterizing it, for instance, as a colonialist or racist enterprise), to challenge Israel's democratic credentials (by calling it an apartheid state, for instance), to favor the dismantling of Israel as a Jewish state, to endorse a "one-state solution" to the Israeli-Palestinian conflict, or to support the BDS campaign aimed at Israel.[131] These are the red lines on Israel that currently determine who can be included and who should be excluded from the organized Jewish community, as well as who can be funded, hosted, and even partnered with. This has been explicitly stipulated in the guidelines issued by the San Francisco Jewish Federation which ruled out providing funding to, or hosting any group they saw as challenging Israel's legitimacy, or was supportive of the BDS movement.[132] Not only do these guidelines try to set limits on what American Jewish organizations can say or do about Israel, they also potentially limit their ability to work with and engage with non-Jewish groups, especially Arab American and Muslim American organizations (in so far as the latter may support BDS aimed at Israel or a Palestinian right of return to Israel, which is regarded within the organized Jewish community as tantamount to denying Israel's right to exist as a Jewish state).

In 2010, Hillel International, the organization that oversees Jewish student life on college campuses across the United States, issued a similar set of guidelines (largely at the behest of Hillel directors and donors) to its campus affiliates about the kinds of activities concerning Israel they could engage in, instructing them not to "partner with, house, or host organizations, groups, or speakers who "deny the right of Israel to exist as a Jewish and democratic state with secure and recognized borders," "delegitimize, demonize, or apply a double standard to Israel," or "support boycott of, divestment from, or sanctions against the State of Israel."[133] Hillel's guidelines effectively barred Jewish student groups from cosponsoring events or conducting activities with Palestinian student organizations, since most of the latter support BDS. They led the Hillel at Harvard University, for example, to pull out of hosting a planned talk by Avraham Burg, a former speaker of the Knesset and former chairman of the Jewish Agency, because a pro-Palestinian group at Harvard was involved in sponsoring the event.[134] The ambiguity of Hillel's guidelines—what, for instance, constitutes "demonizing Israel" or applying a "double-standard" to it—has also made it harder for some campus Hillels to host speakers from the left-wing Israeli NGO Breaking the Silence, since it was accused of being "anti-Israel." It has even become problematic to screen Israeli films that are critical of the Occupation, such as the Oscar-nominated documentaries *Five Broken Cameras* and *The Gatekeepers*.[135]

Many Jewish students are unhappy with Hillel's guidelines on Israel and some have spoken out publicly against them, criticizing them for stifling the kind of open and honest discussion of Israel in a Jewish setting that they are looking for and blaming them for alienating students.[136] A group at Harvard University started a campaign called "Open Hillel" and distributed an online petition, signed by more than 1200 Jewish students, calling upon Hillel's leadership to change its Israel guidelines.[137] Student opposition to Hillel's guidelines gained national attention in December 2013 when the Hillel chapter at Swarthmore College declared itself an "Open Hillel" and announced that it would not abide by Hillel's guidelines on Israel, leading Hillel International's President to threaten Swarthmore Hillel with expulsion from the Hillel network if it did not adhere to the guidelines.[138] Since then, Open Hillel chapters have formed on other college campuses,[139] and in October 2014 the first Open Hillel national conference was held at Harvard. Most of the 350 people who came were young Jewish students from across the country eager to grapple with controversial questions about Israel, Zionism, and the Israeli-Palestinian conflict that are seldom, if ever, discussed within their campus Hillels, and to hear from prominent critics of Israel like Judith Butler and Rashid Khalidi who are prohibited from speaking in Hillels and other mainstream Jewish venues. The collective sentiment at the conference was not only of youthful rebellion against the strictures governing discourse about Israel within the organized American Jewish community, but also strong opposition to Israel's policies toward the Palestinians, especially the Occupation, coupled with a deep concern for the future of Israel, the American Jewish community, and Judaism. In the words of one of the student organizers of the conference: "The security of a Jewish future will depend, not on the might of the Israeli military, but on the empowerment of young Jews to grapple with and act on urgent questions of social justice. We are here, we care, and we want to have these conversations without boundaries and red lines."[140]

Among the participants at the Open Hillel conference were many members of the left-wing group Jewish Voice for Peace (JVP). First established in Berkeley, California, in 1996, JVP has become the bête noire of the organized Jewish community in recent years because of its outspoken support for the BDS campaign against Israel,[141] and its refusal to endorse a two-state solution to the Israeli-Palestinian conflict and hence Israel's continued existence as a Jewish and democratic state.[142] A top official of the Jewish Federations of North America has stated that by "promoting the boycott of goods both inside and outside Israel's Green Line . . . [a]nd by refusing to support the concept of Israel as both a Jewish and democratic state, it [JVP] clearly falls outside the boundaries of being a Zionist organization that is inside the tent of the pro-Israel community."[143] The ADL has gone even further, publicly listing JVP as one of the "ten most influential anti-Israel groups" in the United States.[144] According to the ADL's national director at the time, Abraham Foxman: "The positions and actions taken by Jewish Voice for Peace are anathema to mainstream Jewish organizations. The group's activities, which include partnerships with anti-Israel organizations that deny Israel's fundamental right to exist, put them at the farthest fringe of the Jewish community and would certainly preclude their participation among mainstream organizations."[145]

JVP's example demonstrates clearly that when American Jewish groups do not abide by the communal norms governing acceptable discourse and activism about Israel, they are liable to find themselves ostracized from the organized Jewish community. While J Street has slowly been gaining entry into the Jewish communal tent, JVP has been actively shut out from it. According to Rebecca Vilkomerson, the group's executive director: "The organized mainstream groups are hostile. There are a few groups we can work with, but even the more moderate or progressive ones are scared. And donors make threats. . . . Their real wish is to whitewash us out of the Jewish community no matter how much of a slice of support we have, and really engineer what Jewish community means."[146]

While JVP wants to be included in the organized Jewish community,[147] and Vilkomerson claims that: "We have not set out to be in conflict with the American Jewish community. . . . The mainstream community has come and attacked us,"[148] it has certainly engaged in some very provocative and confrontational tactics. The most famous of its "protest actions" occurred on November 8, 2010, when young JVP activists repeatedly heckled and interrupted Israeli Prime Minister Benjamin Netanyahu's speech at the Jewish Federations' annual General Assembly (a protest described in detail in this book's introduction). The protest was aimed at generating media attention for the launch of JVP's "Young, Jewish and Proud" campaign, and within minutes of the protest, a website appeared with a declaration that invoked the legacy of "Jewish radical intellectuals and refugees," and asserted:

> We refuse to knowingly oppress others, and we refuse to oppress each other. We refuse to be whitewashed. . . . We won't be won over by free vacations and scholarship money. We won't buy the logic that slaughter means safety. We will not quietly witness the violation of human rights in Palestine. . . . We commit ourselves to peace. . . . We commit to re-envisioning "homeland," to make room for justice. We will stand in the way of colonization and displacement. . . . We are committed to the struggle. We are the struggle. . . . We will not stop. We exist. We are young Jews, and we get to decide what that means.[149]

By disrupting the events of mainstream Jewish organizations and programs,[150] JVP's protests have been intended not only to loudly denounce Israel's treatment of the Palestinians and gain maximum publicity for itself, but also to bring attention to the group's exclusion from Jewish communal settings and, more broadly, to what it regards as the suppression of dissent by the organized Jewish community. As Cecilie Surasky, JVP's deputy director, put it when explaining why the group chose to disrupt Prime Minister Netanyahu's speech at the General Assembly: "The organized Jewish community works overtime to silence dissent and marginalize our voices. . . . Groups like ours have been literally banned from Jewish spaces. The fact is that we had to scream to be heard."[151]

It is certainly true that JVP has often been "banned from Jewish spaces." JVP activists cannot participate in events sponsored by local Jewish Federations,[152] nor are they allowed to speak publicly in many

JCCs (such as the one in San Francisco). At universities across the United States, JVP student groups cannot join their campus Hillel societies because Hillel's national guidelines effectively, and deliberately,[153] bar them.[154] On at least two occasions, JVP members have even been subjected to threats and physical violence.[155] Yet, despite being blacklisted by much of the organized Jewish community and even demonized in some circles, JVP has grown rapidly in recent years. Its growth has particularly spiked in the aftermath of Israel's military campaigns against Hamas in the Gaza Strip in December 2008–January 2009 and July–August 2014 ("Operation Cast Lead" and "Operation Protective Edge").[156] The group now claims to have 9,000 dues-paying members (up from just 600 in 2011), 200,000 online supporters, and more than sixty chapters around the country, including many on college campuses.[157] Thus, despite, or perhaps because of its radical image, JVP is attracting increasing Jewish support, especially from young Jews—a fact that is alarming many within the organized Jewish community.

CONCLUSION: THE NEED FOR "RED LINES"

Over the past three decades, a profound shift has taken place in American Jewish attitudes toward Israel, from largely unconditional and uncritical support to a more critical engagement. Though no less attached to Israel emotionally, American Jews have become more willing to question Israeli government policies and even criticize them in public. Consequently, public criticism of Israel, once taboo, is now commonplace and generally accepted (except when Israel is at war). Although dissent about Israel is still controversial and, to many American Jews, unwelcome, if not downright disloyal, it has become more tolerated, even within the organized Jewish community. There is undoubtedly greater acceptance of the need to allow for some diversity of political opinion when it comes to Israel and especially the Israeli-Palestinian conflict. The organized Jewish community now aspires to be a more inclusive "big tent," and its somewhat grudging acceptance of J Street demonstrates that this is more than just rhetoric.

Nevertheless, a big tent is not an open tent. The hostility toward and exclusion of JVP by the organized Jewish community today resembles its treatment of Breira more than three decades ago.[158] Clearly, there is only so much tolerance of dissent within the organized Jewish community. Although it has undoubtedly come a long way since the 1970s when just saying the word "Palestinian" was frowned upon, let alone calling for a Palestinian state, there are still opinions that are considered beyond the pale in the organized Jewish community, in particular opposing Zionism, supporting the BDS movement, or favoring a "one-state" rather than two-state solution to the conflict. The organized Jewish community's "red lines" on Israel, therefore, have not disappeared, they have simply moved and, if recent history is any guide, they may well move again in the future.[159]

It is, however, unlikely that the organized Jewish community will become completely open to all political views about Israel and Zionism. Since the organized Jewish community now routinely equates anti-Zionism with anti-Semitism and many American Jews have come to reflexively associate them, there is probably less tolerance of anti-Zionism today than there was in the past (certainly compared to the 1950s when anti-Zionism was still acceptable within some parts of the Jewish community). Zionism has become, in Shaul Magid's words, "an American Jewish dogma, making non- or anti-Zionism an unspoken heresy."[160] As long as anti-Zionism is linked with anti-Semitism (whether correctly or not), it will not become an acceptable opinion within the organized American Jewish community and those propounding it will continue to be excluded from the communal conversation.

But it is not just the conflation of anti-Zionism with anti-Semitism that limits the political openness of the organized American Jewish community. It is also the community's basic need to define itself. The maintenance and enforcement of certain red lines—wherever they are drawn—not only serves to delegitimize dissident opinions and groups and effectively exclude them from the communal conversation, but also, and more fundamentally, to define the community itself. Drawing red lines is a way of demarcating the political boundaries of the community, and such boundaries help delineate "the community" since communities are defined not only by what their members share, but also by their symbolic boundaries.[161] The organized American Jewish community is no different. The delineation of a "Jewish community" necessarily involves drawing symbolic boundaries, separating those who are inside from those outside. The organized Jewish community's red lines on Israel and Zionism are, therefore, essentially a means of defining its very identity.

If support for Israel did not define the Jewish community, then what would? In an age of accelerating assimilation, declining religious observance, and weakening social ties—when fewer Jews than before work with other Jews, socialize mostly with other Jews, live mainly among other Jews, and, above all, marry other Jews—what defines the American Jewish community other than its stalwart support for Israel? "Israel has become the primary norm of an increasingly secularized Jewish community," Daniel J. Elazar observed in his classic study of the organized American Jewish community, published in 1976.[162] Charles Liebman, another scholar writing in the 1970s, also noted that: "support for Israel has become a boundary-defining aspect of membership in the Jewish community."[163] In a similar vein, the historian David Biale wrote in the mid-1980s: "If in the Middle Ages obedience to Jewish law and to the will of the Jewish community defined a Jew, today, when self-identifying Jews take radically different positions on all other religious, cultural, and political questions, Israel is the one issue over which the lack of belief is treated as heresy."[164] Despite all the changes that have occurred in the American Jewish relationship with Israel over the past thirty years, these observations still ring true today. In the absence of strong social ties and shared religious practices, supporting Israel continues to be the glue that holds the American Jewish community together. But it is now beginning to come unstuck.

3.
THE ARGUMENT ABOUT ISRAEL

Truth is, North American Jews no longer know how to have a civil conversation about Israel.

—Rabbi Eric Yoffie, former president of
the Union for Reform Judaism[1]

On a cold December night in 2013, a large audience had assembled at the 92nd Street Y on the Upper East Side of Manhattan to hear a panel of prominent American Jews discuss the question "What does it mean to be pro-Israel in America today?"—a question that has become perhaps the most vexing and contentious issue in American Jewish life today. What they heard instead was less of a discussion than an ill-tempered shouting match, which culminated when one of the panelists, John Podhoretz, the editor of *Commentary Magazine*, angrily stormed off the stage after arguing with another member of the panel, J Street director Jeremy Ben-Ami, and being booed and jeered by members of the audience.[2] Although Podhoretz later dismissed his walkout from the unruly event as merely "a tempest in a teapot,"[3] it epitomized the current state of American Jewish public discourse about Israel, which is often argumentative, acrimonious, and sometimes outright abusive.[4] The rancorous discussion that took place that evening dramatically displayed not only the lack of agreement over what being pro-Israel means but also the apparent inability to even have a civil discussion about anything to do with Israel. Over the last few years, similar discussions about Israel in synagogues,

Jewish Community Centers (JCCs), and other Jewish venues across the United States have also often degenerated into heated arguments and shouting matches, as tempers flare and accusations are angrily exchanged. Indeed, things have become so bad that in many Jewish communities, public discussions about Israel are now being avoided altogether, or when they do take place, they must be "guided" by facilitators specially trained to encourage civil discourse.

Why has the conversation about Israel within the American Jewish community become so emotionally charged and so difficult to have? What about Israel are American Jews arguing over? How does this argument differ from ones they have had in the past? And what impact is this argument about Israel having upon local Jewish communities? This chapter seeks to answer these questions. I begin by mapping out the current American Jewish public debate over Israel, and particularly over the Israeli-Palestinian conflict—the focus of the debate. I then explain what is significantly different about the debate today from the way American Jews discussed and debated Israel in the past. In doing so, I provide some reasons for why this debate has become so fraught and acrimonious in recent years. The chapter ends by discussing the impact this is having on many Jewish communities throughout the United States, and how some Jewish organizations are responding to this.

MAPPING THE PUBLIC DEBATE: THE FOUR JEWISH CAMPS

No issue looms larger in the American Jewish public debate about Israel than the Israeli-Palestinian conflict. The issue of Israel's policies toward Palestinians, especially those living in the West Bank and Gaza Strip, dominates American Jewish political debate just as it has dominated Israeli political debate for more than four decades since Israel conquered those territories in the 1967 war. There are, to be sure, other Israeli issues of great concern to American Jews, particularly Jewish pluralism and the status of non-Orthodox Judaism in Israel[5]—an issue that directly touches upon American Jews since most are not Orthodox. But the Palestinian issue attracts by far the most sustained attention and generates the most controversy, whether this is because it is regarded as the greatest threat to Israel's security, its international legitimacy, its morality, its identity as a Jewish state, or simply because it has become such a huge global issue and the subject of intense media coverage.

Like the Israeli debate, the debate among American Jews about Israel's policies toward the Palestinians has now been going on for decades, at least since the early 1970s (when Breira was formed). Some of the questions in this long-running debate, therefore, are by no means new: What should Israel do with the territories under its control? Can they be exchanged for peace? Are the Palestinians really willing to make peace with Israel? What are Israel's security needs? Where should its final borders lie? Is building Israeli settlements harmful to the prospects for peace? Is Israel at least partly responsible for the continuation of the conflict with the Palestinians? In addition to these perennial questions, newer ones have arisen in recent years: Is a two-state solution to the Israeli-Palestinian conflict still feasible? Has the Israeli occupation of the West Bank damaged Israeli democracy? Has Israel's treatment of the Palestinians been ethical? Has its use of military force against them been justified? Should the U.S. government be encouraged to apply pressure on Israel to make peace? Is international pressure on Israel, especially in the form of boycotts, sanctions, and divestment, legitimate?

A wide range of views is expressed in the American Jewish public debate on these questions. As such, any attempt to classify and categorize these views is bound to be somewhat reductionist. Nevertheless, with this caveat in mind, it is still possible to distinguish between different political "camps" in this debate. The most conventional distinction made is between "right" versus "left," or "hawks" versus "doves." Neither of these binary divisions, however, adequately captures the different positions in the debate. While often used in Israel, the monikers "hawks" and "doves" wrongly implies that the debate revolves solely around the issue of Israeli national security, when in fact it goes well beyond this. The "right" versus "left" categorization is also problematic since it obscures important differences of opinion within these broad camps. American Jews on the left disagree

TABLE 3.1.

The Four Camps in the American Jewish Debate about the Israeli-Palestinian Conflict

	ZIONISM?	WHO IS AT FAULT?	TWO-STATE SOLUTION?	PUBLIC JEWISH CRITICISM OF ISRAEL?	EXTERNAL PRESSURE ON ISRAEL?
LEFT	Bad/ hijacked/ outdated	Israel	Acceptable, but not realistic and/or preferable	Yes	Yes, including BDS
CENTER-LEFT	Good, as long as it's liberal	Both Israel and Palestinians	Essential and urgently needed	Yes	Yes, but only diplomatic
CENTER-RIGHT	Good	Palestinians	Desirable, but not right now	No	No
RIGHT	Good	Palestinians	Dangerous and/or wrong	Yes, but only right-wing criticism	No

over ideological questions (specifically, the legitimacy and future of Zionism), end goals (a two-state solution or a one-state solution), strategies (especially BDS), and terminology (such as the use of the term "apartheid"). Similarly, there is no agreement among Jews on the right concerning the future of the Israeli settlement enterprise in the West Bank, the desirability of a Palestinian state, or the legitimacy of publicly criticizing Israel and opposing the policies of its governments.

It is more accurate, therefore, to differentiate between four major camps in the debate about the Israeli-Palestinian conflict (these camps are by no means equal in size).[6] Table 3.1 summarizes the different positions of these four camps.

THE CENTER-RIGHT

Attend a pro-Israel rally, an AIPAC conference, a local Jewish Federation event on Israel, or read editorials about Israel in many American Jewish newspapers and the views that one is most likely to hear are those of the center-right (although they may often be described as centrist by those espousing these views). In this perspective, both Zionism and the State of Israel are unquestionably right. Indeed, challenging either is often regarded as tantamount to anti-Semitism. Israel is absolved of any responsibility for its conflict with the Palestinians. It is the latter's stubborn (and self-defeating) refusal to accept the Jewish people's right to establish their own state in their historic homeland that is regarded as the fundamental cause of the conflict. As Alan Dershowitz—perhaps the most prominent American Jewish advocate of the center-right position—matter-of-factly states in his popular book *The Case for Israel*: "Arab rejection of Israel's right to exist has long been the cause of the problem."[7] Likewise, the failure to make peace with the Palestinians is not Israel's fault, but the Palestinians, especially their leaders. Israeli leaders, it is claimed, have repeatedly demonstrated Israel's willingness to compromise with the Palestinians, whereas Palestinian leaders—Yasser Arafat in particular—have consistently been unwilling or unable to accept the "generous" offers made to them.[8] The occasional flare-ups of Israeli-Palestinian violence are also blamed solely on the Palestinians, whether it is due to the extremist groups (most notably Hamas) that are allowed to flourish, or the culture of anti-Israeli and even anti-Semitic "incitement" that is propagated through Palestinian media, school textbooks, and public discourse. Hence, the prospects for Israeli-Palestinian peace depend almost exclusively on the Palestinians—they must first recognize the legitimacy of the Jewish state, decisively reject violence, stop terrorism, and end anti-Israel incitement before peace can be achieved.

This perspective, therefore, affords Israel little, if any, agency in the conflict. Its security measures (such as the barrier in the West Bank) and military actions against Palestinians are seen as purely reactive, defensive, and necessary to protect the lives of Israeli civilians from Palestinian terrorism. Similarly, its settlement building in the West

Bank and East Jerusalem is not regarded as an obstacle to peace with the Palestinians (contrary to prevailing international opinion and the opinion of the U.S. State Department). In Dershowitz's words: "I do not believe that [settlements] are the real barrier to peace. The real barrier has been the unwillingness of many Palestinians, and many Palestinian terrorist groups and nations, to accept the existence of a Jewish state in any part of Palestine."[9]

This does not mean, however, that the center-right supports the expansion of Israeli settlements, only that they do not believe Israeli settlements are the problem they are often made out to be by Palestinians and their supporters. In fact, those on the center-right might well favor the evacuation of at least some outlying Israeli settlements in the West Bank in the context of an overall settlement of the Israeli-Palestinian conflict involving the establishment of a Palestinian state. The center-right does accept the eventual creation of a Palestinian state (just as Benjamin Netanyahu did soon after becoming Israel's prime minister in 2009), but it wants the size and sovereign powers of this future state to be very limited (that is, encompassing much less land than the entire West Bank, Gaza Strip, and East Jerusalem, and without the right to have a military or control over its own airspace and borders).

Although the center-right endorses in principle the creation of a Palestinian state, in practice it does not want one to be established any time soon because this could exacerbate a number of security threats to Israel (above all the threat of Palestinian rocket attacks against Israel's population centers and its main airport). Israeli security is the center-right's foremost concern. It is much more preoccupied with ensuring Israel's security than seeking an elusive and potentially dangerous peace agreement with the Palestinians. While the center-right lauds Israel's economic, technological, and military accomplishments, it continues to perceive Israel as embattled and endangered by threats near and far. The fact that Israel's security is regarded as highly precarious accounts for the center-right's paramount concern for it and aversion to anything that might possibly jeopardize it.

While not a direct security threat to Israel, the center-right is also very worried by what it perceives as a concerted attempt, spearheaded by the Palestinians, to globally "delegitimize" Israel. The BDS campaign is seen as a key part of this effort, which is fuelled, it is claimed, by anti-Semitism. Since delegitimization is regarded as a major strategic threat to Israel, combating the delegitimization of Israel, and by extension the BDS movement, has risen to the top of the center-right's agenda. As a result, it is extremely wary about any criticism of Israel, however well intended, whether from left-wing Jews, liberal journalists, or American government officials, because such criticism can, they say, be exploited by those seeking to delegitimize, and ultimately, defeat the Jewish state.

Finally, the center-right camp staunchly opposes any kind of U.S. government pressure on Israel, even including verbal criticism of Israeli policies and actions. American support for Israel is sacrosanct and maintaining this support is therefore vital. This is considered to be perhaps the most important political task for the American Jewish community. To do this, American Jews should present a united front to American policymakers, avoid public criticism of Israel, and actively defend Israel against its many critics, engaging in what is called *hasbara* (Hebrew for "explanation").

THE RIGHT

The right-wing camp shares the center-right's belief that the predicament of Palestinians (whether those in the West Bank, Gaza Strip, or elsewhere in the Arab world) is solely the fault of Palestinian and Arab leaders, for which Israel bears no responsibility. It also routinely focuses on Palestinian rejectionism, terrorism, and incitement. But the right-wing camp goes further than this, disputing the Palestinians' national rights by claiming that the Palestinians are not the indigenous inhabitants of the land and that they have only recently defined themselves as a distinct nation. As the billionaire casino mogul Sheldon Adelson (a major donor to the right-wing group the Zionist Organization of America), once remarked: "There's no such thing as a Palestinian. Do you know what they are? They call themselves southern Syrians."[10] According to those on the right, the Palestinians are basically an invented, fake nation, and Palestinian nationalism is merely a stalking horse, deliberately designed to delegitimize Israel internationally and disguise the real goal of Arab nationalists and Muslim "fundamentalists" to destroy Israel.

Since the Palestinians have no legitimate claim to national self-determination, as far as the right is concerned, there is no good reason to establish a Palestinian state under any circumstances. Such a state will only serve as stepping-stone for the Palestinians' and Arabs' ultimate goal of destroying Israel. Emphasizing the pervasive hostility to Israel and to Jews in the Arab and Muslim worlds leads the right to regard the possibility of territorial compromise with the Palestinians as a dangerous chimera. The Palestinians—indeed the Arab world as a whole—they maintain are not interested in real compromise and peace with Israel. Driven by deep-rooted anti-Semitism, both secular and religious (that is, based upon the Quran), the Arabs' only objective is to eliminate the Jewish state from their midst. As such, the right fiercely opposes any Israeli territorial withdrawals or concessions since they believe this only encourages more Arab aggression. For this reason, the right strongly condemned the Oslo Accords in the early 1990s and Israel's unilateral withdrawal from the Gaza Strip in 2005. For the right, the "lesson" of the Gaza disengagement and Hamas's subsequent takeover of the Gaza Strip is that Israel should never relinquish its control over territory.

While the center-right tentatively endorses Israel's peace process with the Palestinians (if only for the sake of maintaining Israel's close relationship with the United States and its support in the international community at large), the right has always stridently opposed the peace process as both futile and dangerous. Instead of the formula of "land for peace," the right-wing advocates "peace for peace"—the idea that the Arabs must unconditionally accept Israel's right to exist and renounce violence, and that this will lead to peaceful relations between Jews and Arabs. Since there is little, if any, likelihood of this happening in the foreseeable future, the right does not believe that a solution to the conflict is possible for a long time to come. Rather than vainly hope for peace, all Israel can do is to remain strong, deterring and defeating its many enemies, and staunchly resisting international pressure on it to make territorial concessions.[11]

Unlike the center-right, therefore, the right completely opposes the establishment of a Palestinian state (unless it is located in Jordan), and it rejects even the possibility of a two-state solution to the Israeli-Palestinian conflict. The most it is prepared to offer the Palestinians is some kind of autonomy under Israeli rule. The right's firm opposition to a Palestinian state is based not only on its deep suspicion of Palestinian intentions but also on its conviction that the entire Land of Israel, including all of Judea and Samaria (the West Bank), rightfully belongs to the Jewish people, whether on historical or theological grounds. Nevertheless, those on the American Jewish right tend to offer security arguments to justify Israel's continued control over the West Bank, rather than the historical and religious arguments that those on the Israeli right often make. They stress the risk to Israel if it withdraws from the West Bank, not the historical or divine right of Israel to possess this territory.[12]

As a corollary to the right's belief that Israel should have sovereignty over all of Judea and Samaria, the right also insists that Israel is absolutely entitled to establish Jewish settlements throughout the entire area. Whereas the center-right's attitude toward Israel's settlement enterprise in the West Bank is lukewarm and noncommittal, the right is committed to the settlement project for historical, religious, and security reasons—claiming, for instance, that Israeli settlement building actually promotes peace by demonstrating Israel's strength and determination. The right, therefore, provides financial, political, and moral support to Jewish settlements.

Notwithstanding its support for the Israeli settlement movement, only a minority within the American Jewish right—almost all of them Orthodox and ultra-Orthodox (*haredim*)—really have a strong religious attachment to the Land of Israel, and even fewer believe that an Israeli withdrawal from the West Bank would be a violation of God's will (unlike much of the Israeli right). In general, the American Jewish right is driven more by ideology than by theology or eschatology. Revisionist Zionism and neo-conservatism shape its perspective on the Israeli-Palestinian conflict much more than Judaism does. In recent years, American-style neo-conservatism has exerted a strong influence upon right-wing thinking. Neo-conservative ideas have been

propagated by prominent American Jewish intellectuals (most notably, William Kristol, Norman Podhoretz, and Charles Krauthammer)
and former government officials (such as Elliot Abrams and Richard
Perle), and widely disseminated in publications and websites aimed at
an American Jewish audience (not only the famous *Commentary* magazine, but also the *Jewish Review of Books* and *Mosaic Magazine*, both
of which are funded by the neo-conservative philanthropic foundation, the Tikvah Fund). Neo-conservative Jewish think tanks—the
Jewish Institute for National Security Affairs (JINSA) in Washington, DC, and the Jerusalem Center for Public Affairs and the
Shalem Center in Israel (both of which are funded in part by Sheldon
Adelson)—have also spread neo-conservatism's influence on American Jewish right-wing thought.

In accordance with the neo-conservative worldview, which claims
that the West is at war with Islamic extremism—a view that gained
traction after the September 11, 2001, terrorist attacks in the United
States—the American Jewish right now considers Israel's conflict
with the Palestinians to be part of this broader global struggle.[13] In
the words of Morton Klein, the head of the right-wing group the
Zionist Organization of American (ZOA): "this is an issue of the
entire Arab-Islamic world's enmity toward Israel as a Jewish state and
toward the West as a whole. . . . [I]t's a war against all non-Muslims,
not only against Jews."[14] Seen through this lens, Israel is perceived as
an embattled outpost of Western democracy besieged by the forces of
"Islamofascism."[15] The Palestinian Sunni Islamist group Hamas, the
Lebanese Shi'a organization Hezbollah, and the Islamic Republic of
Iran are all then lumped together as a single enemy, and Israel's ongoing battle against them is linked with the United States' fight against
Al Qaeda, the Islamic State/ISIS, and other jihadist groups around
the world. Just as the United States must be resolute and uncompromising in its war on terror, so too, the right argues, must Israel. This
also means that American diplomatic pressure on Israel or lack of
support for Israel is not only harmful to Israel but also to the United
States, since Israeli and American interests are essentially identical.

Although the right loudly objects to any American government
criticism of Israel, however mild it may be, as well as all left-wing Jew-

ish criticism of Israel, it is itself quite willing to publicly criticize Israeli government policies and actions when it opposes them (as it repeatedly did, for instance, during the Oslo peace process in the 1990s and in the run-up to Israel's disengagement from Gaza in 2005). The right does not share the center-right's aversion to public criticism of Israeli governments, nor its concern for ensuring consensus within the American Jewish community and for projecting American Jewish unity in Washington, DC. Instead, the right is prepared to publicly reject whatever communal consensus exists and openly challenge the policies of Israel's governments. In this respect, if nothing else, the right has something in common with the left and center-left camps.

THE CENTER-LEFT

Zionism is the one belief that the center-left has in common with the right and center-right (which may be why people in the center-left camp often emphasize their Zionism). All three camps share a basic conviction in the justness of Zionism and, accompanying this, a bedrock commitment to Israel's continued existence as a Jewish state. Beyond these fundamentals, however, the center-left position significantly departs from those of the center-right and right. The center-left abhors the militant, maximalist Zionism of the right, and it assails the unapologetic, uncritical Zionism of the center-right for its failure to openly acknowledge and address the past and present wrongdoings of Israel and the Zionist movement.[16] According to its brand of "liberal Zionism" (or "humane and pragmatic Zionism" as the late Leonard Fein characterized it[17]), the claims of Zionism are not absolute.[18] They must be reconciled with the rights of the Palestinians as the indigenous inhabitants of Israel/Palestine. While upholding the historic necessity and justice of the Zionist cause, the center-left believes that just as the Jews have a legitimate claim to the land and a right to national self-determination, so too do the Palestinians. For liberal Zionists, Jewish self-determination cannot be legitimately achieved if it involves the denial of Palestinian self-determination, or endemic discrimination against Israel's own Palestinian citizens (who make up roughly 20 percent of the country's citizenry). This belief means that it is essential for Israel to be a liberal democracy that treats all its citizens equally, and for a Palestinian state to be established in which the Palestinian nation can live freely and exercise its right to self-determination.[19]

For the center-left, a two-state solution to the Israeli-Palestinian conflict—involving a Jewish democratic state of Israel existing alongside a Palestinian state—is the only feasible way for both peoples to achieve their legitimate national aspirations. Thus, while the center-right's grudging and somewhat half-hearted acceptance of the two-state solution is based upon pragmatism, the center-left's passionate and whole-hearted support for it is not only pragmatic, but also normatively grounded. For the center-left, territorial compromise with the Palestinians is not simply seen as the best, indeed only, means to resolve the conflict, but also—and perhaps no less importantly—as fundamentally just. Territorial compromise, then, is a moral commitment for the center-left as much as it is also regarded as a necessary means for Israel to resolve its conflict with the Palestinians.

There is an additional moral dimension to the center-left's support for the establishment of a Palestinian state. Not only is it regarded as a means to satisfy Palestinian national rights, it is also seen as a way of alleviating Palestinian suffering and rectifying, or at least ending Israeli wrongdoing. Israel's establishment in 1948 and its long occupation of the West Bank, Gaza Strip, and East Jerusalem since 1967 has, in the eyes of the center-left, entailed massive Palestinian suffering as it has involved displacement, dispossession, and discrimination, and widespread violence and human rights violations. Whereas the right and center-right either deny or downplay Palestinian suffering, or blame it upon Palestinian and Arab leaders, the center-left holds Israel at least partly, if not mostly, responsible (especially in recent years, since Israel is perceived as the more powerful party). The center-left assigns Israel much more agency in the conflict and, consequently, holds Israel more morally accountable. Israel is not simply seen as the innocent victim of unrelenting Arab aggression and unceasing Palestinian violence. Rather, Israel is also at least partially guilty for perpetuating and exacerbating the conflict. According to the center-left, Israel's own actions and policies toward the Palestinians, particularly since 1967, have often been misguided, self-destructive, and even immoral. This is especially true of Israel's military rule and settlement project in the Occupied Territories, which the center-left considers to be a strategic and moral disaster for Israel and Zionism. Israeli settlements in the West Bank are viewed as serious obstacles to peace with the Palestinians and a stain on Israel's moral character. The center-left, therefore, condemns the continued expansion of Israeli settlements and advocates an Israeli withdrawal from most, if not all, of the West Bank, including the evacuation of most settlements (certainly all those lying east of the separation barrier). It also supports a territorial division in Jerusalem, with the eastern part of the city becoming the capital of a Palestinian state.

Based upon its reading of current demographic trends in Israel and Palestine, which project that Palestinians in Israel and the Palestinian Territories will soon outnumber Jews (if they don't already), the center-left views Israel's continued occupation of the West Bank as seriously jeopardizing Israel's existence as a Jewish and democratic state—it insists that Israel should and must remain both. Once there are more Palestinians than Jews under Israel's control, Israel will be forced to choose between being a democracy and losing its Jewish character, or remaining a Jewish state at the expense of democracy. Hence, Israel must withdraw from the West Bank in order to avoid sacrificing either its Jewishness or its democratic nature—both important values to those on the center-left. Demography, then, motivates the center-left's support for a two-state solution, as much as morality does.

This pressing demographic concern—coupled with the fear that the longer the conflict continues, the harder it will be to resolve as Jewish settlements in the West Bank grow and Israelis and Palestinians lose hope in the possibility of peace—underpins the urgency that the center-left expresses to bringing about the two-state solution. In contrast to those on the center-right who favor the eventual creation of a Palestinian state at some point in the future and only so long as Israel's security needs are met, the center-left wants a Palestinian state established as soon as possible. They argue that time is rapidly running out for the two-state solution.

While increasingly anxious that the two-state solution may soon become unattainable, the center-left is simultaneously very confident that an Israeli-Palestinian peace agreement can be quickly and easily achieved with enough political will. All that is really required is for Israeli and Palestinian leaders to make some courageous decisions and overcome the resistance of extremist groups on both sides. The optimistic belief that a peace agreement is not only possible, but within reach, is a key tenet of the center-left position. The center-left camp adamantly rejects the right's claim that Israel has no Palestinian "partner for peace," insisting that a majority of Palestinians want peace and favor a two-state solution and that there is in fact a moderate Palestinian leadership with whom Israel can negotiate.

This conviction does not mean, however, that the center-left places much confidence on the ability of Israeli and Palestinian leaders to make peace if left entirely to their own devices. Given the failure of the Oslo peace process and more recent Israeli and Palestinian peace efforts, the center-left believes that the United States has a crucial role to play in bringing about a comprehensive peace agreement. In particular, as Israel's most important and trusted ally, the United States should not just broker peace talks, but also, if necessary, apply some diplomatic pressure on both parties, and even perhaps present its own peace plan.[20] Although the center-left opposes a cut-off in American military aid to Israel, it supports more limited forms of U.S. government pressure on Israel—a position that is sharply at odds with that held by the center-right and right. In calling for "active" American engagement in the peace process, the center-left stresses that a resolution of the Israeli-Palestinian conflict is in the interests of the United States, not just Palestinians and Israelis.

Just as the center-left supports and even encourages American government criticism of Israeli policies and actions that undermine the prospects for peace, it also wants the American Jewish community to vocally criticize Israel when it acts against it own best interests (by, for example, building settlements in the West Bank).[21] The center-left asserts that American Jews have the right, and even the responsibility, to publicly criticize Israel and push it, for its own sake, to end its occupation of Palestinian land. The center-left is also willing to openly criticize Israel's use of force against Palestinians. Although it endorses Israel's "right to self-defense" (against Palestinian rocket attacks, for instance), the center-left camp often agonizes over the killing of innocent Palestinians and criticizes what it sees as Israel's "disproportionate" or "indiscriminate" use of force. Even when voicing tepid support for Israeli military campaigns, the center-left also generally calls for a swift end to the violence and asserts that the best means of ensuring Israel's security is through diplomacy and, ultimately, a peace agreement with the Palestinians—a view that echoes that of Israeli-Jewish "doves" and Israel's peace movement (most notably, *Shalom Achshav* ["Peace Now"]).

THE LEFT

Although the center-left camp is frequently critical of Israel, its criticism goes only so far. It opposes the Israeli occupation, but not the State of Israel. It rejects the uncompromising and unapologetic Zionism of the right, but not Zionism itself. It denounces discrimination and racism against Israel's Arab minority, but not Israel's claim or desire to be a "Jewish and democratic state." The left takes issue with what it regards as the center-left's limitations, inconsistencies, and ideological blind spots.[22] Unlike the center-left's measured and moderate criticisms of Israel and its conduct toward the Palestinians, the left's critique is much more wide-ranging and far-reaching.[23] It is not just the Occupation that is wrong, in the left's eyes, but also the Israeli state, specifically its inherent, institutionalized bias against its own Palestinian citizens. The left's goal, therefore, is not simply to end the Occupation, but also to radically transform the State of Israel, if not abolish it altogether (at least as a self-defined Jewish state). It calls for equality and justice in all of Israel/Palestine, not necessarily a Palestinian state in just the West Bank, Gaza Strip, and East Jerusalem.

Emerging from a tradition of American Jewish peace activism,[24] which grew out of the major protest movements of the 1960s and 1970s (the antiwar movement, the civil rights movement, and the women's movement), the left has a strongly universalistic orientation.

It is just as concerned with Palestinian rights as Jewish rights, and since it believes that it is the Palestinians whose rights have been continually violated by Israel, the left focuses on defending and promoting these rights (including, most controversially, the Palestinian "right of return"). As far as the left is concerned, Israel and the prestate Zionist movement (or at least its dominant factions) are primarily the guilty party in the Israeli-Palestinian conflict. It argues that the conflict first started with Zionist colonization and it escalated when Zionists forcibly expelled and dispossessed the Palestinians immediately before and after Israel's establishment in 1948. Since then, successive Israeli governments have continued to systematically dispossess Palestinians and deny them their rights up to the present day. The left, therefore, emphasizes the historic injustices done to the Palestinians and Israel's ongoing oppression of Palestinians, including (but not limited to) the daily violence and human rights abuses perpetrated by Israeli soldiers and settlers in the Occupied Territories. Indeed, those on the left routinely describe Israel as an aggressive, "apartheid state" that flagrantly violates international laws and commits war crimes.[25]

Although the left-wing camp draws upon a long history of Jewish anti-Zionism, socialism, and "Diasporism,"[26] it is not only composed of anti-Zionists, but also non-Zionists, "post-Zionists," "dissident Zionists" (such as cultural or nonstatist Zionists), and disillusioned Zionists. Some on the left may believe that the Zionist movement was fundamentally wrong or misguided from the outset,[27] others that Zionism lost its way or was hijacked over time, and still others that it has simply outlived its usefulness and become anachronistic.[28] But whatever their different views on the history of Zionism, the left-wing camp agrees on the need to challenge the contemporary form of Zionism that prevails both within Israel and the American Jewish community.

What most animates the left, however, is its fierce opposition to the "Occupation." While it shares this opposition with the center-left, the left is willing to endorse more radical and confrontational tactics, by both Jews and Palestinians, to end the Occupation. It rejects Palestinian violence (albeit perhaps not as loudly or firmly as some would like), but it supports all forms of nonviolent Palestinian resistance, including the global BDS campaign launched by Palestinian civil society activists in 2005.[29] Over the last few years, the left's support for BDS has become a major point of contention between it and the center-left, which actively opposes BDS (although some prominent voices on the center-left, such as Peter Beinart, have called for more targeted boycotts of Israeli products made in West Bank settlements). In addition to its BDS advocacy, the left also backs the small movement of conscientious objectors in Israel (that is, Israeli conscripts and reserve soldiers who refuse to serve in the Occupied Territories),[30] and calls for a suspension of American military aid to Israel. Needless to say, these highly controversial positions often make those publicly associated with the left, especially its leading champions such as Judith Butler, pariahs in the American Jewish community. Regardless of this, the left firmly believes that American Jews have not only a right to criticize Israel, but actually an ethical obligation to protest Israeli policies carried out in their name—hence the popular slogan "Not in My Name" that often appears on placards at left-wing demonstrations against Israel.

When it comes to ending the Occupation, the left's disagreement with the center-left is not just about tactics (for example, supporting BDS, opposing U.S. military aid to Israel), but also increasingly about outcomes. More and more people in the left-wing camp, especially the younger generation, now question the feasibility, and even the desirability, of a two-state solution to the Israeli-Palestinian conflict. There is growing skepticism that a two-state solution will ever be achieved given what the left perceives as Israel's continued intransigence. Furthermore, as far as the left is concerned, any American sponsored Israeli-Palestinian peace process is doomed to fail because of the power imbalance between the two sides and the United States government's inability to act as an honest broker. Even in the unlikely event that a Palestinian state of some kind is established, few on the left believe that the weak, impoverished and truncated state that will emerge is likely to satisfy the basic rights and needs of Palestinians, including Palestinian refugees. As such, the left is doubtful, at best, that the two-state solution enthusiastically promoted by the center-left will, in fact, be a solution at all. It might even, they fear, only worsen the conflict.

Having largely abandoned all hope for a two-state solution, many of those on the left now favor a "one-state solution" involving the establishment of a single democratic state, or a binational state, over all the territory of Israel and Palestine. Since the emerging demographics would necessarily entail the end of Israel as a Jewish state, the left's embrace of "one-statism" puts it sharply at odds with the center-left and center-right (although not, ironically, with the right who also do not support the two-state solution, albeit for entirely different reasons).

AMERICAN JEWISH PUBLIC DISCOURSE ABOUT ISRAEL

As the preceding section makes clear, there is a no single, hegemonic view that dominates American Jewish public discourse regarding Israel and the Israeli-Palestinian conflict. There are, at least, four distinct perspectives (right, center-right, center-left, left), and the differences among these competing perspectives are profound. As a result, American Jewish political discourse about Israel is highly fractious and contentious—to say the least! But is this really a new thing? How does American Jewish public discourse about Israel today differ from the past? After all, there has always been debate about Israel among American Jews. Contrary to the popular belief, and nostalgic memory, that once upon a time American Jews all agreed about Israel and wholeheartedly supported it, the historical record is, in fact, replete with examples of American Jewish disagreements about matters concerning Israel.[31] There has never really been a period of complete unanimity of opinion about Israel. And, before Israel's establishment, American Jews deeply disagreed over Zionism itself.[32] Thus, Jack Wertheimer, a historian of American Jewry notes: "Whereas American Jews once argued over whether to support or oppose the Zionist enterprise, and then over whether dissent from Israeli policies was even permissible, they are now arrayed in rival camps, arguing about how Israel should behave."[33] Even the debate among American Jews about Israel's behavior toward the Palestinians is by no means new. It has been going on for decades, at least since the late 1970s.

Although it is important not to forget the earlier history of American Jewish debate about Israel and Zionism, it is no less important to appreciate what is new about the current debate. Three distinctive features stand out in particular: it is more public, more polarized, and more vitriolic.[34] The first, and perhaps most obvious, difference about the debate today from that in the past is that it is happening out in the open, not behind closed doors. Whereas debate about Israel was once largely confined to the conference rooms of American Jewish organizations or the living rooms of American Jewish families, it has now spilled out into the open. It is conducted very publicly, in American and Israeli media, on the Internet, in Jewish community centers and synagogues, on campuses, even on the streets of big American cities.

As the debate between American Jews over Israel and the Israeli-Palestinian conflict has become increasingly open—and because Israel and its conflict with the Palestinians is a subject of intense, even unparalleled, media interest—the debate has attracted a lot of attention in the American, and even international, media.[35] Almost anything to do with the Israeli-Palestinian conflict gets written about and reported on because there is such a huge amount of interest in the conflict. As such, more than ever before, the American Jewish debate about Israel takes place in the glare of the media. Even relatively minor incidents can quickly become inflated into major news stories. In December 2012, for example, the *New York Times* featured two news articles about a dispute among members of an upper west side Manhattan synagogue (*B'nei Jeshurun*) after three of its rabbis wrote a public letter welcoming the United Nations General Assembly's upgrading of Palestine to nonmember observer state status.[36]

Today, therefore, Jewish communal conflicts and controversies over Israel are extensively reported in the mainstream American media, as well as in Jewish and Israeli media. This coverage, of course, further fuels these conflicts and controversies. As such, the contemporary debate about Israel within the American Jewish community is no longer kept within the community and away from public attention, as it generally used to be. In the words of one observer: "If once upon a time Jews held a line not to hang our dirty laundry in public, the American public square has become a Jewish laundromat."[37]

As this quote suggests, another part of the reason for the more public nature of American Jewish debate about Israel today is the gradual erosion over the past three decades of the traditional communal norm governing Jewish public discourse (discussed in the previous chapter) that strongly inhibited many American Jews from publicly questioning, debating, and challenging Israeli policies and practices. Nowadays, there is much less inhibition about criticizing Israel. By and large, American Jews feel more confident and entitled to openly express their own opinions about Israel, even critical ones (which is not to say that they may have no trepidation in doing so). Consequently, there is a much freer Jewish public discussion about Israel—a development that one commentator has even likened to glasnost in the Soviet Union in the late 1980s.[38] While this is certainly hyperbole, it is true that there has been a sweeping liberalization in American Jewish public discourse about Israel. Whereas in the past, this discourse was limited and restrained, especially when compared to the lively, often raucous, public discussion that took place in Israel, over the past two decades or so the public discussion about Israel among American Jews has gradually come to more closely resemble the discussion among Israelis themselves, with all the rancor that goes with it.

It is not just that American Jews are more willing to openly discuss and debate Israel and the Israeli-Palestinian conflict, they also have many more available public forums in which they can do so today. The advent of the Internet, including social media like Facebook and Twitter, means that there are now countless outlets for debate today.[39] The Internet has created new spaces for Jewish communal debate and has enabled more people to participate in these debates. As Ari Kelman writes: "The Internet has made information far more accessible, enabled new venues for communal debate, discussion, and engagement, allowed more voices into the Jewish communal conversation."[40] The Internet's massive popularity and ubiquity means that it has now become a primary arena in which Jewish communal debate about Israel (as well as a host of other subjects) is conducted. Consequently, it has played a key role in opening up the American Jewish debate about Israel and allowing many more American Jews to participate in it.[41] According to one individual who has spent decades working within the organized American Jewish community: "The Internet has democratized the way the [Jewish] community discusses issues."[42] Major established Jewish organizations that once dominated the communal discussion about Israel are now unable to do so because they "no longer have sole proprietorship over the content of communal Jewish debate, nor do they control the venues in which those debates take place."[43] While large, mainstream Jewish organizations have lost their ability to dominate the discussion about Israel within the Jewish community, individuals and small groups of people have been empowered as the Internet has made it much easier to share opinions, spread messages, organize politically, and mobilize others.[44] Moreover, nowadays individuals and small groups can have a disproportionate political impact since a website promoting one person's political view can appear the same as one representing the view of thousands of people. This means that minority, dissenting views that were once easy to ignore, can be now be loudly heard. Among other things, this helps to publicize and spread Jewish dissent about Israel. As one left-wing Jewish blogger has written: "The burgeoning of online media and political blogs has meant communication has become decentralized and democratized. Instead of begging your local Jewish paper to publish your letter to the editor or demonstrating outside the local Israeli consulate during a war, you could publish your views widely and instantaneously. You could compete in the marketplace of ideas and win readers by the strength of your arguments, the quality of your writing and the passion of your personal vision of what Israel should be."[45]

The second distinctive feature of the contemporary debate about Israel among American Jews is that it tends to be highly polarized. In the words of Peter Joseph, the chairman of the Israel Policy Forum, a decidedly centrist pro-Israel organization: "In the American Jewish dialogue on Israel, extreme polarization reigns."[46] While that may be something of an exaggeration, it is undoubtedly the case that the debate over the Israeli-Palestinian conflict is frequently dominated by voices from the left and right, while more moderate voices are drowned out. This is due, in part, to the commercial preferences of the media, for which conflict and shrill polemics of all sort sell

111

(advertising, newspapers, and so on). But it is also because both the left- and right-wing perspectives have been bolstered by events over the last fifteen years or so. The left and the right interpreted the collapse of the Oslo peace process and the outbreak of the second Intifada in 2000 as a kind of vindication of their views. To the right, it meant that the Palestinians were not interested in peace and that henceforth Israel must simply defeat Palestinian terror with as much force as needed, while the left concluded that greater international and American Jewish pressure had to be brought to bear on Israel if the Occupation was ever to end.[47] Subsequent events in the years since then, such as the Gaza withdrawal in 2005 and "Operation Cast Lead" in 2008–2009, have only served to reinforce these views and gain new adherents to them. In response to these events, and the prevailing sense of pessimism about the Israeli-Palestinian peace process, growing numbers of American Jews (particularly young ones) have gravitated to the left- and right-wing camps.[48]

Although most American Jews still hold opinions about the conflict that are closer to the center-left or center-right position—as the next chapter will discuss in-depth—the poles in the American Jewish public debate about Israel have been strengthening. They are highly vocal and becoming louder. The left is becoming ever more vociferous in its criticism of Israeli government policies and more outspoken in its support for boycotting, divesting from, and sanctioning Israel, while the right is no less strident in its opposition to any kind of Israeli territorial compromise with the Palestinians and in its denunciations of those, Jews and non-Jews, who they regard as insufficiently supportive of Israel.

Both the left and right seem, at times, to be feeding off each other, using the other's positions as counter-points and presenting the other as bogeymen in order to rally new supporters to their cause. The polemics between the left and the right have become ever more harsh. Each side vilifies the other. The left accuses the right of supporting Israeli colonialism, racism, and fascism, while the right accuses the left of condoning Palestinian terrorism and global anti-Semitism. The left dismisses the right as heartless zealots; the right dismisses the left as assimilated, disloyal, "self-hating" Jews.

This kind of invective has become all too common in the current American Jewish debate about Israel and the Israeli-Palestinian conflict. Not only has the debate become much more public and polarized than it used to be, it has also become much more combative, acrimonious, and vitriolic—and not just between those on the far-left and right of the political spectrum. In general, both in public and in private, political discussions about Israel among American Jews are becoming fraught, heated, and often vituperative.[49] They quickly degenerate into insults, ad hominem attacks, angry diatribes, and plain rudeness.[50] In the words of Rabbi Steve Gutow, the president of the Jewish Council for Public Affairs (one of the largest organizations in the American Jewish community): "The level of anger, the venom in words, demagoguery at times seems to be overtaking Jewish life."[51] In a similar vein, a journalist for Israel's *Ha'aretz* newspaper has noted that: "As a topic of conversation, Israel has become a poison infecting every area of American-Jewish life—from organizations to families."[52]

J Street president Jeremy Ben-Ami has gone even further, claiming: "the state of the Israel conversation [in the American Jewish community] is putting the heart and soul of the American Jewish community at risk."[53] And Rabbi Rick Jacobs, the president of the Union for Reform Judaism (the largest Jewish denominational movement in the United States, with about 1.5 million members), issued the same dire warning in his address to the annual General Assembly of Jewish Federations in 2012, declaring that: "incivility, divisiveness and corrosiveness . . . increasingly threatens to tear our own Jewish community apart."[54]

If there is one thing that almost everyone involved in American Jewish life today agrees on, it is that the communal debate over Israel is increasingly ugly and uncivil. Senior officials working within the organized Jewish community are deeply concerned by the trend of growing incivility in American Jewish public discourse about Israel.[55] Many leading Jewish public figures—rabbis, activists, writers, and heads of major Jewish organizations—now regularly lament the prevalent "toxic discourse" about Israel and its policies, characterized by a lack of civility and extreme animosity among Jews.[56]

What accounts for this lack of civility in contemporary Jewish public discourse surrounding Israel? Four major factors can be identified.

First, and foremost, the debate about Israel is very emotionally charged because it is deeply personal for many, if not most, of the individuals involved in the debate. This infuses the debate with a passionate intensity that can easily turn nasty. For many of the participants/combatants in the debate, Israel is an important part of their identity, whether positively or negatively, and their engagement with Israel consumes a lot of their time and energy. For many, the debate is also about much more than Israel and its policies toward the Palestinians. It is also about Jewish identity, Jewish collective memory, and Judaism itself. As one of the main protagonists in this debate, J Street's Jeremy Ben-Ami, puts it: "The discussion we're having is not just about Israel or about policy—it's about the soul of the Jewish community here in the States."[57] The debate, in other words, is not only about what Israel should do and what kind of a state it should be, but also, and perhaps more fundamentally, about who American Jews are, what their community stands for, and what its purpose should be.[58] The clashing perspectives in the debate tend to reflect profoundly different Jewish worldviews and Jewish identities. Thus, the right harbors a strong sense of victimhood, and identifies Jews as victims, and by extension, the Jewish state as a victim (this view is common on the Israeli right as well). Based upon a very bleak view of Jewish history, which emphasizes endemic anti-Semitism and the perennial persecution of Jews, the right believes that deep-rooted, sometimes latent, anti-Semitism drives a lot of the opposition to Israel and global criticism of Israel. Those on the left, by contrast, often emphasize Jewish power and "privilege" both in the United States and in Israel and the moral responsibilities that come with it.[59] Jews and the Jewish state, they believe, are not always innocent victims, and the "lesson" of Jewish history is not that Jews must remain vigilant and militant in the face of constant danger, but that Jews must be especially sensitive to, and stand up against, discrimination and persecution in general, especially when it is being carried out by Jews themselves. The shared collective memory of Jewish victimhood (and of the Holocaust in particular), therefore, evokes very different responses on the left and the right. In the words of Marc Ellis, another prominent voice in the American Jewish debate over Israel: "Though many see the Jewish civil war as a battle over politics, . . . the battle is really over Jewish memory and what that memory calls Jews to in the present."[60] The second reason why the debate about Israel is often so virulent is that it is influenced by the wider political climate in the United States in which it is taking place. Intense partisanship, rancorous political debate, and incivility have dramatically increased in American politics in recent years,[61] and this certainly affects the tenor of the political debate among American Jews too. As Donniel Hartman suggests: "the recent increase in acrimony in the American political discourse between the right and the left may have had a significant negative impact on the Jewish community's culture of public debate. Jewish discourse on Israel seems to be mimicking Fox News versus MSNBC."[62]

Third, American Jewish public debate is also influenced by the political debate in Israel, which is often very heated and ill tempered. As Israeli politics has been imported into the American Jewish community, the way that American Jews discuss Israel has increasingly come to resemble the way Israeli Jews do. American Jews now argue combatively about Israeli politics and its policies toward the Palestinians just like Israeli Jews, if not more so.

Fourth, and finally, the Internet has had a major impact upon the tone of the debate. In addition to broadening the public debate over Israel, allowing many more people to participate in it and have their voices heard, the instantaneity and anonymity that the Internet provides has also made the debate much shriller and angrier (blogs, Facebook posts, and online comment sections especially encourage shrill rhetoric and angry diatribes). The net result, according to one British Jewish participant in this debate: "It is as if the unregulated discourse of the online universe let loose the Jewish dogs of war . . . the Israel-Palestine debate now often observes the law of the jungle."[63]

COMMUNAL CONFLICT AND AVOIDANCE: THE IMPACT UPON JEWISH COMMUNITIES

In his now classic study of the organized American Jewish community first published in 1976, Daniel Elazar emphasized the importance it placed on maintaining communal consensus and avoiding public controversies: "[T]he avoidance of conflict is a major principle in the American Jewish community," he wrote. Elazar goes on to explain that: "In the aftermath of the Holocaust and because of the continuing crisis affecting the Jewish world, no issue is allowed to emerge as a matter of public controversy in the American Jewish community if it is felt that this might threaten the unity of the community. Open community conflict therefore tends to be confined to marginal matters."[64] How times have changed! Now more than three decades later, the American Jewish community is currently being torn apart by the fierce and very public communal battle that is raging over Israel. As Steven Windmueller, another seasoned observer of the American Jewish community, wrote in 2010: "The once-understood communal principle of governing by consensus has given way in these times to the presence of political positions that firmly divide the Jewish community into ideological camps. Increasingly, one finds that in place of a shared discourse and a commitment to civility, the communal debate [over Israel] often deteriorates to sloganeering and, at times, name-calling."[65]

No subject provokes more conflict and controversy within the American Jewish community today than Israel. It has been described as "a catalyst for divisiveness,"[66] and "the most volatile, wedge issue in the [American] Jewish community."[67] Disagreements about the Israeli-Palestinian conflict and Israel's policies toward the Palestinians are by far the biggest source of conflict. The American Jewish public debate over Israel is not merely an elite preoccupation, limited to some public intellectuals, journalists, activists, and communal leaders. It has penetrated right down to the grassroots of the Jewish community, and swept up members of synagogues, JCCs, Jewish Federations, Jewish Community Relations Councils (JCRCs), Jewish film festival boards, and Jewish student associations. "In synagogues, campuses and JCC's, fierce and emotional battles are fought between right and left that not only challenge the status quo but also create a sense of unease and foreboding," one observer writes.[68] Another comments that: "The debate [over Israel] has been heating up wildly around the country over the past few years, escalating from shouting to name-calling and efforts—mostly by the right—to have opponents excluded from community forums, parades, JCCs, Hillels, and more. It's not going to get better any time soon."[69]

As these quotes indicate, the intensifying communal conflict over Israel has spread far and wide. Synagogues, JCCs, Jewish film festivals, and university campuses have all become public battlegrounds for this communal conflict.[70] All across the United States, but especially in its major cities with large Jewish populations,[71] the increasingly toxic nature of the American Jewish public debate about Israel and its policies is having a pernicious impact upon local Jewish communities. It is dividing and polarizing community members, stoking communal tensions, and even ruining personal friendships.[72] According to Rabbi Sheldon Lewis, a longtime rabbi in Palo Alto in the Bay Area of San Francisco (home to about half a million Jews): "Our communities have really been torn apart surrounding Israel. People have attacked each other personally, friendships have ended, people have left synagogues because of it and have even disappeared entirely from the community."[73] In many local Jewish communities today, the situation has become so bad that it is almost impossible to have an open, honest, and polite discussion about Israel, and especially about the Israeli-Palestinian conflict. All too often, the discussion that does take place is either very guarded, or else its gets very heated and acrimonious, frequently degenerating into vitriol and diatribes. Consequently, when it comes to discussing Israel in many Jewish communities, there is a growing tendency toward either bitter argument or outright avoidance—shouting or silence.[74]

For many American Jews today, the argument about Israel has become so toxic that they have become extremely wary of talking about Israel at all. Rabbi Rick Jacobs, the head of the Reform movement, bluntly acknowledges that: "Conversations about Israel often get polarized, so we've stopped having them."[75] Similarly, Arnold Eisen, the Chancellor of the Jewish Theological Seminary in New York (the leading institute and rabbinical training academy of the Conservative movement) ruefully admits: "honest discussion about Israel [within the American Jewish community] is largely shut down. Some rabbis will speak their minds; but people don't want to fight and there is a disinclination to argue about Israel."[76] In fact, in many synagogue congregations, there is now an unofficial moratorium on discussing Israel, or at least the Israeli-Palestinian conflict, in order to stop people fighting about it, and some synagogues have reduced their Israel-related activities in order to avoid sparking a controversy or crisis within the community.[77]

There is probably no one in the American Jewish community more acutely aware of the difficulty and danger of discussing Israel today than local rabbis.[78] Their jobs, indeed their livelihoods, depend upon their ability to rise above the communal fray, to bring congregants together, and to articulate in their sermons and speeches their community's hopes, fears, and beliefs. Since expressing solidarity with Israel has long been a central feature of American Jewish communal life and religious practice, rabbis are often expected to publicly express their support for and commitment to Israel and encourage this support and commitments among their congregants. These tasks, however, have become almost impossible to perform for many rabbis today, especially those working in Reform and Conservative synagogues (where communal divisions over Israel are most common). Many say that they feel intimidated and even afraid to talk about Israel to their congregations, and some have even been told by their boards not to talk about Israel.[79] Rabbis fear that voicing any criticism of Israel's policies toward the Palestinians may antagonize some members of their congregations and could even risk their jobs.[80] Such fears are now widespread among rabbis as well as others working within the organized Jewish community, as Ethan Felson, the vice president of the Jewish Council for Public Affairs states: "One of the concerns we have—and we hear this over and over again from rabbis and community leaders—people are afraid to discuss Israel. People fear for their jobs, their professional lives if they have these conversations."[81]

In response to the widespread atmosphere of anxiety and trepidation about discussing Israel within the American Jewish community today, and in an effort to prevent such discussions when they do occur from degenerating into incivility, there have been a number of civility initiatives and intra-Jewish dialogue projects launched over the last few years.[82] This began in 2010, when the Jewish Council for Public Affairs (JCPA) introduced a "civility campaign," passing a resolution during its annual meeting that year calling for an end to "a level of un-civility, particularly over issues pertaining to Israel, that has not been witnessed in recent memory." The JCPA also produced guidelines for community events in which participants are reminded: "we gather as a community to discuss and debate, but not to degrade. Our goal is a civil and constructive discussion."[83] Since then, other major organizations within the American Jewish establishment (such as the AJC, the ADL, and the Conference of Presidents) have followed suit, issuing their own statements and resolutions emphasizing the importance of civility in communal discourse.

On a local level, some Jewish communities have started their own civility initiatives. After the debate about Israel in the Jewish community in San Francisco and the Bay Area became so vitriolic, the Jewish Federation of San Francisco and the local JCRC promoted a "Year of Civil Discourse" in 2011. Its declared purpose was "to elevate the level of discourse within the Jewish community, and increase the ability of Jewish institutions to have more respectful and informed conversations about Israel and other contentious issues." As part of this initiative, local communal leaders, officials, and rabbis were trained in how to handle discussions about "difficult" and "sensitive issues" in their communities, above all issues concerning Israel.[84] There were also a series of facilitated dialogue groups bringing together some local community members with opposing points of view about Israel.[85] In 2014, a similar initiative was launched in New York by the local JCRC there. It stated: "Differences of opinion regarding the State of Israel now too often serve as a cause for American Jewish communal discord and even acrimony. When disagreement becomes hostile it frays the bonds of our community. The consequences of such disconnectedness are profound and severe. We must ask ourselves what we can do to listen with more patience, to hear each other and ourselves with greater clarity, and not to impugn the character or motivations of those with whom we disagree."[86] The JCRC in New York hired someone to serve as "director of Jewish intra-communal affairs," giving them the job of trying to foster more civility among Jews around the issue of Israel. This person organized a series of facilitated dialogue groups called "Israel Talks," in which members of the community sat in small groups and were encouraged by a facilitator to share their personal feelings about Israel (rather like a group therapy session). The point of such gatherings, in the words of the organizer, was "to have people listen and try to understand someone else's views."[87] After attending one of these dialogue groups, Gary Rosenblatt, the editor and publisher of a widely circulated American Jewish newspaper lamented in his weekly editorial: "It's a shame that we've come to the point where we need a communal organization to foster respectful dialogue among Jews discussing Israel, which has become such a hot-button issue. But that's the reality."[88]

CONCLUSION: FROM SOLIDARITY TO DISCORD

The current American Jewish debate about Israel is unprecedented in many ways. It is more public, more polarized, and more acrimonious than ever before. It is no longer an elite preoccupation, but a debate in which growing numbers of American Jews are now engaged on an almost daily basis. While this has allowed many more people to freely voice their different opinions about Israel and its conflict with the Palestinians, it has also often led to angry arguments, personal attacks, and ruined relationships. Indeed, the debate about Israel has become so ugly in many Jewish communities that communal groups have had to respond by promoting civility initiatives and dialogue groups, and even hiring people to facilitate discussions about Israel.

But even if the American Jewish argument about Israel could be more civil, it will remain divisive. However politely they may disagree, the fact remains that the solidarity that American Jews once felt when it came to Israel is now a distant memory.

In the years following the 1967 war, Israel was the great unifying cause of American Jewish politics (along with the campaign to free Soviet Jewry). American Jews marched in the streets, held fundraisers, and lobbied their elected officials in support of Israel. These activities became staples of American Jewish communal life, and they served the crucial function of bringing American Jews together, physically and emotionally. As much as they helped Israel, they helped local Jewish communities express a common bond and find a common mission. Supporting Israel, then, gave American Jews a sense of unity and purpose. Nowadays, the unifying effect that supporting Israel had upon Jewish communities has greatly diminished, if not ceased altogether. Far from uniting American Jews, the issue of Israel increasingly divides them, and local Jewish communities face the possibility of being torn apart by these divisions. Israel has become a challenge, even a problem, for many Jewish communities as they struggle to accommodate different, often clashing opinions about it. Arguments about Israel have become the primary source of conflict within Jewish communities, so much so that many (especially rabbis) are now wary of discussing Israel at all. As one commentator writes: "Israel has visibly shifted from being a uniting force into being a disruption to North American Jewish life, the black sheep, the uncomfortable topic that nobody wants to talk about because discussing Israel means fighting about Israel."[89]

There are still times, however, when many, perhaps most, American Jews are united in support of Israel—when it is under violent attack. When Israel is at war, there is always a surge of American Jewish solidarity with it, and with each other (often, wars prompt populations to "rally 'round the flag"). A sense of emergency and heightened threat unifies American Jews (and Israeli Jews), albeit only temporarily. Once the violence ebbs, and the sense of emergency and threat diminish, debates resume and divisions quickly resurface. The outbreak of the second Intifada, for example, halted the fierce debate that American Jews had been having over the Oslo peace process. Most American Jews immediately rallied to Israel's side (this was apparent in the large public demonstrations held in support of Israel, increased donations to Israel, and the "solidarity missions" of Jewish organizations to Israel).[90] For instance, on April 15, 2002, after a wave of Palestinian suicide bombings, over 100,000 Jews gathered in Washington, DC, to express their solidarity with Israel in what was the largest pro-Israel rally ever by American Jews. Speaking at the rally, Rabbi Marvin Hier, the founder and dean of the Simon Wiesenthal Center in Los Angeles, declared that: "This is a message to the American government and to the world that the support for Israel in the American Jewish community and among friends of Israel in the non-Jewish community is wall-to-wall, from left to right."[91] But this "wall-to-wall" support did not last long. Political divisions soon reappeared within the American Jewish community, particularly after the Bush administration proposed a "Road Map" to end the second Intifada and restart Israeli-Palestinian peace talks in the summer of 2003.[92] This pattern has also been evident during other wars and rounds of violence involving Israel since the end of the second Intifada (notably, the second Lebanon War in 2006, "Operation Cast Lead" in 2008–2009, and "Operation Protective Edge" in 2014[93]).

Moments of American Jewish unity when it comes to Israel are now short-lived and rare. The more normal state of affairs is fractious debate among American Jews. How accurately this debate reflects American Jewish public opinion about the Israeli-Palestinian conflict is the subject of the next chapter.

4.

THE EROSION OF CONSENSUS

Put two Jews in a room, and you'll get three opinions.

—David Ben-Gurion, Israel's first Prime Minister[1]

The increasingly polarized and vitriolic argument about Israel raging within the American Jewish community, described in the previous chapter, certainly gives the impression that American Jews are now deeply divided over the Israeli-Palestinian conflict. But is this public debate actually reflective of the views of American Jewry at large? How polarized are American Jews in their views about the conflict? Are they really as divided as they seem? What consensus, if any, exists, and has it changed over time? In this chapter, I answer these questions by examining what surveys of American Jews tell us about American Jewish public opinion regarding the Israeli-Palestinian conflict. I will draw upon numerous public opinion polls that have been conducted over the past two decades to dissect the views of American Jews about the conflict, and outline the major trends in American Jewish public opinion. In particular, for recent American Jewish views about the Israeli-Palestinian conflict, I will use the Pew Research Center's 2013 "A Portrait of Jewish Americans," since it is the largest and most comprehensive national survey of American Jews in more than a decade; and to trace trends in American Jewish public opinion over time, I will use the "Annual Survey of American Jewish Opinion," commissioned by the American Jewish Committee (AJC).[2]

AMBIVALENT CENTRISTS

In the American Jewish debate about the Israeli-Palestinian conflict, those on both the left and right often assert that the majority of American Jews share their views, and they frequently claim to speak on behalf of this silent majority. Although no doubt politically convenient, such claims, on both sides, do have some factual basis. In their views about the Israeli-Palestinian conflict, most American Jews lean a bit left and a bit right. That is, they agree with the center-left on some questions and they agree with the center-right on others. They are, in short, centrists (much like Israeli Jews).[3] They support a two-state solution to the Israeli-Palestinian conflict and they continue to believe that such a solution is still possible. A majority (61 percent in the Pew survey) also believes that a future Palestinian state could co-exist peacefully with Israel.[4] However, most American Jews, like most Israeli Jews, are pessimistic about the chances of achieving a peace agreement between Israel and the Palestinians. They are also persistently distrustful of the Palestinians (again, just like Israeli Jews[5]). In the Pew survey, three-quarters of American Jews did not believe that the current Palestinian leadership (led by Palestinian Authority President Mahmoud Abbas) was making a sincere effort to reach a peace agreement with Israel,[6] and in the AJC survey that year, three-quarters of American Jewish respondents agreed with the statement: "The goal of the Arabs is not a peaceful two-state agreement with Israel, but rather the destruction of Israel" (similar numbers agree with this statement every year the question is asked).

Most American Jews are, therefore, ambivalent centrists. They want peace and favor some Israeli territorial concessions,[7] but they also worry about Israeli security and are highly suspicious about Palestinians' intentions. They agree with the center-right about the potentially severe security threat Israel could face if it withdraws from territory in the West Bank, and they agree with the center-left about the major demographic threat to Israel's future as a Jewish and democratic state if it continues to hold onto this territory and effectively rule over the Palestinian population within it.[8] They are torn between these conflicting beliefs. They want Israel to end the Occupation, but they do not want Israel to take any security risks. They want Palestinians to have a state of their own, but they do not want this state to be a threat to Israel in any way.[9] They are, in Steven Cohen's apt phrase, "conditional doves."[10]

The deep ambivalence that most American Jews feel concerning a land-for-peace deal with the Palestinians is mirrored in their views about Israel's use of force against Palestinians. Whenever Israel undertakes military actions against Palestinians, a solid majority of American Jews consistently, perhaps instinctively, backs Israel. Yet, most American Jews also doubt the effectiveness of Israel's wars and military campaigns. For instance, in a national survey carried out in March 2009 shortly after the conclusion of Israel's "Operation Cast Lead" against Hamas in the Gaza Strip, three-quarters of American Jews approved of Israel's war in Gaza, and most (69 percent) did not believe that its military campaign was disproportionate (contrary to much international public opinion at the time).[11] But most American Jews (59 percent) also did not believe that "Operation Cast Lead" improved Israeli security. In other words, American Jews strongly support Israel's use of force even though they doubt its utility.

However conflicted they may be, the centrist orientation of the majority of American Jews regarding the Israeli-Palestinian conflict is remarkably stable and enduring.[12] For the last quarter of a century, most American Jews have consistently supported the Israeli-Palestinian peace process (since it began with the U.S.-sponsored Madrid peace conference in 1991), while remaining suspicious of Palestinian intentions. For example, in a poll taken almost a year after the signing of the "Declaration of Principles" between Israel and the PLO on the White House lawn on September 13, 1993, two-thirds of American Jews expressed support for the agreement (this was actually down from 75 percent who initially supported it), yet far fewer (44 percent) thought that the Palestinians were interested "in a true and lasting peace with Israel," with 42 percent believing that the Palestinians were not interested in this.[13] There was even greater distrust of the PLO, with a slight majority (53 percent) of those surveyed agreeing with the view that "the PLO is determined to destroy Israel,"[14] and only 18 percent agreeing that "the PLO [could] be relied upon to honor its agreements and refrain from terrorist activity against Israel."[15] While their support for the Oslo peace process declined slightly over time, throughout the years of the peace process (1993–2000) there was still a solid majority of American Jews in favor of it—although the minority of American Jews who opposed it were so vocal and strident they gave the impression that there was much more opposition to the peace process among American Jews than there actually was.[16]

When the Oslo peace process collapsed and the second Intifada broke out, the vast majority of American Jews blamed the Palestinians for the failure to make peace and for the renewal of Israeli-Palestinian violence (in the 2002 AJC survey, 80 percent thought the Palestinians were responsible for the violence). Most American Jews also supported the aggressive military actions of the Israeli government then led by Prime Minister Ariel Sharon in response to the wave of Palestinian suicide bombings that took place at the height of the second Intifada. Almost two-thirds (62 percent) thought that the U.S. government should give the Sharon government a "free hand" to take whatever actions it wanted in responding to terrorist attacks, and nearly four out of five American Jews supported the "targeted assassination" of suspected Palestinian terrorists.[17] Nevertheless, throughout the second Intifada (2000–2005), most American Jews continued to support the establishment of a Palestinian state and favored the dismantling of at least some Jewish settlements in the West Bank. In fact, American Jewish support for the establishment of a Palestinian state "in the current situation" increased slightly during the course of the second Intifada (from 53 percent support in 2001 to a peak of 57 percent in 2004). The majority of American Jews, then, were hawkish in their views about how Israel should respond to Palestinian terrorism,[18] but dovish in their views about how Israel should resolve its conflict with the Palestinians.

This "hawkish dovishness" still typifies the views of most American Jews when it comes to the Israeli-Palestinian conflict. In this respect, there has been no change in American Jewish opinion over the years. According to the AJC surveys, there has also been little, if any, change in American Jewish views about some other issues in the

Israeli-Palestinian conflict.[19] For example, most American Jews (like Israeli Jews) have been consistently opposed to a division of Jerusalem.[20] Nevertheless, there have been some significant shifts of opinion over time. Most notably in the AJC surveys, American Jews have gradually become more supportive of dismantling some, but not all, Israeli settlements in the West Bank in the context of a peace agreement with the Palestinians.[21]

DIVISIONS AMONG AMERICAN JEWS

American Jewry as a whole, then, is not as polarized in its views about the Israeli-Palestinian conflict as the public debate suggests (this is hardly surprising, since public debates tend to be dominated by the most ideologically committed and politically mobilized, and those who shout loudest are most often heard in the media, however unrepresentative they may be).[22] Nor has there been as much change in American Jewish public opinion over the years as media reports often suggest (or some people would like to believe). Nevertheless, while there is still a consensus among American Jews on some matters concerning Israel's conflict with the Palestinians, on others there are deep divisions. In particular, surveys show that the establishment of a Palestinian state and the future of Israel's settlements in the West Bank are highly divisive issues among American Jews.

In the annual AJC surveys, American Jews are consistently divided in their views about the establishment of a Palestinian state, with roughly half generally favoring this and half opposing it (see figure 4.1).[23] On the question of what should happen to Jewish settlements in the West Bank in the framework of a peace agreement with the Palestinians, while a solid majority of American Jewish respondents in the AJC surveys consistently supports the dismantling and evacuation of some or all Israeli settlements, a significant minority—ranging from between 35 to 45 percent—opposes the dismantling of any settlements (see figure 4.2).[24] In the 2013 AJC survey, for example, 43 percent were opposed to the dismantling of any Jewish settlements, while 56 percent favored the dismantling of some or all settlements (just 12 percent of those surveyed wanted all Jewish settlements to be

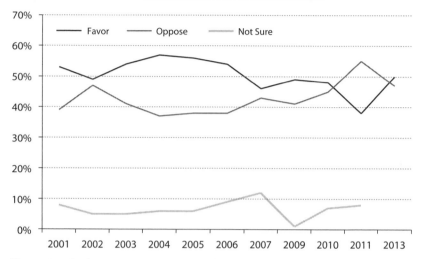

Figure 4.1. In the current situation, would you favor or oppose the establishment of a Palestinian state? Data from American Jewish Committee.

dismantled). The lack of agreement among American Jews regarding Israeli settlements is also evident in other recent surveys. In the 2013 Pew survey, 44 percent of American Jews said that the continued construction of settlements in the West Bank hurt Israel's security, compared to 46 percent who thought that settlement building makes no difference or actually helps Israeli security;[25] and in a poll of American Jewish voters conducted on behalf of J Street following the November 2014 midterm Congressional elections, 28 percent wanted Israel to stop all settlement construction in the West Bank, 52 percent wanted Israel to stop construction beyond the major settlement blocs, and 20 percent wanted Israel to continue building settlements anywhere in the West Bank.[26] These survey results clearly demonstrate that American Jews are very divided in their attitudes toward Israel's settlement project. Given the controversy that surrounds this project in Israel and the constant international and American criticism of it, such divisions are to be expected.

Underlying the divisions within American Jewish public opinion about the Israeli-Palestinian conflict are larger political differences among various subgroups of American Jews. Three stand out as most important in

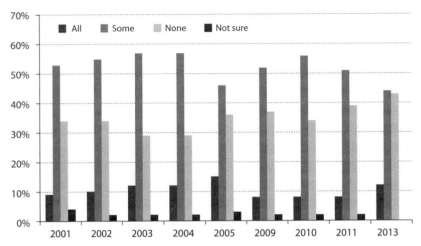

As part of a permanent settlement with the Palestinians, should Israel be willing to dismantle all, some, or none of the Jewish settlements in the West Bank?

Figure 4.2. As part of a permanent settlement with the Palestinians, should Israel be willing to dismantle all, some, or none of the Jewish settlements in the West Bank? Data from American Jewish Committee.

terms of the impact they have upon shaping opinions about the conflict: (1) the differences between Orthodox and non-Orthodox Jews; (2) the differences between liberals and conservatives, Democrats, and Republicans; and (3) the differences between younger and older Jews.

THE DENOMINATIONAL DIVIDE

Divergent American Jewish opinions about the Israeli-Palestinian conflict (as well as other political issues) correlate closely with different religious denominations.[27] The religious spectrum and the political spectrum in the American Jewish community are almost identical— with more religious Jews generally falling on the right and more secular Jews falling on the left (needless to say, not all religious Jews are on the right and not all secular Jews are on the left). Orthodox Jews, just like their counterparts in Israel, have long held the most right-wing and hawkish views within the American Jewish community, while Reform Jews and unaffiliated Jews (that is, those who do not identify

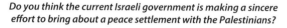

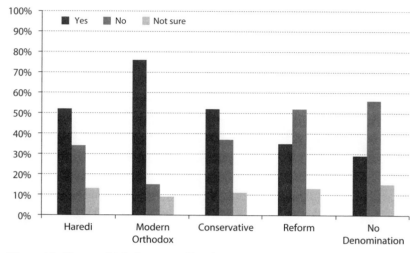

Figure 4.3. Do you think the current Israeli government is making a sincere effort to bring about a peace settlement with the Palestinians? (By religious denomination.) Data from Pew Research Center.

with any denomination) are often the most left-wing and dovish; and Conservative Jews are typically more centrist, with views somewhere in the middle (much the same way as Conservative Judaism lies between Reform Judaism and Orthodox Judaism) (see figure 4.3).[28]

More broadly, on most matters concerning Israel and the Palestinians, the biggest division in American Jewish opinion is simply between Orthodox and non-Orthodox Jews. In the Pew survey, for example, a majority of Orthodox Jews (61 percent) did not think that Israel and a future Palestinian state could coexist peacefully, whereas most non-Orthodox Jews thought that this would be possible.[29] Similar findings appear in numerous other surveys over many years. In the mid-1990s, at the height of the Oslo peace process, polls showed that American Jewish opposition to the peace process was largely concentrated within the Orthodox community. In a survey taken in September 1995, 64 percent of Orthodox Jews opposed the Rabin government's peace policy, while roughly three-quarters of non-Orthodox Jews supported it (77 percent of Reform Jews and 74 percent of Conservative Jews).[30] A decade later, in a 2005 survey, a large majority of Orthodox Jews (69 percent) was opposed to the establishment of a Palestinian state, whereas a majority of non-Orthodox Jews wanted a Palestinian state to be established. In the same survey, most Orthodox Jews (65 percent) opposed dismantling any West Bank settlements in a peace deal with the Palestinians, compared with only 36 percent of Conservative, 31 percent of Reform, and 32 percent of unaffiliated Jews who felt this way.[31]

Orthodox Jews, who currently make up around 10 percent of the American Jewish population, are therefore much more likely than non-Orthodox Jews to oppose a Palestinian state and any dismantling of Jewish settlements in the West Bank. They are much less supportive of Israeli territorial compromise with the Palestinians in general than are other Jews.[32] Conversely, they are much more supportive of Israeli settlement building in the West Bank than non-Orthodox Jews are.[33] The issue of Jewish settlements in the West Bank divides Orthodox and non-Orthodox American Jews more than any other single issue in the Israeli-Palestinian conflict. While most Orthodox Jews have always strongly supported the settlement project and still do (in many cases financially as well), most non-Orthodox Jews have come to view the settlements as a major threat to Israel's future as a Jewish and democratic state. These radically different attitudes to the Israeli settlement enterprise surely stem in part from the fact that Orthodox American Jews have a very different view of settlers and settlements than non-Orthodox American Jews because they are much more likely to have family or friends who actually live in West Bank settlements and many have probably visited such settlements themselves. Furthermore, over the last few decades it has become very common for young modern Orthodox American Jews to spend a year or two after high school studying in yeshivas and seminaries in Israel before returning to the United States to go to college. Not only does this experience have a powerful impact upon their religious beliefs and practices, it also affects their political beliefs and attitudes.[34] Cumulatively, the attendance of so many young Orthodox Jews at yeshivas in Israel (some of which are located in the West Bank and East Jerusalem) has had a profound impact upon the culture and politics of modern Orthodox American Jews, resulting in a stricter adherence to

131

Orthodox religious practices and a stronger commitment to Israel.[35] It has also, no doubt, generated greater sympathy and support for the settlement project.[36]

THE IDEOLOGICAL AND PARTISAN DIVIDE

In addition to the long-standing religious divide between Orthodox and non-Orthodox American Jews over the Israeli-Palestinian conflict, there is also a growing divide between politically conservative Jews and liberal Jews. Although a commitment to liberalism has traditionally been a major feature of American Jewish identity and politics,[37] and an important source of cohesion for American Jews,[38] by no means all American Jews adhere to this aspect of the American Jewish "creed." While liberals still greatly outnumber conservatives in the American Jewish community—in the Pew survey, half of American Jews described themselves as liberal, while only 20 percent described themselves as conservative (the rest, 30 percent, were self-declared moderates),[39]—the minority of American Jews who are politically conservative are often highly vocal, especially when it comes to Israel. They are also disproportionately represented in the organized American Jewish community.[40]

Politically conservative Jews tend to be more emotionally attached to Israel than liberal Jews,[41] and much more hawkish in their views concerning the Israeli-Palestinian conflict.[42] Compared with liberals and moderates, they are consistently more opposed to Israeli territorial concessions to the Palestinians,[43] including a division of Jerusalem,[44] and they are less willing to dismantle Israeli settlements in the West Bank.[45] Indeed, in the Pew survey, the majority of conservative Jews (63 percent) thought that building settlements in the West Bank either helped Israel's security or made no difference to it. Most liberal Jews (60 percent), by contrast, thought that settlement building undermined Israeli security. In recent years, during which successive right-wing governments have ruled Israel, politically conservative Jews have been much more supportive of Israeli government policies and actions than politically liberal Jews. While the latter have become increasingly critical of Israeli governments and were highly

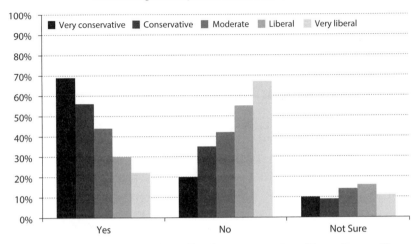

Do you think the current Israeli government is making a sincere effort to bring about a peace settlement with the Palestinians?

Figure 4.4. Do you think the current Israeli government is making a sincere effort to bring about a peace settlement with the Palestinians? (By political orientation.) Data from Pew Research Center.

skeptical of the Netanyahu government's willingness to make peace with the Palestinians, conservative Jews have staunchly defended Israeli governments and strongly backed the Netanyahu government in particular (see figure 4.4).[46] Conservatives were also much more likely than liberals to blame the Palestinians for the failure to reach a peace agreement, and were much less likely than liberals to believe that the Palestinians truly want peace with Israel.[47] Finally, and perhaps unsurprisingly, Jewish conservatives have been critical of the level of U.S. support for Israel during the Obama administration, with 57 percent of conservatives in the Pew survey saying that the United States does not support Israel enough (by contrast, most American Jews, 56 percent, said they were satisfied with the current level of U.S. support for Israel).

Fierce criticism of the Obama administration's policy toward Israel, and President Obama in particular, by politically conservative American Jews has been a prominent feature of American Jewish public discourse in recent years (despite the fact that the vast majority of American Jews have always supported President Obama and have approved of his handling of U.S.-Israel relations). This criticism has

133

been one indication of a growing partisan divide in American politics vis-à-vis the Israeli-Palestinian conflict. Simply put, while Democrats have gradually become more critical of Israel, Republicans have become much more supportive. Since the collapse of the Oslo peace process and the terrorist attacks in the United States on September 11, 2001, there has been a growing "sympathy gap" between Republicans and Democrats with the former sympathizing much more strongly with Israel than with the Palestinians.[48] In line with this general trend, in surveys Jewish Republicans have been much more sympathetic toward Israel's Netanyahu government than Jewish Democrats,[49] and much less supportive of the establishment of a Palestinian state.[50]

THE GENERATIONAL DIVIDE

Along with religiosity and political orientation, age also has a significant impact upon the divisions of opinion among American Jews regarding the Israeli-Palestinian conflict. Although they are, at least for the most part, emotionally attached to Israel, young American Jews are more critical of it than their parents and grandparents. This is clearly evident in the data gathered by the Pew survey. For instance, only a quarter of Jews aged 18 to 29 believed that the Israeli government was making a "sincere effort" to reach a peace agreement compared to 43 percent of those aged over 50 (see figure 4.5A), and half of young American Jews thought that settlement building undermined Israeli security.[51] Even more strikingly, young Jews are also more critical of U.S. government support for Israel, with a quarter of them in the Pew survey saying that the United States supports Israel too much, compared with only 5 percent of Jews aged 50 and older.[52] The Pew survey also showed that young, non-Orthodox American Jews are less suspicious of the Palestinians, and more hopeful about the prospects for peaceful coexistence between Israel and a future Palestinian state. They were more than twice as likely as older (over 50) non-Orthodox American Jews to think that the Palestinian leadership was making a sincere effort to bring about a peace agreement with Israel; and three-quarters of them (76 percent) believed that Israel and an independent Palestinian state could peace-

A.   Do you think the current Israeli government is making a sincere
effort to bring about a peace settlement with the Palestinians?

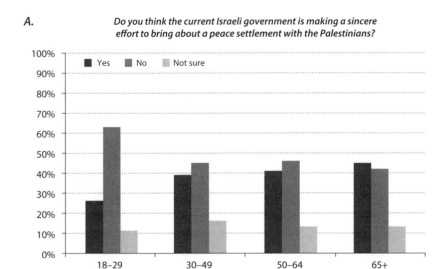

Figure 4.5A. Do you think the current Israeli government is making a sincere effort to bring about a peace settlement with the Palestinians? (By age.) Data from Pew Research Center.

B.   Is there a way for Israel and an independent
Palestinian state to coexist peacefully?

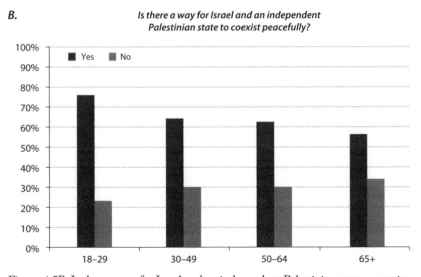

Figure 4.5B. Is there a way for Israel and an independent Palestinian state to coexist peacefully? Data from Pew Research Center.

fully coexist, compared to 63 percent of non-Orthodox Jews between the ages of 50 and 64, and 56 percent of those over 65 (see figure 4.5B).

Crude statistics, however, cannot really capture the nuanced attitudes of young American Jews to Israel's conflict with the Palestinians and how profoundly they differ from those of older generations. This passage written by a young Jewish American in the summer of 2010 powerfully conveys this difference in attitude:

> For many Jews my age, who love Israel and strive to nourish her efforts to thrive in a hostile region, defending her actions in Gaza has too often become an immense moral struggle that requires the suspension of our values as human beings and, notably, the suspension of our values as Jews. Where many older American Jews see a faultless and holy entity struggling simply and nobly to exist, we of the younger persuasion see a government—a special government, presiding over a place near and dear to our hearts, but a government nonetheless—with the capacity to make wrong decisions in light of a tortuous history. Some among my mother's friends rejoice in violent attacks on Palestinians who seek to harm Israel, while my friends cringe at the initiation of bloodshed by Jews. We see their aggressive stance as zealotry and paranoia; they see our discomfort as abandonment and naiveté.[53]

Such an attitude is quite common among well-educated, liberal, young American Jews, and many of them have flocked to join groups on college campuses like J Street U, Open Hillel, and, further to the left, Jewish Voice for Peace. This does not necessarily mean, however, that young Jews are always critical of Israel, or that they are politically alienated from it, as some have claimed.[54] In fact, a large survey of young American Jews taken before and after the 2014 Gaza War found that a vast majority thought that Israel's actions in the war were mostly or completely justified, and most also said they felt support for Israel during the war. This was true regardless of their political orientation, with 78 percent of self-described liberals viewing Israel's conduct in the war as mostly or completely justified compared to just 21 percent who viewed it as unjustified (although most young liberal

Jews viewed Israel's conduct in the war as justified, they were less likely to hold this view than moderates or conservatives).[55] There are a number of factors that help account for the different attitudes between younger and older American Jews toward the Israeli-Palestinian conflict. First, younger Americans in general have significantly different views than older Americans on a host of current social and political issues.[56] With regard to the Israeli-Palestinian conflict, they tend to be more critical of Israel and more sympathetic toward the Palestinians.[57] Second, just as other young Americans are more likely than older Americans to have liberal attitudes, young American Jews are more socially and politically liberal than older Jews (in fact, young American Jews are even more liberal than non-Jewish Americans in their age group).[58] Third, younger American Jews, especially college students, are more likely than their parents or grandparents to be acquainted with the Palestinians and to have been more exposed to the Palestinian narrative.[59] Fourth, since they have grown up long after the Holocaust, their political beliefs are less strongly shaped by it,[60] and this also probably affects their attitudes toward Israel and the Israeli-Palestinian conflict because support for Israel is strongly linked to the collective Jewish memory of the Holocaust (as Holocaust consciousness became stronger in the 1960s and 1970s, for example, so too did support for Israel). Finally, perhaps the biggest reason why young American Jews tend to be more dovish and more critical of Israel is because they are much more likely than older Jews to be the offspring of intermarried couples. Intermarriage undoubtedly has an impact upon the political attitudes and opinions of the children of such unions. Young American Jews whose parents are intermarried are not only more liberal than other Jews, but also significantly less attached to Israel. As such, it is hardly surprising that this rapidly growing subgroup within the American Jewish population has very different views about the Israeli-Palestinian conflict than other American Jews.

Will the political attitudes of young non-Orthodox Jews toward Israel significantly change, as they grow older? Will they become less dovish in their views about the Israeli-Palestinian conflict (assuming, of course, that the conflict remains unresolved)? While only time will tell, there is good reason to believe that the "dovishness" of young, non-Orthodox American Jews will endure over time because once political attitudes and identities are formed in adolescence and young adulthood they tend to remain fairly stable throughout a person's life. If this turns out to be the case, then the existing divisions of opinion among Americans Jews, especially between the Orthodox and non-Orthodox, will only widen and become more entrenched. The American Jewish public consensus about the Israeli-Palestinian conflict—already narrower than it once was—is therefore likely to continue to erode, if not completely disappear, in the future.

Figure 1. Yeshiva students from New Jersey march along Fifth Avenue in the annual Celebrate Israel parade in New York City, May 31, 2015. Photo Credit: Gili Getz.

Figure 2. Young supporters of Israel marching in the annual Celebrate Israel parade in New York City, June 1, 2014. Photo Credit: Gili Getz.

Figure 3. Marchers representing liberal and left-wing Jewish organizations such as the New Israel Fund, Americans for Peace Now, Partners for Progressive Israel, and T'ruah: The Rabbinic Call for Human Rights participating in the Celebrate Israel parade in New York City, May 31, 2015. Photo Credit: Gili Getz.

Figure 4. Right-wing demonstrators from Americans for a Safe Israel heckling left-wing marchers at the 2015 Celebrate Israel parade in New York City, May 31, 2015. Photo Credit: Gili Getz.

Figure 5. Ultra-Orthodox Jews protesting the Celebrate Israel parade in New York City, June 2, 2013. Photo Credit: Gili Getz.

Figure 6. American Jewish protester at a demonstration in New York City during the 2014 Gaza War, August 2014. Photo Credit: Gili Getz.

Figure 7. Jewish Voice for Peace (JVP) protester at a demonstration in New York City during the 2014 Gaza War, August 2014. Photo Credit: Gili Getz.

Figure 8. Members of Jewish Voice for Peace (JVP) at a pro-Palestinian demonstration in New York City, August 2014. Photo Credit: Gili Getz.

Figure 9. Audience member at the inaugural Open Hillel conference at Harvard University, October 2014. Photo Credit: Gili Getz.

Figure 10. A student member of Open Hillel protests outside the 2015 General Assembly of the Jewish Federations of North America in Washington, DC, November 8, 2015. Photo Credit: Gili Getz.

Figure 11. J Street's 2012 National Conference in Washington, DC, March 2012.
Photo Credit: Gili Getz.

Figure 12. Peter Beinart speaking at the 2012 J Street National Conference in
Washington, DC, March 2012. Photo Credit: Gili Getz.

Figure 13. U.S. Senator Chuck Schumer speaking at AIPAC's Policy Conference in Washington, DC, March 2014. Photo Credit: Gili Getz.

Figure 14. Morton Klein, president of the Zionist Organization of America (ZOA), speaking at a demonstration outside Senator Chuck Schumer's New York office, March 2015. Photo Credit: Gili Getz.

Figure 15. Rival protesters outside Senator Chuck Schumer's New York office, August 2015. Photo Credit: Gili Getz.

5.
THE FRACTURING OF THE PRO-ISRAEL LOBBY

Anyone who thinks that Jewish groups constitute a homogeneous "lobby" ought to spend some time dealing with them.

—Former U.S. Secretary of State George Shultz[1]

When many, perhaps most, people in the United States and around the world think of American Jews and Israel, what immediately comes to their minds is the so-called pro-Israel lobby, sometimes simply (and inaccurately) referred to as the "Jewish lobby."[2] Whether reviled or admired, the power of the pro-Israel lobby has long been the stuff of legend. Both its detractors and its supporters alike view the lobby, especially AIPAC, as enjoying immense influence in the corridors of power in Washington, DC. This perception has itself fuelled the lobby's power, as politicians fear incurring its supposedly mighty wrath.[3] Indeed, the pro-Israel lobby is widely regarded as the second most powerful domestic lobby in the United States, behind only the "gun lobby" (led by the National Rifle Association). So powerful is the pro-Israel lobby, according to some observers, that not only is it almost single-handedly responsible for American government support for Israel, it is also the driving force behind U.S. foreign policy toward the Middle East as a whole. It has even been (falsely) accused of masterminding the U.S. invasion of Iraq and the overthrow of Saddam Hussein in 2003,[4] and orchestrating the imposition of mounting economic sanctions against Iran for its nuclear program over the past decade, not to mention other more far-fetched accusations of conspiracies and cover-ups. Chronicling and denouncing the alleged machinations and misdeeds of the pro-Israel lobby has become something of a cottage industry, with books, magazines, and websites devoted to the task.

The most famous, or notorious, indictment of the pro-Israel lobby to appear in recent years was published in 2007 by two prominent professors of International Relations at elite universities, John Mearsheimer and Stephen Walt.[5] In their highly controversial book *The Israel Lobby and U.S. Foreign Policy*, they blamed it for what they described as the American government's pro-Israel "bias," especially for the United States' failure to hold Israel to account for its aggressive military actions and human rights violations or to pressure it to make the necessary concessions to the Palestinians for the sake of peace. These charges sparked a fierce public debate, which was both polarized and often highly personal. The book's strongest critics denied that the pro-Israel lobby had any influence at all upon U.S. policy-making,[6] while its defenders often asserted that the lobby effectively determined U.S. Middle East policy.[7] The two mild-mannered professors themselves were hailed by some as courageous heroes who spoke "truth to power,"[8] and assailed by others as anti-Semitic villains who simply recycled age-old conspiracy theories.[9]

What was lost in all the controversy, however, was any recognition that the pro-Israel lobby, whatever its purported power, is internally diverse and politically divided. It is certainly not the monolith it is often made out to be.[10] Ironically, while the public debate and controversy over *The Israel Lobby* was raging, concerted efforts by some liberal American Jews were taking place behind the scenes to create a lobby group to counter AIPAC's influence. These efforts led to the establishment of J Street in 2008 (less than a year after *The Israel Lobby* was published). Although it was not the first center-left group to become part of the pro-Israel lobby, J Street's rapid expansion and growing political activism has not only challenged AIPAC, but also undoubtedly contributed—for better or for worse (depending on your point of view)—to the further splintering of the pro-Israel lobby.

This chapter describes the formation and subsequent fragmentation of the pro-Israel lobby. In doing so, I argue that after a century of highly effective lobbying on behalf of the Zionist movement and subsequently the State of Israel, the pro-Israel lobby is becoming more organizationally fragmented and politically divided than ever before, and that this may well undermine its political influence in the future. The more fractured and divided the pro-Israel lobby becomes, the less able it is to speak with one voice to American policymakers, and the less willing they will probably be to listen to it. But while the growing divisions within the pro-Israel lobby might eventually threaten its political power, these divisions accurately reflect the divisions within the American Jewish community regarding Israel, and particularly the Israeli-Palestinian conflict. The fracturing of the pro-Israel lobby mirrors the fracturing over Israel of American Jewry at large. A more divided lobby, therefore, is also a more representative one.

WHAT IS THE PRO-ISRAEL LOBBY?

It is important at the outset to clearly define what I mean by the term "pro-Israel lobby" because all too often the term is used in a vague and slippery manner. In their book, for instance, Mearsheimer and Walt define the "Israel Lobby" as "a convenient shorthand term for the loose coalition of individuals and organizations that actively work to shape U.S. foreign policy in a pro-Israel direction."[11] They go on to state that: "To be part of the lobby . . . one has to actively work to move American foreign policy in a pro-Israel direction. For an organization, this pursuit must be an important part of its mission and consume a substantial percentage of its resources and agenda. For an individual, this means devoting some portion of one's professional or personal life (or in some cases, substantial amounts of money) to influencing U.S. Middle East policy."[12] The problem with this definition of the pro-Israel lobby is that it is too broad and elastic. According to Mearsheimer and Walt, it is not only composed of formal lobbying organizations (most notably AIPAC), but also think tanks (such as the Washington Institute for Near East Policy and the Jewish Institute for National Security Affairs), and numerous individual

149

American Jews, Christian evangelicals, and neo-conservative policy-makers, pundits, and thinkers (including the latter in the pro-Israel lobby is particularly problematic because although neo-conservatives, both Jewish and gentile, may indeed be pro-Israel in their sympathies, their foremost concern is with the United States).

Instead of this broad usage of the term, I define the pro-Israel lobby more narrowly to refer solely to an assortment of formal organizations that try to influence American policy toward Israel in a direction that they believe is in Israel's interests.[13] The pro-Israel lobby, then, is composed of groups who actively lobby the U.S. government on issues concerning Israel. What distinguishes these groups from other organizations involved in lobbying the U.S. government on Middle East issues is that every group in the pro-Israel lobby is motivated by a fundamental concern for Israel's welfare and a commitment to ensuring Israel's existence as a Jewish state (the fact that they want Israel to exist as a Jewish state is what differentiates pro-Israel lobby groups from non-Zionist or even anti-Zionist Jewish groups that are outside the pro-Israel lobby). In trying to influence U.S. government policy concerning Israel, the pro-Israel lobby engages in a wide variety of activities. As its name suggests, lobbying lawmakers in Congress and policymakers and officials in the Executive Branch is a major part of the work of the pro-Israel lobby. This lobbying is done regularly rather than intermittently, and involves not only promoting or opposing particular policy initiatives or pieces of legislation (at times even drafting the legislation itself), but also just maintaining good relationships with elected politicians and government bureaucrats and keeping them informed about issues concerning Israel (one way this is done is by taking politicians on "study missions" to Israel).[14] The pro-Israel lobby also utilizes dozens of political action committees (PACs) that raise money, pool it, and then donate it to their preferred candidates for their election campaigns (this way, they can contribute more money to political campaigns than individual donors are permitted). Campaign contributions from pro-Israel PACs (which totaled about $12 million in the 2014 election cycle, not including super-PAC contributions)[15] can help ensure support for Israel from politicians, and help defeat politicians considered to be unsympathetic to Israel. Finally, pro-Israel groups also engage in regular outreach to religious groups, ethnic groups,[16] trade unions, journalists,[17] and students.[18] In doing so, they seek to attract supporters, gain domestic allies, build co-alitions, and influence the opinion of certain segments of the Ameri-can public, as well as the public opinion of Americans in general.

Although political lobbying is by no means the only kind of pro-Israel advocacy that American Jews (and non-Jews) engage in, and pro-Israel advocacy efforts are increasingly directed at a number of different audiences extending well beyond Washington, DC, elected officials at the highest levels of the U.S. government remain the pri-mary target of the pro-Israel lobby's activities. It is in Washington, DC, that the pro-Israel lobby is still most active and most influential, and it is there that the fragmentation of the Israel lobby has become most apparent. In order to understand this fragmentation and put it into historical perspective, it is necessary to briefly tell the history of the pro-Israel lobby from its emergence as a Zionist lobby in the interwar years, through its consolidation and growth in the decades after World War II, to its splintering beginning in the 1990s and con-tinuing to the present day.

A SHORT HISTORY OF THE PRO-ISRAEL LOBBY

What is now a large, diverse, well-financed, and highly sophisticated lobby began as a single, small, and weak organization, with minimal support among American Jews, let alone from American policymak-ers. On July 4, 1898 (less than a year after the first Zionist Congress in Basel, Switzerland), an assortment of local Zionist clubs and *Hovevei Zion* ("Lovers of Zion") societies gathered together in New York City and formed the Federation of American Zionists (FAZ). In its early years, the group devoted itself to building support for Zionism among American Jews, a difficult task since Zionism's call for mass Jewish emigration and settlement in Palestine held little appeal to most American Jews at the time (many of whom were new immigrants). It was during World War I, under the new leadership of Louis D. Brandeis, that the FAZ first began lobbying the U.S. government (as well as the British government) on behalf of the Zionist movement.

Brandeis, together with Rabbi Stephen Wise, another leading figure in the FAZ, used their personal connections with President Woodrow Wilson to lobby for the Zionist cause. In 1917, this lobbying helped convince Wilson and his secretary of state Edward House to endorse Britain's plan to issue a statement of support for the establishment of a Jewish national home in Palestine. When the British government then issued its famous Balfour Declaration, the Wilson administration publicly declared its support for the declaration, against the advice of its own State Department. Subsequent Zionist lobbying on Capitol Hill resulted in a joint Congressional resolution supporting Britain's Balfour Declaration (the resolution passed unanimously in September 1922).

In 1918, the FAZ became the Zionist Organization of America (ZOA). After Brandeis lost the leadership of the ZOA in 1921, the organization was beset with internal divisions and leadership rivalries. Over the next two decades, it mainly focused on providing philanthropic support to the Zionist enterprise in British Mandatory Palestine, but in the mid- to late 1930s it also lobbied American policymakers to oppose British plans to limit Jewish immigration into Palestine. In 1936, for instance, Wise (who became head of the ZOA in 1935) appealed to President Roosevelt to urge the British not to suspend all Jewish immigration to Palestine, a policy change they were considering as a means of appeasing mounting Arab opposition to the Zionist movement. Roosevelt did so, and Britain continued to allow Jewish immigration to Palestine until British Prime Minister Neville Chamberlain sharply curtailed it with the White Paper of 1939.

Wise's appeal to Roosevelt, and Brandeis's earlier lobbying of Wilson, typified the approach of the Zionist lobby during its half-century of existence (from 1898 to 1948). Unable to mobilize much grassroots support, and lacking resources, the Zionist lobby largely relied upon the high-level personal connections of its most prominent leaders to achieve its goals. In this respect, it operated much like Jewish politics had traditionally operated in the Diaspora, using *Shtadlanim* ("court Jews") to intercede with rulers on behalf of the Jewish community's interest. Only in 1939 did the ZOA actually set up a formal lobbying organization in Washington run by a full-time lobbyist. Headed by

Rabbi Isadore Breslau, the American Zionist Bureau, as it was called, was in existence for only two years before it was closed due to lack of funds. The outbreak of World War II and the desperate plight of European Jews trying to flee Nazi-occupied Europe led to the formation of the American Emergency Committee for Zionist Affairs (AECZA, later renamed the American Zionist Emergency Council [AZEC]), an umbrella group that represented all the major American Zionist organizations of the time (the ZOA, Hadassah, and two smaller groups—Mizrahi, the religious Zionist organization, and Poalei Zion, the Labor Zionist organization). During the war, AZEC, led by Rabbi Abba Hillel Silver, lobbied Congress to encourage the British to change its policy on Palestine and allow Jewish immigration. As part of this effort, AZEC's lobbying office in Washington recruited and trained Jewish activists around the country to lobby their representatives and senators. By the end of World War II, AZEC had established a national network of activists to engage in grassroots activism to supplement its efforts on Capitol Hill. After the war, this network of activists made an important contribution to the Zionist lobby's efforts to build American political support for Jewish statehood. AZEC helped convince Congress to support Jewish statehood (in the 1944 election, support for Jewish statehood became part of the platforms of both the Democratic and the Republican parties—in large part as a result of Zionist lobbying and both parties' attempts to win the support of Jewish voters). AZEC activists also reached out to governors, state legislatures, mayors, churches, and trade unions to get them to voice support for Jewish statehood. They even set up two front groups to attract non-Jewish supporters to the Zionist cause—the Christian Council on Palestine (for clergymen) and the American Palestine Committee (which had 75 regional chapters and 15,000 members nationwide).

AZEC's public campaign in support of Jewish statehood played an important role in helping the State of Israel come into existence. By rallying Jewish and non-Jewish supporters to the cause of Jewish statehood, AZEC succeeded in making it a domestic political issue within the United States. This undoubtedly influenced the stance of the Truman administration toward the future of Palestine. By winning support for the Zionist cause in Congress, among Jewish voters, and within American public opinion in general, AZEC increased the political pressure on the Truman administration to support the partition of Palestine and the establishment of an independent Jewish state. This partly accounts for President Truman's immediate recognition of the State of Israel in May 1948 (like President Wilson before him, this went against the State Department's advice). The Zionist lobby, therefore, was instrumental in securing American support for Israel's establishment (though other factors, personal, political, and strategic, were also responsible).[19]

Israel's establishment in 1948 marks the end of the first phase of American Jewish lobbying on behalf of Zionism and Israel. During the fifty-year period from 1898 to 1948, the Zionist lobby emerged, gradually gained the backing of most American Jews, and made support for Zionism and Jewish statehood part of American domestic politics, thereby influencing U.S. foreign policy, most notably under presidents Wilson and Truman. These were no small achievements. The second phase in the history of the pro-Israel lobby was even more successful. From the beginning of the 1950s to the early 1990s, the pro-Israel lobby was consolidated and streamlined. The once fractious and unruly Zionist lobby became (with the prodding of Israeli and American governments) a much more cohesive and centralized pro-Israel lobby. It also became, not coincidently, a major player in American politics and foreign policymaking. In doing so, it helped transform America's relationship with Israel, and turn the United States into Israel's closest and most reliable ally.

The consolidation and streamlining of the pro-Israel lobby took place in the early 1950s with the formation of its two "flagship" organizations, AIPAC and the Conference of Presidents of Major American Jewish Organizations (Conference of Presidents). There was a clear division of labor between them, with AIPAC focusing on Congress and the Conference of Presidents on the Executive Branch (this division of labor still exists to some extent[20]). The Conference of Presidents was formed when Henry Byroade, an aide to then Secretary of State John Foster Dulles, suggested to Nahum Goldmann, the head of the World Jewish Congress, that the American Jewish community should speak with one voice to the White House and State Department. Following this suggestion, Goldmann, together with Abba Eban (then Israel's ambassador to the United States) and Philip Klutznick (the head of B'nai B'rith, the oldest American Jewish organization) organized a gathering of the leaders of all the major American Jewish organizations in March 1954. This led to the formation of the Conference of Presidents, which was to serve as the voice of the American Jewish community to the U.S. administration on issues concerning Israel.

Unlike the Conference of Presidents, which was a coalition of many organizations, AIPAC started as just a one-man operation. In 1951, Isaiah "Si" Kenen, an American Jew who had been working for the Israeli embassy in Washington, began working as the Washington representative of the American Zionist Council (the successor organization to AZEC). Operating quietly behind the scenes, Kenen cultivated relationships with members of Congress and succeeded in getting modest amounts of American aid for the fledgling Jewish state ($65 million in U.S. economic assistance to Israel in 1951 and $73 million in 1952). In 1954, worried that the American Zionist Council was about to be investigated by the Eisenhower administration for carrying out lobbying activities that violated its tax-exempt status, Kenen set up the American Zionist Committee for Public Affairs as an independent domestic lobbying group (thereby allowing it to engage in an unlimited amount of congressional lobbying). In 1963, he changed the name of the organization to the American Israel Public Affairs Committee (AIPAC) in order to attract the support of non-Zionist American Jewish leaders.

AIPAC's primary mission was, and is, to strengthen the relationship between the United States and Israel. In the 1950s, this was no easy task, as the Eisenhower administration was more concerned with gaining Arab allies in the Cold War than helping Israel. AIPAC could not stop U.S. aid to Arab states, nor could it prevent the Eisenhower administration from pressuring Israel to completely withdraw from the Sinai, which it had seized in the 1956 Suez War. In its early years, therefore, AIPAC had little success in winning U.S. support for

155

Israel. This began to change after Israel's stunning military victory in the 1967 war demonstrated to American policymakers the country's potential strategic value to the United States. The following year AIPAC helped convince the Johnson administration to sell Israel F-4 Phantom jet fighters (thereby legitimizing the sale of advanced U.S. weaponry to Israel). Nevertheless, the pro-Israel lobby was not the driving force behind the warming relationship between the United States and Israel after 1967. The biggest increase in U.S. arms sales to Israel occurred in the 1970s under the Nixon administration. The pro-Israel lobby was not responsible for this increase. Rather, it was President Nixon's and his secretary of state Henry Kissinger's belief that U.S. military assistance to Israel served American strategic interests in the Cold War. This motivated their decision to substantially increase U.S. arms sales to Israel and upgrade the U.S.-Israeli relationship.

It was not until the 1980s that the pro-Israel lobby, and AIPAC in particular, really came to national attention and began to acquire the fearsome reputation it has today. Ironically, it was a defeat that, in the words of J. J. Goldberg, "created the myth of AIPAC."[21] In 1981, AIPAC together with the Conference of Presidents and the National Community Relations Advisory Council (NCRAC, now called the Jewish Council for Public Affairs) tried to prevent the Reagan administration's proposed sale of AWACs (airborne warning and command system) reconnaissance planes to Saudi Arabia. Although they succeeded in getting the House of Representatives to oppose the sale, the Senate approved it and the sale went ahead. Despite failing to achieve its goal, the lobby's AWACs campaign demonstrated its abilities, especially AIPAC's influence in Congress. Henceforth, AIPAC was considered a force to be reckoned with.

Over the next decade AIPAC went from being a small Washington-based lobbying group controlled by the major national Jewish organizations to become a large, independent national organization with a mass membership. Under the leadership of Thomas Dine (a former congressional staffer) from 1980 to 1993, AIPAC's annual budget increased from $1.2 million to $15 million (between 1980 and 1990),[22] its staff grew from several dozen to 150, and its membership expanded to more than 55,000.[23] Dine developed a nationwide network of members so that AIPAC could influence every member of Congress. He also expanded AIPAC's lobbying activities, so that it not only dealt with Congress but also with the Federal bureaucracy, especially the Departments of State, Defense, and Commerce. It was not just Dine's leadership, however, that turned AIPAC into the pre-eminent organization in the pro-Israel lobby. American and Israeli policymakers also played a part. The Reagan administration preferred dealing with AIPAC over other American Jewish pro-Israel groups because it was a single-issue organization, unlike the liberal and left-of-center American Jewish groups, which opposed the Republican and conservative Reagan administration on a host of domestic issues.[24] Similarly, Israel's Likud Party under Yitzhak Shamir preferred AIPAC (and the Conference of Presidents) to other more democratic and hence unpredictable and uncontrollable national Jewish organizations (NCRAC in particular, which was sidelined).[25]

Augmenting AIPAC's growing power in the 1980s were pro-Israel PACs, which emerged and proliferated due to changes in campaign-finance laws. Pro-Israel PACs first appeared in the 1980 congressional elections, and in 1982, Nat PAC, a national pro-Israel PAC based in Washington, DC, was established. In that year, pro-Israel PAC money helped to defeat Congressman Paul Findley from Illinois, a prominent critic of Israel, and in the next election in 1984, pro-Israel PACs claimed an even bigger victory with the defeat of Senator Charles Percy (R-IL), the chairman of the Senate Foreign Relations Committee (who had supported the sale of advanced aircraft to Saudi Arabia).[26] Pro-Israel PACs quickly became a highly effective (and discreet) means of rewarding or punishing elected politicians for their track record on issues concerning Israel. By the end of the 1980s, there were dozens of pro-Israel PACs.

Just when some commentators were beginning to decry the pro-Israel lobby's outsize political influence,[27] it lost its biggest battle ever. In the fall of 1991, AIPAC and the Conference of Presidents went up against the George H. W. Bush administration over U.S. loan guarantees to Israel. The Bush administration wanted to delay Congressional approval of Israel's request for $10 billion in U.S. loan guarantees to help it pay for the absorption of immigrants from the Soviet Union in order to pressure the Shamir government in Israel to stop settlement building in the Occupied Territories. Opposed to the Bush administration's linkage of loan guarantees to the issue of the settlements, the Conference of Presidents organized a national advocacy day on September 12, 1991, when over 1,000 Jewish leaders came to Washington, DC, to lobby Congress for the loan guarantees. In response, during a press conference that day, President Bush described himself as "one lonely little guy" who was "up against some powerful political forces."[28] With this single remark, President Bush galvanized American public opinion behind him and turned Congress against immediately approving the loan guarantees (which it was poised to do). The Bush administration ultimately succeeded in delaying the loan guarantees until the left-of-center Rabin government came to power in Israel.

The first cracks in the united front that the pro-Israel lobby presented to U.S. policymakers occurred in the midst of the battle over loan guarantees when Americans for Peace Now (APN, originally called American Friends of Peace Now when it was established in 1983 to support the Israeli organization, Peace Now) publicly came out in support of the Bush administration's suspension of loan guarantees. This was also the first time that an American Jewish organization actively lobbied in Washington, DC, against the policies of an Israeli government. Although politically insignificant at the time, it marks a watershed in the history of the pro-Israel lobby and American Jewish pro-Israel advocacy more generally. From that point on, the lobby has steadily lost its unity and shared mission. Instead of working together to promote U.S. support for Israel, the pro-Israel lobby has increasingly fractured into a host of rival groups with competing political orientations and agendas. The different groups in the pro-Israel lobby seldom agree among themselves on what American or Israeli policies they favor, and they rarely, if ever, act in unison. As a result, since the early 1990s, policymakers in Washington, DC, and beyond have heard from a growing cacophony of pro-Israel voices, rather than the chorus that their predecessors were accustomed to hearing.

More than anything else, it was the Oslo peace process that led to the fracturing of the pro-Israel lobby. While its cohesion first started to fray during the battle over loan guarantees, it really unraveled after the signing of the Oslo Accords between Israel and the PLO in 1993 during the first term of the Clinton administration. The lobby was deeply divided over the peace process, with different groups lobbying U.S. policymakers for and against it.[29] While left-of-center groups like Americans for Peace Now and the newly formed Israel Policy Forum lobbied in support of the peace process and the U.S. government's role in it (and later, between 1996 and 1999, for pressure to be applied on Israel's right-wing Prime Minister Benjamin Netanyahu to continue it[30]), right-wing groups like the ZOA and Americans for a Safe Israel lobbied against it. The ZOA veered sharply to the right under the leadership of Morton Klein (who became its president in December 1993), an outspoken opponent of the Oslo Accords who, unlike previous ZOA leaders, was willing to publicly criticize Israeli governments.[31] Not only did the ZOA openly oppose the peacemaking policy of the Rabin government in Israel, it actively sought to use the U.S. Congress to derail the peace process (by trying to stop U.S. financial assistance to the newly created Palestinian Authority and trying to move the American Embassy from Tel Aviv to Jerusalem).[32] For example, in 1994, the ZOA, along with the Orthodox Union and some Evangelical Christian pro-Israel groups (such as the Christian Israel Public Action Campaign) successfully lobbied Congress to pass the Specter-Shelby Amendment, which linked U.S. aid to the Palestinian Authority (PA) to State Department certification that the PA was complying with the Oslo Accords (the Rabin government opposed this amendment).[33] The following year, against the explicit wishes of the Rabin government in Israel, the ZOA tried, but failed, to persuade Congress not to give the PA $500 million in American aid.[34] Prime Minister Rabin himself complained about this interference, stating: "Never have we witnessed an attempt by American Jews to lobby against the policy of a democratically elected Israeli government."[35]

The ZOA's lobbying in the mid-1990s was also a direct challenge to AIPAC. Having long enjoyed unrivalled leadership in the pro-Israel lobby, AIPAC now faced a competitor. It was also caught in the middle between pro-Israel groups to its right and left, and it faced criticism and attacks from both sides. This was only one of the challenges that AIPAC encountered during the years of the Oslo peace process. The advent of the peace process posed major difficulties for AIPAC. After years spent staunchly defending Israel's refusal to negotiate with the PLO and make territorial concessions to it, AIPAC had to suddenly shift to supporting these things. It had to lobby Congress for American aid to the Palestinian Authority, headed by Israel's long-time nemesis PLO leader Yasser Arafat. This abrupt reversal of position was very difficult for AIPAC to make. It own leadership was divided over the peace process, and it had to contend with internal discontent, as many of its supporters were uncomfortable with the sea-change in AIPAC's positions.[36] It was torn between having to support the peacemaking policies of the Clinton Administration and the Rabin government and the views of its more hawkish and right-wing membership.

AIPAC's relationship with Israel's Labor-led government, and Prime Minister Yitzhak Rabin himself, was tense and frosty from the start.[37] Senior figures in the Israeli government privately complained that AIPAC was not doing all that it could to support the peace process, and in some instances was even attempting to undermine it (notably, when it joined with the ZOA to lobby Congress to pass a bill requiring the United States to move its embassy from Tel Aviv to Jerusalem, despite behind-the-scenes objections from the Rabin government). Yossi Beilin, the Deputy Foreign Minister in the Rabin government and one of the initiators of the Oslo Accords, later wrote that: "When Israel asked the United States to lend assistance to co-operative projects in the Middle East and to finance the activities of the Palestinian Authority . . . , AIPAC felt it would be awkward for it to be involved in lobbying members of Congress for such purposes. During those years [the mid-1990s], AIPAC officials went about their work on the issue of Palestinian aid as if frozen by the sight of a ghost."[38] However reluctantly, AIPAC did lobby for U.S. aid to the PA (much to the displeasure of some of its major donors and many of its members, leading some to join the reinvigorated, stridently anti-Oslo ZOA). But AIPAC's support for the Oslo peace process was half-hearted at best. According to Neil Sher, its executive director from 1994 to 1996, "getting AIPAC to support Oslo, and what the Israeli government wanted to do, was like pulling teeth."[39] Keith Weissman, another AIPAC employee at the time, has gone even further, claiming that: "AIPAC couldn't act like they were rejecting what the government of Israel did, but the outcry in the organization about Oslo was so great that they found ways to sabotage it."[40]

The collapse of the Oslo peace process and the outbreak of the second Intifada allowed AIPAC and the Conference of Presidents to return to more comfortable and familiar roles. They no longer had to publicly promote a peace process that their leaders and members were divided over. Instead, they could throw the full weight of their support behind Israel's efforts to combat Palestinian terrorism. It is much easier for both organizations to publicly defend Israel when it is embattled and under attack than when it is pursuing peace and territorial compromise. As their somewhat tepid support for the Oslo peace process demonstrated, they find it harder to lobby in favor of Israeli peace initiatives than lobby in support of Israeli military actions. With Israel under attack during the second Intifada, therefore, AIPAC and the Conference of Presidents once again took the lead in mobilizing American Jewish and U.S. government support for Israel, and AIPAC enjoyed a surge of support.[41] After the terrorist attacks against the United States on September 11, 2001, and the onset of the George W. Bush administration's "war on terror," they were also operating in a very favorable domestic political climate, with Israel and the United States now widely perceived as fighting against a common enemy in the form of Islamic extremism.

The renewed sense of unity and purpose that the second Intifada generated for the pro-Israel lobby, however, was short-lived. Divisions quickly resurfaced. In April 2002, at the height of the second Intifada, a group of dovish, left-wing American Jews who opposed the Sharon government's aggressive military response to the second Intifada (involving, among other things, the IDF's reoccupation of large parts of the West Bank and the "targeted killing" of Palestinian terrorists) formed a new nationwide grassroots organization called *B'rit Tzedek v'Shalom* (Jewish Alliance for Justice and Peace) to mobilize the Jewish community and lobby members of Congress for a resumption of the peace process and a two-state solution to the conflict. The following year, it initiated a petition calling for Jewish settlers in the West Bank to be given financial incentives to return to Israel (the petition garnered 10,000 signatures and was delivered to President George W. Bush and Prime Minister Ariel Sharon on April 14, 2004); and it campaigned in support of the Geneva Accord (a model Israeli-Palestinian peace agreement negotiated by Yossi Beilin and Yasir Abd Rabbo, which was strongly opposed by the Sharon government). As part of this campaign, *Brit Tzedek v'Shalom* activists personally delivered copies of the Geneva Accord (and Swiss chocolates) to every member of Congress, and the group ran an advertisement in Capitol Hill's *Roll Call* newspaper.

After the second Intifada died down in 2005 (it had no official end), the disagreements and divisions within the pro-Israel lobby became more pronounced. Prime Minister Sharon's 2005 plan to unilaterally withdraw from the Gaza Strip and from four small West Bank settlements divided the lobby along the usual lines, with right-wing groups vociferously opposing the plan and those on the left supporting it (despite their skepticism of Sharon's motives and future intentions). Once again, AIPAC and the Conference of Presidents were internally divided over the disengagement from Gaza,[42] although both organizations eventually voiced support for it.[43] The lobby was similarly divided when Israeli-Palestinian peace talks resumed under Sharon's successor as prime minister (and leader of the Kadima Party), Ehud Olmert. Right-wing groups (like the ZOA, American Friends of Likud, and the Orthodox Union) campaigned against the renewal of peace talks in the run-up to the Annapolis summit meeting between Prime Minister Olmert and PA President Mahmoud Abbas convened by the Bush administration in November 2007.[44] They also vocally opposed Prime Minister Olmert's stated willingness to make territorial concessions on Jerusalem, declaring that Jerusalem must remain Israel's undivided capital.[45] After the summit took place, the Orthodox Union publicly criticized Olmert for his willingness to negotiate over Jerusalem and for not defending Israel's right to Jerusalem during his speech at the summit.[46] Clearly annoyed, Olmert personally responded to this criticism, asking rhetorically: "Does any Jewish organization have a right to confer upon Israel what it negotiates or not?" He went on to insist that: "The government of Israel has a sovereign right to negotiate anything on behalf of Israel."[47]

Although AIPAC and the Conference of Presidents supported the peace talks between Olmert and Abbas (just as they had previously supported, however halfheartedly, the Oslo peace process), both were frequently accused of having "tilted to the right" over the years.[48] Leaders of liberal American Jewish groups who were themselves members of the Conference of Presidents even made this accusation.[49] Both organizations were loudly criticized for not doing enough to promote peace between Israel and the Palestinians,[50] and some critics went so far as to argue that: "AIPAC and the Presidents Conference have kept the United States from taking steps that many believe are essential if peace is ever to come to the region."[51] Amid this growing criticism of the pro-Israel lobby—fueled in large part by Mearsheimer and Walt's best-selling book (and their earlier working paper and article in the *London Review of Books*[52])—J Street was launched in April 2008, billing itself as "the political home for pro-Israel, pro-peace Americans."[53] Claiming that, in the words of its founder Jeremy Ben-Ami, "the loudest voices that American politicians hear come from one part of the pro-Israel community, leading them to believe that the entirety of the American-Jewish community has only one perspective on this issue and this conflict,"[54] the group sought to represent the "moderate voice" of most American Jews, who were pro-Israel, but critical of its policies toward the Palestinians, and who favored a more assertive American role in the peace process (that is, one that applied pressure on both Israel and the Palestinians). The "moderate voice" of the majority of American Jews, J Street argued, has generally been drowned out by "the loudest eight percent" of American Jews who are the most vocal, single-minded, right-wing, and uncritical in their support for Israel.[55] This was a thinly veiled criticism of much of the pro-Israel lobby, and AIPAC in particular. Although Jeremy Ben-Ami himself said that, "I'm very consciously not interested in portraying our organization as anti-AIPAC,"[56] commentators in the media immediately hailed J Street as AIPAC's rival and potential usurper.[57]

Whether it wanted to or not, J Street was undoubtedly an unprecedented challenge to AIPAC.[58] Led by Jeremy Ben-Ami, a former

Clinton administration aide with a lot of "inside-the-beltway" political experience, and backed by some major financiers (including, controversially, the liberal philanthropist George Soros), J Street was unlike any of the dovish American Jewish groups that came before it (such as APN). What most differentiated it from its predecessors was that J Street had its own PAC (JStreetPAC), allowing it to both endorse and raise election campaign money for politicians supportive of its agenda (other dovish pro-Israel groups were prohibited from doing this because of their 501(c)(3) tax status). In doing so, J Street recognized the close connection in American politics between campaign funding and political influence.[59] Within months of its establishment, by the time of the U.S. elections in November 2008, JStreetPAC had raised nearly $570,000 for forty-one U.S. congressional candidates.[60] This was more than any other pro-Israel PAC in the country,[61] leading the *Washington Post* to describe J Street's PAC as "Washington's leading pro-Israel PAC."[62] JStreetPAC has given even more money in subsequent elections. In the 2010 midterm elections, it raised $1.5 million, nearly triple what it had raised in 2008, and amounting to 30 percent of all pro-Israel PAC money; and in the 2012 elections, it distributed $1.8 million to seventy-one congressional candidates (seventy of whom won their races), 35 percent of all pro-Israel PAC funding and half of all pro-Israel PAC contributions to Democratic candidates. J Street also made a number of high-profile endorsements in the 2012 election cycle, including senatorial candidate Tim Kaine and Senator Dianne Feinstein, a prominent Jewish legislator who was then chairwoman of the Senate Intelligence Committee. In Tim Kaine's Virginia Senate race—which he won—J Street's contribution of $160,000 made the organization one of his leading PAC donors.

In addition to establishing the largest pro-Israel PAC, J Street also quickly built a national network of supporters (well over 100,000 of them). With its financial firepower, a rapidly growing cadre of activists, and well-publicized ties to the Obama administration, J Street soon became the leading left-of-center pro-Israel lobby group, and attracted lots of positive press coverage, most notably a cover story in the *New York Times Magazine*.[63] A little over a year after it was founded, one observer wrote: "While other dovish Jewish groups have attempted, over the years, to influence America's Mideast policy debates, none has managed to generate anything comparable to J Street's potent combination of grassroots enthusiasm, inside-the-Beltway political cachet and media buzz."[64] Within just a few years, J Street went from being a small start-up (with only four full-time staff members) to becoming a major player in the pro-Israel lobby (with a staff of fifty). Its operating budget increased from roughly $1.5 million in 2008 to almost $7 million in 2013.[65]

J Street's rise was clearly visible at its annual national conferences in Washington, DC. Every year, they drew bigger crowds and more prominent speakers. About 1,500 people attended its first conference in October 2009, which featured a keynote speech by then U.S. national security adviser James L. Jones. By the time of its fourth conference, in 2013, there were more than 2,800 attendees, and speeches by U.S. Vice President Joe Biden, U.S. Middle East envoy Martin Indyk, and Israel's then minister of justice and lead peace negotiator Tzipi Livni. J Street had clearly emerged as a group that American and Israeli policymakers could not afford to ignore.[66] Indeed, Israeli officials initially tried hard to do so—Michael Oren, then Israel's ambassador to the United States, famously declined an invitation to speak at J Street's inaugural conference—but they eventually had to acknowledge that J Street was "significant," as one senior Israeli government official succinctly put it.[67]

However significant it is, J Street still has a long way to go before it can match, or even exceed, AIPAC's political clout. Although J Street has had some successes in Congress—for example, in December 2012, when its lobbying helped to prevent an amendment to the National Defense Authorization Act that would have reduced U.S. aid to the PA and shut down the PLO's office in Washington, DC, to punish the Palestinians for seeking nonmember state status in the United Nations[68]—it has not been able to persuade Congress to apply any pressure on the Israeli government or even express any criticism of it regarding its policies toward the Palestinians.[69] In both chambers of Congress, at least, AIPAC continues to exercise unrivaled influence on anything to do with Israel. The bills supporting Israel that it drafts or promotes often receive almost unanimous support in both the House of Representatives and the Senate. Indeed, one Capitol Hill staffer has said that: "We can count on well over half the House—250 to 300 members—to do reflexively whatever AIPAC wants."[70] AIPAC's influence also means that, in the words of one congressman (who wanted to remain anonymous): "Congress would never pass a resolution that was in any way critical of anything Israel has done."[71] Although AIPAC has much less influence within the White House, it can still effectively limit the room for maneuver of any U.S. administration on issues concerning Israel and the Israeli-Palestinian conflict because American presidents are generally wary of trying to exert strong pressure on Israeli governments in the face of broad Congressional opposition. This helps explain why President Obama backed down from his early confrontation with the Netanyahu government in 2009 over his demand for an Israeli settlement freeze as he tried to restart the stalled peace process between Israel and the Palestinians.

Despite the recent emergence of newer, high-profile, well-financed, and politically savvy groups on both its left (J Street) and its right (the Emergency Committee for Israel, a neo-conservative organization established in 2010 with close links to the Republican Party and to conservative Christian evangelicals[72]), AIPAC remains the preeminent organization within the pro-Israel lobby. As Robert Wexler, a former Democratic congressman, states: "AIPAC is still by a factor of a hundred to one the premier lobbying organization for the Jewish community."[73] AIPAC is still easily the biggest and wealthiest group in the lobby,[74] with over 100,000 dues-paying members, hundreds of staff working in seventeen regional offices across the United States, and a large pool of wealthy donors, many of them also major contributors in U.S. election campaigns.[75] Its revenue continues to grow—rising from $14.5 million in 2000 to about $70 million in 2013[76]—enabling it to far outspend other pro-Israel groups.[77] According to the Center for Responsive Politics, for instance, AIPAC spent about $3 million on lobbying in 2014, compared to only $400,000 by J Street.[78] AIPAC also continues to attract new members, more and more of them non-Jewish. Its annual conference in Washington, DC, has become a dazzling showcase of its popularity and power. Fourteen thousand people from across the country attended its 2014 conference (up from 8,000 in 2008),[79] and more than two-thirds of Congress showed up for the gala dinner, making it the year's second-largest gathering of legislators (surpassed only by the president's State of the Union address), and the largest kosher dinner served in the United States.

There are many factors that account for AIPAC's unrivalled influence, but four are most crucial. First and foremost is its large national membership. AIPAC uses this grassroots base to establish and maintain relations with congressmen and senators in their local districts. As J. J. Goldberg writes: "The real key to AIPAC's clout . . . is its ability to mobilize its members as a disciplined army of volunteer lobbyists across the country."[80] The fact that many AIPAC activists are deeply devoted and focused on a single issue—supporting and "protecting" Israel—augments their political influence because single-issue voters and donors have a disproportionate influence in American politics.

Second are its unofficial ties with a large network of pro-Israel PACs. Although AIPAC itself cannot legally raise money for election candidates or publicly endorse politicians, it gives clear signals about who should receive political donations and who should not. One way it does this is through producing the "AIPAC Insider," which is "a kind of political report card . . . which gives information on every legislator's voting record on bills, amendments, and other Congressional initiatives that AIPAC deems important."[81] Furthermore, AIPAC's national board members include major fundraisers and donors to both political parties. Indeed, according to Douglas Bloomfield, a former legislative director at AIPAC: "If you want to be a player at AIPAC, you have to be a significant giver both to AIPAC and to politicians."[82]

A third important reason for AIPAC's influence is the constant access its professional lobbyists have with congressional staff members and executive branch officials, and the work that they quietly do behind the scenes in support of legislation in Congress. Finally, AIPAC's influence rests upon its appearance as a pragmatic, non-ideological, centrist organization. Both inside the beltway and inside the American Jewish community, AIPAC is careful to present itself in this manner. As then AIPAC spokesman Josh Block once put it: "AIPAC is not an ideological organization, unlike others on the fringe left or fringe right, who are attempting to promote specific ideological positions that America should then pressure Israel to adopt."[83] AIPAC has largely succeeded in positioning itself in the center of the pro-Israel lobby, with J Street to its left and groups like the ZOA and ECI to its right. Although this has meant that it is often criticized from both sides,[84] such criticism has actually helped it to portray itself, and be perceived by many, as centrist and mainstream.[85]

Of course, how centrist AIPAC really is, is very much open to debate, especially among American Jews. On the one hand, unlike the ZOA, AIPAC does officially endorse the principle of territorial compromise and the goal of Palestinian statehood, and it has lobbied to maintain and even increase American aid to the Palestinian Authority (a stance that lost it the support of one of its biggest donors, the billionaire casino magnate Sheldon Adelson).[86] On the other hand, unlike J Street, AIPAC does not push for peace talks to actually bring about a Palestinian state any time soon, and it strongly opposes any kind of American diplomatic pressure on Israel. Similarly, unlike the ZOA, AIPAC does not promote Israeli settlement building; but, unlike J Street, it does not oppose the expansion of Israeli settlements. Its position on Israeli settlement building is that it is neither illegal—since Israel is supposedly not legally an "occupying power" according to the Geneva Conventions—nor an obstacle to peace.[87] In any case, the Israeli-Palestinian peace process is not AIPAC's primary concern. Stopping Iran's nuclear program and maintaining U.S. aid to Israel are AIPAC's top priorities. For the past decade in particular, the specter of a nuclear-armed Iran has dominated AIPAC's political agenda, while the peace process has been, at most, a secondary issue. And, while AIPAC has supported the peace process, its public statements about it are vague, generally avoiding specific and highly contentious issues, such as Israeli settlement building or the details of a final peace agreement.[88] In doing so, AIPAC has been able to remain largely above the fray as American Jewish groups on the left and right battle over the Israeli-Palestinian conflict, Israel's policies, and the role of the United States in the peace process. This does not mean, however, that AIPAC has been untouched by the fracturing of the pro-Israel lobby. On the contrary, AIPAC, like the rest of the lobby, has been profoundly affected by the lobby's fragmentation.

CONCLUSION: THE EFFECTS OF FRAGMENTATION

I have argued in this chapter that the pro-Israel lobby is not nearly as united as it once was. Contrary to its popular image, the lobby is far from monolithic. Instead, it is deeply divided between left-wing, right-wing, and more centrist groups—so much so, in fact, that it may be more accurate now to refer to three, distinct Israel lobbies, rather than just one.[89] These divisions are not new. In fact, as the history of the lobby shows, it has been fracturing for a long time. Beginning in the 1990s, the growing divisions within the American Jewish community over the Israeli-Palestinian conflict, and especially over the Oslo peace process, have spilled over into the pro-Israel lobby. Hence, just as the wider American Jewish consensus over Israel has eroded over time, so too has the unity of the lobby. This has had a number of important consequences for pro-Israel advocacy in Washington, DC, and beyond.

The most direct consequence of the fragmentation of the pro-Israel lobby is that it can no longer speak to the U.S. government with a single voice as it did in earlier eras. Although there has always been a plethora of American Jewish organizations, when it came to pro-Israel lobbying, for decades pretty much the only voices that American policymakers heard were those of AIPAC and the Conference of Presidents (and they always said basically the same thing). Nowadays, this is far from being the case. While AIPAC undoubtedly still has the loudest voice in Washington, DC, it is by no means the only one that policymakers hear. Instead, there is now a veritable cacophony of discordant voices, each claiming to be "pro-Israel."

This has been strikingly evident during the years of the Obama administration. When President Obama, for instance, publicly demanded in 2009 that the Netanyahu government stop building Jewish settlements in the West Bank and East Jerusalem in order to get the Palestinians to resume peace talks with Israel, some groups within the pro-Israel lobby (such as J Street) supported him, while others (such as AIPAC) opposed the president. Similarly, some groups within the lobby (for example J Street) wanted the United States to vote in favor of a UN Security Council resolution in February 2011

169

that criticized Israel for expanding settlements, while others (including AIPAC) wanted the Obama administration to veto the resolution (which is what it did). More generally, J Street and other center-left groups within the lobby have persistently called for the Obama administration to be more engaged and assertive in trying to broker peace between Israel and the Palestinians, while right-wing groups like the ZOA and Emergency Committee for Israel (ECI) have adamantly opposed this, and AIPAC and the Conference of Presidents have stayed silent. Center-left groups themselves have not always supported the same thing—for example, J Street opposed the Palestinian bid for UN membership in 2012, while APN supported it.

Nor have the disagreements within the lobby been restricted to issues concerning the Israeli-Palestinian conflict. In fact, during the Obama administration's second term in office, while the peace process has been stalled, U.S. policy toward Iran's nuclear program—an issue critical to Israeli security—has been the focus of even greater discord within the pro-Israel lobby. Some groups (especially AIPAC) have lobbied Congress to impose more sanctions on Iran, while others (most notably, J Street) have opposed new sanctions; and when the United States, together with Britain, France, Germany, Russia, and China (the so-called P5+1) announced a framework agreement with Iran in April 2015 that would restrict, but not end, its nuclear program in exchange for a lifting of sanctions, the accord was hailed by J Street and strongly criticized by AIPAC and right-wing groups such as the ECI and the ZOA. Even before the agreement itself was announced, while painstaking diplomatic negotiations between Iran and the P5+1 were taking place in Lausanne, Switzerland, the pro-Israel lobby was split when John Boehner, then Republican leader of the House of Representatives, controversially invited Prime Minister Netanyahu to give a speech on the subject of Iran's nuclear program to a joint session of Congress on March 3, 2015, just two weeks before an Israeli election, and without the Obama administration's prior approval.[90] When a comprehensive nuclear agreement with Iran (formally known as the Joint Comprehensive Plan of Action) was finally reached in July 2015, the lobby was publicly divided, with AIPAC, and the AJC, ADL, ZOA, ECI, and Orthodox Union all lobbying

Congress hard to reject the deal, and the left-of-center groups J Street and APN energetically lobbying in favor of it.[91] So intense was the battle among these pro-Israel groups that J Street spent about $5 million on advertising in support of the nuclear deal, while AIPAC spent more than $20 million opposing the deal.[92] Both groups also met with hundreds of members of Congress in a determined effort to persuade them to vote for or against the nuclear agreement, and they participated in a fractious meeting in the White House with President Obama and Vice President Biden.[93]

As the lobbying fight over the Iranian nuclear deal made vividly clear, nowadays Congress and the White House hear many different views from a variety of pro-Israel lobby groups. Consequently, it is hard for them to know which one, if any, actually represents the opinion of most American Jews. Whereas American officials and politicians once believed that AIPAC and the Conference of Presidents spoke on behalf of the American Jewish community, most, if not all, are now well aware that this is no longer the case (if it ever was). As Joe Biden, then the Democratic Party vice-presidential nominee bluntly stated in the run-up to the 2008 U.S. election: "[AIPAC] doesn't speak for the entire Jewish community or for the State of Israel. . . . No one in AIPAC or any other organization can question my support of Israel."[94] Today, no single organization within the pro-Israel lobby can credibly claim to represent the American Jewish community. This makes it much harder for members of Congress to know whom to listen to and, more broadly, to know what American Jews think about a particular issue. Consequently, in the future they may become less inclined to pay as much attention to the lobby.

Some American Jewish leaders have voiced concern over this development. Abraham Foxman, the longtime head of the ADL, for example, has expressed his unease over how J Street's lobbying might "confuse Congress" about what is pro-Israel. "Those [members of Congress] who want to stand up and be for Israel want to know, where is the Jewish community?" Foxman explained in an interview, "And now they're going to get another voice that says that if you want to be for Israel, you should be against settlements and against building in East Jerusalem. It complicates life."[95] Malcolm Hoenlein, the executive vice chairman of the Conference of Presidents, puts it more succinctly, stating: "In our unity, lies our strength."[96]

Not surprisingly, J Street's leader, Jeremy Ben-Ami, takes a very different view. "It may be that no single voice can or should speak on behalf of all Jewish Americans on any issue," Ben-Ami says, "let alone on Israel, where passions and feelings run so deep."[97] For Ben-Ami, getting American politicians to become more aware of the fact that American Jews disagree about the Israeli-Palestinian conflict has actually been one of J Street's biggest achievements so far. In an interview in J Street's headquarters in Washington, DC, he said: "Five years ago [before J Street was founded] there was no sense in this town that there were two points of view in the Jewish community. Today I would say that eighty percent of people in this town are aware that there is a division in the Jewish community on this issue [the Israeli-Palestinian conflict]. Just awareness of the existence of diversity of debate is a huge victory."[98]

If one major effect of the fragmentation of the pro-Israel lobby has been to highlight the political divisions among American Jews and undermine the notion that any group within the lobby can speak on behalf of the American Jewish community as a whole, another major effect has been to fundamentally call into question the very meaning of the term "pro-Israel." With so many different pro-Israel groups expressing different views and advocating for different policies, it is no longer clear to policymakers (or anyone else for that matter) what position or policy actually is pro-Israel.[99] As a reporter for the *Washington Post* wrote in July 2015 about the clash among pro-Israel groups over the nuclear agreement with Iran: "The battle in Congress over whether to approve the nuclear deal with Iran is fueling a separate but related argument over another long-debated question: What does it mean to be 'pro-Israel'?"[100] Is it pro-Israel to support or oppose a nuclear agreement with Iran? Is providing U.S. economic assistance to the Palestinian Authority pro-Israel or not? Is it pro-Israel to advance the peace process, even when the Israeli government is reluctant? Is supporting Palestinian statehood pro-Israel? The answers to these questions depend upon which pro-Israel groups you ask. Even the designation of a particular group as pro-Israel is hotly debated, most clearly in J Street's case. There is no agreement anymore on what policies and which groups are pro-Israel. While AIPAC used to enjoy a near-monopoly on the use of the pro-Israel label, it has now lost its control over the term. Instead, the use of the pro-Israel moniker is now contested, and, remarkably, even AIPAC has been accused of not being pro-Israel.[101]

The term "pro-Israel" once had a clear, widely accepted meaning —it meant supporting Israel, which, in turn, meant supporting its government. The mission of pro-Israel groups was, by extension, also clear. Their purpose was to staunchly defend the actions and policies of whatever Israeli government was in power, and to try to ensure as much U.S. support as possible for that government. This has long ceased to be the case. Since the early 1990s, pro-Israel groups have been promoting their own political perspectives and preferred policies, which are often at odds with those of the government in Israel. Being pro-Israel, they contend, sometimes means lobbying against the policies and wishes of its government, or directly lobbying Israeli governments themselves. Pro-Israel groups on both the left and right have repeatedly done this. Left-wing groups, for instance, have opposed Israeli settlement building, the 2008–2009 Gaza War, and a possible Israeli military strike against Iran's nuclear facilities; while right-wing groups have opposed the peace process, the 2005 disengagement from Gaza, and any possible future division of Jerusalem. Morton Klein, the leader of the ZOA, has boasted of this, saying: "We criticized Rabin and Ehud Barak and Ehud Olmert when they made their offers [to the Palestinians]. We fought against the Gaza withdrawal like crazy on the Hill."[102] Perhaps nothing better encapsulates the profound changes that the pro-Israel lobby has undergone than the fact that the head of its oldest organization now publicly takes pride in opposing the policies of Israel's governments.

6.
THE CHALLENGE TO THE
JEWISH ESTABLISHMENT

If the leaders of groups like AIPAC and the Conference of Pres-
idents of Major American Jewish Organizations do not change
course, they will wake up one day to find a younger, Orthodox-
dominated, Zionist leadership whose naked hostility to Arabs and
Palestinians scares even them, and a mass of secular American
Jews who range from apathetic to appalled.

—Peter Beinart[1]

Although most American Jews have never heard of him, Malcolm Hoenlein—or just Malcolm, as many call him—has been described as "one of the most powerful people, politically, in the United States" and "the most powerful Jew in the Western world."[2] Since his early days working on the campaign to free Soviet Jewry in the 1970s, Hoenlein has been at the forefront of American Jewish politics. For more than a quarter of a century, he has been at the helm of the Conference of Presidents of Major American Jewish Organizations (Conference of Presidents), the organization that serves as the community's unofficial mouthpiece, speaking to American presidents, Israeli prime ministers, and foreign leaders from around the world. He is the ultimate insider in the organized Jewish community, the savvy powerbroker who knows everyone who is anyone, the tireless consensus-builder who quietly works behind the scenes to forge a semblance of unity among the fractious fifty-two groups that comprise his umbrella organization, and the passionate activist who tries to mobilize the masses of American Jews. He is also an Orthodox Jew and a diehard supporter of Israel, widely believed to harbor hawkish, right-wing views (although he insists that he is a pragmatist who is motivated only by "what's practical, what helps the security of Israel and the Jewish people"[3]). No other person in recent years has been as central in managing and, at times, orchestrating the American Jewish community's collective response to almost every major issue and crisis concerning Israel.[4] As a result, he has often been a lightning rod for the communal conflict over Israel, attacked by those on both the left and right for his organization's stances on the Israeli-Palestinian conflict.

Hoenlein himself is unperturbed by all the criticism. "We are always going to be seen by anyone who disagrees with us as to the left or right,"[5] he nonchalantly tells me. Nor is he concerned about divisions over Israel within the American Jewish community, as he is convinced that there is still a consensus among American Jews when it comes to Israel (which he confidently believes he represents). What does concern him though is the "next generation's involvement [with Israel]." "I am concerned about sustaining the political base," he says. But while Hoenlein worries about young American Jews feeling apathetic toward Israel, in the eyes of many, his organization disregards or even disdains the views of American Jews, especially younger ones, who do actually care about Israel but are critical of its treatment of Palestinians. When the members of the Conference of Presidents refused to allow J Street to join their ranks in April 2014, it was widely seen not only as a rejection of J Street (a group that Hoenlein is completely dismissive of, categorically asserting that "J Street is marginal and will become more so"[6]), but also a repudiation of its approach of criticizing Israel while supporting it.[7] Many observers saw the Conference of Presidents's vote over J Street's application for membership, which took place in a secret ballot held in its midtown Manhattan office, as a test of the American Jewish establishment's inclusivity and tolerance—a test that it had failed badly. As one commentator wrote in Israel's *Ha'aretz* newspaper: "In rejecting J Street, the conference chose exclusion over inclusion, intolerance over understanding, division over agreement, a bunker mentality over open mindedness."[8] J Street's president Jeremy Ben-Ami made much the same point in his own reaction to the vote, stating: "This is what has been wrong with the conversation in the Jewish community. People whose views don't fit with those running longtime organizations are not welcome, and this is sad proof of that."[9]

By excluding J Street, the Conference of Presidents appeared to be intolerant of criticism of Israel, even when it comes from Jewish groups that proclaim themselves to be pro-Israel. Critics immediately lambasted the organization as unrepresentative and out of touch with the views of American Jews when it came to Israel.[10] "By keeping J Street out," one wrote, "the conference shot itself in the foot, eroding its claim to represent the entire Jewish community."[11] J Street itself posted on its website a sarcastic thank you note addressed to Malcolm Hoenlein, saying: "Thank you for finally making it clear that the Conference of Presidents is not representative of the voice of the Jewish community."[12] Even some members of the Conference of Presidents publicly criticized it, most notably Rabbi Rick Jacobs, the head of the Reform movement, who accused it of "being beholden to a large number of small right wing groups that do not adequately represent the diversity of the American Jewish community." Jacobs went so far as to threaten to withdraw his organization from the Conference of Presidents unless its structure and decision-making process were reformed.[13] "This much is certain," he declared, "we will no longer acquiesce to simply maintaining the facade that the Conference of Presidents represents or reflects the views of all of American Jewry."[14]

The Conference of Presidents found its very legitimacy called into question amid the controversy over its rejection of J Street. Other organizations in the so-called American Jewish establishment, such as the Federations movement, AIPAC, and Hillel, have also been assailed in recent years for their failure to adequately represent the diversity of American Jewish opinion regarding Israel. Indeed, the American Jewish establishment as a whole has come under persistent attack for its alleged failure to reflect the changing politics of the Jewish community concerning Israel. Critics frequently accuse it of being intolerant, reactionary, and out of step with American Jewish opinion.[15] It is also routinely castigated for being self-serving, primarily concerned with perpetuating itself and slavishly following the demands of a small co-terie of "mega-donors," rather than representing the views and prior-ities of American Jews, especially on the hot-button subject of Israel. While some of these criticisms are by no means new—the leadership of the organized Jewish community has long been criticized for being undemocratic and unrepresentative[16]—at a time of growing commu-nal conflict over Israel, the American Jewish establishment faces per-haps its greatest challenge ever. How can it speak on behalf of Ameri-can Jews when so many of them are bitterly divided over Israel? How can it represent a communal consensus on Israel when that consensus is eroding? How can it support Israel, and not alienate young Jews who are critical of it? In other words, how can it lead a divided Jewish community and act in a polarized political climate?

In this chapter, I evaluate the current critique of the American Jewish establishment and examine the challenge that it faces today. I argue that its underlying problem is not that it is entirely unrepresen-tative, but that it only represents a small segment of American Jewry, which is more right-wing and religious than the majority of American Jews. Most American Jews, especially younger ones, are largely, if not entirely, disconnected from the American Jewish establishment, and thus effectively disenfranchised. This disconnect between the Jewish establishment and the Jewish masses, however, has less to do with the establishment's stances vis-à-vis Israel and its conflict with the Pales-tinians, and more to do with broader social, cultural, economic, and technological changes within the Jewish community and the United States in general. Together, these changes threaten the very survival of the American Jewish establishment, and by extension, its ability to represent and collectively mobilize the Jewish community. Not only are the major Jewish organizations that have long dominated Amer-ican Jewish politics accused of being undemocratic, unrepresentative, and out of touch, but also they are steadily losing ground to newer, niche organizations that have been able to take advantage of new sources of funding and new technologies (especially the Internet). As a result, long-established Jewish organizations are less attractive and less relevant to younger generations of American Jews. Instead, younger Jews are embracing new vehicles of activism and different issues (most notably, social justice and the environment). In short, the organizational landscape of the American Jewish community is changing in ways that will have profound implications for American Jewish support for Israel in the future.

THE ESTABLISHMENT UNDER ATTACK

No article in recent times has provoked as much controversy in American Jewish public life as Peter Beinart's 2010 essay in the *New York Review of Books* titled "The Failure of the American Jewish Establishment."[17] In it, Beinart, a prominent young American Jewish journalist known to be a staunch supporter of Israel, delivered a blistering attack on the American Jewish establishment, assailing it for what he described as its slavish devotion to supporting the increasingly illiberal, intolerant, and oppressive policies of right-wing Israeli governments. "Not only does the organized American Jewish community mostly avoid public criticism of the Israeli government," Beinart wrote, "it tries to prevent others from leveling such criticism as well."[18] By refusing to criticize Israeli government policies, Beinart argued, the American Jewish establishment was not only betraying the values of liberal Zionism, but also alienating young liberal American Jews from Israel and Zionism. As he put it: "For several decades, the Jewish establishment has asked American Jews to check their liberalism at Zionism's door, and now, to their horror, they are finding that many young Jews have checked their Zionism instead."[19]

Beinart's article, and his subsequent book *The Crisis of Zionism*, in which he expanded upon his critique of the American Jewish establishment for its uncritical support of Israel (accusing it of being obsessed with Jewish victimhood and failing to recognize that Jews now have power and are no longer vulnerable victims),[20] generated a huge amount of attention in the American Jewish community.[21] They were the topic of packed public debates,[22] panel discussions at Jewish conferences,[23] dozens of op-eds and reviews in the Jewish press, and heated arguments in the Jewish blogosphere. Reactions ranged from wildly enthusiastic support (when Beinart spoke at J Street's national conference in 2011, for example, he was greeted like a rock star by the young members of J Street U and his image was even emblazoned on T-shirts with the slogan "Beinart's army"), to vicious ad hominem attacks (one critic called him "a self-hating Jew" and a "shame to the Jewish community"[24]). Beinart had obviously touched a raw nerve in the Jewish community.

While those on the right inevitably took issue with Beinart's characterization of Israel as an oppressor of Palestinians, much of the public discussion focused on his claim that young American Jews were becoming alienated from Israel because of its policies toward the Palestinians and the "failure of the American Jewish establishment" to criticize those policies. Experts on American Jewry pointed out that, in fact, young American Jews were not becoming alienated from Israel—surveys showed that they were no less attached to Israel than previous generations of young Jews—and that those who were alienated from Israel tended to be alienated from Jewish life in general, not just Israel. This was largely due to assimilation, not opposition to Israeli government policies.[25] These rebuttals of Beinart's argument were correct—he overstated the extent of young American Jewish alienation from Israel and, at the very least, exaggerated the role that Israeli policies play in this—but they ignored a key part of his wider argument. None of the criticism challenged his depiction of the American Jewish establishment, particularly groups like the Conference of Presidents, AIPAC, and the ADL, as merely a mouthpiece of Israeli governments, and acting as "intellectual bodyguards for Israeli leaders who threaten the very liberal values they profess to admire."[26]

The fact that this part of Beinart's scathing portrayal of the American Jewish establishment elicited no objections, amid all the uproar and debate about his work, suggests that such a view is, at a minimum, noncontroversial, if not commonplace. Indeed, in liberal and left-wing circles in the American Jewish community, there is a widespread perception that the Jewish establishment is run by a right-wing cabal that seeks to enforce a narrow pro-Israel dogma. It is taken for granted that this establishment does not represent the liberal majority of American Jewry. As J Street's Jeremy Ben-Ami has stated:

"The majority of American Jews . . . do not feel that they have been well represented by [American Jewish] organizations that demand obedience to every wish of the Israeli government."[27] How accurate is this view? Is the American Jewish establishment as right-wing and unrepresentative as its critics claim?

To begin to answer this question, one must first define what the term "the American Jewish establishment" actually refers to. What exactly is the Jewish establishment? Is it just a small clique of powerful advocacy organizations as Beinart implies, or is it a much larger assortment of organizations that are engaged in every facet of American Jewish life as others have suggested?[28] A broader definition of the American Jewish establishment would include not only the most prominent advocacy organizations (AIPAC and the Conference of Presidents), but also the so-called defense organizations (such as the ADL and the AJC), religious organizations (such as the Union for Reform Judaism, the Rabbinical Assembly, and the Rabbinical Council of America), educational organizations (for instance, the Hebrew Union College-Jewish Institute of Religion and the Jewish Theological Seminary), philanthropic organizations (like the American Jewish Joint Distribution Committee, B'nai B'rith, and Hadassah), and umbrella organizations (the Jewish Federations of North America and the Jewish Council for Public Affairs). One could also include local Jewish federations, Jewish Community Centers, and even synagogues within this definition.[29]

Clearly, it is impossible to generalize about the political makeup and orientation toward Israel of such a wide variety of organizations. Each organization is distinct, with a different mission, different membership (or lack thereof), and different governance structure. Some are very centralized and top-down, with powerful leaders, others are decentralized and bottom-up (the Jewish Council for Public Affairs, for example, has a nationwide network of community relations councils). Some focus exclusively on Israel (most notably, AIPAC), while others deal with Israel along with a range of other issues (the AJC, for example). This diversity means that the American Jewish establishment is not monolithic or politically homogeneous.[30] Those running these organizations, working within them, volunteering for them, or financially supporting them are likely to hold a range of political views on Israel and the Israeli-Palestinian conflict. To simply categorize them all as right wing and reactionary is grossly inaccurate. If anything, the most common and natural tendency among these organizations is to be avowedly centrist when it comes to Israel and the Israeli-Palestinian conflict. They seek to represent a consensus position (AIPAC, the Conference of Presidents, the ADL, and the AJC, for example, all support a two-state solution), and they generally avoid taking stances on controversial issues (the public opposition of many organizations in the Jewish establishment to the July 2015 nuclear agreement with Iran is a highly notable recent exception to this general tendency).[31] That is why they rarely, if ever, publicly condemn Israeli settlement building, even when their leaders privately bemoan it (as many, in fact, do[32]). Almost instinctively, the major organizations in the American Jewish establishment are reluctant to criticize Israeli policies, and their support for Israel is automatic and unconditional. Yet, even they occasionally voice criticisms and concerns about the policies, actions, and statements of Israeli governments and politicians—the ADL and AJC, for instance, both publicly expressed their opposition to recent legislation introduced in the Knesset that sought to restrict foreign funding to human rights NGOs in Israel.

The centrist orientation vis-à-vis Israel of much of the American Jewish establishment basically reflects the views of many, if not most, American Jews, who as chapter 4 discussed are also generally centrists in their attitudes toward Israel's conflict with the Palestinians. Indeed, when asked in surveys whether "traditional Jewish organizations" did a good job of representing their views on Israel, a large plurality of American Jews (just under half of those surveyed) answered affirmatively.[33] Even young American Jews—who Beinart argued are increasingly alienated from Israel and the American Jewish establishment—are not as critical of mainstream Jewish organizations as media reports often suggest. In a 2011 survey of young Jews living in New York (those between the ages of 18 and 34), for instance, only around a quarter of them thought that "Jewish organizations were too quick to defend Israel" (which was about the same figure as those aged between 35 and 49, and just slightly more than those aged over 65).[34]

Only a minority of American Jews, therefore, is really critical of the American Jewish establishment's politics regarding Israel. Most are either reasonably satisfied or simply unaware and apathetic. "Like leaders in mass societies everywhere in the world today," J. J. Goldberg observed in his 1996 book on American Jewish politics, "the leaders of the Jewish community are caught between a militant minority that makes it opinions known at every opportunity, and a large, tolerant majority that rarely shows its face."[35] There are both right-wingers and left-wingers in the "militant minority" that is vocally critical of the Jewish establishment—antipathy toward the establishment may be the one thing that both sides agree on! As Goldberg wrote, "Right-wing Jewish populists regularly skewer the major organizations for being too liberal, too conciliatory, and too cautious in responding to intergroup conflict. Left-wing populists savage them just as harshly for being too supportive of conservative regimes, whether in Washington or Jerusalem."[36] The same is true today. Those on the right chastise Jewish establishment organizations for not defending Israel aggressively enough,[37] while those on the left castigate them for uncritically supporting Israel. In this respect, nothing has changed, except for the fact that this criticism from the left and the right is now louder and more constant than ever before.

What makes the American Jewish establishment especially subject to criticism is the fact that its leadership is not elected by the American Jewish community. At best, only a handful of American Jews get to vote on the leadership of Jewish organizations, and even when elections do take place they are rarely competitive. Most of the leaders of the most prominent organizations in the Jewish establishment are unelected and some have been in place for decades (Abraham Foxman, for instance, headed the ADL for 28 years until his retirement in 2015, and David Harris has been in charge of the AJC for more than 25 years). The organized American Jewish community is not a democracy. It is run by an oligarchy.[38] This is typical of Diaspora Jewish communities (although in some cases, such as the UK and France, there is at least a formal system of elections for leadership positions, even if most Jews do not vote).[39] Most American Jewish leaders are appointed by governing boards (composed largely, if not entirely, of major donors), and they generally come to power by volunteering for leadership positions, networking, and donating large sums of money.[40] This helps account for the fact that wealthy, older men dominate the leadership positions of organizations in the Jewish establishment; whereas women, young people, and the less affluent are grossly under-represented. Although these organizations would probably love to have more women and young people involved in leadership positions, the amount of time and money needed to ascend to them tends to militate against this.

An unelected leadership, however, is not necessarily unrepresentative. The leadership of the American Jewish establishment can still be considered representative if it reflects the political, ideological, and cultural orientation of the majority of the community.[41] But, which community? The American Jewish community at large, or the much smaller organized Jewish community? According to John Ruskay, the longtime head of the Jewish Federation of New York: "This is not a representative democracy in which everyone has the right to vote. People vote here by getting involved. So the question needs to be recast: are the present organizations of the American Jewish community appropriately representing those that are engaged in them?"[42] The answer to this question is surely yes. The leadership of the American Jewish establishment does a good job of representing the opinions of Jews who belong to their organizations and are actively engaged in the Jewish community. The leaders themselves openly acknowledge this, claiming to represent only engaged and affiliated Jews, not all American Jews. Malcolm Hoenlein, for instance, has stated: "We [the Conference of Presidents] represent the views of affiliated Jews, Jews who belong to something—an organization, a synagogue—Jews whose voices are heard through their representatives, who sit at the Conference of Presidents."[43] Similarly, Steven Bayme, a leading official in the AJC, notes that: "Jewish organizations are representative of those within the Jewish community who care enough about Jewish public affairs to become involved in communal institutions. Sadly, that percentage is rather small, but it does not mean the organizations themselves are undemocratic or unrepresentative."[44] Abraham Foxman of the ADL put it more bluntly, telling a reporter in response to criticism that the American Jewish establishment did not represent the views of American Jewry, who were much more critical of Israel: "You know who the Jewish establishment represents? Those who care."[45]

"In all polities," John Ruskay commented in an interview, "the issue is not what all public opinion is, but who is ready to act, who are the activists."[46] In the American Jewish "polity," those most involved and "ready to act" tend to be more hawkish, right-wing, and religious than the average American Jew.[47] Today, many of the most active participants in major Jewish organizations are politically conservative and religiously Orthodox.[48] As such, they exercise a disproportionate influence in the organized Jewish community simply because they are more likely to attend meetings, to donate money, and to protest.[49] In Ruskay's words: "Those on the center-right are more likely to arrive at a meeting, and arrive on the street to protest than those on the center-left. They arrive. They're in your email. They're in your office. They're at your meeting. They're on the street."[50] The same is true of Orthodox Jews—themselves generally right-wing—who have become increasingly politically active within the organized American Jewish community, especially in pro-Israel activism.[51] Steven Bayme even claims that there is an "incipient Orthodox ascendancy among Jewish communal activists."[52] This is at least part of the reason why many organizations in the American Jewish establishment (such as AIPAC and the AJC) have "tilted to the right" in recent years. Simply put, when the center-left does not show up, the center-right wins.[53]

THE REAL FAILURE OF THE AMERICAN JEWISH ESTABLISHMENT

The problem with the American Jewish establishment, therefore, is not that it is unrepresentative, but that it only really represents a small and shrinking segment of American Jewry, and one that differs in many ways from most American Jews.[54] The majority of American Jewry is disconnected from, and uninterested in the Jewish establishment. This disconnect is, arguably, the real "failure" of the American Jewish establishment. It is failing to attract American Jews, particularly younger ones,[55] into the ranks of the organized Jewish community (to be fair, this is not entirely, or even mostly, its fault).[56] This failure has been happening for a long time. Three decades ago, Daniel J. Elazar noted in his book *Community and Polity* that: "a great change taking place in American Jewish community life is the decline in membership of the mass-based Jewish organizations."[57] This change was evident in the findings of successive National Jewish Population Surveys. From 1970 to 1990, American Jewish membership in Jewish organizations significantly declined from 43 percent to just 28 percent.[58] In the National Jewish Population Survey of 2000–2001, only 24 percent of American Jews reported belonging to a Jewish organization other than a synagogue or JCC.[59] More recent surveys of American Jews, such as those conducted by the AJC and the Pew Research Center, have found even lower levels of affiliation to Jewish organizations, especially among non-Orthodox Jews. In the 2013 Pew Survey, less than one in five Jews (18 percent) reported belonging to a Jewish organization other than a synagogue.[60] Thus, for a long time now, non-Orthodox American Jews have not been joining American Jewish organizations (or, for that matter, non-Orthodox religious movements) as much as they once did. Consequently, the membership of many organizations in the American Jewish establishment is shrinking and aging (a fact that is immediately apparent when attending meetings of these organizations, which tend to be largely populated by older Jews).[61]

Many establishment organizations not only have fewer members than in the past, but also fewer donors.[62] And, as the numbers of American Jews joining and donating to major Jewish organizations has steadily declined since the 1970s, these organizations have had to increasingly rely upon large donations from a small number of donors. In the words of Jack Wertheimer: "ever growing percentages of Jewish philanthropy are contributed by a continually declining number of Jewish givers."[63] This is not simply because many Jewish organizations have fewer members. It is also because of changes in fundraising methods and strategies,[64] and changing patterns in Jewish philanthropy.[65] Nevertheless, whether born out of necessity or choice, Jewish organizations have become more dependent on a small number of very rich people. Indeed, some local Jewish federations are financially dependent upon the support of just one or two major donors. Inevitably, this gives such individuals a huge influence in these federations. In Boston, for example, Seth Klarman, a billionaire hedge fund manager, is a major donor to the local Jewish federation (the Combined Jewish Philanthropies), and wields a great deal of influence in it and, by extension, in the JCRC (since the local JCRC is mostly funded by the Federation).[66] By far the best-known and most influential "megadonor" to American Jewish organizations is the billionaire casino magnate Sheldon Adelson (his personal wealth is estimated at over $20 billion, making him one of the richest men in the world). Adelson is the single largest donor in the American Jewish community, and is reported to have donated over $200 million to Jewish and Israeli causes (which is just a fraction of the amount he has spent supporting the Republican Party and conservative causes in American politics).[67]

Major donors dominate the governing boards, and undoubtedly influence the decision-making of many, if not most, mainstream American Jewish organizations—the more money one donates, the more access and influence one enjoys. This is by no means a new development. Very rich individuals have long had a dominant role in Jewish communal life.[68] It is also probably unavoidable given the dependence of Jewish organizations and the projects they fund on voluntary financial contributions.[69] Thus, J. J. Goldberg notes: "Big givers have played a key role in setting policy in every Jewish organization for as long as there have been organizations. In a voluntary community, funded by voluntary donations, this may be inevitable."[70] But while wealth has always been (and will surely remain) a major determinant of power within the organized American Jewish community: "The challenge confronting Jewish organizations today is that, despite being desperate for funding, they must resist being turned into personal fiefdoms of unaccountable billionaires."[71] In an age of "mega donors" and a diminishing number of small donors, major American Jewish organizations are at risk of becoming too financially dependent on a few donors and being controlled by them. In short, the leadership of the American Jewish establishment is in danger of becoming a plutocracy.

THE ALTERNATIVE TO THE ESTABLISHMENT

Although the American Jewish establishment seems quite content for now to rely upon the financial support of a small number of big donors, it is acutely aware of the need to bring in younger Jews. Indeed, nothing appears to concern the establishment more than attracting young American Jews. It sponsors studies, symposia, and social events in a desperate attempt to find ways to connect with young Jews and get them involved in the organized Jewish community.[72] Yet, despite their best efforts, the organizations of the Jewish establishment are still struggling to attract Jews in their twenties and thirties.[73] Young Jews, it seems, are simply not interested in joining establishment Jewish organizations (especially if they have to pay to do so). This is not, however, because they reject the Jewish establishment—they barely even know about it[74]—but because they have very little interest in it, and do not care about it. Establishment Jewish organizations are just irrelevant to them.[75] This is also true of Jewish institutions in general, which is why very few young unmarried Jews are affiliated with Jewish institutions of any kind (synagogues, JCCs, Jewish Federations, or other Jewish organizations).

But, contrary to the popular stereotype of "millennials" (that is, those born in the 1980s and 1990s) as obsessed with consumerism and careerism, young American Jews (like other young Americans) are not simply apathetic (although, of course, some surely are). Although they are disconnected from the organized Jewish community, they are not necessarily uninterested in Judaism and Jewish culture or disengaged from Jewish life. As sociologists Steven M. Cohen and Ari Y. Kelman have argued, the fact that young American Jews do not join mainstream, established Jewish institutions does not mean that they do not have strong Jewish identities, or don't want to be involved in collective Jewish activities.[76] In fact, a 2011 study of Jews in New York (by far the largest Jewish community in the country) revealed that while younger Jews (those between the ages of 18 and 34) were more detached from organized Jewish life, they were actually more likely to study Jewish topics or participate in adult Jewish education than older Jews, though they're apt to do so informally. They were also much more likely to belong to an online Jewish group than belong to or participate in an established Jewish organization.[77]

If young American Jews are more "Jewishly engaged" than many believe them to be, then why are they generally not involved in establishment Jewish organizations? There are certainly many reasons for this, but a major one is the fact that the priorities of the Jewish establishment are not the same as those of young Jews. In the eyes of many younger American Jews, the Jewish establishment is seen as too narrowly focused on the issues of Israel and anti-Semitism. For decades now, these two issues—supporting Israel and fighting anti-Semitism—have dominated the agenda of Jewish establishment organizations.[78] Above all, over the last few decades, the activities, resources, and energies of major American Jewish organizations have become more and more focused on Israel (this is partly because, as fundraising has become more difficult for Jewish organizations, it is easier for them to raise money on the issue of Israel than on other issues).[79] Though young Jews care about Israel, and worry about anti-Semitism, these concerns are less important to them than they are to older Jews. Thus, while the leadership of the Jewish establishment— mostly men in their fifties, sixties, and seventies—incessantly warn about rising anti-Semitism and threats to Israel's security (not entirely without reason, it should be noted), they appear to be completely out of touch with the interests of young Jews, who are more concerned with cultural creativity, spirituality, social justice, and the environment than with Israel and anti-Semitism.[80] A generational divide, therefore, is at the heart of the estrangement of young American Jews from the Jewish establishment (as it was, no doubt, for previous generations of young Jews).

While younger Jews mostly steer clear of Jewish establishment organizations, they have flocked toward Jewish social justice and environmental groups (such as American Jewish World Service, Bend the Arc, Avodah, and Hazon). Though certainly not a new phenomenon, Jewish social justice and environmental activism has flourished over the past decade or so, largely because of its popularity with younger Jews (for whom *tikkun olam*, "repairing the world," has become something of a catchphrase).[81] In fact, "Jewish social justice organizations were created, in part, as an alternative to the organized Jewish community, especially as the mainstream groups set their internal focus on Jewish identity and their external focus on the security of Israel and fighting anti-Semitism."[82] Some of these Jewish social justice organizations have rapidly grown from being very small, shoestring operations into large, well-staffed, and well-financed organizations.[83] The growth of the American Jewish World Service (AJWS) has been perhaps the most impressive. In 2001, AJWS had fourteen staff members, an income of just over $5.5 million, and less than 7,000 donors. A decade later, in 2011, it employed more than a hundred staff members, with an income of almost $50 million, and more than 50,000 donors (that year, it provided $36 million in grants to promote human rights in the developing world).[84]

The expansion and proliferation of Jewish social justice and environmental groups in recent years is part of a broader "new wave of Jewish organizing" that has been taking place.[85] Since the late 1990s, there has been an explosion in the number of Jewish "start-up" organizations, cultural projects, learning initiatives, independent prayer groups, and other kinds of organized activities.[86] For instance, in just two years from 2008 to 2010, the number of Jewish start-ups doubled from 300 to 600, despite the economic recession in the United States at the time.[87] Funded in many cases by private Jewish foundations practicing "venture philanthropy," as well as by some Jewish establishment organizations, these new Jewish organizations and initiatives are generally local, small-scale, low budget, decentralized, nonhierarchal, and highly participatory. As such, they offer younger Jews an appealing alternative to large, establishment Jewish organizations, which are much more rigid, hierarchical, and less participatory.[88] Thus, Jack Wertheimer writes: "Where once formal organizations were the name of the game, today establishment institutions have been augmented and, in many cases, challenged by hundreds of start-ups and many new types of affinity organizations."[89] Another observer, Joshua Avedon, goes further, suggesting that: "If the mainstream Jewish community doesn't get hip to what is driving the new start-ups soon, a whole parallel universe of Jewish communal life might just rise up and make the old structure irrelevant."[90]

The new Jewish organizations that have sprung up differ dramatically from their establishment counterparts not only in terms of their size, structure, decision-making style, and membership, but also in terms of their leaderships. A survey of almost 4,500 leaders of Jewish establishment and "nonestablishment" organizations showed that the leaders of nonestablishment organizations tend to be much younger than the leaders of establishment organizations, and are also less likely to be male.[91] The survey also revealed significant differences in their sociocultural attitudes, worldviews, and political opinions about Israel. The leaders of nonestablishment organizations had a less particularistic and more universalistic orientation than their counterparts in establishment organizations, feeling less of a sense of responsibility "to take care of Jews in need around the world."[92] They also had less of a sense of threat and did not see the world as such a dangerous place for Jews or for Israel. Whereas the leaders of Jewish establishment organizations "see a great need to defend Jewish interests at home, in Israel, and around the world against threats from various anti-Semitic and anti-Israel forces,"[93] the leaders of nonestablishment organizations were not nearly as worried about anti-Semitism and Israel's security.[94] Only a small minority of nonestablishment leaders (18 percent) thought it was "important to defend Israel against unfriendly critics," compared with 53 percent of establishment leaders.[95] These young Jewish leaders were also less supportive of Israeli government policies and more "dovish" in their views about the Israeli-Palestinian conflict than the leaders of establishment organizations—for instance, 20 percent of establishment leaders said they felt "bothered by Israel's treatment of Palestinians," compared to almost half of the leaders of nonestablishment organizations.[96]

What, then, are the implications of all of this for American Jewish support for Israel?

CONCLUSION: THE DECLINE OF THE ESTABLISHMENT

Collectively, the American Jewish establishment has contributed enormously to Israel's development, if not its very survival. Since the founding of the state—in fact, even before—the organizations of the

Jewish establishment have raised and channeled hundreds of millions of dollars to the state and to a host of Israeli causes. A walk around any Israeli city or town, any university, museum, or hospital provides abundant evidence of this massive financial support, as they are filled with plaques and signs acknowledging major donations from American Jewish organizations (especially from Federations). In addition to raising vast sums of money for Israel, these organizations have also politically mobilized the American Jewish community on Israel's behalf. They have put support for Israel at the top of the communal agenda. They have turned out the masses to demonstrate and parade in solidarity with Israel, organized them to lobby their elected representatives to support Israel, and constantly encouraged, even persuaded, American Jews to fervently care about Israel. They have also diligently defended Israel in the court of public opinion, both domestically and internationally. Indeed, at times, the public diplomacy of major American Jewish organizations in Israel's defense has dwarfed that of the Israeli government (and probably been more effective). It is no exaggeration to say that the American Jewish establishment has been Israel's best champion inside and outside the Jewish community, nationally and even globally.

In a period of growing tensions and sharpening divisions over Israel within the American Jewish community, the establishment's ability to continue to perform this crucial role is being severely tested. It can no longer legitimately claim to express a communal consensus over Israel since that consensus is unraveling, and it can no longer speak plausibly on behalf of American Jews when so few of them are affiliated in any way with Jewish establishment organizations. It cannot lead American Jewry any longer, with its own leadership widely seen as out of touch and unrepresentative. It lacks popular legitimacy, not simply because its leaders are unelected, but because American Jews are now more politically divided. And it faces new competition from an array of newer, nimbler, niche organizations that appear more innovative and more interesting, especially in the eyes of younger American Jews.

This does not necessarily mean that the American Jewish establishment is becoming obsolete, or that it is doomed. It would be premature to declare that the Jewish establishment is dying, as some observers already do.[97] A more modest assessment is that, in the words of Steven M. Cohen, "none of the components of the so-called establishment community is in particularly good shape; all seem stable at best or challenged at worst."[98] American Jewish establishment leaders themselves recognize that some of their organizations will disappear, as the once-mighty American Jewish Congress already has.[99] As Malcolm Hoenlein stated in an interview: "I think many [Jewish] organizations will ultimately go out of business or become marginalized."[100] But whichever establishment organizations survive, and some surely will, one thing seems clear—the American Jewish establishment as a whole will be smaller and weaker. It will be unable to determine the Jewish community's political agenda or claim to speak on its behalf. It is already less relevant and less influential today than it was in the past due to declining rates of affiliation and the proliferation of new Jewish organizations, new funding sources, and new technologies. The near-monopoly over organized Jewish life and politics that the American Jewish establishment once enjoyed has given way to a more "competitive and individualized marketplace."[101] In this marketplace, establishment organizations must compete with new organizations for patrons, and individuals can pick and choose which Jewish organizations or groups, if any, they wish to join, and which specific cause they want to support based upon their own particular views and beliefs. And in this increasingly competitive market, supporting Israel, especially uncritically supporting Israeli governments (as most Jewish establishment organizations still do), is just not as popular as it was in the past.

7.
THE POLARIZATION OF
AMERICAN JEWRY

In the late twenty-first century, there may be two Judaisms in the United States. They will represent contrasting viewpoints and have little contact with each other.

—Dana Evan Kaplan[1]

In a speech in Washington, DC, on May 4, 2012, Ambassador Michael Oren, then Israel's ambassador to the United States (who was himself born and raised in the United States) told an audience of young American Jews how shocked he was by the difference in attitudes between American Jews and Israelis: "on the same day that my son was worrying about his raw recruits [in the IDF] and my daughter about rockets in Beersheva, a portion of the American Jewish community was debating whether or not to buy Ahava hand products [which are made in the West Bank]. Something is wrong here. Terribly wrong," he complained. He went on to lament the growing divide between the two communities:

When I grew up in this country, the slogan of the United Jewish Appeal was "We are One." Today, that same logo is more likely to raise eyebrows than funds. No doubt, a majority of American Jews care deeply about the security of Israel and oppose those seeking to undermine it. And even some of those calling for boycotts do so out of a sense of caring—I'd say misplaced sense of caring—about Israel. And yet, sometimes it seems that we, Israelis and American Jews, not only inhabit different countries but different universes, different realities. . . . Ironically, at a time when support for Israel in this country is at a near all-time high—indeed it's one of the few truly bipartisan issues—we Jews seem increasingly divided. Let me be clear: at stake is not merely Israel's policies or rights of American Jews to criticize them. At stake is nothing less than the unity of a Jewish people.[2]

Rarely, if ever, has a senior Israeli government official so openly acknowledged the fact that many American Jews now support a boycott of Israeli goods produced in the West Bank, and even more remarkably acknowledged that they might do so because they care about Israel (and not because they are anti-Israel, as they are often accused of being). No less surprising is Ambassador Oren's frank admission that, despite all the official rhetoric of American Jewish solidarity with Israel, there is, in fact, a growing divide between American Jews and Israelis.[3] But what the ambassador failed to concede is that the divide is not simply between Jews in the United States and Israel, but also among Jews in America and among Jews in Israel. While it is obviously true that American and Israeli Jews have "different realities" and, consequently, different perceptions and attitudes, it is no less true that both groups are themselves internally divided. In fact, secular, left-wing Israeli Jews are likely to have much more in common, at least politically, with secular, liberal American Jews than with other Israeli Jews, and vice versa. In other words, the bigger divide is not between Israelis and American Jews, but between secular, liberal Jews and more religious, right-wing Jews in both Israel and the United States (and, for that matter, in other Jewish communities in the Diaspora). The division is not primarily geographic, then, but political and religious. And this division is what really threatens Jewish unity, both in the United States and, to a lesser extent, in Israel.[4]

Peter Beinart neatly summarizes the divide between American Jews: "More and more observers recognize that there are really two Jewish Americas. One is older, richer, more Republican, more Orthodox, and more interested in shielding Israel from external pressure than pursuing a two-state solution. The other is younger, more secular, less tribal, overwhelmingly Democratic, less institutionally affiliated and deeply troubled by Israel's direction."[5] This chapter explores some of the differences between these "two Jewish Americas" and what they might mean for American Jewish support for Israel in the future. I argue that there is a major divide in the American Jewish community between religious conservatives and secular liberals—a divide that basically mirrors that between these two groups within the American population at large. Moreover, this divide is steadily widening over time due to an ongoing process of polarization between American Jews who are more religiously Orthodox, more politically conservative, and more attached to Israel; and American Jews who are less religiously observant, more politically liberal, and often more critical of Israel. The different views of Orthodox and non-Orthodox Jews on issues concerning Israel, and particularly the Israeli-Palestinian conflict, are just one manifestation of the broader divide between them. Non-Orthodox Jews, especially younger ones, also increasingly embrace an individualistic approach to Judaism and a more pluralistic view of Jewish identity, whereas Orthodox Jews still adhere to a more traditional monistic view of Judaism, and a more particularistic, ethnocentric approach to Jewish identity. The polarization between the non-Orthodox majority of American Jews and the Orthodox minority (who currently make up around 10 percent of the American Jewish population, of which 6 percent are ultra-Orthodox and 3 percent Modern Orthodox[6]) poses a severe challenge to the future cohesion of the American Jewish community, threatening to split it into two. In the more distant future, however, if non-Orthodox Jews continue to assimilate, intermarry, and have far fewer children than Orthodox Jews, over time the Orthodox could gradually come to dominate the American Jewish community.

Before proceeding, some quick caveats are necessary. I am not claiming in this chapter that American Jewry is already polarized; only that it is becoming polarized. As my analysis in chapter 4 of American Jewish public opinion concerning the Israel-Palestinian conflict made clear, American Jews are not as divided in their views about the conflict as their public debate often suggests. There are certainly strong disagreements between them, but it is important not to exaggerate the depth and extent of divisions among American Jews.[7] It is also important to bear in mind that American Jewry has never been unified, politically or religiously, and there have previously been periods of intense communal conflict.[8] Most recently, from the mid-1980s to the mid-1990s, there were serious disputes and tensions between American Jews of different religious denominations, primarily over the question of "who is a Jew" and the issues of patrilineal descent, conversion to Judaism, and intermarriage. This interdenominational conflict—particularly between Orthodox and non-Orthodox (principally, Reform and Conservative) Jews—was so severe that one observer, the journalist Samuel Freedman, called it a "struggle for the soul of American Jewry,"[9] and another, Jack Wertheimer, went so far as to characterize American Jews as "a people divided."[10] The fact that this interdenominational conflict subsequently died down (although it has not completely ended), and religious tensions among American Jews have calmed in recent years, suggests that such characterizations were hyperbolic, or at least premature. It also serves to remind us that passions can cool over time, tensions can ease, and conflicts can be ameliorated, if not entirely resolved. There is, therefore, nothing inevitable about the polarization of American Jewry described in this chapter.

Nevertheless, while the intensity of the current American Jewish conflict over Israel might subside in the future—especially if/when Israel comes under serious attack[11]—there is little reason to expect an end to divisive debates about Israel among American Jews. Jack Wertheimer, who has extensively studied both the American Jewish debates over Judaism and over Israel, has provided a clear summary of the difference between these debates: "the longest and most vituperative debates in American Jewish life over the last three decades have been about Israel," he writes. "Other divisive issues, such as the role of women in Jewish life or the religious status of homosexuals, were resolved relatively swiftly within the individual denominations. However disagreements over Israeli policies in the territories and the proper relationship between synagogue and state in the Jewish state go on and on, and become increasingly bitter. They seem to have become a permanent feature of American Jewish culture, both causing and demonstrating deep fissures in the American Jewish community."[12]

NON-ORTHODOX VERSUS ORTHODOX JEWS

For some time now, many of the most impassioned public debates in societies around the world pit secular liberals against religious conservatives (whether they are Christian, Muslim, Hindu, or Jewish). In the United States, they line up against each other in the fierce debates over abortion, gay marriage, and school prayer—to name just a few examples. In Israel, they are on opposite sides of the long-running debate over the future of the Occupied Territories, especially the West Bank. In many other countries, they battle it out over the separation between religion and state. Indeed, numerous commentators have claimed that the primary axes of political and cultural conflict today is the divide between secular liberals and religious conservatives.[13] While many, perhaps most, people do not fall neatly into either "camp," and not every political issue or outcome can be reduced to a "culture war,"[14] the differences in political perspectives, moral attitudes, and possibly even psychology,[15] between secular liberals and religious conservatives are undoubtedly at the heart of a lot of contemporary debates and disagreements.

There is also a major divide between secular liberals and religious conservatives underlying the debate over Israel among American Jews. In my analysis of American Jewish public opinion regarding the Israeli-Palestinian conflict in chapter 4, I noted that there are significant differences of opinion between Jews who are politically liberal and those who are conservative, and between non-Orthodox and Orthodox Jews. In both cases, the former are significantly more critical of Israel's policies toward the Palestinians, and more willing to support far-reaching Israeli concessions to them (such as a division of sovereignty over Jerusalem). What must be emphasized here is that liberal Jews and non-Orthodox Jews (especially Reform, Reconstructionist, post-denominational, and nonaffiliated Jews) are not simply more "dovish" than politically conservative and Orthodox Jews (including the ultra-Orthodox[16]), but that non-Orthodox Jews are also much more likely to be politically liberal and Orthodox Jews more likely to be conservative. Extensive survey data demonstrates that religiosity has the biggest impact upon the political divisions among American Jews, as religious denomination is consistently most strongly correlated with political beliefs.[17] In other words, the more religiously observant you are, the less politically liberal you are. Orthodox Jews, on one end of the religious spectrum, are more politically conservative than other American Jews, while secular (nonaffiliated) Jews at the other end of the religious spectrum are the most liberal (with Conservative, Reform, and Reconstructionist Jews falling between these two poles).[18] Thus, political divisions overlap with religious divisions and reinforce each other, exacerbating intra-Jewish conflict. As Laurence Kotler-Berkowitz writes: "the overlap between religious and political cleavages may make the task of developing communal consensus particularly daunting, since multiple and reinforcing divisions—as opposed to cross-cutting ones—make for higher barriers, less common ground, and greater mistrust among sectors of a community."[19]

In the American Jewish debate about the Israeli-Palestinian conflict, therefore, more secular liberal "doves" are generally arrayed on one side against more religious conservative "hawks" (there are, of course, also some secular "hawks" and religious "doves" within the American Jewish community). While most Orthodox Jews, including the ultra-Orthodox, remain staunchly supportive of Israel,[20] non-Orthodox Jews are finding it harder and harder to support the actions and policies of Israeli governments toward the Palestinians. Israel's treatment of Palestinians—both those in the Occupied Territories and those who are citizens of Israel—is becoming a growing problem for secular liberal Jews, and they are increasingly outspoken in criticizing it. It is a problem for them not only because their support for Israel is in tension with their own commitment to human rights and liberal values like equality and fairness, but also because among their non-Jewish liberal friends, colleagues, and even family members, Israel is increasingly perceived as a kind of pariah state, an illegal occupier and a violent oppressor of Palestinians. For secular liberal Jews who have their own qualms and misgivings about supporting Israeli governments, the negative view of Israel that is now common among liberals and leftists makes it even harder for them to support the country. In a column in the *Jewish Daily Forward* (a liberal American Jewish newspaper), the writer Jay Michaelson captured the current predicament of many liberal American Jews:

> In my social circles, supporting Israel is like supporting segregation, apartheid or worse. . . . I don't think advocates of Israel understand exactly how bad the situation is on college campuses, in Europe, and in liberal or leftist social-political circles. Supporting Israel in these contexts is like supporting repression, or the war in Iraq, or George W. Bush. It's gotten so bad, I don't mention Israel in certain conversations anymore, and no longer defend it when it's lumped in with South Africa and China by my friends. This is wrong of me, I know, but I've been defending Israel for years, and it's gotten harder and harder to do so.[21]

It is not just about Israeli politics and the Israeli-Palestinian conflict that non-Orthodox and Orthodox Jews disagree. They also sharply disagree over American domestic politics. While non-Orthodox Jews consistently and overwhelmingly vote for the Democratic party in U.S. elections—at much higher rates than white voters in general (and despite well-financed efforts by the Republican Jewish Coalition to woo them)—the majority of Orthodox Jews are supporters of the Republican Party. In the 2013 Pew Survey of American Jews, 57 percent of Orthodox Jews said they identified with or leaned toward the Republican Party, compared with just 18 percent of other Jews.[22] In fact, Orthodox Jews are far more Republican than Americans in general—39 percent of whom identify as Republican or lean Republican. Thus, the Pew survey notes that: "the only other U.S. religious groups that are as conservative and Republican as Orthodox Jews are white evangelical Protestants and Mormons."[23] Politically, Orthodox Jews have more in common with evangelical Christians and others on the religious right in the United States than they do with non-Orthodox Jews, especially on controversial social issues like abortion and same-sex marriage, and on issues concerning the separation of "church and state" (such as government funding of "parochial"/religious schools).[24]

The wide gulf in political attitudes and opinions between Orthodox and non-Orthodox Jews has been strikingly evident in recent years during Obama's presidency. While most American Jews have strongly supported President Obama—overall, around 74 percent of American Jews voted for President Obama in 2008 and about 70 percent in 2012—he has been deeply unpopular among Orthodox American Jews. For many, he has become a figure of loathing, subject to relentless hostility and criticism. While some of the accusations often hurled against him—that he is really a Muslim and/or an anti-Semite—are simply malicious and ludicrous, the more serious criticism leveled against him is that he is insufficiently supportive of Israel or understanding of its security needs. The belief that President Obama is not "pro-Israel" is widely held among Orthodox American Jews (but not by American Jews in general),[25] and this belief has undoubtedly motivated much of their opposition to him, including at the polls. When it comes to voting in presidential elections, the issue of Israel is much more important to Orthodox Jews than it is to non-Orthodox Jews,[26] which is largely why far fewer of them have voted for Obama.

These political differences between non-Orthodox and Orthodox Jews reflect deeper sociocultural differences, particularly concerning their Jewish identities and practices.[27] Jack Wertheimer summarizes these differences in the following manner: "[Orthodox Jews] attend synagogue services, observe religious rituals, give to Jewish causes, travel to Israel, send their children to study in Israel, and immerse their children in intensive programs of formal and informal Jewish education at rates far exceeding Jews who identify with the other movements."[28] Hence, according to Wertheimer: "It appears that Jewish identification carries an entirely different valence in the lives of Orthodox Jews."[29] The 2013 Pew Survey supports this conclusion. Nearly 90 percent of Orthodox Jews (87 percent) and two-thirds of Conservative Jews (69 percent) said that being Jewish was very important in their lives, but only a minority (43 percent) of Reform Jews felt this way, and just one-in-five (22 percent) of Jews who were unaffiliated with any Jewish denomination.[30] This does not mean, however, that non-Orthodox Jews do not care about being Jewish (even among the unaffiliated, 87 percent of those in the Pew survey said they were proud to be Jewish).[31] For many non-Orthodox Jews, while they value their Jewish identity, the way they conceive of this identity substantially differs from the way in which Orthodox Jews do. Instead of understanding Jewishness and Judaism as entailing a set of individual obligations and communal commandments, many non-Orthodox Jews, especially younger ones, now approach Jewishness and Judaism as a source of personal meaning and spirituality.[32] Being Jewish for them is more of a personal choice than a religious definition, and they define their Jewish identities and Judaism itself in their own individual ways—what Dana Evan Kaplan refers to as "privatized Judaism."[33] More than ever before, non-Orthodox Jews are choosing not only whether they want to be Jewish or not, but also the content and meaning of their Jewishness. Some selected Jewish rituals and culture, not commandments, are what matter to most to them. Describing the emergence of the "postmodern Jewish self" in their book *The Jew Within*, Steven Cohen and Arnold Eisen argued that non-Orthodox American Jews now approach Judaism as part of an individualistic search for meaning and self-fulfillment, one that is directed by "the sovereign self."[34] Needless to say, this highly personal, individualistic, and ad hoc approach to Judaism common among non-Orthodox American Jews differs markedly from the more communal, restrictive, and rule-bound approach of most Orthodox Jews,[35] especially from the more insular ultra-Orthodox.

Not only do many non-Orthodox Jews increasingly take a novel, alternative approach to Judaism, but also, and even more importantly, they are becoming less committed to what is known as "Jewish peoplehood."[36] In the 2013 Pew Survey, for instance, secular, unaffiliated Jews were much less likely than other Jews to feel a strong sense of belonging to the Jewish people and to believe that they have a special responsibility to care for Jews in need around the world.[37] This helps explain why hardly any of the most secular Jews in the Pew survey (those defined in the survey as "Jews of no religion") belonged to Jewish organizations (just 4 percent) and few gave money to Jewish charities (20 percent). Orthodox Jews, by contrast, were much more likely than other Jews to belong to Jewish organizations and donate to Jewish causes.[38]

There are many reasons why non-Orthodox American Jews are less committed to "Jewish peoplehood" today. Some are simply assimilating into the American "melting pot," and shedding their Jewish identities altogether.[39] American Judaism itself is becoming "post-ethnic" in the context of a wider multicultural and multiracial society.[40] The collective belief in a shared ethnicity upon which American Jewish identity was traditionally based is eroding, and with it the accompanying collective sense of solidarity and responsibility. This is particularly true for younger non-Orthodox Jews,[41] for whom their Jewish identity is just one of their many identities,[42] with the whole concept of "Jewish peoplehood" seeming to many of them too tribal and exclusivist, even racist. Solidarity with other Jews—Jewish "tribalism"—is becoming passé, much to the consternation of some American Jewish commentators who bemoan the universalism and cosmopolitanism of today's young non-Orthodox American Jews.[43] But it is not just because tribalism has fallen out of fashion in a multicultural and multiethnic America that accounts for the weaker sense of collective solidarity and responsibility felt by young non-Orthodox American Jews.[44] It is also because they have grown up in a world in which Jews are more powerful and more privileged than ever before, especially in the United States. Since they do not see the world as such a threatening and hostile place for Jews, they are much less inclined to divide the world into "us" and "them" (Jews and non-Jews), as older generations of Jews have done,[45] and taking care of other Jews is less of a priority for them.

Among the reasons for the decline of "Jewish peoplehood" among non-Orthodox American Jews—and the biggest sociocultural difference between them and Orthodox Jews—is surely the simple fact that so many of them are intermarried or the children of intermarried couples.[46] Since the early 1970s, intermarriage rates have skyrocketed among American Jews, rising from less than 20 percent of American Jews to almost 60 percent between 2005 and 2013, according to the Pew survey. Among non-Orthodox Jews, the rate of intermarriage is even higher, at 71 percent, while it is practically nonexistent among Orthodox Jews (98 percent of married Orthodox Jews in the Pew survey had a Jewish spouse).[47] Equally significant is the fact that the percentage of Jewish adults who are the offspring of intermarriages is also dramatically rising: just 18 percent of Jewish "baby boomers" have one Jewish parent, compared with 24 percent of "generation X" (those born between 1965 and 1980), and nearly half (48 percent) of Jewish "millennials" (born after 1980).[48] Most young non-Orthodox Jews, therefore, have parents who are intermarried. This undoubtedly shapes their understanding of their Jewish identities and their attachment to "Jewish peoplehood," since intermarriage weakens Jewish ethnicity and peoplehood.[49] As sociologists Steven Cohen and Ari Kelman have written: "Intermarriage represents and advances more open and fluid group boundaries along with a commensurate drop in Jewish tribalism, collective Jewish identity and Jewish Peoplehood."[50]

Cohen and Kelman have also claimed that increasing intermarriage among non-Orthodox Jews is largely responsible for undermining American Jewish attachment to Israel, especially among the young. Emphasizing survey data that show that Jews who are raised in intermarried families, or who are themselves intermarried, express less emotional attachment to Israel,[51] they argue that the high rate of intermarriage is therefore likely to reduce the overall level of non-Orthodox American Jewish attachment to Israel over time. In their words: "All things considered, we think that non-Orthodox Jews in America, as a group, are growing more distant from Israel and will continue to do so."[52] Other American Jewish sociologists (most notably Theodore Sasson, Leonard Saxe, and Charles Kadushin) have vigorously challenged this prediction of declining attachment to Israel, pointing to evidence indicating that travel to Israel by young Jewish adults, especially on the hugely popular Taglit-Birthright tours, significantly increases emotional attachment to Israel. Since more and more young Jews are participating in "Israel-experience" programs such as Birthright, these scholars suggest that this participation is actually strengthening American Jewish attachment to Israel, and counteracting rising intermarriage, since Birthright participants are also more likely to go on to marry other Jews (relative to a control group of nonparticipants).[53] Whether mass youth travel to Israel will be enough to sustain, or even raise, the current level of American Jewish attachment to Israel in the future is very much open to question. The long-term impact of the Birthright program remains to be seen, and since only a minority of young American Jews participate in it, it would be premature, at best, to assume that Birthright alone will ensure that non-Orthodox American Jews remain emotionally attached to Israel in the future.

What is clear is that young non-Orthodox American Jews are not very attached to Israel—in the Pew survey, for example, less than a third (30 percent) of them thought that "caring about Israel is essential to being Jewish"—and they are much less attached to Israel than older Jews.[54] Although this might well change as they grow older (as some sociologists argue, based upon past experience, which shows that attachment to Israel increases with age[55]), current trends among non-Orthodox Jews—particularly, the gradual erosion of the ethnic dimension of Jewish identity; the greater emphasis upon Judaism and Jewish identity as a personal choice and source of meaning; and the disengagement of young Jews from Jewish establishment organizations that have played a key role in encouraging Jewish support for Israel (discussed in the previous chapter)—all suggest that their attachment to Israel is likely to decline in the future.[56] Above all, the steadily growing secularism of non-Orthodox Jews portends a long-term erosion in their emotional connection to Israel because the more secular Jews are, the less attached they are to Israel.[57] Or, to put it another way, the less important being Jewish is to them, the less important Israel is to them.

The causal connection between religiosity and attachment to Israel is also evident on the other end of the secular-religious spectrum, as the most religiously observant American Jews also care about Israel the most. Thus, in the Pew survey, three-quarters (77 percent) of Modern Orthodox Jews said they feel very attached to Israel, compared to just under a quarter of (24 percent) of Reform Jews.[58] Orthodox American Jews are also twice as likely as Reform Jews to visit Israel, and most American immigrants (*olim*) to Israel are Orthodox.[59] Religiosity also influences American Jewish political behavior regarding Israel, as it has been demonstrated that synagogue attendance significantly increases the salience of Israel as a basis for political behavior. This is partly because synagogue attendance strengthens ethnic consciousness (the aforementioned sense of "Jewish peoplehood"), leading to an increased concern with Jewish interests and encouraging collective action on behalf of Jews. It is also because individuals regularly attending synagogue services are more likely to encounter "persuasive communication" about the importance of Israel (in rabbis' weekly sermons, for example), and participate in cultural and symbolic activities that highlight the role of Israel as crucial to Jewish identity (most obviously, reciting the "Prayer for the State of Israel," which is said in most synagogues on every Sabbath and Jewish holiday).[60]

If non-Orthodox Jews do become increasingly detached from Israel, then Orthodox Jews are almost certain to remain strongly attached. This is bound to have implications for American Jewish support for Israel in the future. Its intensity might not be diminished because, as Ephraim Tabory notes, "Orthodox support [for Israel] might be stronger and more action oriented than more lackadaisical or ambivalent support by non-Orthodox Jews,"[61] but its base will be much narrower. Supporting Israel could become merely an Orthodox cause, not one that unites most American Jews. This might also affect wider American political support for Israel as it would exacerbate the partisan divide over Israel that is already developing. Since Orthodox Jews tend to support the Republican party (as do evangelical Christians, who are also staunch supporters of Israel), supporting Israel would become a Republican cause, and no longer a bipartisan one. Non-Orthodox American Jewish support for Israel, ambivalent though it is, is therefore important in ensuring that Israel remains a bipartisan cause in American domestic politics, which, in turns, helps secure continued American diplomatic, military, and economic assistance to Israel. The potential erosion of support for Israel among non-Orthodox American Jews is thus ultimately a long-term threat to U.S. government support for Israel. However devoted and mobilized Orthodox Americans Jews are concerning Israel, they cannot completely compensate for a decline in non-Orthodox American Jewish commitment to Israel.

Even if free trips to Israel for young Jewish adults and other kinds of programs (like synagogue programs to encourage interfaith couples to raise Jewish children) prevent "distancing" from Israel among non-Orthodox American Jews in the future, there will still be a big difference between their level of emotional attachment to Israel and that of Orthodox Jews. This difference, along with others that I have discussed in this chapter, adds to the sense of alienation that is growing between Orthodox and non-Orthodox Jewry in the United States. [62] Indeed, arguably the greatest challenge that American Jewry faces in the future is not alienation and estrangement from Israel, but from each other. In the words of one Israeli observer: "The distancing of Orthodox and non-Orthodox Jews from one another may be more significant for a united Jewish people than the distancing of Diaspora Jews from support for Israel as a political entity."[63]

CONCLUSION: THE ASCENDANCE OF THE ORTHODOX

Today, the major divide in American Jewry is no longer between the three major denominations (Orthodox, Conservative, and Reform), but between Orthodox Jews and non-Orthodox Jews.[64] In this chapter, I have shown that this divide is not just a religious one, but also a political divide. Orthodox and non-Orthodox American Jews are increasingly divided by religion *and* politics. They strongly disagree about religious issues (as they have for a long time)—over fundamental questions such as what Judaism is, who a Jew is, and what role women should have in Jewish life—and they now also vehemently disagree about political issues, especially concerning Israel—over questions like what kind of a state Israel should be, where its final borders should be, and what should eventually happen to Jewish settlements in the West Bank.

There is no reason to believe that this wide divide will narrow in the future. On the contrary, it can be expected to grow, given current social and demographic trends within the American Jewish community. In particular, the data indicates that, as a whole, American Jewry is simultaneously becoming more secular and more religious. That is, there is "movement in two opposing directions" by the more and less religiously observant parts of American Jewry.[65] There is, in other words, a process of polarization taking place.[66] This polarization is clearly apparent in the Pew survey data, which shows that the two poles of the Jewish identity spectrum are growing larger—the most secular ("Jews of no religion," now roughly one-in-five Jews),[67] and the most religious (Orthodox, and especially ultra-Orthodox Jews)[68]—while the middle (Conservative and Reform Jews) is stable, at best.[69] Commentators have pessimistically predicted that the polarization between Orthodox and non-Orthodox Jews threatens to create a "permanent rift within American Jewry."[70] Even more gloomily, one commentator laments that: "The American Jewish community is coming apart at the seams. Its vital center is collapsing and the entire group is increasingly polarized by runaway growth at both extremes: religious fundamentalism on one end, secular non-belief on the other."[71]

If one future scenario is that the American Jewish community will slowly split into two—one mostly composed of Orthodox Jews and the other of non-Orthodox Jews—another, and probably more likely one, is that the community will just become much more Orthodox, and especially ultra-Orthodox, over time. The reason for this is simple: the Orthodox have more children than the non-Orthodox. Nearly half of all Orthodox parents have 4 or more children (48 percent), compared with just 9 percent of non-Orthodox Jewish parents. Non-Orthodox Jews have a much lower birthrate than Orthodox Jews (1.7 children compared to the Orthodox birthrate of 4.1 children), and a lower marriage rate (they also marry much later).[72] While the Orthodox birthrate is well above the U.S. average of 2.2 children per adult, the non-Orthodox birthrate is well below what demographers refer to as the "replacement level" of 2.1. This means that the population of non-Orthodox Jews will probably sharply decline, while the population of Orthodox Jews will rapidly increase (although some Orthodox Jews will surely become non-Orthodox).[73] Although they constitute only 10 percent of the American Jewish population today, Orthodox Jews could well become a quarter of the total U.S. Jewish population by 2050, and eventually maybe even the majority of American Jews (they already make up 27 percent of all Jewish children, and 35 percent of all Jewish children under the age of 5). The American Jewish community of the future, then, might even be composed largely of ultra-Orthodox (*haredi*) Jews and a small remnant of secular Jews and part-Jews.[74]

The changing demographic profile of New York's Jewish community —which now numbers more than 1.5 million and is the largest in the United States and the world's largest Jewish community outside Israel—offers a glimpse of this possible future: over the last thirty years, the percentage of Jewish households in New York that were Orthodox has risen from 13 percent in 1981 to 32 percent in 2011. In New York City itself, the epicenter of the organized American Jewish community, 40 percent of the Jewish population is now Orthodox. Most of these are actually ultra-Orthodox Jews. Moreover, the startling fact that two out of three Jewish children living in the New York region are Orthodox (even more in the city) suggests that the Jewish community of New York will become increasingly religious, if not *haredi*.[75]

This potential demographic change could have major long-term political implications for American Jewry and for Israel. American Jewish politics would shift to the right as Orthodox Jews gradually come to outnumber non-Orthodox. The future American Jewish community would be more politically conservative, more Republican, and even more supportive of Israel. The long American Jewish love affair with liberalism and the Democratic Party would come to an end, and the Republican Party will finally be able to do what it has tried and largely failed to do for the past three decades—prise American Jewish voters away from their historic attachment to the Democrats. And if the American Jewish community becomes more politically conservative and abandons its traditional support for liberalism, it will only further alienate the already shrinking number of non-Orthodox, liberal Jews in its midst. Rather than remain within the organized Jewish community, they could well become completely estranged from it, thereby reinforcing its religious and right-wing orientation. The growing religiosity of American Jewry might also weaken future American Jewish support for religious pluralism in Israel, Arab civil rights and Arab-Jewish co-existence, Israeli-Palestinian peace, and a host of other causes currently popular with liberal, non-Orthodox Jews. (There is nothing inherently contradictory between Judaism and support for peace, tolerance, and human rights, but in practice, Orthodox Jews are far less committed to these causes.) The most important and influential Jewish community in the Diaspora could be slowly transformed from a bastion of progressive social values and Jewish religious pluralism to a redoubt of ultra-Orthodoxy, thereby strengthening the growing power of the *haredim* in Israel.[76]

Demography, of course, is not destiny. One must be cautious about making future predictions based upon current trends, but it seems safe to say that the predominantly secular, liberal American Jewish community of today is endangered. Although still relatively small in number, Orthodox Jews are already exerting a growing cultural and political influence in the American Jewish community (and in American domestic politics at large).[77] Indeed, reflecting on the remarkable resurgence of Orthodox American Jews since the end of World War II and their increasing cultural visibility, vitality, and political power, one expert has declared "the triumph of Orthodoxy."[78] Perhaps this is a bit premature, but Orthodox Jews themselves are now full of self-confidence and in a triumphalist mood.[79] As the *New York Times* columnist David Brooks observed after visiting the thriving Orthodox Jewish enclave of Midwood, Brooklyn: "Once dismissed as relics, they now feel that they are the future."[80]

CONCLUSION

Quarrel has always been a Jewish norm, and controversy a pri-
mary instrument for the development of Jewish culture and Jew-
ish religion.

—Leon Wieseltier[1]

In this book, I have examined in depth the current American Jewish conflict over Israel. In doing so, I have traced its roots in the evolving attitude that American Jews have toward Israel, dissected the vigorous public debate among American Jews about the Israeli-Palestinian conflict, and explored the impact this debate is having within the American Jewish community, and upon the pro-Israel lobby in Washington, DC. I have also analyzed American Jewish public opinion concerning the Israeli-Palestinian conflict, looked at the challenges facing the American Jewish establishment, and described the polarization now occurring between Orthodox and non-Orthodox American Jews. I have tried to do all this as objectively as possible, with the intention of elucidating the American Jewish conflict over Israel, not taking sides in it (although, inevitably, my own personal opinions and biases shape my analysis).

I hope that the reader will have gained a deeper understanding of why American Jews are now arguing so publicly and so bitterly over Israel, and over the Israeli-Palestinian conflict in particular. I also hope that by appreciating the underlying changes in American Jewry's attitude toward Israel, in American Jewish opinion about the conflict, in the organized American Jewish community, and in American Jewry at large, the reader will have come to recognize that the conflict over Israel is deeply rooted and not merely a passing phenomenon, or simply a response to the latest policies and actions of the Israeli or American government. My central argument, in fact, has been that the American Jewish conflict over Israel reflects broader shifts in the American Jewish community. It is not just a reaction to events six thousand miles away in Israel and Palestine. It is also a consequence of changes in American Jewish attitudes toward Israel (from unconditional support to critical engagement), and of other changes in the American Jewish community, and in American society at large. In short, the conflict is really about American Jews, as much as it is about Israel (just as the earlier American Jewish embrace of Israel was also partly about American Jews themselves).

As such, it would be foolish to expect that this conflict will suddenly end. Whatever happens in Israel and whatever Israel does, American Jews are likely to debate and disagree with each other about it (just as Jews have traditionally done about many things). The political consensus over Israel that once reigned within the American Jewish community, which was represented by the American Jewish establishment and the pro-Israel lobby, has been unraveling for some time. Although there are still some points of broad agreement among American Jews—they are not as polarized as their public debate suggests—there are sharpening political divisions over Israeli policies toward Palestinians, and these divisions overlap with religious divisions, exacerbating intra-Jewish conflict. Thus, there is little chance that increasingly secular, liberal, "dovish" Jews will reach a consensus about the Israeli-Palestinian conflict with more religious, conservative and "hawkish" Jews. On the contrary, as long as the Israeli-Palestinian conflict continues—and, sadly, it shows no signs of ending—the political divisions among American Jews, especially between the Orthodox and non-Orthodox, will only continue to widen. In the long run, this poses a very serious challenge to the cohesion of the American Jewish community.

Another equally serious challenge to the American Jewish community is the incivility and intolerance that frequently accompanies the debate over the Israeli-Palestinian conflict. In some local Jewish communities, this debate has become so nasty that a moratorium on talking about Israel has effectively been put into place. Many rabbis, communal officials, Jewish educators, and even students are now afraid to discuss Israel and freely express their opinions about the conflict. There is a pervasive atmosphere of trepidation, even intimidation, within the organized American Jewish community today when it comes to Israel. Certain opinions (most notably, support for BDS) are taboo, and some American Jewish groups are shunned (J Street), and even blacklisted (Jewish Voice for Peace). Such intolerance, however it is justified by opponents of liberal Jews, only serves to alienate a younger generation of American Jews, who are more critical of Israel and less interested in joining the organized Jewish community. If their views are ignored and their voices silenced, they will simply walk away from the organized Jewish community, as many have already done.

But it is not just important for the organized Jewish community to allow debate and dissent in order to retain and attract young American Jews. Above all, it is important because such debate and dissent already exists, and will not go away. Censorship, red lines, and blacklists cannot put the proverbial genie back in the bottle. American Jews have been vocally criticizing Israel, even at times condemning it, for years, and there is simply nothing that the American Jewish establishment, or its wealthy benefactors, can do to stop this. To try to do so is futile, if not counterproductive. Instead, American Jewish establishment leaders, and major donors, must accept, albeit reluctantly, that American Jewish dissent over Israel will not disappear. If anything, it will only intensify as long as Israel's conflict with the Palestinians remains unresolved. They must, therefore, learn to deal with, and accept, public debate and dissent over Israel. So too, must American Jews in general. However much some may nostalgically look back to the time when there was a broad feeling of unity surrounding Israel, they must realize that the unity they once enjoyed (which was never as pronounced or prolonged as many believe) is now a thing of the past. Support for Israel is no longer the great unifier of American Jewry that it was after 1967. Israel is now actually becoming a divisive, rather than a unifying force in American Jewish life. In the future, supporting Israel may well be even less of a common denominator among American Jews, if non-Orthodox Jews grow more detached from Israel and care less about it. To be sure, there will probably still be times when many, perhaps most, American Jews will come together to support Israel—when it is under violent attack by its enemies—but these occasions will be fleeting. The more normal and enduring state of affairs will be American Jewish division, not unity, over Israel. Like their communal leadership, American Jews must accept this and learn to live with it. Failing to do so could end up splitting the American Jewish community apart. That is, unless it becomes increasingly Orthodox in composition.

The deep-rooted and far-reaching American Jewish conflict over Israel that this book describes also has clear implications for Israeli and American political leaders. The former should acknowledge that although most American Jews, including younger ones, still care about Israel, their continued support—emotional and political—cannot be taken for granted. The days when Israeli governments could count on the unequivocal support of American Jews are long gone. American Jews are now much less willing to simply back Israeli government policies than they once were, and increasingly, they want their own opinions taken into account by Israeli policymakers. Even leaders of American Jewish establishment organizations have become frustrated by what is widely perceived to be the tendency of Israeli governments to ignore American Jewish concerns and feelings.[2] Abraham Foxman, the ADL's longtime leader, publicly voiced this complaint in a forum on Israel's future held in New York in June 2015: "I think we [American Jews] have signed up for Israel," he said. "Some unreservedly, others with some more reservations. I don't think Israel understands, appreciates, values, respects this partner—this side of the partnership. . . . There needs to be a lot more sensitivity and education in Israel as to the value of this community beside sending checks or in a moment of crisis, running to Congress."[3] These very frank remarks coming from a leading figure in the American Jewish establishment should make Israeli political leaders take notice. If they want continued American Jewish political support—and they surely do—they will have to listen more to American Jewish opinion and not simply expect unconditional support from American Jews.

Instead, Israeli leaders should expect growing American Jewish pressure to change Israel's policies, especially toward Palestinians in the Occupied Territories. Growing numbers of American Jews, even a majority now, are dissatisfied with Israel's treatment of the Palestinians and deeply worried about Israel's ability to remain a Jewish and democratic state if it continues to effectively rule over Palestinians in the West Bank and East Jerusalem. They want Israel to stop its continued expansion of Jewish settlements, and resume serious peace talks with the Palestinians aimed at achieving a two-state solution to the conflict. While there is now serious doubt about whether such a solution is still possible, the fact that the current right-wing Israeli government led by Prime Minister Netanyahu has publicly declared its unwillingness to establish a Palestinian state in the near future is a cause of much consternation among liberal American Jews. They face the frightening prospect of Israel becoming increasingly illiberal, and increasingly isolated in the international community. As this happens, many liberal American Jews, especially younger ones, will turn away from Israel in despair, or even disgust. To avert this, Israeli policymakers, foremost among them Prime Minister Netanyahu, should recommit Israel to the goal of establishing a Palestinian state as quickly as possible. Otherwise, American Jewish support for Israel, at least among the non-Orthodox, is bound to erode. Not only will this undermine the American Jewish relationship with Israel, but also it will affect U.S. government policy toward Israel (despite the unflagging support for Israel among Orthodox Jews and evangelical Christians).

Finally, American policymakers must remember that no single group speaks on behalf of American Jews on the subject of Israel and the Israeli-Palestinian conflict—not even AIPAC, despite its preeminence among pro-Israel groups. They should also realize that a majority of American Jews would actually welcome a more activist and assertive U.S. policy toward the conflict, one that might help to finally bring about peace.[4] For too long, many American politicians on both sides of the aisle have studiously avoided any criticism of Israel at least partly out of a concern not to lose Jewish voters and campaign donors (although the electoral importance of pro-Israel evangelicals is an even greater concern for many Republicans). They have shown too much deference to the preferences of a highly mobilized minority of American Jews, and ignored the wishes of the quieter majority who favor a more evenhanded U.S. role in brokering an end to the conflict. While this is unlikely to change any time soon given the nature of American politics, one can only hope that more American politicians, both Democrats and Republicans, will have the awareness that President Obama clearly has when he told an interviewer in May 2015:

[Y]ou should be able to say to Israel, we disagree with you on this particular policy. We disagree with you on settlements. We think that checkpoints are a genuine problem. We disagree with you on a Jewish-nationalist law that would potentially undermine the rights of Arab citizens. And to me, that is entirely consistent with being supportive of the State of Israel and the Jewish people. . . . But you can't equate people of good will who are concerned about those issues with somebody who is hostile towards Israel. And you know, I actually believe that most American Jews, most Jews around the world, and most Jews in Israel recognize as much.[5]

President Obama is correct in his belief that most American Jews accept that Israel can be criticized, and do not equate all criticism of Israel with hostility to it (though a sizable and vocal minority certainly does).[6] Just as most American Jews have come to believe that one can care about Israel and criticize its policies, so too should American politicians. Whether such criticism will lead to major changes in Israeli policies is a different question entirely, one that this book does not address. Nevertheless, it is hard to believe that any Israeli government, including the present one, is completely immune to criticism, and that an increase in this criticism, by American Jews and others, will not eventually encourage, if not compel, Israeli policymakers to alter Israel's present course. If that happens, then the American Jewish conflict over Israel, though divisive and often acrimonious, may turn out to have been productive.

NOTES

INTRODUCTION

1. Cain Burdeau, "Protesters Interrupt Netanyahu New Orleans Speech," *Huffington Post*, last updated May 25, 2011; available at www.huffington post.com/2010/11/08/netanyahu-new-orleans-protesters_n_780700.html (accessed November 9, 2015).
2. YouTube, "Israel/Palestine: Young Jews Protest Netanyahu at Jewish GA," uploaded on November 9, 2010; available at www.youtube.com/watch?v= xjLm6d2Mzgg#t=13 (accessed November 9, 2015).
3. Rae Abileah, "Jewish Values vs. Israeli Policies: Why Five Young Jews Disrupted PM Netanyahu in New Orleans," *Mondoweiss*, November 9, 2010.
4. Josh Nathan-Kazis, "Jewish Voice for Peace Activists Interrupt Bibi at GA," *Forward*, November 8, 2010. One observer later explained the audience's angry reaction to the protesters: "'The charged emotional reaction of the crowd to the protesters reflects the cultural undercurrent that characterizes the Federation's core constituency, one that sees activists with the views like those held by JVP as implacably beyond the pale, 'traitors,' and 'delegitimizers.'" Joanna Steinhardt, "What Really Happened at the GA," *Zeek*, November 29, 2010.
5. Daniel J. Elazar, *Community and Polity: The Organizational Dynamics of American Jewry* (Philadelphia: The Jewish Publication Society, 1995), pp. 102–103.
6. Charles S. Liebman and Steven M. Cohen, *Two Worlds of Judaism: The Israeli and American Experiences* (New Haven, CT: Yale University Press, 1990), p. 85.
7. Daniel J. Elazar, *Community and Polity*, p. 24.
8. The size of the American Jewish population ranges widely depending on who you count as being Jewish. The most recent figure estimated the total Jewish population to be 6.7 million, including 4.2 million adults who are "Jewish by religion," 1.2 million adults of no religion, and 1.3 million children being raised as Jews or partly as Jews. The Pew Research Center, "A Portrait of Jewish Americans: Findings from a Pew Research Center Survey of U.S. Jews," October 2013.
9. Sergio DellaPergola, World Jewish Population, 2010.

10. The American Jewish community's importance in American politics is reflected in the fact that the White House has a person specifically designated as a liaison to the community. The liaison's job is to regularly meet with and speak with leaders of the organized Jewish community and update them about the administration's policies, particularly concerning Israel. Neil Rubin, *American Jewry and the Oslo Years* (New York: Palgrave Macmillan, 2012), p. 22.

11. Neil Rubin, *American Jewry and the Oslo Years*, p. 20.

12. Peter Y. Medding, "The New Jewish Politics in America," in Robert S. Wistrich, ed. *Terms of Survival: The Jewish World since 1945* (New York: Routledge, 1995), p. 94.

13. J. J. Goldberg, *Jewish Power: Inside the American Jewish Establishment* (Reading, MA: Addison-Wesley, 1996), p. 4.

14. This was the case, for example, with the Azerbaijani government in the 1990s. Yossi Shain and Tamara Cofman Wittes, "Peace as a Three-Level Game: The Role of Diasporas in Conflict Resolution," in Thomas Ambrosio, ed., *Ethnic Identity Groups and U.S. Foreign Policy* (Westport, CT: Praeger, 2002), p. 187.

15. Yossi Shain and Tamara Cofman Wittes, "Peace as a Three-Level Game" p. 179.

16. Steven T. Rosenthal, *Irreconcilable Differences? The Waning of the American Jewish Love Affair with Israel* (Hanover, NH: Brandeis University Press), 2001, p. xv.

17. From the 1950s to the late 1980s, most donations to Israel by American Jews were given to the Jewish Agency for Israel (an Israeli quasi-governmental body) for the resettlement of immigrants, social welfare provision, and economic development. Since then, American Jews have given more of their money to nongovernmental organizations in Israel.

18. Josh Nathan-Kazis, "26 Billion Bucks: The Jewish Charity Industry Uncovered," *Forward*, March 28, 2014.

19. For instance, in 2007 American Jews donated an estimated $2 billion to Israel. Eric Fleisch and Theodore Sasson, *The New Philanthropy: American Jewish Giving to Israeli Organizations* (Waltham, MA: Cohen Center for Modern Jewish Studies, 2012).

20. Charles S. Liebman, *Pressure without Sanctions: The Influence of World Jewry on Israeli Policy* (Cranbury, NJ: Associated University Presses, 1977), p. 55.

21. Quoted in Liebman, *Pressure without Sanctions*, p. 225.

22. Lahav Harkov, "32% of Israelis Believe US Jews Should Stay Out of Peace Process," *Jerusalem Post*, June 18, 2013.

23. Theodore Sasson, *The New American Zionism* (New York: New York University Press, 2013), pp. 57–59.

24. There are currently approximately 60,000 American Jews who are settlers in the West Bank, constituting an estimated 12 to 15 percent of all Jewish settlers. Judy Maltz, "60,000 American Jews Live in the West Bank, New Study Reveals," *Ha'aretz*, August 27, 2015.

25. Yossi Shain and Tamara Cofman Wittes, "Peace as a Three-Level Game," p. 177.

26. Jim Rutenberg, Mike McIntire, and Ethan Bronner, "Tax-Exempt Funds Aid Settlements in West Bank," *New York Times*, July 5, 2010.

27. David Landy, *Jewish Identity and Palestinian Rights: Diaspora Jewish Opposition to Israel* (London: Zed Books, 2011).

28. See, for instance, Daniella Peled, "British Jews Ever So Carefully Begin to Criticize the Occupation," *Ha'aretz*, February 27, 2015; "Italian Jews Grapple with J Street-Style Rift on Israel," *Jewish Telegraphic Agency*, January 20, 2014; Vicky Tobianah, "Montreal Jewish Festival Cancels Panels by Anti-Birthright Activist," *Ha'aretz*, November 3, 2013; Dan Goldberg, "Australian Jewish Conference Cancels Far-left Speakers, Renewing Controversy," *Ha'aretz*, June 5, 2012; "Jewish Umbrella Considers Booting Australian Group for Settlement Boycott Call," *Jewish Telegraphic Agency*, April 5, 2013; "Aussie Umbrella Body Slams Jewish Group for Promoting West Bank Goods Boycott," *Jewish Telegraphic Agency*, June 5, 2013.

29. Netanyahu directly addressed American Jews through a special live webcast on August 4, 2015, in which he warned of the great dangers the Iran nuclear deal posed to Israel and encouraged his audience to lobby their members of Congress to block the deal. American Jews could watch the webcast on their computers and cell phones, as well as in group viewings held by Jewish organizations. Rebecca Shimoni Stoil, "PM to Make Direct Appeal to US Jews in Bid to Thwart Iran Deal," *Times of Israel*, July 31, 2015. See also "Netanyahu Urges U.S. Jews to Oppose Iran Deal," *Jewish Telegraphic Agency*, August 4, 2015.

30. Nathan Diament, the executive director of the advocacy center of the Orthodox Union (which represents Orthodox American Jewish synagogue congregrations) described the effort to oppose the nuclear deal with Iran as "the biggest mobilization in the community that we have ever seen." Quoted in Julie Hirschfeld Davis, "Lobbying Fight over Iran Nuclear Deal Centers on Democrats," *New York Times*, August 17, 2015.

31. The most reliable survey of American Jewish public opinion regarding the Iranian nuclear deal, conducted on behalf of the *Los Angeles Jewish Journal* shortly after the agreement was announced, found that American Jews supported the deal 49 percent to 31 percent (more than Americans in general), and that 54 percent of American Jews wanted Congress to approve the deal, compared with 35 percent who opposed Congressional approval. "Poll: Most of American Jews Think Congress Should Approve Iran Deal," *Ha'aretz*, July 24, 2015. See also Todd Gitlin and Steven M. Cohen, "On the Iran Deal, American Jewish 'Leaders' Don't Speak for Most Jews," *Washington Post*, August 14, 2015.

32. On August 28, 2015, President Obama spoke directly to American Jews about the Iran nuclear deal via a live webcast. A few weeks before, he personally met with twenty leaders from an array of Jewish groups on the same day that Prime Minister Netanyahu addressed American Jews through another

live webcast. See "Obama to Meet with Jewish Leaders for First Time since Iran Deal," *Jewish Telegraphic Agency*, August 3, 2015; "Obama to Seek American Jews' Support for Iran Deal in Webcast," *Jewish Telegraphic Agency*, August 21, 2015; Jonathan Weisman, "Obama Tries to Soothe Divided Jewish Community on Iran Deal," *New York Times*, August 28, 2015.

33. Jonathan Weisman, "Obama Tries to Soothe Divided Jewish Community on Iran Deal," *New York Times*, August 28, 2015. See also Debra Nussbaum Cohen, "Iran Deal Fight Splits American Jews," *Ha'aretz*, July 21, 2015; Jonathan Mark, "Jews Bitterly Divided on Iran," *New York Jewish Week*, July 29, 2015.

34. Roger Cohen, "Iran and American Jews," *New York Times*, August 17, 2015.

35. Chemi Shalev, "Fractured American Jewish Community Is First Victim of Iran Nuclear Deal," *Ha'aretz*, August 16, 2015. Even more dramatically, Greg Rosenbaum, the chairman of the National Jewish Democratic Council, told a *New York Times* reporter: "We are on the verge of fratricide in the Jewish community, and it has to stop." Quoted in Jonathan Weisman and Alexander Burns, "Iran Deal Opens a Vitriolic Divide among American Jews," *New York Times*, August 28, 2015. See also Rabbi Michael Knopf, "Will Partisan Fight over Iran Deal Permanently Polarize Jewish Americans?" *Ha'aretz*, July 30, 2015.

36. Gary Rosenblatt, "Iran Deal Driving Jews Farther Apart," *New York Jewish Week*, August 12, 2015.

37. Barak Ravid, "Diplomat Warns: U.S. Jews Aren't United behind Israel on Iran Deal," *Ha'aretz*, July 30, 2015.

CHAPTER 1: THE CHANGING AMERICAN JEWISH RELATIONSHIP WITH ISRAEL

1. Jeremy Ben-Ami, *A New Voice for Israel: Fighting for the Survival of the Jewish Nation* (New York: Palgrave Macmillan, 2011), p. 152.

2. "Get Ready to Celebrate: Thousands of Marchers, Performers, Bands and Floats Set for Annual Celebrate Israel Parade up Fifth Avenue on Sunday, June 3," Press Release, May 14, 2012; available at: http://celebrateisraelny.org/wp-content/uploads/2011/12/Parade-press-release-5-14-12.pdf (accessed May 16, 2012).

3. Gary Rosenblatt, "Raining on the Parade," *Jewish Week*, June 5, 2012.

4. The groups were the New Israel Fund, Ameinu, Americans for Peace Now, B'Tselem USA, Partners for Progressive Israel, and Rabbis for Human Rights–North America. A similar campaign was waged, ultimately unsuccessfully, prior to the parades in 2013, 2014, and 2015. See Debra Nussbaum Cohen, "Who Has the Right to Celebrate Israel?" *Ha'aretz*, April 6, 2014; Amanda Borschel-Dan, "No BDS Supporters for New York Celebrate Israel Parade," *Times of Israel*, February 13, 2015.

5. Michael Miller, the head of the Jewish Community Relations Council of New York, declared in a newspaper interview after the 2012 parade: "The parade once again brought out the spirit of support that we in New York have for Israel, whether we are on the right or on the left, religious or not, Jewish or not. 35,000 marchers prove that despite the difference that people may have about this or that matter on Israel's agenda, we all support the core struggle of Israel and identify with it." Quoted in Chemi Shalev, "Orthodox Make Big Showing at Salute to Israel Parade," *Ha'aretz*, June 4, 2012.

6. Even before Israel's founding, the Zionist movement gained vital diplomatic support—most significantly in the form of the Balfour Declaration issued by Great Britain in 1917—due in part to the prevalent, but mistaken, belief that Jews around the world were staunch supporters of Zionism.

7. In a March 2012 survey, only 4 percent of American Jews said that Israel was the most important issue for them in voting for president in the 2012 election. Robert P. Jones and Daniel Cox, "Chosen for What? Jewish Values in 2012: Finding from the 2012 Jewish Values Survey," Public Religion Research Institute: Washington, DC, March 2012, p. 11. The low importance normally given to Israel by American Jewish voters, however, may well be because there are few, if any, candidates in American elections who do not tout their pro-Israel credentials, thereby assuring most American Jews that this is not a factor they need to consider when choosing between two candidates. If a politician was widely perceived as not being pro-Israel, this could affect the voting behavior of many American Jews.

8. A survey conducted in 2008 found that nearly half of American Jews talked about Israel only "a few times a year" (26 percent), "hardly ever" (16 percent), or "never" (3 percent). J Street, "National Survey of American Jews, Conducted between 29 June–3 July 2008."

9. Fifty-seven percent of American Jews have never visited Israel. Pew Research Center, "A Portrait of Jewish Americans: Findings from a Pew Research Center Survey of U.S. Jews," October 2013, p. 85.

10. Many American Jews are quite ignorant about Israel. In a November 2012 survey, for example, almost one in five American Jews (18 percent) did not know that Benjamin Netanyahu was the prime minister of Israel. Among American Jews aged between 18 and 30, 42 percent did not know who he was. J Street, "Post-Election Survey of 800 American Jewish Voters Conducted on November 6, 2012."

11. Pew Research Center, "A Portrait of Jewish Americans." The survey was based on interviews with 3,500 Jews in all 50 states.

12. Ibid., p. 14.

13. Among Jews 65 and older, about half (53 percent) said that caring about Israel was essential to what being Jewish meant to them, whereas only 32 percent of Jews under age 30 felt this way. Ibid., p. 55.

14. Fifty-eight percent of Conservative Jews and 55 percent of Orthodox Jews say caring about Israel is essential to what being Jewish means to them, compared to just 42 percent of Reform Jews. Ibid., p. 57.

NOTES TO CHAPTER 1

15. Extensive survey data indicates that attachment to Israel among American Jews varies according to factors such as age, strength of Jewish identity, and denominational affiliation. Young Jews, for example, are generally less attached to Israel than older ones, and Orthodox Jews are the most attached to Israel.

16. In the National Jewish Population Survey of 2000–2001 (based on a nationally representative sample of approximately 4,500 Jews), 63 percent of American Jews described themselves as very or somewhat attached to Israel. Jonathon Ament, "Israel Connections and American Jews: United Jewish Communities Report Series on the National Jewish Population Survey 2000–2001," United Jewish Communities, Report, 12, August 2005, p. 41. Similarly, in the 2013 Pew Survey, 69 percent of American Jews said they felt emotionally attached to Israel, with 30 percent feeling "very attached" and 39 percent feeling "somewhat attached" to Israel. Pew Research Center, "A Portrait of Jewish Americans," p. 82.

17. Theodore Sasson, Benjamin Phillips, Charles Kadushin, and Leonard Saxe, et al., "Still Connected: American Jewish Attitudes about Israel," (Waltham, MA: Cohen Center for Modern Jewish Studies, Brandeis University, August 2010), p. 9.

18. In regular surveys sponsored by the American Jewish Committee between 2000 and 2005, a significant minority of American Jews who said that being Jewish was either very important or somewhat important to them (around 45 percent in the surveys) described themselves as feeling somewhat distant or very distant to Israel. Joel Perlmann, "American Jewish Opinion about the Future of the West Bank: A Reanalysis of American Jewish Committee Surveys," Levy Economics Institute of Bard College, Working Paper No. 526, December 2007, pp. 12–13.

19. Judith Butler, "No, It's Not Anti-semitic," *London Review of Books* vol. 25, no. 16 (August 2003).

20. Gideon Shimoni, "Reformulations of Zionist Ideology since the Establishment of the State of Israel," in Peter Medding, ed., *Values, Interests and Identity: Jews and Politics in a Changing World* (New York: Oxford University Press, 1995), p. 11.

21. Charles S. Liebman and Steven M. Cohen, *Two Worlds of Judaism: The Israeli and American Experiences*, p. 17.

22. Ibid., p. 19.

23. Ibid., p. 18.

24. Steven M. Cohen, "Israel in the Jewish Identity of American Jews: A Study in Dualities and Contrasts," David Gordis and Yoav Ben Horin, eds., *Jewish Identity in America* (Los Angeles: Wilstein Institute, 1991), p. 128. Cohen notes that "attachment to Israel is correlated with perceptions of Arab hostility and with perceptions of American Gentile hostility (to Jews and to Israel). . . . [V]iewing the world as generally antagonistic to Jews and to Israel comports with a high level of caring about Israel." Cohen, "Israel in the

Jewish Identity of American Jews," in Gordis and Ben Horin, eds., *Jewish Identity in America*, p. 128.

25. Paradoxically, although fear of anti-Semitism, at home and abroad, partially motivates American Jewish support for Israel, pro-Israel activism by Americans Jews is driven more by a sense of confidence and security in the United States. After all, it was only after American Jews felt more comfortable and secure in the United States, from the late 1960s onward, that they became much more confident about expressing their support for Israel. Charles S. Liebman and Steven M. Cohen, *Two Worlds of Judaism*, p. 41.

26. Liebman, *Pressure without Sanctions*, pp. 199–200.

27. For detailed ethnographic studies of Birthright Israel tours, see Shaul Kelner, *Tours That Bind: Diaspora, Pilgrimage, and Israeli Birthright Tourism* (New York: New York University Press, 2010); Jasmin Habib, *Israel, Diaspora and the Routes of National Belonging* (Toronto: University of Toronto Press, 2004); Leonard Saxe and Barry Chazan, *Ten Days of Birthright Israel: A Journey in Young Adult Identity* (Waltham, MA: Brandeis University Press, 2008).

28. Kelner, *Tours That Bind*, p. 196. Interestingly, since Israeli governments provide some of the funding for Birthright Israel, they clearly accept this goal, despite the fact that it conflicts with the tenets of classical Zionism— specifically the notion that all Jews should live in Israel and that Jewish life in the Diaspora is ultimately doomed.

29. "Birthright Celebrates Its 500,000[th] Participant," *Times of Israel*, June 13, 2015.

30. Pew Research Center, "A Portrait of Jewish Americans."

31. For most American Jews, supporting Israel is actually not one of the most important elements of their Jewish identity. In two surveys taken years apart (in 1965 and 1989), most American Jews ranked supporting Israel quite low on a list of what was "essential to being a good Jew." J. J. Goldberg, *Jewish Power*, pp. 148–149. More recently, in a 2012 survey, only 20 percent of American Jews said that supporting Israel was most important to their Jewish identity, compared to 46 percent who cited a commitment to social equality as being most important. Nevertheless, support for Israel was ranked as more important to Jewish identity than either religious observance or cultural tradition. Robert P. Jones and Daniel Cox, "Chosen for What? Jewish Values in 2012: Finding from the 2012 Jewish Values Survey" (Washington, DC: Public Religion Research Institute, 2012), p. 9.

32. In a survey of Reform Jews conducted in 1970, for instance, 80 percent of respondents regarded support for Israel as essential to being a "good Jew." Jack Wertheimer, "American Jews and Israel: A 60-Year Retrospective," in *American Jewish Yearbook 2008* (New York: American Jewish Committee, 2008), p. 63.

33. Arthur Hertzberg, ed., *The Zionist Idea: A Historical Analysis and Reader* (Philadelphia: Jewish Publication Society, 1997), p. 625.

34. Steven T. Rosenthal, *Irreconcilable Differences?*, p. xv.

35. Dan Senor and Saul Singer, *Start-up Nation: The Story of Israel's Economic Miracle* (New York: Twelve, 2009).

36. Jack Wertheimer, "American Jews and Israel: A 60-Year Retrospective," p. 79.

37. In the 2000–2001 NJPS study, for example, 72 percent of Orthodox Jews said they were strongly attached to Israel, compared to 54 percent of Conservative Jews and only 22 percent of Reform Jews. In the Pew survey, 77 percent of Modern Orthodox Jews said they felt very attached to Israel, compared to just 24 percent of Reform Jews. Pew Research Center, "A Portrait of Jewish Americans," p. 82.

38. Ibid., p. 86.

39. Although Reform Judaism was initially hostile toward Zionism before Israel's establishment, since 1948 the Reform movement has embraced Israel as the spiritual and cultural center of the Jewish people. Yossi Shain, *Kinship and Diasporas in International Affairs* (Ann Arbor: University of Michigan Press, 2008), p. 75.

40. Jack Wertheimer, "American Jews and Israel: A 60-Year Retrospective," p. 16. Israel's religious significance is expressed most clearly in the "Tefila Li'shlom Ha-Medina" (Prayer for the Welfare of the State), recited in synagogue services on the Sabbath and on religious festivals.

41. Shain, *Kinship and Diasporas in International Affairs*, p. 75.

42. Ibid., pp. 74–75.

43. Shaul Magid observes that "Zionism for American Jews was, and arguably remains, largely a project about American Jewish identity." Shaul Magid, "Butler Trouble: Zionism, Excommunication, and the Reception of Judith Butler's Work on Israel/Palestine," *Studies in American Jewish Literature* vol. 33, no. 2 (2014): 238.

44. Salman Rushdie, *Imaginary Homelands: Essays and Criticism, 1981–1991* (London: Granta Books, 1991).

45. Steven T. Rosenthal, "Long-distance Nationalism: American Jews, Zionism, and Israel," in Dana Evan Kaplan, ed., *The Cambridge Companion to American Judaism* (New York: Cambridge University Press, 2005), p. 212.

46. Jack Wertheimer, "American Jews and Israel: A 60-Year Retrospective," p. 79.

47. Steven M. Cohen, "Are American and Israeli Jews Drifting Apart?" (New York: American Jewish Committee, 1989), p. 4.

48. Charles S. Liebman, "Religious Trends among American and Israeli Jews," in Robert S. Wistrich, ed., *Terms of Survival: The Jewish World since 1945*, p. 307.

49. Arthur Hertzberg, "Afterword," in Arthur Hertzberg, ed., *The Zionist Idea: A Historical Analysis and Reader* (Philadelphia: Jewish Publication Society, 1997), p. 624.

50. On the profound impact of *Exodus* on American Jews, see M. M. Silver, *Our Exodus: Leon Uris and the Americanization of Israel's Founding Story* (Detroit: Wayne State University Press, 2010).

51. Jonathan Sarna, "A Projection of America as It Ought to Be: Zion in the Mind's Eye of American Jews," in Allon Gal, ed., *Envisioning Israel: The*

Changing Images and Ideals of North American Jews (Jerusalem and Detroit: Magnes Press and Wayne State University Press, 1996), p. 41.

52. Sarna, "A Projection of America as It Ought to Be," pp. 41–42.

53. Shaul Magid, "Butler Trouble," p. 240.

54. Rosenthal, *Irreconcilable Differences?*, pp. 25–26.

55. Zohar Segev, "American Zionists' Place in Israel after Statehood: From Involved Partners to Outside Supporters," *American Jewish History* vol. 93, no. 3 (2007): 277–302.

56. Rosenthal, "Long-distance Nationalism," p. 212.

57. According to Ben-Gurion, Zionism was based "on the conviction that we do not form part of the peoples among whom we lived, that we had no intention of remaining in *galut* (exile), and that out deepest aspiration was to return personally to Zion." Quoted in Gideon Shimoni, "Reformulations of Zionist Ideology since the Establishment of the State of Israel," in Peter Medding, ed., *Values, Interests and Identity: Jews and Politics in a Changing World* (New York: Oxford University Press, 1995), p. 12.

58. This is hardly surprising given the fact that early Zionist thinkers ignored American Jewry, as Ilan Troen wrote: "America was beyond the pale of Zionist theoreticians." S. Ilan Troen, "Beyond Zionist Theory: Coming to Terms with the American Jewish Experience," in Allon Gal and Alfred Gottschalk, eds., *Beyond Survival and Philanthropy: American Jewry and Israel* (Cincinnati: Hebrew Union College Press, 2000), p. 64.

59. Steven M. Cohen, "Israel in the Jewish Identity of American Jews: A Study in Dualities and Contrasts," in David Gordis and Yoav Ben Horin, eds., *Jewish Identity in America* (Los Angeles: Wilstein Institute, 1991), pp. 122–123.

60. Charles S. Liebman, "Diaspora Influence on Israel: The Ben-Gurion-Blaustein 'Exchange' and Its Aftermath," *Jewish Social Studies* vol. 36, no. 3/4 (1974): 271–280.

61. Jonathan Sarna, "The Question of Shlilat Ha-Galut in American Zionism," in Allon Gal and Alfred Gottschalk, eds., *Beyond Survival and Philanthropy*, p. 60.

62. Ibid., pp. 60–61.

63. The American Zionist movement was born in July 1898 (a year after the first Zionist Congress in Basel, Switzerland), when the Federation of American Zionists (FAZ, renamed the Zionist Organization of America in 1918) held its founding convention in New York. Other Zionist organizations later emerged, notably Hadassah, the women's Zionist organization; Mizrahi, the religious Zionist organization; and Poale Zion, the Labor Zionist organization.

64. For the history of Zionism within the American Jewish community before 1948, see Melvin I. Urofsky, *American Zionism from Herzl to the Holocaust* (Garden City, NY: Anchor Press, 1975); Naomi W. Cohen, *The Americanization of Zionism, 1897–1948* (Hanover, NH: Brandeis University Press/ University Press of New England, 2003); Naomi W. Cohen, *American Jews and the Zionist Idea* (New York: Ktav Publishing House, 1975); Mark Raider,

The Emergence of American Zionism (New York: New York University Press, 1998).

65. Magid, "Butler Trouble," p. 239.

66. Although the American Zionist movement attracted a growing number of supporters—membership in the ZOA had grown to over 200,000 Jews in 1945 compared to only 8,400 in 1932—Zionists were still a small minority in the American Jewish community. Rosenthal, *Irreconcilable Differences?*, p. 16.

67. Not all varieties of Zionism in Europe insisted that all Jews should live in the Jewish homeland or state. The "cultural Zionism" espoused by Ahad Ha'am accepted the existence of a Jewish Diaspora even after the establishment of Jewish statehood. According to Ahad Ha'am, the Jewish state would be a "spiritual center" for Diaspora Jewry. In this cultural Zionist view, Jewish life in the Diaspora would be inferior to that in the Jewish homeland and culturally dependent on it.

68. Rosenthal, *Irreconcilable Differences?*, p. 15. The concept of *shlilat hagolah* ("negation of the Diaspora") was also noticeably absent from American Zionism. Sarna, "The Question of Shlilat Ha-Galut in American Zionism," pp. 59–63. For a discussion of the concept of Shlilat Ha-galut in Zionist thought, see Yosef Gorny, "Shlilat Ha-Galut: Past and Present," in Gal and Gottschalk, eds., *Beyond Survival and Philanthropy*, pp. 41–58.

69. Quoted in Sarna, "The Question of Shlilat Ha-Galut in American Zionism," p. 59.

70. Quoted in Yossi Shain, *Kinship and Diasporas in International Affairs* (Ann Arbor: University of Michigan Press), 2008, p. 99.

71. Under Brandeis's leadership, membership in the FAZ/ZOA massively increased from just 12,000 in 1914 to over 176,000 in 1919. Martin J. Raffel, "History of Israel Advocacy," in Alan Mittleman, Jonathan Sarna, and Robert Licht, eds., *Jewish Polity and American Civil Society* (Lanham, MD: Rowman and Littlefield, 2002), p. 105.

72. Rosenthal, *Irreconcilable Differences?*, p. 13.

73. *Truman Memoirs*, quoted in Rosenthal, *Irreconcilable Differences?*, p. 20.

74. Between 1945 and 1948, American Jews donated around $400 million to Israel. Steven T. Rosenthal, "Long-distance Nationalism: American Jews, Zionism, and Israel," in Dana Evan Kaplan, ed., *The Cambridge Companion to American Judaism*, p. 211.

75. Steven T. Rosenthal writes that: "Without the support of American Zionists, who never had any intention of forsaking their adopted homeland, the Jewish state would very likely never have been born." Rosenthal, *Irreconcilable Differences?*, p. 21.

76. The concern about being accused of having "dual loyalties" may have inhibited American Jews from engaging in political advocacy for Israel. Shain, *Kinship and Diasporas in International Affairs*, p. 55.

77. Rosenthal, *Irreconcilable Differences?*, p. 27.

78. Shain, *Kinship and Diasporas in International Affairs*, p. 55.

79. See, for example, Marshall Sklare and Joseph Greenblum, *Jewish Identity on the Suburban Frontier: A Study of Group Survival in the Open Society* (New York: Basic Books, 1967).

80. Nathan Glazer, *American Judaism* (Chicago: University of Chicago Press, 1957), p. 115.

81. By 1967, American Jews had purchased $850 million worth of Israel Bonds. Shain, *Kinship and Diasporas in International Affairs*, p. 56.

82. Although most scholars of American Jewry regard the 1967 war as a watershed event in American Jewish relations with Israel, not all scholars share this view. See Chaim Waxman, "The Limited Impact of the Six Day War on American Jews," in Eli Lederhendler, ed., *The Six Day War and World Jewry* (Bethesda: University Press of Maryland, 2000), pp. 99–116.

83. Lucy Dawidowicz, "American Public Opinion," in Morris Fine and Milton Himmelfarb, eds., *American Jewish Year Book 1968* (New York: American Jewish Committee, 1968), p. 205.

84. J. J. Goldberg, *Jewish Power*, p. 137.

85. Cohen and Liebman, 2000, p. 5.

86. Rosenthal, *Irreconcilable Differences?*, p. 33.

87. Ibid., p. xv.

88. Jonathan Woocher, *Sacred Survival: The Civil Religion of American Jews* (Bloomington: Indiana University Press, 1986).

89. Daniel J. Elazar, *Community and Polity: The Organizational Dynamics of American Jewry*, p. 107. In a similar vein, Rosenthal writes that "worship of Israel became the supreme basis of American Jewish identity" after 1967. Rosenthal, *Irreconcilable Differences?*, p. 33.

90. Monty Noam Penkower, "American Jewry and the Holocaust: From Biltmore to the American Jewish Conference," *Jewish Social Studies* vol. 47, no. 2 (1985): 95–114.

91. Rosenthal, *Irreconcilable Differences?*, pp. 16–17.

92. Lynn Rapaport, "The Holocaust in American Jewish Life," in Dana Evan Kaplan, ed., *The Cambridge Companion to American Judaism*, pp. 187–208.

93. Disputing the common view that "Holocaust consciousness" did not begin to develop among American Jews until the mid-1960s, Michael Staub argues that "far from being silent—either out of horror at the magnitude of Nazi crimes or out of respectful sensitivity toward the trauma of survivors—Jewish commentators of a variety of political persuasions already in the 1940s, 1950s, and early 1960s made analogies to the mass murder of European Jewry when debating domestic political issues or explaining its purported 'lessons' for America." Michael E. Staub, "Holocaust Consciousness and American Jewish Politics," in Marc Lee Raphael, ed., *The Columbia History of Jews and Judaism in America* (New York: Columbia University Press, 2008), p. 315.

94. J. J. Goldberg, *Jewish Power*, pp. 145–146. Morse's book *While Six Million Died* accused the Roosevelt administration of deliberately failing to save

Jewish lives during the Holocaust. Arthur D. Morse, *While Six Million Died: A Chronicle of American Apathy* (New York: Random House, 1968).

95. J. J. Goldberg, *Jewish Power*, p. 146.

96. Staub, "Holocaust Consciousness and American Jewish Politics," pp. 313–336.

97. Steven Bayme, *American Jewry Confronts the Twenty-First Century* (Jerusalem: Jerusalem Center for Public Affairs, 2010), p. 38.

98. This narrative continues to underpin the annual "March of the Living," in which Jewish teenagers from around the world visit the notorious Nazi concentration and death camp Auschwitz-Birkenau and then Israel. The fact that the trip ends in Israel accords with the "Holocaust to rebirth" narrative and evokes the belief that the Jewish state's existence now ensures that Jews are no longer defenseless.

99. Deborah Dash Moore, "Introduction," in Deborah D. Moore, *American Jewish Identity Politics* (Ann Arbor: University of Michigan Press, 2009), pp. 10–29.

100. Staub, "Holocaust Consciousness and American Jewish Politics," p. 326.

101. Ibid., pp. 326–327.

102. Sara Hirschhorn, "The Origins of the Redemption in Occupied Suburbia? The Jewish-American Makings of the West Bank Settlement of Efrat, 1973–87," *Middle Eastern Studies* vol. 51, no. 2 (2015): 269–284.

103. Rosenthal, *Irreconcilable Differences?*

104. In a survey of American Jewish opinion conducted by the AJC in 1983, for example, 48 percent of respondents agreed with the statement that they were "often troubled by the policies of the current Israeli government [led by Menachem Begin]," compared to only 29 percent who disagreed. J. J. Goldberg, *Jewish Power*, p. 216.

105. The Begin government launched a massive settlement drive in the West Bank and Gaza Strip. When it came to power in 1977, there were 24 Jewish settlements in the West Bank and Gaza, inhabited by 3,200 people. By the time of Begin's retirement in 1983, there were 106 settlements (98 in the West Bank, and 8 in Gaza), with the number of residents increasing to 28,400. Not only did the number of settlements and settlers increase, but also the type and location of settlements changed during this period as a large number of settlements were established in central locations in the West Bank and in close proximity to local Palestinian populations—an area that would form the basis of any territorial compromise. Ilan Peleg, *Begin's Foreign Policy, 1977–1983: Israel's Move to the Right* (Westport, CT: Greenwood, 1987), 110–111.

106. Rosenthal, *Irreconcilable Differences?*, pp. 54–55.

107. Ibid., p. 64.

108. Marla Brettschneider, *Cornerstones of Peace: Jewish Identity Politics and Democratic Theory* (New Brunswick, NJ: Rutgers University Press, 1996), p. 30.

109. Rosenthal, *Irreconcilable Differences?*, p. 73.

110. After the Sabra and Shatila massacre, support grew within American Jewry for the dovish Israeli Peace Now movement, founded in 1979, and "Friends

of Peace Now" chapters were formed in many cities across the United States. Soon after, in 1983, a national organization was established called "American Friends of Peace Now" (later renamed Americans for Peace Now [APN]). Starting out with just $6,000 in the bank, a decade later, in 1993, APN's annual budget was almost $1.3 million.

111. Albert Vorspan, "Soul Searching," *New York Times Magazine*, May 8, 1988.

112. Rosenthal, *Irreconcilable Differences?*, p. xix.

113. Ibid., p. 111.

114. Ibid., pp. 105, 112.

115. Ibid., p. xix.

116. Cited in ibid., p. 111.

117. Ibid., p. xix.

118. In his account of the "waning of the American Jewish love affair with Israel," Steven Rosenthal claims that the cumulative impact of the Lebanon war, the Pollard spy scandal, the first Palestinian Intifada, and the "Who is a Jew?" controversy led to the growing disillusionment with Israel. In doing so, he attributes all the responsibility for American Jewish disaffection with Israel to the actions and policies of Israeli governments. Rosenthal, *Irreconcilable Differences?*

119. Because Jonathan Pollard was an American Jew who stole U.S. intelligence secrets and gave them to Israel, his spying threatened to open up American Jews to the charge of dual-loyalty.

120. Howard Schuman and Amy Corning, "Generational Memory and the Critical Period: Evidence for National and World Events," *Public Opinion Quarterly* vol. 76, no. 1 (Spring 2012): 1–31.

121. See, for example, Jonathan Chait, "Israel Is Making It Hard to Be Pro-Israel," *New York Magazine*, July 2014. For more on American Jewish attitudes toward the IDF's conduct in its asymmetrical wars, see Shmuel Rosner and Michael Herzog, "Jewish Values and Israel's Use of Force in Armed Conflict: Perspectives from World Jewry" (Jerusalem: Jewish People Policy Institute, 2015).

122. See Benny Morris, *1948: A History of the First Arab–Israeli War* (New Haven, CT: Yale University Press, 2008); Benny Morris, *The Birth of the Palestinian Refugee Problem Revisited* (Cambridge, UK: Cambridge University Press, 2004); Benny Morris, *Israel's Border Wars 1949–1956: Arab Infiltration, Israeli Retaliation, and the Countdown to the Suez War* (Oxford, UK: Clarendon Press, 1993).

123. Norman Finkelstein, *Knowing Too Much: Why the American Jewish Romance with Israel Is Coming to an End* (New York: OR Books, 2012).

124. Steven M. Cohen, "Are American and Israeli Jews Drifting Apart?" (New York: American Jewish Committee, 1989), p. 4.

125. In a survey of American Jews taken in 1986, for example, only a third knew that Menachem Begin and Shimon Peres were members of different political parties. Steven M. Cohen, "Ties and Tensions: The 1986 Survey of American

Jewish Attitudes toward Israel and Israelis" (New York: American Jewish Committee, 1987), p. 36. Similarly, a decade later in a 1996 survey, a majority of American Jews did not know that Shimon Peres and Benjamin Netanyahu belonged to different political parties. "In the Aftermath of the Rabin Assassination: A Survey of American Jewish Opinion about Israel and the Peace Process," conducted for the American Jewish Committee by Market Facts, January 10–16, 1996, p. 8.

126. Steven T. Rosenthal, *Long-distance Nationalism: American Jews, Zionism, and Israel*, p. 209.

127. Liebman, *Pressure without Sanctions*, p. 198.

128. Ibid., p. 48, italics in original.

129. Theodore Sasson, *The New Realism: American Jewish Views about Israel* (New York: American Jewish Committee, 2009), p. 26.

130. Jack Wertheimer, "American Jews and Israel: A 60-Year Retrospective," in *American Jewish Yearbook 2008*, p. 79.

131. Liebman, *Pressure without Sanctions*, p. 200. Liebman accurately compared the relationship that most American Jews had with Israel to the relationship they had with their local synagogue. They rarely attended synagogue services and were quite ignorant about what happened in the service, but it was still important to them that such services took place and that the synagogue existed. Similarly with Israel, most American Jews never went there and most knew very little about the country, but it was important for them that Israel existed. Ibid., p. 209.

132. Liebman, *Pressure without Sanctions*, p. 209. Liebman argued that American Jewry's lack of interest in Israel's policies was one of the main reasons why American Jews at the time did not try to pressure Israel to change these policies. Ibid., p. 202.

133. Rosenthal, *Long-distance Nationalism: American Jews, Zionism, and Israel*, p. 211.

134. Israel's flag, not the menorah, the two tablets of the Ten Commandments, or the scroll of the Torah, is in fact the most widely used Jewish symbol today.

135. Theodore Sasson, "Mass Mobilization to Direct Engagement: American Jews' Changing Relationship to Israel," *Israel Studies* vol. 15, no. 2 (2010): 191.

136. Much of the readership, somewhere between 30 and 60 percent, of the online English-language versions of major Israeli newspapers is based in the United States, and they are mostly American Jews. In total, there are at least a dozen English-language online newspapers, radio stations, and television channels that operate from Israel. Gilad Halpern, "Home and Away: Israel's English-language Media and Its Jewish-American Readers," unpublished paper, 2015.

137. Jonathon Ament, "Israel Connections and American Jews: United Jewish Communities Report Series on the National Jewish Population Survey 2000–2001," p. 41.

138. Uzi Rebhun, "Recent Developments in Jewish Identification in the United States: A Cohort Follow-Up and Facet Analysis," *Papers in Jewish Demography 1997*, eds. Sergio DellaPergola and Judith Even, The Avraham Harman

Institute of Contemporary Jewry, p. 268; Jonathon Ament, "Israel Connections and American Jews: United Jewish Communities Report Series on the National Jewish Population Survey 2000–2001," p. 41. Pew Research Center, "A Portrait of Jewish Americans," p. 85.

139. On the expansion of courses about Israel at American universities, see Janet Krasner Aronson, Annette Koren, and Leonard Saxe, "Teaching Israel at American Universities: Growth, Placement, and Future Prospects," *Israel Studies* vol. 18, no. 3 (Fall 2013): 158–178.

140. These works began appearing in the 1980s. Some notable examples were Benny Morris, *The Birth of the Palestinian Refugee Problem, 1947–1949* (Cambridge, UK: Cambridge University Press, 1987); Avi Shlaim, *Collusion across the Jordan: King Abdullah, the Zionist Movement, and the Partition of Palestine* (Oxford, UK: Clarendon Press, 1988); Zeev Sternhell, *The Founding Myths of Israel: Nationalism, Socialism and the Making of the Jewish State* (Princeton, NJ: Princeton University Press, 1998). *Tikkun* magazine, founded in 1986 and edited by Michael Lerner, helped bring this work to the attention of American Jews.

141. Theodore Sasson, "The New Realism: American Jewish Views about Israel."

142. Theodore Sasson, "Mass Mobilization to Direct Engagement," p. 176.

143. Sasson, "Mass Mobilization to Direct Engagement," pp. 185–186. See also, Theodore Sasson, *The New American Zionism*.

144. Major national and world events that occur during a person's late childhood, adolescence, or early adulthood leave a lasting impression on people's memories, attitudes, and worldviews (Karl Mannheim, "The Problem of Generations," in *Essays on the Sociology of Knowledge*, London: Routledge and Kegan Paul, 1952, pp. 292–299). Thus, historians and sociologists refer to "generational memory" to describe how formative events and collective memories differ between generations. Howard Schuman and Amy Corning, "Generational Memory and the Critical Period: Evidence for National and World Events," *Public Opinion Quarterly* vol. 76, no. 1 (Spring 2012): 1–31.

145. Sylvia Barack Fishman, Rachel S. Bernstein, and Emily Sigalow, "Reimagining Jewishness: Younger American Jewish Leaders, Entrepreneurs, and Artists in Cultural Context," in Jack Wertheimer, ed. *The New Jewish Leaders: Reshaping the American Jewish Landscape* (Waltham, MA: Brandeis University Press, 2011), p. 174.

146. Cohen and Kelman, "Beyond Distancing."

147. For example, in a study conducted in 2010 when presented with Israeli and Turkish statements regarding the May 2010 flotilla incident (in which Israeli soldiers and pro-Palestinian activists clashed as the activists tried to bypass the Israeli naval blockade of the Gaza Strip), younger American Jews were less likely to agree with the Israeli statement. Rather, a plurality of the group aged 18–29 felt that the truth was probably about halfway between the Turkish and Israeli statements. Theodore Sasson et al., *Still Connected: American Jewish Attitudes about Israel*, p. 15.

148. In a 2012 survey of non-Orthodox American Jews under 35 years old, 40 percent opposed Israeli settlement construction (while only 22 percent supported it), and 45 percent said that Israel is not acting as if it wants peace with the Palestinians. Chemi Shalev, "Poll: Young American Jews Are Growing More Attached to Israel," *Ha'aretz*, July 9, 2012.

149. An online survey of 1,157 self-identified Jewish college students in the United States conducted in 2014 found that while Israel was most commonly cited as "the most crucial issue concerning young Jewish people today," only 35 percent of those surveyed felt that supporting Israel was very important to being Jewish. Ariela Keysar and Barry M. Kosmin, "The Demographic Survey of American Jewish College Students 2014," cited in Derek M. Kwait, "First Results of the Jewish Student Survey Are In!" New Voices, September 15, 2014, available at http://newvoices.org/2014/09/15/jewishstudentsurvey results1/ (accessed October 10, 2014).

150. For a good expression of this attitude, see Dana Goldstein, "Why Fewer Young American Jews Share Their Parents' View of Israel," *Time*, September 29, 2011.

151. Pew Research Center, "A Portrait of Jewish Americans."

152. See, for instance, Rosenthal, *Irreconcilable Differences?*

153. The "distancing hypothesis" has been the subject of prolonged debate among scholars of American Jewry. For the "distancing" claim, see Steven M. Cohen, "Are American and Israeli Jews Drifting Apart?," and Steven M. Cohen, "Did American Jews Really Grow More Distant from Israel, 1983–1993?— A Reconsideration," in Allon Gal, ed., *Envisioning Israel: The Changing Ideals and Images of North American Jews* (Jerusalem and Detroit: Magnes Press and Wayne State University Press, 1996), pp. 352–373; Steven M. Cohen and Ari Y. Kelman, "Beyond Distancing: Young Adult American Jews and Their Alienation from Israel" (New York: Andrea and Charles Bronfman Philanthropies, 2007); Steven M. Cohen and Ari Y. Kelman, "Thinking about Distancing from Israel," *Contemporary Jewry* vol. 30 (2010): 287–296; Steven M. Cohen and Ari Y. Kelman, "Distancing Is Closer than Ever," *Contemporary Jewry* vol. 30 (2010): 145–148. For the counter-argument, see Theodore Sasson, Benjamin Phillips, Graham Wright, Charles Kadushin, and Leonard Saxe, "Understanding Young Adult Attachment to Israel: Period, Lifecycle and Generational Dynamics," *Contemporary Jewry* vol. 32 (2012): 67–84; Theodore Sasson, Charles Kadushin, and Leonard Saxe, "On Sampling, Evidence and Theory: Concluding Remarks on the Distancing Debate," *Contemporary Jewry* vol. 30 (2010): 149–153. For useful overviews of the debate about the "distancing hypothesis," see Shmuel Rosner and Inbal Hakman, *The Challenge of Peoplehood: Strengthening the Attachment of Young American Jews to Israel in the Time of the Distancing Discourse* (Jerusalem: Jewish People Policy Institute, 2011); Ron Miller and Arnold Dashefsky, "Brandeis v. Cohen et al.: The Distancing from Israel Debate," *Contemporary Jewry* vol. 30 (2009): 155–164.

154. The question of whether American Jewry and Israel were "drifting apart" was the subject of a symposium organized by the American Jewish Committee in New York City on November 4, 1989.

155. Rosner and Hakman suggest that one reason why the claim of distancing is so popular in the American Jewish community is because it serves a variety of political, organizational, philanthropic, and denominational interests. Rosner and Hakman, *The Challenge of Peoplehood*, pp. 20–23.

156. Some surveys have shown that young Jews feel less attached to Israel than older ones. For instance, in a 2007 survey less than half of American Jews under the age of 35 agreed with the statement, "Israel's destruction would be a personal tragedy." Cohen and Kelman, "Beyond Distancing."

157. Sasson et al., "Still Connected: American Jewish Attitudes about Israel." See also Sasson, *The New American Zionism*, pp. 138–143.

158. Theodore Sasson, Charles Kadushin, and Leonard Saxe, "Trends in American Jewish Attachment to Israel," *Contemporary Jewry* vol. 30 (2010).

159. Steven M. Cohen, "Israel in the Jewish Identity of American Jews: A Study in Dualities and Contrasts," in David Gordis and Yoav Ben Horin, eds., *Jewish Identity in America* (Los Angeles: Wilstein Institute, 1991), p. 131.

160. In the 1990s, the reallocation of communal funds by Jewish Federations away from Israel and toward local needs was widely interpreted as evidence of American Jewish distancing from Israel. For this view, see Rosenthal, *Irreconcilable Differences?*, p. 172.

161. The AJC annual surveys show no decline in American Jewish attachment to Israel since 2001, with between two-thirds to three-quarters of American Jews consistently reporting feeling either "very close" or "fairly close" to Israel (72 percent in 2001, 73 percent in 2002, 74 percent in 2003, 75 percent in 2004, 77 percent in 2005, 76 percent in 2006, 70 percent in 2007, 67 percent in 2008, 69 percent in 2009, 74 percent in 2010, 68 percent in 2011). The Pew Report states that "emotional attachment to Israel has not waned discernibly among American Jews in the last decade." Pew Research Center, "A Portrait of Jewish Americans," p. 13.

162. Recent research even suggests that attachment to Israel may actually be increasing among young non-Orthodox American Jews. A 2012 survey of non-Orthodox American Jews below the age of 35 found that they were much more attached to Israel than those between the ages of 35 and 44. The likely reason for this is the fact that younger Jews are more likely to have visited Israel due to the "Birthright Israel" program—what Steven Cohen has called the "Birthright Bump." Chemi Shalev, "Poll: Young American Jews Are Growing More Attached to Israel," *Ha'aretz*, July 9, 2012.

163. Steven M. Cohen, "Disturbed or Distant? They're Not the Same," *ejewish philanthropy*, February 24, 2012; available at http://ejewishphilanthropy.com/disturbed-or-distant-theyre-not-the-same/ (accessed November 9, 2015). Even being ashamed of Israel, as some American Jews now claim to be, implies some sense of attachment to it since we are only ashamed of people, groups, or countries that we feel we belong to in some sense. We might be ashamed of a member of our family, for example, but we do not feel ashamed by the actions of someone who is completely unrelated to us. Shame, like embarrassment, implies an existing emotional attachment.

164. A survey of rabbinical students of the Jewish Theological Seminary (affiliated with the Conservative movement), for instance, found that they were strongly attached to Israel but also critical of it, with most holding dovish views on the Israeli-Palestinian conflict and left-wing views on Israeli policy issues. Steven M. Cohen, "JTS Rabbis and Israel, Then and Now: The 2011 Survey of JTS Ordained Rabbis and Current Students," *Jewish Political Studies Review* vol. 24 (2012): 59–98.

165. Shain, *Kinship and Diasporas in International Affairs*, p. 68.

166. Jack Wertheimer, "American Jews and Israel: A 60-Year Retrospective," p. 74.

CHAPTER 2: THE END OF "ISRAEL, RIGHT OR WRONG"

1. Quoted in Ron Kampeas, "ADL's Foxman Explains His 'Yes' on J Street, ZOA's Klein His 'No,'" *Jewish Telegraphic Agency*, April 29, 2014.

2. Available at https://www.facebook.com/notes/all-thats-left-anti-occupation -collective/press-release-bennett-interrupted/455238114551564 (accessed July 15, 2013).

3. Marla Brettschneider, *Cornerstones of Peace: Jewish Identity Politics and Democratic Theory* (New Brunswick, NJ: Rutgers University Press, 1996), p. 1.

4. Quoted in Laurence J. Silberstein, "American Jewry's Identification with Israel Problems and Prospects," in Alan T. Levenson, ed., *The Wiley-Blackwell History of Jews and Judaism* (Oxford, UK: Wiley-Blackwell, 2012), p. 619.

5. Rosenthal, *Irreconcilable Differences?*, p. 1.

6. Ibid., p. xiii.

7. Steven M. Cohen and Charles S. Liebman, "Israel and American Jewry in the Twenty-First Century," in Allon Gal and Alfred Gottschalk, eds., *Beyond Survival and Philanthropy* (Cincinnati: Hebrew Union College Press, 2000), p. 13.

8. Jeremy Ben-Ami, *A New Voice for Israel: Fighting for the Survival of the Jewish Nation* (New York: Palgrave Macmillan, 2011), p. 155.

9. Pew Research Center, "A Portrait of American Jews," p. 14.

10. Arthur Hertzberg, "World Jewry Is Not an Amen Chorus," *Ha'aretz*, January 7, 2004.

11. Gary Rosenblatt, "When Israel Becomes a Source of Embarrassment," *Jewish Week*, March 8, 2011.

12. Uri Misgav, "On July 4, Marking the Independence of American Jewry," *Ha'aretz*, July 4, 2013.

13. According to a study on American Jewish philanthropy, in 2007 U.S.-based not-for-profit groups raised $40 million for Israeli settlements and $46 million for progressive groups in Israel (groups that advocate for civil rights, human rights, women's rights, democracy, and co-existence). The New Israel Fund alone raised $29 million in 2007. Eric Fleisch and Theodore Sasson, *The New Philanthropy: American Jewish Giving to Israeli Organizations*, p. 6.

See also Josh Nathan-Kazis, "U.S. Groups Raise $40 Million for Settlements," *Forward*, May 1, 2012.

14. Daniel Abraham, the founder of Slim Fast Foods and a major donor to the Democratic Party, funded two nonprofit organizations (One Voice and V15) that actively campaigned for a change in government in the run-up to the Israeli election in March 2015.

15. Steven Bayme, "American Jewry Confronts the Twenty-First Century," p. 35.

16. Rabbi Jill Jacobs, "Diaspora Jews Want to Be Israel's partners—Not Only Its Donors," *Ha'aretz*, March 11, 2013.

17. There are some rare occasions when left-wing and right-wing American Jews have found a common reason to criticize Israel. See, for instance, Ron Kampeas, "From Left to Right, American Jews Are Criticizing Israeli Anti-boycott Law," *Jewish Telegraphic Agency*, July 12, 2011.

18. Criticism of Israeli government policies occurred within the Jewish Student Movement in the late 1960s and early 1970s, which emerged out of the wider left-wing student movement and counterculture of the era. Aliza Becker, "The American Jewish Peace Movement for a Two-State Solution to the Israeli-Palestinian Conflict: An Overview of National Initiatives, 1969–2012," (Washington, DC: Brit Tzedek v'Shalom, 2013).

19. Groups like the Committee on New Alternatives in the Middle East (CONAME) in the early 1970s, Breira in the mid-1970s, and New Jewish Agenda in the early 1980s.

20. Individuals like Balfour Brickner, Philip Klutznick, Ted Mann, Rabbi Alexander Schindler, Rabbi Joachim Prinz, and Rabbi Arthur Hertzberg.

21. Albert Vorspan, "Soul Searching," *New York Times Magazine*, May 8, 1988.

22. Arthur Hertzberg, "World Jewry Is Not an Amen Chorus," *Ha'aretz*, January 7, 2004.

23. Ron Kampeas, "Defending Israel, Mainstream U.S. Groups Critique It," *Jewish Telegraphic Agency*, January 11, 2011.

24. Jeremy Ben-Ami, *A New Voice for Israel*, p. xiii.

25. Rabbi Jill Jacobs, "Diaspora Jews Want to Be Israel's Partners."

26. Caryn S. Aviv and David Shneer, *New Jews: The End of the Jewish Diaspora* (New York: New York University Press, 2005).

27. In the past few years, especially since the 2008–2009 Gaza War and the publication of the "Goldstone Report," there has been a concerted effort by some right-wing groups (most notably Im Tirzu) and political parties in Israel (such as Yisrael Beiteinu) to vilify and discredit certain liberal and left-wing nongovernmental organizations (B'Tselem, Breaking the Silence, Zochrot, and the New Israel Fund, in particular), and to restrict freedom of speech in Israel, specifically calls for boycotts of Israel and/or its West Bank settlements or "slandering" the IDF. See, for instance, Isabel Kershner, "Israeli Rights Groups View Themselves as Under Siege," *New York Times*, April 5, 2010; Isabel Kershner, "Israel Bans Boycotts against the State," *New York Times*, July

11, 2011; Edmund Sanders, "Israel Struggles with Free-speech Rights," *Los Angeles Times*, July 31, 2011.

28. Tony Judt was particularly denounced for his 2003 article in the *New York Review of Books* titled "Israel: The Alternative." In it, Judt described the Jewish state as a "dysfunctional anachronism" in today's world, and suggested that it should eventually become a binational state. Tony Judt, "Israel: The Alternative," *New York Review of Books*, October 23, 2003. Judith Butler, a professor at the University of California-Berkeley, has been attacked for her vocal support for the international "Boycott, Divestment, and Sanctions" (BDS) campaign against Israel. Norman Finkelstein has been a bête noire for many within the American Jewish community since the publication of his controversial book *The Holocaust Industry: Reflections on the Exploitation of Jewish Suffering* (New York: Verso, 2000).

29. See, for instance, Jonathan Tobin, "Anti-Zionists Must Not Be Allowed to Hijack the Jewish Community," *Commentary*, February 21, 2014.

30. Magid, "Butler Trouble," pp. 248–251.

31. Peter Beinart received scorn and withering personal criticism for his 2012 book *The Crisis of Zionism*. See, Bret Stephens, "Peter Beinart's False Prophecy," *Tablet Magazine*, March 26, 2012; Sol Stern, "Beinart the Unwise," *Commentary*, April 1, 2012; Daniel Gordis, "A Dose of Nuance: Peter Beinart's Mis-identity Crisis," *Jerusalem Post*, April 11, 2012. Thomas Friedman was accused of abetting anti-Semitism for suggesting in one of his columns that Israeli Prime Minister Benjamin Netanyahu received a standing ovation in the U.S. Congress because of the pro-Israel lobby's influence there. See Jonathan S. Tobin, "Thomas Friedman and the New Anti-Semitism-Part One," *Commentary*, December 14, 2011.

32. Hody Nemes, "Feud over Israel Erupts at Jewish Institutions," *Forward*, February 24, 2014; Uriel Heilman, "Hosting Israel critics? Jewish Institutions Damned if They Do, Damned if They Don't," *Jewish Telegraphic Agency*, February 25, 2014; Michael Kaplan, "Boycott Israel Backer Judith Butler Pulls Out of Jewish Museum Appearance," *Forward*, February 2, 2014.

33. Lisa Wangsness, "Newton Synagogue Cancels Talk by Critic of Israeli Policies," *Boston Globe*, November 17, 2010. This has not been the only time when representatives of J Street have been prevented from speaking in local synagogues.

34. Kim Severson, "Jewish Book Event in Atlanta Cancels Author's Talk on Zionism, and Uproar Follows," *New York Times*, November 13, 2012.

35. Marc Fisher, "For Jewish Groups, a Stand-off between Open Debate and Support of Israel," *Washington Post*, May 28, 2014.

36. Ben-Ami, *A New Voice for Israel*, p. 133.

37. Heilman, "Hosting Israel Critics?"

38. Rachel Corrie was a young American activist in the pro-Palestinian International Solidarity Movement who was crushed to death by an Israeli bulldozer while protesting in the Gaza Strip on March 16, 2003.

39. The invitation for Cindy Corrie to speak was what generated the most out-
    rage. On the controversy, see Matthai Kuruvila, "Documentary Sparks Uproar
    at Jewish Film Fest," *San Francisco Chronicle*, July 25, 2009; Stacey Palevsky,
    "At Festival, Rachel Corrie Film Is a Lightning Rod," *J Weekly*, July 27, 2009.

40. "JCF Policy on Israel-Related Programming by Its Grantees, February 18,
    2010"; available at http://sfjcf.wordpress.com/2010/02/18/policy/ (accessed
    October 15, 2012).

41. Alan Snitow and Deborah Kaufman, "A Chill in San Francisco," *Forward*,
    April 23, 2010. For a more positive opinion on the guidelines, see "Drawing
    a Line in the Bay," *Forward Editorial*, March 26, 2010.

42. Nathan Guttman, "JCCs Are a New Front in the Culture War on Israel,"
    Forward, March 23, 2011.

43. Ibid.

44. Marc Fisher, "For Jewish Groups, a Stand-off between Open Debate and
    Support of Israel," *Washington Post*, May 28, 2014.

45. Nathan Guttman, "Theater J Scales Back Show as Pro-Israel Critics Pressure
    Washington D.C. Troupe," *Forward*, October 18, 2013; Marc Fisher, "For
    Jewish Groups, a Stand-off between Open Debate and Support of Israel,"
    Washington Post, May 28, 2014.

46. Nathan Guttman, "DCJCC Cancels Theater J's Middle East Festival,
    Prompting Censorship Debate," *Forward*, November 25, 2014.

47. Peter Marks, "Artistic Director Ari Roth Is Fired from Theater J," *Washington
    Post*, December 18, 2014.

48. Jeremy Ben-Ami, for instance, claims that the "campaign against dissent"
    has been "extraordinarily effective" and that "[t]he overall atmosphere in the
    United States when it comes to discussing Israel is becoming one of intim-
    idation and fear." Jeremy Ben-Ami, *A New Voice for Israel*, pp. 133–134. The
    same claim has been made about the political atmosphere concerning Israel
    in other Jewish communities in the Diaspora such as Britain and France.
    Antony Lerman, for example, writes that "outside of Israel the atmosphere
    surrounding controversial issues has in recent years become ever more
    oppressive. . . . [A] new fundamentalism has taken hold." Antony Lerman,
    "Touching a Raw Nerve," in Anne Karpf, Brian Klug, Jacqueline Rose, and
    Barbara Rosenbaum, eds., *A Time to Speak Out: Independent Jewish Voices on
    Israel, Zionism and Jewish Identity* (London, UK: Verso, 2008), p. 164. Sim-
    ilarly, Jonathan Freedland, a prominent Jewish newspaper columnist in the
    United Kingdom, claims that: "People [within the British Jewish commu-
    nity] are frightened to say what they feel [about Israel]." Quoted in David
    Landau, "Alive and Well," *Economist*, July 28, 2012. For a similar claim about
    the French Jewish community, see Esther Benbassa, "How One Becomes a
    Traitor," in Nathalie Debrauwere-Miller, ed., *Israeli-Palestinian Conflict in the
    Francophone World* (New York: Routledge, 2010), pp. 232–249.

49. For instance, the documentary film *Between Two Worlds: The American Jewish
    Culture Wars*, which explored the divisions within the Jewish community

over Israel and the attempts to suppress criticism of Israel was, ironically, not screened in many Jewish film festivals because of pressure from funders, board members, or local community members. Deborah Kaufman, "The Jewish Community's Drift Toward the Right," *Tikkun*, July 13, 2012.

50. According to Kenneth Bob (the leader of the left-wing American Zionist group Ameinu), Jewish institutions and synagogues often feel obligated to "balance" a left-wing speaker with a right-wing speaker. Thus, the expression of left-wing criticism of Israel is permissible in Jewish communal settings as long as it can be countered and rebutted. The same is not true of right-wing opinions about Israel, which are often expressed in Jewish venues without being "balanced" with a left-wing opinion. Author interview with Kenneth Bob, November 10, 2011.

51. Since the controversy over the screening of the film about Rachel Corrie, for example, the San Francisco Jewish film festival has continued to show films that are critical of Israel—among the films shown at its 2012 festival, for instance, were "The Law in These Parts" and "My Neighborhood," both of which are highly critical of the Israeli occupation of the West Bank and East Jerusalem—and the director of the film festival insists that despite the fallout from the Rachel Corrie episode, the festival is still willing to screen controversial films about Israel. Judy Maltz, "At Jewish Film Fests, Lights, Camera, Controversy!" *Ha'aretz*, July 31, 2012. Others, however, claim that the San Francisco Jewish Film Festival has become more cautious about the films it screens concerning Israel and the groups that it partners with. Author interview with filmmakers Deborah Kaufman and Alan Snitow, November 11, 2013.

52. In recent years, the question of whether Jews should publicly criticize Israel has been a major subject of debate within a number of Diaspora Jewish communities, not just in the United States. See, for instance, Simon Rocker, "Shock over Senior UK Jewish Leader's Bibi Criticism," *Jewish Chronicle*, November 18, 2010; Ben Weinthal, "German Jews Feud over Criticizing Israel," *Forward*, March 9, 2007; Ben Cubby, "Jewish Coalition Calls for Open Debate on Palestine," *Sydney Morning Herald*, March 6, 2007.

53. J. J. Goldberg, *Jewish Power: Inside the American Jewish Establishment*, p. 206.

54. Steven M. Cohen, "Israel in the Jewish Identity of American Jews: A Study in Dualities and Contrasts," in David Gordis and Yoav Ben Horin, eds., *Jewish Identity in America* (Los Angeles: Wilstein Institute, 1991), p. 131.

55. Quoted in Glen Frankel, *Beyond the Promised Land: Jews and Arabs on a hard road to a new Israel* (New York: Simon & Schuster 1994), p. 222.

56. Israeli leaders have often voiced this opinion. Prime Minister Shamir, for example, bluntly stated during the first Intifada: "When Israel decides, the Jews of America must support it. We are on the front line." Quoted in Albert Vorspan, "Soul Searching," *New York Times Magazine*, May 8, 1988.

57. Quoted in Sol Stern, "Menachem Begin vs. the Jewish Lobby," *New York Magazine*, April 24, 1978.

58. For example, Rabbi Eric H. Yoffie, the past president of the Union for Reform Judaism, has argued that: "Zionism brought Israel into existence and bestowed upon Jews everywhere a role in determining the character of the Jewish state. While final authority rests with Israel's citizens, whether Jewish or other, Israel is not primarily the state of Israelis; it is the state of the Jewish people. Israel invites Jews of every country in the Diaspora not only to visit frequently, contribute financially, and generate support for its policies, but also to engage in its affairs, participate in its debates, and offer criticism of its actions. Expressing criticism, even harsh criticism, requires no special permission from Israeli or Diaspora leaders; the right to do so is inherent in the Zionist mission." Eric H. Yoffie, "Muzzled by the Minority," *Reform Judaism*, September 27, 2014.

59. J. J. Goldberg, "Criticize Away," *Havruta* no. 8, February 2012.

60. Jeremy Ben-Ami, *A New Voice for Israel*, p. 160.

61. In a national survey taken in 1981, for instance, 57 percent of American Jews disagreed with the statement: "American Jews should not publicly criticize the policies of the government of Israel"; and in a 2007 survey, 52 percent disagreed and only 26 percent agreed with this statement. Steven M. Cohen, "Ties and Tensions: The 1986 Survey of American Jewish Attitudes toward Israel and Israelis," American Jewish Committee, 1987, pp. 58–59; Cohen and Kelman, "Beyond Distancing,"

62. In a November 2012 survey, 46 percent of American Jews agreed that it is better for Israel when the American Jewish community "speaks with a unified voice regarding Israeli government policy," compared to 30 percent who disagreed with this. With regards to their own interests, 40 percent of American Jews agreed with the statement: "The interests of American Jews are best served when the Jewish community speaks with a unified voice regarding Israeli government policy," whereas 36 percent believed that "the interests of American Jews are best served when different voices in the Jewish community express their differences regarding Israeli government policy." J Street's Post-Election Survey of 800 American Jewish voters conducted on November 6, 2012.

63. Thirty-one percent of American Jews surveyed in November 2012 said that they were bothered when American Jews disagreed publicly with Israeli government policy. J Street's Post-Election Survey of 800 American Jewish voters conducted on November 6, 2012.

64. Author interview with Malcolm Hoenlein, Executive Vice Chairman of the Conference of Presidents, conducted in New York City on October 31, 2011.

65. According to Kenneth Jacobson, the deputy director of the ADL, his organization is willing to publicly criticize Israel on internal issues like racism against Arabs and religious pluralism, but it refrains from criticizing Israel on issues of security and the peace process. Author interview with Kenneth Jacobson, October 27, 2011.

66. Steven Rosenthal goes so far as to describe the injunction against American Jewish criticism of Israel's security policies as "an eleventh commandment for American Jews." Rosenthal, *Irreconcilable Differences?*, p. 123.

67. See, for instance, Gal Beckerman, "Conversion Bill Sparks Unusual Push Back from Diaspora Jews," *Forward*, March 26 2010.

68. Ron Kampeas, "Defending Israel, Mainstream U.S. Groups Critique It," *Jewish Telegraphic Agency*, January 11, 2011; "U.S. Jewish Groups Take Israel's Government to Task over 'Jewish State' Bill," *Jewish Telegraphic Agency*, December 3, 2014.

69. For information about this task force, see its website, www.iataskforce.org/.

70. See "U.S. Jewish Groups Slam Rabbis Anti-migrant Decrees," *Jewish Telegraphic Agency*, June 11, 2010; Ron Friedman, "Do Not Send These Children Away, Foxman Pleads," *Jerusalem Post*, October 20, 2010.

71. Ron Kampeas, "Defending Israel, Mainstream U.S. Groups Critique It," *Jewish Telegraphic Agency*, January 11, 2011.

72. On the eve of the Annapolis summit meeting between Israeli Prime Minister Olmert and Palestinian Authority President Mahmoud Abbas in November 2007, for instance, Malcolm Hoenlein said in an interview that when it comes to the issue of the future of Jerusalem: "It's a question where everyone has a right, if not an obligation to speak out." Quoted in Ron Kampeas and Ami Eden, "Debate Erupts over Role of Jewish Groups," *Jewish Telegraphic Agency*, November 19, 2007. In the same interview, Hoenlein himself publicly criticized Israel's deputy prime minister at the time, Haim Ramon, for his stated willingness to give up Israeli control over some Arab neighborhoods in East Jerusalem in the framework of a final peace agreement with the Palestinians. See also James D. Besser, "New Coalition to Fight Any Division of Jerusalem," *Jewish Week*, October 18, 2007; Shlomo Shamir, "Reform Head: U.S. Jews Must Not Oppose Compromise on Jerusalem," *Ha'aretz*, December 23, 2007.

73. Author interview with Dan Fleshler, board member of Ameinu and Americans for Peace Now, October 13, 2011.

74. According to Goldberg, the real injunction concerning Diaspora Jewish criticism of Israel is: "Diaspora Jews should never tell Israel what to do (unless they're telling it to be more hardline)." J. J. Goldberg, "Criticize Away," *Havruta* no. 8, February 2012.

75. See, for instance, Leonard Fein, "How Big a Tent," *Forward*, March 31, 2011; Nathan Guttman, "How Big Is Jewish 'Tent' on Israel?" *Forward*, November 8, 2011.

76. The group deliberately chose a Hebrew name in order to signify its commitment to Israel. Marla Brettschneider, *Cornerstones of Peace: Jewish Identity Politics and Democratic Theory*, p. 42.

77. At the time, the ruling Labor Party preferred to hand the West Bank over to Jordanian control in return for a peace agreement, while the Likud wanted Israel to permanently keep the territory.

78. Jack Wertheimer, "Breaking the Taboo: Critics of Israel and the American Jewish Establishment," in Allon Gal, ed., *Envisioning Israel* (Detroit: Wayne State University Press, 1996), pp. 397–419.

79. "Breira Statement of Purpose," quoted in Steven T. Rosenthal, *Irreconcilable Differences?*, p. 36. Steven Rosenthal argues that "Breira's real 'sin' in the eyes

of the [American Jewish] establishment was to go public with its criticism of Israel and to urge others to do so, thereby destroying the illusion of unity that the mainstream organizations had labored so mightily to build." Rosenthal, *Irreconcilable Differences?*, p. 37.

80. Quoted in Wertheimer, "Breaking the Taboo," p. 399.

81. Marla Brettschneider writes that Breira was the target of "a smear campaign designed to delegitimize the organization." Brettschneider, *Cornerstones of Peace*, p. 46.

82. Quoted in Rosenthal, *Irreconcilable Differences?*, p. 38.

83. Quoted in Brettschneider, *Cornerstones of Peace*, p. 44.

84. Rosenthal, *Irreconcilable Differences?*, pp. 38–39.

85. B'nai B'rith came under a lot of external pressure to stop its Hillel rabbis from being involved in Breira. After initially resisting this pressure, it eventually issued guidelines stating that its employees were "expected to take into account the effects of conduct, including the expression of opinions that conflict with the objectives of B'nai B'rith and its maintenance and growth . . . and also weigh the effects of actions and speech . . . upon the fulfillment of the responsibilities of [a] . . . staff position." Quoted in Wertheimer, "Breaking the Taboo," p. 403.

86. Brettschneider, *Cornerstones of Peace*, pp. 43–44.

87. Rosenthal, *Irreconcilable Differences?*, p. 39.

88. Breira's methods were also very conventional. It never organized any demonstrations or sit-ins, nor did its members disrupt any meetings. It just produced pamphlets and a small magazine, sent out letters to its members, and arranged for some Israeli politicians and former generals to speak to Jewish audiences in the United States. Brettschneider, *Cornerstones of Peace*, p. 43.

89. Brettschneider, *Cornerstones of Peace*, pp. 42–43; Becker, *The American Jewish Peace Movement for a Two-State Solution to the Israeli-Palestinian Conflict*.

90. Brettschneider, *Cornerstones of Peace*, p. 41.

91. Becker, *The American Jewish Peace Movement for a Two-State Solution to the Israeli-Palestinian Conflict*.

92. Wertheimer, "Breaking the Taboo," p. 416.

93. For a detailed history of New Jewish Agenda, see Ezra Berkley Nepon, *Justice, Justice Shall You Pursue: A History of New Jewish Agenda* (Philadelphia: Thread Makes Blanket Press, 2012).

94. Wertheimer, "Breaking the Taboo," p. 410; Rosenthal, *Irreconcilable Differences?*, p. 120. Unlike Breira, New Jewish Agenda was a multi-issue Jewish organization, but it became increasingly focused on the issue of Israeli-Palestinian peace.

95. Becker, *The American Jewish Peace Movement for a Two-State Solution to the Israeli-Palestinian Conflict*.

96. Quoted in Wertheimer, "Breaking the Taboo," p. 409.

97. Becker, *The American Jewish Peace Movement for a Two-State Solution to the Israeli-Palestinian Conflict*.

98. Whereas local Breira chapters only managed to be admitted into the JCRCs of New Haven and San Francisco, New Jewish Agenda chapters gained admission into local Jewish councils or Jewish federations in Kansas City, New Haven, Ann Arbor, Santa Fe, and, most significantly, Los Angeles. Wertheimer, "Breaking the Taboo," p. 411.

99. Becker, *The American Jewish Peace Movement for a Two-State Solution to the Israeli-Palestinian Conflict.*

100. Wertheimer, "Breaking the Taboo," p. 412.

101. This also explains why APN was admitted into the Conference of Presidents, as Marla Brettschneider argues: "the difference between the fates of Breira and APN . . . is directly related to the developing ability of the [American Jewish] community to open its ears, to tolerate and work with dissent." Brettschneider, *Cornerstones of Peace*, p. 55.

102. Jeremy Ben-Ami, *A New Voice for Israel*, p. 106.

103. See for instance, Morton Klein, "J Street Should Rescind Its Invitation to Al-Marayati," *Jewish Telegraphic Agency*, September 9, 2009; Lenny Ben-David, "Protecting the Quarterback in the White House," *Jerusalem Post*, September 13, 2009; Isi Leibler, "J Street's 'Pro-Israel' Stance Is Phoney," *Guardian*, October 26, 2009; Natasha Mozgovaya, "Dershowitz Lays into J Street in AIPAC Conference Dust-up," *Ha'aretz*, March 22, 2010.

104. Rabbi Eric Yoffie, the president of the Union for Reform Judaism, publicly rebuked J Street for its stance on the Gaza War, describing it as "morally deficient, profoundly out of touch with Jewish sentiment and also appallingly naïve." Quoted in James Traub, "The New Israel Lobby," *New York Times Magazine*, September 13, 2009.

105. Hilary Leila Krieger, "J Street Donors Include Muslims, Arabs," *Jerusalem Post*, August 14, 2009.

106. Author interview with Rachel Lerner, Senior Vice President of J Street for Community Relations, December 6, 2013.

107. In March 2011, the Knesset Immigration, Absorption and Public Diplomacy Committee even held a hearing to determine whether J Street could call itself "pro-Israel." During the occasionally raucous meeting, which was unprecedented in the history of the Knesset, the chairman of the committee, Likud MK Danny Danon asserted that: "J Street is pro-Palestinian and not pro-Israel." Another member of the committee, Kadima MK Otniel Schneller, told J Street's director Jeremy Ben-Ami, who came in person to testify before the committee, that: "You are not Zionists and you do not care about Israeli interests." Quoted in Rebecca Anna Stoil, "Raucous Knesset Committee Debates J Street," *Jerusalem Post*, March 23, 2011. See also Ethan Bronner, "U.S. Group Stirs Debate on Being 'Pro-Israel,'" *New York Times*, March 24, 2011.

108. Morton A. Klein and Daniel Mandel, "ZOA Report: J Street—Siding with Israel's Enemies," April 8, 2013; available at http://zoa.org/2013/04/10196411 -zoa-report-j-street-siding-with-israels-enemies/ (accessed August 4, 2014).

109. See the film's website, http://thejstreetchallenge.com/ (accessed August 9, 2014).

110. J Street's rapid growth was partly the result of its "friendly takeovers" of other like-minded organizations. In May 2009, J Street took over the Jewish campus group the Union of Progressive Zionists to form J Street U, enabling it to reach out to college students. In January 2010, it took over *Brit Tzedek v'Shalom* (Jewish Alliance for Justice and Peace), acquiring its network of 50,000 grassroots activists and 40 local chapters. Nathan Guttman, "J Street Makes a Strategic Acquisition," *Forward*, September 4, 2009.

111. In the Pew Research Center's 2013 survey of American Jews, 48 percent said they doubted that the Netanyahu government was making a sincere effort to achieve a peace agreement with the Palestinians, compared to 38 percent who trusted the Israeli government's sincerity. Only 26 percent of young American Jews (those aged between 18 and 29) believed that the Israeli government was making a "sincere effort" to come to a peace settlement. Pew Survey, p. 89.

112. Peter Beinart, "Establishment's Rebuff Highlights J Street's Success in Changing Jewish America," *Ha'aretz*, May 7, 2014.

113. Israeli diplomats and politicians (including members of the right-wing Likud Party) now regularly attend J Street's annual conference in Washington, DC. According to an anonymous senior government official in Israel, the Israeli government regards J Street as "significant." The same official even described J Street as a friend, albeit one with whom the Israeli government had disagreements. Ron Kampeas, "J Street and Israel Are Still Arguing—But on Friendlier Terms," *Jewish Telegraphic Agency*, March 27, 2012.

114. Author interview with Rachel Lerner, Senior Vice President of J Street for Community Relations, December 6, 2013.

115. J Street's Boston chapter, for example, became a member of the Boston JCRC despite heavy lobbying against its inclusion by CAMERA, a Jewish media watchdog group. See Naomi Zeveloff, "J Street Accepted in Some, Not All, Cities," *Forward*, December 23, 2011. J Street chapters in Baltimore, Atlanta, and San Francisco have also been admitted into their local JCRCs.

116. The Jewish Student Union at the University of California, Berkeley, however, has twice rejected J Street U's application to become a member. "Berkeley Jewish Student Union Rejects J Street affiliate," *Jewish Telegraphic Agency*, October 11, 2013.

117. Author interview with Rachel Lerner, Senior Vice President of J Street for Community Relations, December 6, 2013.

118. Ibid.

119. Ben-Ami, *A New Voice for Israel*, p. 105.

120. Ron Kampeas, "J Street Confab's Message: We've Arrived," *Jewish Telegraphic Agency*, September 24, 2013.

121. Quoted in James Traub, "The New Israel Lobby," *New York Times Magazine*, September 13, 2009.

122. Author interview with Rachel Lerner, Senior Vice President of J Street for Community Relations, December 6, 2013.

123. J Street failed to win the support of the two-thirds majority of the entire Conference of Presidents, or 34 of the 51 member groups, that it needed to join the organization (it received only 17 votes in favor of its membership, with 22 votes against it, and 3 abstentions). Nathan Guttman, "J Street Fails Badly in Bid for Admission to Presidents Conference," *Forward*, April 30, 2014.

124. J.J. Goldberg, "Blackballing J Street: Who Voted How," *Forward*, May 4, 2014.

125. Some American Jewish leaders publicly criticized the vote as "misguided" and "destructive." Rabbi Julie Schonfeld, "Fear and Exclusion of J Street Is Misguided and Destructive," *Ha'aretz*, May 2, 2014. Others defended it, claiming that: "the vote represented the consensus of the American Jewish community, which regards J Street and its policies to lie beyond the pale." Rabbi Pesach Lerner, "J Street Belongs outside the Pale," *Times of Israel*, May 4, 2014.

126. AIPAC and the AJC, two other major establishment organizations in the Conference of Presidents, either abstained or voted against J Street's application for membership (neither organization publicly stated its position). J.J. Goldberg, "Blackballing J Street," *Forward*, May 4, 2014.

127. See, John Ruskay, "Combating Delegitimization Requires a Big Tent," *Jewish Week*, February 15, 2011.

128. Quoted in Chemi Shalev, "J Street U Takes on Jewish Community's 'Hypocrisy' on Occupation," *Ha'aretz*, January 22, 2015.

129. Martin Raffel, the senior vice president of the JCPA, has stated: "Those who can unequivocally express support for Israel as the democratic homeland of the Jewish people, I think in general ought to be welcomed inside the tent . . . ." Quoted in Julie Wiener, "The Delegitimization Dance," *Jewish Week*, November 30, 2010. Similarly, William Daroff, the vice president for public policy and director of the Washington office of the Jewish Federations of North America (JFNA) has stated: "We must have a big tent of organizations and belief. Not everyone will agree on many of the specifics. . . . But we embrace those organizations and individuals who hold core beliefs in Israel as a democratic Jewish state that is the eternal home of the Jewish people." Quoted in Stewart Ain, "Consensus Seen Taking Shape on Boycotts," *Jewish Week*, March 15, 2011.

130. The "Israel Action Network" was launched by the Jewish Federations and the Jewish Council for Public Affairs to combat the "delegitimization of Israel," but it lacks a working definition of "delegitimization," and its first major campaign was gathering over 100,000 signatures to an online petition against the Palestinians' "Unilateral Declaration of Independence" (that is, the Palestinian attempt to secure UN recognition of a Palestinian state) in September 2011—a Palestinian initiative that explicitly accepted a two-state solution to the Israeli-Palestinian conflict and thus Israel's existence. On the Israel Action Network, see Martin Raffel and Michael Kotzin, "Introducing

the Israel Action Network," *Jerusalem Post*, October 26, 2010; James Besser, "Jewish Federations Join Fight against Israel Delegitimization, but Is That Smart?" *Jewish Week*, October 26, 2010.

131. Within the organized American Jewish community, it is widely believed that the real purpose of the global BDS campaign is not to end Israel's occupation of the West Bank and East Jerusalem, but to delegitimize Israel's right to exist as a Jewish state. The BDS campaign is also seen as one-sided, solely holding Israel responsible for the continuation of the Israeli-Palestinian conflict, and resting on an unfair and inaccurate analogy between Israel and Apartheid-era South Africa. Not only is it forbidden in the organized Jewish community to support BDS, it is difficult—and quite rare—to even have a public discussion about it in Jewish communal settings. A prominent Conservative synagogue on the Upper West Side of Manhattan, for example, backed out of a contract to host a Jewish panel discussion about equality and democracy in Israel out of concern that the event might involve a discussion of BDS (even though the synagogue was not sponsoring the event, but merely renting out its space, and two of the four speakers on the panel were opponents of BDS). In the words of the synagogue's rabbi, "the conversation about whether there should be an economic assault on the state of Israel, which would turn Israel into a pariah state on the scale of South Africa—that's not a conversation that we want to explore the merits of here. It's beyond the pale." Rabbi Jeremy Kalmanofsky, quoted in Sigal Samuel, "Fear Of BDS Spreads to Ansche Chesed," *Open Zion*, March 11, 2013; available at www.thedailybeast.com/articles/2013/03/11/fear-of-bds-spreads-to-ansche-chesed.html (accessed March 15, 2013).

132. For the San Francisco Federation guidelines, see "JCF Policy on Israel-Related Programming by Its Grantees, February 18, 2010"; available at http://sfjcf.wordpress.com/2010/02/18/policy/ (accessed October 15, 2012).

133. Hillel's "Guidelines for Campus Israel Activities"; available at www.hillel.org/israel/guidelines.htm (accessed May 25, 2012). For the background to the issuing of these guidelines by Hillel, see John B. Judis, "Hillel's Crackdown on Open Debate Is Bad News for American Jews," *New Republic*, January 6, 2014. Judis writes that: "These guidelines represented a final step in transforming Hillel from an umbrella organization for Jews on campus to a member of a pro-Israel coalition."

134. In November 2012, Harvard's Hillel also refused to host an event called "Jewish Voices against the Occupation" because it was cosponsored by a pro-Palestinian group that supported BDS. Julie Wiener, "Swarthmore Hillel Picks Fight over Campus Group's Israel Guidelines," *Jewish Telegraphic Agency*, December 11, 2013.

135. John B. Judis, "Hillel's Crackdown on Open Debate Is Bad News for American Jews," *New Republic*, January 6, 2014. See also Shaul Magid, "Who Is Boycotting Whom: National Hillel Guidelines, Dissent, and Legitimate Protest," *Zeek*, January 10, 2014; available at http://zeek.forward.com/articles/117993/ (accessed November 11, 2015).

136. Lex Rofes and Simone Zimmerman, "Pluralism in Hillel Must Extend to Israel," *Jewish Telegraphic Agency*, May 22, 2013; Jacob Plitman, "Hillel and Its Donors Repress Real Conversation about Israel," *Jewish Week*, December 15, 2013.

137. See the group's website, at http://www.openhillel.org (accessed January 7, 2014).

138. Derek Kwait, "Hillel Threatens Its Swarthmore Chapter with Expulsion over Israel Dispute," *Forward*, December 20, 2013; Laurie Goodstein, "Members of Jewish Student Group Test Permissible Discussion on Israel," *New York Times*, December 28, 2013.

139. For example, in February 2014, the Jewish student group at Vassar College joined the "Open Hillel" movement. Hody Nemes, "Vassar Jewish Students Break with Hillel on Israel," *Forward*, February 28, 2014.

140. Naomi Dann, "Want to Engage Young Jews? Look to Open Hillel," *Forward*, October 13, 2014; available at http://blogs.forward.com/forward-thinking/ 207280/want-to-engage-young-jews-look-to-open-hillel/?utm_source=Sail thru&utm_medium=email&utm_term=Opinion&utm_campaign=Opinion %202014-10-13#ixzz3G3xfwZdR (accessed October 13, 2014).

141. JVP initially campaigned for a limited boycott of Israeli companies operating in the West Bank and a selective divestment from companies that profit from Israel's occupation of the West Bank (such as the American corporation Caterpillar and the investment firm TIAA-CREF). In 2015, its board of directors voted to embrace the global BDS movement and call for a complete boycott of Israel and divestment from all Israeli companies. Evan Serpick, "Embracing Israel Boycott, Jewish Voice for Peace Insists on Its Jewish Identity," *Forward*, March 28, 2015.

142. JVP is officially neutral on the question of whether there should be one state or two states in Israel/Palestine. In the words of Rebecca Vilkomerson: "We do not take a position on one or two states. It's not our place as American Jews to take a position on that." Quoted in Gal Beckerman, "JVP, Harsh Critic of Israel, Seeks a Seat at the Communal Table," *Forward*, April 22, 2012. Many within the American Jewish community, however, see this stance as disingenuous and believe that JVP, or at least many of its members secretly harbor a desire for a binational state, especially because the group supports a right of return for Palestinian refugees to Israel. (JVP does not call for the return of all Palestinian refugees to Israel, but it wants Israel to acknowledge the Palestinian refugees' right of return and it calls for a "mutually agreed, just solution based on principles established in international law including return, compensation and/or resettlement.") See http://jewishvoiceforpeace.org/ content/jewish-voice-peace-faq#refugees (accessed November 10, 2015).

143. William Daroff, the vice president for public policy and director of the Washington office of the JFNA, quoted in Stewart Ain, "Consensus Seen Taking Shape on Boycotts," *Jewish Week*, March 15, 2011.

144. See http://www.adl.org/assets/pdf/israel-international/Top-10-Anti-Israel -Groups-in-America.pdf (accessed September 21, 2013).

145. Evan Serpick, "Embracing Israel Boycott, Jewish Voice for Peace Insists on Its Jewish Identity," *Forward*, March 28, 2015.

146. Interview with Rebecca Vilkomerson, executive director of Jewish Voice for Peace, October 20, 2011.

147. Gal Beckerman, "JVP, Harsh Critic of Israel, Seeks a Seat at the Communal Table," *Forward*, April 22, 2012.

148. Ibid.

149. Available at http://www.youngjewishproud.org/about/ (accessed September 21, 2013).

150. JVP activists have also disrupted a Birthright Israel conference in New York in November 2011.

151. Quoted in Joanna Steinhardt, "What Really Happened at the GA," *Zeek*, November 29, 2010.

152. Interview with Rabbi Alissa Wise, director of campaigns for Jewish Voice for Peace and founding co-chair of the JVP Rabbinical Council, November 3, 2011. Members of JVP's youth wing, for instance, have not been allowed to set up a booth at "TribeFest," an annual gathering of young Jews organized by the Jewish Federations of North America.

153. Sharon Ashley, the former director of Hillel's Center for Israel Engagement, has acknowledged that: "The reason these guidelines were created is because of extreme left-wing [Jewish] groups denying the existence of Israel." Interview with Sharon Ashley, November 7, 2011.

154. In March 2011, for example, the Hillel Society at Brandeis University refused to accept Brandeis's JVP chapter as a member when it applied to join. Stewart Ain, "Consensus Seen Taking Shape on Boycotts," *Jewish Week*, March 15, 2011.

155. On November 14, 2010, members of the Jewish group StandWithUs disrupted a local chapter meeting of JVP in Berkeley, California, and in the ensuing scuffle a StandWithUs activist pepper-sprayed two JVP members. Another incident occurred on February 2, 2011, when Estee Chandler, a JVP activist in Los Angeles, found a poster on her front porch with the words "WANTED for treason and incitement against Jews." The poster also featured her picture, her workplace, and the names of her family members.

156. As a result of "Operation Cast Lead," JVP's mailing list went from 20,000 to 85,000 between November 2008 and March of 2009. JVP gained 60,000 online supporters and 25 new chapters as a result of "Operation Protective Edge." Interview with Rebecca Vilkomerson, executive director of Jewish Voice for Peace, October 20, 2011. Author correspondence with Rebecca Vilkomerson, October 16, 2014.

157. Evan Serpick, "Embracing Israel Boycott, Jewish Voice for Peace Insists on Its Jewish Identity," *Forward*, March 28, 2015.

158. One can certainly see some parallels in Jack Wertheimer's description of the organized Jewish community's response to Breira: "Some organizations refused to send speakers to programs that also included Breira representatives.

Some agonized over whether they would be granting legitimacy to Breira if they elected individuals associated with the dissenting group to positions of influence within their own organizations. And still others debated the wisdom of bringing Breira into the communal tent, a step that might provide some leverage to temper the group's provocative policies, or whether to treat Breira as an outcast and thereby make it serve as an object lesson to other dissident groups." Wertheimer, "Breaking the Taboo," pp. 403–404.

159. While supporting BDS is currently a "red line," it is becoming more legitimate in the Jewish community to support a limited boycott of products from Israeli settlements (something that is now advocated, for instance, by Americans for Peace Now). See Dov Waxman and Mairav Zonszein, "The Boycott Debate: No Longer Taboo in Progressive Pro-Israel Circles," *Dissent*, March 29, 2011. Some prominent liberal voices in the Jewish community are already arguing that supporting boycotts of Israel should not necessarily be grounds for exclusion from the Jewish community. See Leonard Fein, "How Big a Tent," *Forward*, March 31, 2011.

160. Magid, "Butler Trouble," p. 239.

161. Anthony P. Cohen, *The Symbolic Construction of Community* (London: Tavistock, 1985).

162. Daniel J. Elazar, *Community and Polity: The Organizational Dynamics of American Jewry*, p. 441.

163. Liebman, *Pressure without Sanctions*, p. 200.

164. David Biale, *Power and Powerlessness in Jewish History* (New York: Schocken Books, 1986), p. 188.

CHAPTER 3: THE ARGUMENT ABOUT ISRAEL

1. Eric H. Yoffie, "Muzzled by the Minority," *Reform Judaism*, September 27, 2014.

2. The other panelist that evening was David Harris, the executive director of the American Jewish Committee, and the moderator was Jane Eisner, the editor of the *Jewish Daily Forward*. What particularly aroused the ire of some members of the audience was Podhoretz's harsh language, such as his comment that the Hillel Society at Swarthmore College "deserve to be spat upon" for its willingness to invite anti-Zionist speakers.

3. John Podhoretz, "A Ludicrous Follow-Up to Last Night's Mess," *Commentary*, December 17, 2013; available at http://www.commentarymagazine.com/2013/12/17/a-ludicrous-follow-up-to-last-nights-mess/ (acessed December 18, 2013).

4. Chemi Shalev, "'Pro-Israel' Discussion in New York Ends in Walkout, Insults and Recriminations," *Ha'aretz*, December 17, 2013.

5. "American Jews Want More Pluralistic Israel: Poll," *Jewish Telegraphic Agency*, May 22, 2014. For a detailed discussion of the role of American Jews in cam-

paigning for Jewish pluralism in Israel, see Yossi Shain, "The Transnational Struggle for Jewish Pluralism," in Thomas Banchoff, ed., *Democracy and the New Religious Pluralism* (Oxford, UK: Oxford University Press, 2007), pp. 85–112.

6. For a similar taxonomy see, Mitch Chanin and Rebecca Ennen, *Guidebook for Deliberation about the Israeli-Palestinian Conflict* (Philadelphia: Jewish Dialogue Group, 2013); for more categories, see Keith Kahn Harris, *Uncivil War: The Israel Conflict in the Jewish Community* (London: David Paul, 2014).

7. Alan Dershowitz, *The Case for Israel* (New Jersey: John Wiley & Sons, 2003), p. 70.

8. Yasser Arafat's rejection of Prime Minister Ehud Barak's peace offer at the Camp David summit in July 2000 and Mahmoud Abbas's failure to accept Prime Minister Ehud Olmert's peace proposal in late 2008 are most often cited as examples of this.

9. Dershowitz, *The Case for Israel*, pp. 176–177.

10. Josh Nathan-Kazis, "Sheldon Adelson Wants Nuclear Strike on Iran—Says Two-States 'Russian Roulette,'" *Forward*, October 23, 2013.

11. This view echoes the "Iron Wall" strategy famously proposed by the founder of Revisionist Zionism, Vladimir "Ze'ev" Jabotinsky back in the early 1920s, although Jabotinsky himself recognized the Arabs as an indigenous people who had national rights. For more on Jabotinsky's concept of the Iron Wall, see Lenni Brenner, *The Iron Wall: Zionist Revisionism from Jabotinsky to Shamir* (London: Zed Books, 1984); Ian Lustick, "To Build and to Be Built By: Israel and the Hidden Logic of the Iron Wall," *Israel Studies* vol. 1, no. 1 (Spring 1996): 196–223.

12. Theodore Sasson, "The New Realism: American Jewish Views about Israel," pp. 14–15. The reason that maintaining the integrity of *Eretz Yisrael* (the Land of Israel) and ensuring permanent Jewish control over it is not a theme in right-wing American Jewish public discourse, whereas it is frequently expressed in right-wing Israeli-Jewish discourse, may be because this aspiration will not resonate with most American Jews for whom the Land of Israel is much less important than it is to Israeli Jews. As Charles Liebman and Steven Cohen observed: "The territory of Israel is of major importance to Israeli Jews, but decidedly peripheral to American Jews." Charles S. Liebman and Steven M. Cohen, *Two Worlds of Judaism: The Israeli and American Experiences* (New Haven, CT: Yale University Press, 1990), p. 67. They also noted: "It is fair to say that to most American Jews, even those with strong interests in Jewish life and Israeli matters, land constitutes an instrument of Israeli security; to the Israeli, it is often an end in itself." Ibid., p. 74.

13. This view is also common on the evangelical Christian right, with whom the American Jewish right is closely allied (for example, the right-wing pro-Israel organization the Emergency Committee for Israel was founded in 2010 by American Jewish neo-conservative William Kristol and Gary Bauer, a leader on the evangelical Christian right).

14. Quoted in Ruthie Blum Leibowitz, "Interview with Morton Klein: 'American Jews grasp the reality of the situation much more than they ever did,'" *Jerusalem Post*, February 25, 2009.
15. For an expression of this view see, Norman Podhoretz, *The Long Struggle against Islamofascism* (New York: Doubleday, 2007).
16. The center-left is also highly critical of the center-right for its refusal to brook liberal Zionist dissent.
17. Leonard Fein, "My Battered Zionism: Liberal Zionists Speak Out," *Huffington Post*, April 26, 2012.
18. The center-left's "liberal Zionism" is part of a long tradition of left-wing and Labor Zionism (represented in Israel today by the Meretz and Labor parties). It is not by accident that many of the most active members of the center-left camp were involved in their teenage years in Labor Zionist youth movements such as Habonim Dror. Keith Kahn Harris, *Uncivil War: The Israel Conflict in the Jewish Community*, pp. 48–49.
19. In recent years, the American Jewish journalist Peter Beinart has made this argument most forcefully and famously in his book *The Crisis of Zionism* (New York: Times Books, 2012). The book was described as "a call to arms for liberal Jewry." In the words of one commentator: "It is, or may come to be, the 'Little Red Book' of left-leaning American Jewish intellectuals, the 'Liberal Manifesto' of sophisticated Jews who insist on clinging to their old-style Zionism, even if it no longer exists." Chemi Shalev, "Is Archliberal Peter Beinart Good for the Jews?" *Ha'aretz*, March 22, 2012.
20. This view developed on the center-left over the past decade in response to the perceived intransigence of Israeli governments. Author interview with Dan Fleshler, board member of Ameinu and Americans for Peace Now, New York, October 13, 2011.
21. In the words of Rabbi Arthur Hertzberg, a leading voice on the center-left during his lifetime: "We who love Israel have an obligation to say what we believe. We have for a century or more helped and supported the Zionist endeavor in the state of Israel. We have long lived with the notion that Israeli governments, from right to left, have tried to inculcate in us—that they determine policy, and we are privileged to say amen on cue. This nonsense is now bankrupt. . . . A Jewish revolt is now brewing." Arthur Hertzberg, "World Jewry Is Not an Amen Chorus," *Ha'aretz*, January 7, 2004.
22. See, for instance, Antony Lerman, "The End of Liberal Zionism," *New York Times*, August 22, 2014.
23. Keith Kahn-Harris, *Uncivil War: The Israel Conflict in the Jewish Community*, p. 50.
24. The American Jewish left is also influenced by the tradition of the radical left in Israel, involving groups like *Matzpen*, which was active in the 1960s and 1970s, and more recently the Arab-Jewish group *Ta'ayush* (meaning "coexistence" or "life in common").
25. Those on the center-left reject the blanket description of Israel as an "apartheid state," but some are willing to apply this description to Israeli rule in the West Bank.

26. David Landy, *Jewish Identity and Palestinian Rights: Diaspora Jewish Opposition to Israel*, p. 41. On "Diasporism," see also Allan Arkush, "From Diaspora Nationalism to Radical Diasporism," *Modern Judaism* vol. 29, no. 3 (2009): 326–350.

27. Some anti-Zionists contend that Jewish power and statehood is contrary to Jewish ethics. See, for instance, Marc H. Ellis, *Israel and Palestine Out of the Ashes: The Search for Jewish Identity in the Twenty-First Century* (London: Pluto Press, 2002); Marc H. Ellis, *Judaism Does Not Equal Israel* (New York: The New Press, 2009).

28. This was the view of the writer Tony Judt, a devout Labor Zionist in his youth, who briefly became a prominent figure on the American Jewish left after he wrote a much-publicized article in the *New York Review of Books* in 2003 in which he advocated a binational state in Israel/Palestine. Tony Judt, "Israel: The Alternative," *New York Review of Books*, October 23, 2003.

29. The American Jewish left also supports BDS because of the importance it places on working with Palestinians and pro-Palestinian activists.

30. The Israeli group *Yesh Gvul* (meaning "There Is a Limit"), founded in 1982 during the first Lebanon War, has led this movement in Israel.

31. See, for instance, Steven Rosenthal's study of American Jewish debates about Israel in the 1980s and early 1990s. Steven Rosenthal, *Irreconcilable Differences?*

32. Naomi W. Cohen, *American Jews and the Zionist Idea*.

33. Jack Wertheimer, "American Jews and Israel: A 60-Year Retrospective," in *American Jewish Yearbook 2008*, p. 74.

34. Noam Sheizaf, "Our Brothers, Ourselves," *Ha'aretz*, January 4, 2011.

35. For instance, an article in the *New York Times* describes the American Jewish community as "increasingly vexed by debate over Israel within its ranks." The article goes on to note: "Debates over Israel appear to be intensifying across the Jewish organizational world." Michael Paulson, "Jewish Groups Consider Including J Street, a Critic of Israel," *New York Times*, April 29, 2014. See also, Rachel Zoll, "Israel No Longer a Cause That Unifies US Jews," *Associated Press*, June 8, 2014.

36. Sharon Otterman and Joseph Berger, "Cheering U.N. Palestine Vote, Synagogue Tests Its Members," *New York Times*, December 4, 2012; Joseph Berger, "Rabbis Apologize for Tone of E-Mail on U.N. Vote," *New York Times*, December 6, 2012.

37. Yehuda Kurtzer, "Presidents, Relevance, and Naming Some Elephants," *Times of Israel*, May 1, 2014.

38. Tony Karon, "Is a Jewish Glasnost Coming to America? Despite a Backlash, Many Jews Are Questioning Israel," *Tom.Dispatch.com*, September 13, 2007.

39. People now constantly air and share their personal thoughts, criticisms, and concerns about Israel via social media.

40. Ari Y. Kelman, "The Reality of the Virtual: Looking for Jewish Leadership Online," in Jack Wertheimer, ed., *The New Jewish Leaders: Reshaping the American Jewish Landscape*, p. 216.

41. This has also happened in the public debate about Israel within the British Jewish community as discussed by Keith Kahn-Harris in his book, *Uncivil War: The Israel Conflict in the Jewish Community*.
42. Author interview with Martin Raffel, senior vice president of JCPA, October 24, 2011.
43. Kelman, "The Reality of the Virtual: Looking for Jewish Leadership Online," p. 215.
44. Kahn-Harris, *Uncivil War*, p. 83.
45. Richard Silverstein, "The Blogging Wars," in Anne Karpf, Brian Klug, Jacqueline Rose, and Barbara Rosenbaum, eds., *A Time to Speak Out: Independent Jewish Voices on Israel, Zionism and Jewish Identity*, pp. 165–166.
46. Peter A. Joseph, "Moderates Must Speak Out," *Jewish Telegraphic Agency*, May 7, 2012.
47. Interview with Rabbi Alissa Wise, director of campaigns for Jewish Voice for Peace and founding co-chair of the JVP Rabbinical Council, November 3, 2011.
48. The Second Intifada and the Gaza War in 2008/9, in particular, provoked a lot of left-wing Jewish criticism and activism and dramatically increased support for left-wing Jewish groups. Adam Horowitz and Philip Weiss, "American Jews Rethink Israel," *Nation*, October 14, 2009.
49. This is also true of current debates about Israel within other Diaspora Jewish communities. As Brian Klug has written: "[I]n today's Jewish world an unhealthy climate of debate has developed when the subject is Israel or Zionism. Jeering and sneering substitute for the give and take of argument, disagreement degenerates into abuse." Brian Klug, "A Time to Move On," in Anne Karpf, Brian Klug, Jacqueline Rose, and Barbara Rosenbaum, eds., *A Time to Speak Out*. For a detailed analysis of the negative characteristics of this debate within the British Jewish community see, Keith Kahn-Harris, *Uncivil War*, pp. 88–116.
50. I have witnessed this and personally experienced this on numerous occasions. For instance, when giving a public talk at a synagogue in a Boston suburb in May 2014, I was repeatedly heckled and rudely interrupted by some extremely irate members of the audience. Many other academics and journalists who give public talks about Israel in Jewish venues have had similar unpleasant experiences.
51. Author interview with Rabbi Steve Gutow, president and CEO of the Jewish Council for Public Affairs, October 17, 2011.
52. Brian Schaefer, "How to Survive a Conversation on Israel," *Ha'aretz*, April 16, 2014.
53. Ben-Ami, *A New Voice for Israel*, pp. 125–126.
54. Quoted in Chemi Shalev, "Ambassador Oren Rebukes Israel's Jewish Critics as Reform Leader Urges Acceptance," *Ha'aretz*, November 13, 2012.
55. Author interview with Ethan Felson, vice president of the Jewish Council for Public Affairs, November 7, 2011.

56. Donniel Hartman, "Jewish Peoplehood and the Toxic Discourse around Israel," *Havruta* no. 8 (February 2012): 22–31.

57. Quoted in Noam Sheizaf, "Our Brothers, Ourselves," *Ha'aretz*, January 4, 2011.

58. The same was true of the ferocious debate among Israeli Jews that took place in the 1990s over the Oslo peace process. Like American Jews today, Israeli Jews then were not just having a political disagreement, but an argument over their own collective identity and the identity and purpose of their state. See Dov Waxman, *The Pursuit of Peace and the Crisis of Israeli Identity: Defending/Defining the Nation* (Palgrave Macmillan: New York, 2006).

59. Interview with Rabbi Alissa Wise, director of campaigns for Jewish Voice for Peace and founding co-chair of the JVP Rabbinical Council, November 3, 2011.

60. Marc Ellis, *Israel and Palestine Out of the Ashes: The Search for Jewish Identity in the Twenty-First Century*, p. 47.

61. As the editors of a symposium on political civility in a political science scholarly journal write: "Name calling and ad hominem attacks that were once associated with talk radio and cable television pundits have made their way into the halls of governing institutions, which no longer serve as sacred spaces one-step removed from bare-knuckled politics." J. Cherie Strachan and Michael R. Wolf, "Political Civility," *PS: Political Science & Politics* vol. 45 (July 2012): p. 401.

62. Donniel Hartman, "Jewish Peoplehood and the Toxic Discourse around Israel," *Havruta* no. 8 (February 2012): p. 29.

63. Richard Silverstein, "The Blogging Wars," in Anne Karpf, Brian Klug, Jacqueline Rose, and Barbara Rosenbaum, eds., *A Time to Speak Out*, p. 169.

64. Elazar, *Community and Polity: The Organizational Dynamics of American Jewry*, pp. 416–417.

65. Steven Windmueller, "The New Angry American Jewish Voter," *Jewish Journal*, August 10, 2010.

66. Eric H. Yoffie, "Muzzled by the Minority," *Reform Judaism*, September 27, 2014.

67. Author interview with Rabbi Melissa Weintraub, February 21, 2010.

68. Chemi Shalev, "American Jews and the Israeli Right: The End of a Beautiful Friendship," *Ha'aretz*, May 23, 2014.

69. J. J. Goldberg, "On Independence Day, the Difficulties of Loving Israel and Each Other," *Forward*, May 5, 2014.

70. See, for examples, Nathan Guttman, "Philadelphia Feud Erupts over Federation Embrace of Anti-J Street Film," *Forward*, March 28, 2014; Nathan Guttman, "JCCs Are the New Front Line in the Culture War on Israel," *Forward*, March 23, 2011; Peter Schworm, "Brandeis Groups Clash on Israel Stance," *Boston Globe*, March 11, 2011; Simone Zimmerman, Jeremy Elster, Isaiah Kirshner-Breen, and Alon Mazor, "J Street U Bounced by Berkeley Group," *Forward*, December 16, 2011.

71. In smaller and more rural Jewish communities, particularly in the south and southwest of the United States, there is less public debate about Israel, and when it does occur it tends to be less acrimonious—perhaps because there is

often less social distance between the members of these communities, which can ameliorate conflicts.

72. This is a common consequence of incivility. J. Cherie Strachan and Michael R. Wolf, "Political Civility," *PS: Political Science & Politics* vol. 45 (July 2012): p. 402.

73. Quoted in Noam Sheizaf, "Our Brothers, Ourselves," *Ha'aretz*, January 4, 2011. In recent years, there have been numerous stories in the American Jewish press of people cancelling their memberships in synagogues because of disagreements over Israel. See, for instance, Gary Rosenblatt, "At B'nai Jeshurun, Congregants Quit to Protest Their Clergy's Criticism of Mayor's Support for AIPAC," *New York Jewish Week*, February 24, 2014.

74. Elisheva Goldberg, "Can Brooklyn Jews Talk Civilly about Israel?" *Forward*, April 8, 2014.

75. Chemi Shalev, "Reform Rabbi Rick Jacobs: American Jews Are 'Afraid' to Talk about Israel," *Ha'aretz*, November 13, 2012. Rabbi Steve Gutow, president of the JCPA, has also stated that: "People over and over say they can't talk about Israel in their synagogue." Author interview with Rabbi Steve Gutow, president of JCPA, October 17, 2011.

76. Quoted in David Landau, "Alive and Well," *Economist*, July 28, 2012.

77. Noam Sheizaf, "Our Brothers, Ourselves," *Ha'aretz*, January 4, 2011.

78. See, for instance, Laurie Goodstein, "Talk in Synagogue of Israel and Gaza Goes from Debate to Wrath to Rage," *New York Times*, September 22, 2014.

79. A national survey of American rabbis (based on the responses of 552 mostly Reform and Conservative congregational rabbis, hence not a fully representative sample) conducted in October 2013 revealed a widespread reticence and unease among non-Orthodox rabbis about openly expressing their views on Israel and the Israeli-Palestinian conflict. Fifty-nine percent of the rabbis surveyed expressed some level of fear about honestly expressing their opinions and feelings about Israel and its conflict with the Palestinians, and one in five of the rabbis said that they feared "significant professional repercussions" if they voiced their true opinions about Israel or particular Israeli government policies. About a third of the rabbis reported that they had refrained on occasion from expressing their opinions about Israel. Rabbis holding dovish views about the Israeli-Palestinian conflict were particularly fearful of openly expressing their views on the conflict (almost three-quarters of dovish rabbis—74 percent—were fearful of publicly expressing their true views, compared to 45 percent of hawkish rabbis.) Steven M. Cohen and Jason Gitlin, "Reluctant or Repressed? Aversion to Expressing Views on Israel among American Rabbis," *A Report of the Jewish Council for Public Affairs, New York, October 8, 2013*, pp. 10–12; Dina Kraft, "American Rabbis Fearful of Expressing Dovish Views on Israel, Study Finds," *Ha'aretz*, October 9, 2013.

80. Ron Kampeas, "As Israel Debates Rage, Jewish Professionals Face Employment Repercussions," *Jewish Telegraphic Agency*, April 8, 2011.

81. Quoted in Ron Kampeas, "As Israel Debates Rage, Jewish Professionals Face Employment Repercussions," *Jewish Telegraphic Agency*, April 8, 2011. See

also Laurie Goodstein, "Talk in Synagogue of Israel and Gaza Goes from Debate to Wrath to Rage," *New York Times*, September 22, 2014.

82. Debra Nussbaum Cohen, "American Jews Learn to Talk with Other American Jews about Israel," *Ha'aretz*, April 23, 2015.

83. The JCPA now sponsors a civility initiative called "Resetting the Table" run by Rabbi Melissa Weintraub and Eyal Rabinovitch, which has worked with numerous local Jewish Federations, synagogues, and Hillel chapters. Debra Nussbaum Cohen, "American Jews Learn to Talk with Other American Jews about Israel," *Ha'aretz*, April 23, 2015.

84. Dan Pine, "'Year of Civil Discourse': Teaching Jews How to Disagree Minus the Vitriol," *Jweekly.com*, September 16, 2010.

85. Ron Kampeas, "As Israel Debates Rage, Jewish Professionals Face Employment Repercussions," *Jewish Telegraphic Agency*, April 8, 2011.

86. "Keep Israel Debate Respectful, N.Y. Jewish Leaders Tell Community," *Jewish Telegraphic Agency*, March 11, 2014.

87. Jonathan Cummings, the JCRC's director of Intra-Communal Affairs, quoted in Gary Rosenblatt, "Tough Conversations," *Jewish Week*, August 6, 2014. See also Elisheva Goldberg, "Can Brooklyn Jews Talk Civilly about Israel?" *Forward*, April 8, 2014.

88. Gary Rosenblatt, "Tough Conversations," *Jewish Week*, August 6, 2014.

89. Allison Kaplan Sommer, "Has Israel Become the Black Sheep of the North American Jewish Family?" *Ha'aretz*, November 7, 2014.

90. Although there was a surge of American Jewish support for Israel during the early years of the second Intifada (2001–2003), there was a massive drop in American Jewish tourism to Israel. The scarcity of American Jews visiting Israel during the second Intifada and the cancellation of some youth tours to Israel (such as the Reform Movement's youth tour in 2001) due to security concerns, was bitterly condemned by Israeli officials, who saw this as evidence of a lack of solidarity with Israel.

91. Quoted in Nick Anderson, "Pro-Israel Demonstration Draws Tens of Thousands to Washington," *Los Angeles Times*, April 16, 2002.

92. Ofira Seliktar, "The Changing Identity of American Jews, Israel and the Peace Process," in Danny Ben Moshe and Zohar Segev, eds. *Israel, the Diaspora and Jewish Identity* (Brighton, UK: Sussex Academic Press, 2007), p. 132.

93. See, for instance, Hody Nemes, "American Jews Rally Mostly to Israel's Side as Gaza Conflict Rages—Minority Objects," *Forward*, July 30, 2014.

CHAPTER 4: THE EROSION OF CONSENSUS

1. This popular quip has been attributed to David Ben-Gurion. Vincent Brook, "Introduction: Seeing Isn't Believing," in Vincent Brook, ed., *You Should See Yourself: Jewish Identity in Postmodern American Culture* (New Brunswick, NJ: Rutgers University Press, 2006), p. 2.

2. The AJC-sponsored annual surveys, beginning in 1983, are useful because they are conducted on a regular basis, with the same methodology (until the 2012 survey), and feature the same questions (respondents are regularly asked about three of the main "final status issues" of the Israeli-Palestinian peace process: Palestinian statehood; the future of Jewish settlements in the West Bank; and the future status of Jerusalem), thereby providing consistent results from year to year, which allows for meaningful comparisons to be made. The AJC surveys, however, include only people who identify themselves as Jewish by religion and exclude "Jews of no religion"—who now constitute 22 percent of the American Jewish population according to the Pew Survey. Since "Jews of no religion" are secular, or cultural Jews, who generally feel less attached to Israel, they may well have more liberal and dovish opinions about the Israeli-Palestinian conflict. By excluding their opinions, therefore, the AJC surveys do not provide a completely accurate representation of American Jewish opinion. The AJC annual surveys are available at www.ajc.org/site/c.ijITI2P HKoG/b.846741/k.8A33/Publications__Surveys/apps/nl/newsletter3.asp (accessed December 17, 2014).

3. The centrist orientation of most American Jews is also evident in their attitudes toward Israel as a Jewish state and democratic state. Unlike those on the right who emphasize the primacy of Israel's Jewish character or those on the left who worry more about its democratic nature, most American Jews regard Israel as both a Jewish and democratic state and they want it to remain so in the future. They oppose discrimination against Arab citizens of Israel and support their integration into Israeli society, but they also oppose abolishing the special privileges for Jews in Israel (especially the country's Law of Return) and eliminating its Jewish symbols and cultural practices. Theodore Sasson, "The New Realism: American Jewish Views about Israel," p. 41.

4. Pew Survey, p. 87.

5. Unlike Israeli Jews, American Jews in general are less likely to have a zero-sum view of the Israeli-Palestinian conflict. Ella Ben Hagai, Eileen L. Zurbriggen, Phillip L. Hammack, and Megan Ziman, "Beliefs Predicting Peace, Beliefs Predicting War: Jewish-Americans and the Israeli-Palestinian Conflict," *Analyses of Social Issues and Public Policy* vol. 13, no. 1 (2013): 286–309.

6. Pew Survey, p. 89.

7. In a survey of 800 American Jewish voters conducted on behalf of J Street at the time of the 2014 midterm congressional elections, three-quarters of American Jews (76 percent) said they supported an Israeli-Palestinian peace agreement that would involve a division of Jerusalem. "J Street—National Post-Election Survey: November 4, 2014." However, in the annual AJC surveys a majority of American Jews has consistently opposed the division of Jerusalem as part of a peace agreement with the Palestinians. In the 2011 AJC Survey (the last time the question was asked), 59 percent opposed a division of Jerusalem in a peace agreement, up from 50 percent a decade earlier in 2001. This discrepancy is probably due to the way in which survey

questions about Jerusalem are formulated. When asked in a single-item survey question, a majority opposes the division of Jerusalem, but a sizable majority supports a division when it is mentioned among many items as part of a comprehensive peace agreement.

8. In the November 2014 J Street survey, 78 percent of American Jews believed that "a two-state solution is necessary to strengthen Israeli security and ensure Israel's Jewish democratic character." "J Street—National Post-Election Survey: November 4, 2014"; available at http://libcloud.s3.amazonaws.com/ 862/89/0/112/1/jstreet-national-election-night-final-results.pdf (accessed November 9, 2015).

9. Relatively few American Jews have a strong ideological commitment to Israeli sovereignty over the West Bank. Theodore Sasson, "The New Realism: American Jewish Views about Israel," pp. 38–39.

10. Steven M. Cohen, "Amoral Zionists, Moralizing Universalists and Conditional Doves," *Moment* vol. 14 (August 1989): 56–57.

11. In another poll taken by the Anti-Defamation League, the vast majority of American Jews (79 percent) thought that Israel's military actions in Operation Cast Lead were appropriate, and 81 percent blamed Hamas for the war. Eric Fingerhut, "Poll: U.S. Jews Overwhelmingly Back Gaza Operation," *Jewish Telegraphic Agency*, January 29, 2009. More recently, 80 percent of American Jews approved of "Operation Protective Edge," Israel's military campaign against Hamas in July–August 2014. "J Street—National Post-Election Survey: November 4, 2014."

12. This does not mean that American Jewish opinion about the Israeli-Palestinian conflict is not affected by developments in Israel, the Palestinian territories, and the wider Middle East. Changes in American Jewish public opinion have occurred in response to such developments. Support for the establishment of a Palestinian state, for instance, fluctuates from year to year largely in response to regional events. The biggest decline in support—a 10 point drop—occurred between 2010–2011, probably in reaction to the outbreak of the so-called Arab Spring and the regional instability it generated. American Jewish opinion also shifted slightly to the right in reaction to the outbreak of the second Intifada. In the 2002 AJC annual survey, 82 percent of American Jewish respondents agreed with the statement "the goal of the Arabs is not the return of occupied territories but rather the destruction of Israel," compared to 73 percent who agreed in 2001, and 69 percent who agreed in 2000. American Jewish Committee, *Annual Survey of American Jewish Opinion*, 2000, 2001, 2002.

13. Renae Cohen, "The Israeli Peace Initiative and the Israel-PLO Accord: A Survey of American Jewish Opinion in 1994" (New York: The American Jewish Committee, 1995), pp. 3–6.

14. Ibid., p. 6.

15. Ibid., pp. 3–4.

16. There was overwhelming support among American Jews for the "Declaration of Principles" between Israel and PLO signed on the White House lawn

on September 13, 1993. In a poll taken that month, 90 percent of American Jews regarded the mutual recognition between Israel and the PLO as a positive development, and 74 percent supported Israel's withdrawal from the Gaza Strip and the West Bank town of Jericho. Steven T. Rosenthal, *Irreconcilable Differences?*, p. 125.

17. Steven M. Cohen, "An Ambivalent Loyalty," *Ha'aretz*, January 24, 2003.

18. Underlying this hawkish attitude was a growing concern among American Jews with Islamist extremism, especially after the September 11, 2001, terrorist attacks, which led many American Jews to believe that Israel and the United States faced a common enemy, whether it was Al Qaeda, Hamas, or even the PLO. For instance, in the AJC's survey of American Jewish opinion carried out in 2001, 44 percent of American Jewish respondents said that Yasser Arafat was Israel's Bin Laden. American Jewish Committee, *2001 Annual Survey of American Jewish Opinion*; available at www.ajc.org/site/apps/nl/content2.asp?c=ijITI2PHKoG&b=838459&ct=1051683 (accessed December 17, 2014).

19. Interview with David Harris, AJC executive director, New York, January 23, 2014.

20. In general, more educated, more politically liberal, and less religiously observant American Jews are more supportive of compromising on the status of Jerusalem in the context of a comprehensive peace agreement with the Palestinians than less educated, more conservative, and more religious Jews. Theodore Sasson et al., *Still Connected: American Jewish Attitudes about Israel*, pp. 24–25. This is the same among Israeli Jews.

21. When asked in the AJC survey in 1994 whether Israel should dismantle Jewish settlements in the West Bank and Gaza as part of a permanent settlement with the Palestinians, just over half of American Jews (52 percent) answered no, while 37 percent said yes. In the AJC survey ten years later (during the second Intifada), only 29 percent of respondents said that Israel should not dismantle any West Bank settlements, whereas 69 percent now thought that Israel should dismantle either all (12 percent) or some (57 percent) of its settlements. More recently, in the 2013 AJC survey, a smaller majority (56 percent) continued to favor the dismantling of all or some Jewish settlements in the West Bank, with a significant minority (43 percent) opposed to this.

22. Interview with David Harris, AJC executive director, New York, January 23, 2014.

23. For instance, in the 2010 AJC survey, 48 percent of respondents supported the establishment of a Palestinian state "in the current situation," and 45 percent opposed it; and in the 2013 AJC survey, 50 percent of respondents supported it, while 47 percent were opposed.

24. A plurality of American Jewish respondents in the AJC surveys consistently favors dismantling some settlements, rather than all of them or none of them.

25. Twenty-nine percent of respondents in the Pew survey thought that continued West Bank settlement construction made no difference to Israeli security, while 17 percent believed that it helps Israel's security. Pew Survey, p. 91.

26. "J Street—National Post-Election Survey: November 4, 2014."

27. A statistical analysis of the results of the annual AJC surveys between 2000 and 2005 demonstrated that American Jewish opinions about the future of the West Bank and East Jerusalem are closely correlated with denominational differences. Joel Perlmann, "American Jewish Opinion about the Future of the West Bank: A Reanalysis of American Jewish Committee Surveys," Levy Economics Institute of Bard College, Working Paper No. 526, December 2007.

28. In the 2013 Pew survey, for example, three-quarters (76 percent) of Modern Orthodox Jews thought that the right-wing Israeli government led by Prime Minister Netanyahu was sincerely trying to make peace with the Palestinians, compared with 51 percent of Conservative Jews, 35 percent of Reform Jews, and only 29 percent of nondenominational Jews.

29. Seventy-two percent of nondenominational Jews, 62 percent of Conservative Jews, and 58 percent of Reform Jews thought this was possible. Pew Survey, p. 87.

30. "American Jewish attitudes Towards Israel and the Peace Process," a public opinion survey conducted for the American Jewish Committee by Market Facts, August 7–15, 1995. Similarly, in a January 1996 survey (taken not long after the assassination of Prime Minister Rabin by an Orthodox Israeli Jew), a majority of Orthodox respondents (56 percent) were opposed to the peace process, whereas an overwhelming majority of non-Orthodox Jews supported it (80 percent of Conservative and 85 percent of Reform Jews). "In the Aftermath of the Rabin Assassination: A Survey of American Jewish Opinion about the Israel and the Peace Process," conducted for the American Jewish Committee by Market Facts, January 10–16, 1996, p. 11.

31. AJC Annual Survey, 2005.

32. Joel Perlmann, "American Jewish Opinion about the Future of the West Bank: A Reanalysis of American Jewish Committee Surveys," Levy Economics Institute of Bard College, Working Paper No. 526, December 2007, pp. 17–19.

33. In the Pew survey, 47 percent of non-Orthodox Jews thought that the continued building of Israeli settlements undermined Israel's security, compared with just 16 percent of Orthodox Jews. Pew Research Center, "A Portrait of Orthodox American Jews," August 26, 2015; available at www.pewforum.org/2015/08/26/a-portrait-of-american-orthodox-jews/ (accessed August 27, 2015). Similarly, in a national survey of American Jewish opinion carried out in March 2009, opposition to Israeli settlement building was highest among unaffiliated and Reform Jews (69 percent and 64 percent, respectively). In contrast, 80 percent of Orthodox Jews supported the expansion of Israeli settlements. J Street Survey, 2009.

34. Samuel C. Heilman, "Jews and Fundamentalism," *Jewish Political Studies Review* vol. 17, nos. 1–2 (Spring 2005).

35. Steven Bayme, "American Jewry Confronts the Twenty-First Century," pp. 30–31. A commitment to Israel has become a much more prominent part of

Orthodox Judaism than Reform or Conservative Judaism. According to one expert: "Orthodox Jews are not only more 'Jewishly oriented' than their non-Orthodox brethren, but they are also more inclined to express their Jewishness by strongly identifying with Israel." Eliezer Don-Yehiya, "Orthodox and Other American Jews and Their Attitude to the State of Israel," *Israel Studies* vol. 17, no. 2 (2012): p. 124.

36. This is partly because Orthodox American Jews who have studied in modern Orthodox yeshivas in Israel are likely to have been exposed to messianic religious Zionism since it is a pervasive ideology in such institutions.

37. According to Charles S. Liebman and Steven M. Cohen: "liberalism is not merely a characteristic [of non-Orthodox American Jews] but clearly a major component of their understanding of what it means to be a Jew." Charles S. Liebman and Steven M. Cohen, *Two Worlds of Judaism: The Israeli and American Experiences*, p. 97. On social issues (such as abortion and same-sex marriage), for example, American Jews are much more liberal than other Americans.

38. Laurence A. Kotler-Berkowitz, "Ethnic Cohesion and Division among American Jews: The Role of Mass-level and Organizational Politics," *Ethnic and Racial Studies* vol. 20, no. 4 (1997): 797–829.

39. Pew Survey. In a survey of American Jews' political values conducted in 2012 (sponsored by the Workmen's Circle), three times as many American Jews identified as liberal than as conservative.

40. "Why Supporting Israel Isn't All in the Family Anymore," *Forward*, June 23, 2014.

41. A cross-tabulation of the raw survey data gathered by the Pew Research Center in its 2013 survey of American Jews conducted by Steven M. Cohen found that conservatives were more attached to Israel than liberals. For instance, 57 percent of conservatives believed that "caring about Israel is essential to being Jewish," compared to 32 percent of liberals. This finding buttresses the results of a national survey of American Jews conducted by the Workmen's Circle in 2012, which revealed for the first time a divide between non-Orthodox Jews who identified as political conservatives and those who identified themselves as liberals and moderates. In this survey, conservatives expressed much more attachment to Israel than liberals and moderates—with 46 percent of conservatives describing themselves as being very attached to Israel, compared with 32 percent of liberals; and 65 percent of conservatives saying they were "pro-Israel to a great extent," as opposed to 41 percent of liberals (figures for political moderates were similar to those of liberals).

42. One possible explanation for why conservatives are much more hawkish than liberals when it comes to Israel can be found in the work of the social psychologist Jonathan Haidt. According to Haidt, liberals and conservatives have fundamentally different moral intuitions (they are intuitions because they are not subject to reason). Liberals only focus on fairness and compassion, while the values of loyalty, sanctity, and respect for authority are also important to conservatives. Haidt argues that these different moral intuitions

underpin political disagreements between conservatives and liberals. Jonathan Haidt, *The Righteous Mind: Why Good People Are Divided by Politics and Religion* (New York: Knopf, 2013). Applying this argument to the American Jewish community suggests that American Jewish conservatives place greater importance on intra-Jewish loyalty and loyalty to Israel, while American Jewish liberals are more likely to stress the need for compassion toward the suffering of Palestinians and the need for Israel to treat Palestinians fairly.

43. Joel Perlmann, "American Jewish Opinion about the Future of the West Bank: A Reanalysis of American Jewish Committee Surveys," Levy Economics Institute of Bard College, Working Paper No. 526, December 2007, p. 22.

44. In a June 2010 survey, 59 percent of liberal and moderate American Jews supported a division of Jerusalem, whereas 66 percent of conservative Jews opposed any compromise on Jerusalem. The survey was based on the responses of 1,243 American Jews and was conducted by the firm Knowledge Networks on behalf of Brandeis University's Cohen Center for Modern Jewish Studies. Theodore Sasson, Benjamin Phillips, Charles Kadushin, and Leonard Saxe, "Still Connected: American Jewish Attitudes about Israel."

45. Ibid.

46. In the 2013 Pew survey, most politically conservative Jews (58 percent) believed that the Netanyahu government was "making a sincere effort to bring about a peace settlement with the Palestinians," whereas most liberal Jews (59 percent) did not (self-described "moderates" were almost evenly split). I am grateful to Steven Cohen for providing me with a breakdown of this data.

47. See the results of the 2012 Workmen's Circle survey.

48. On the growing partisan divide over the Arab-Israeli conflict see, Jonathan Rynhold, *The Arab-Israeli Conflict in American Political Culture* (New York: Cambridge University Press, 2015), pp. 88–91. At least part of the reason for the growing gap in partisan support for Israel is the fact that Evangelical Christians, most of whom are Republicans, have become such strong supporters of Israel. Amnon Cavari, "Religious Beliefs, Elite Polarization, and Public Opinion on Foreign Policy: The Partisan Gap in American Public Opinion toward Israel," *International Journal of Public Opinion Research* vol. 25, no. 1 (Spring 2013): 1–22.

49. In the Pew survey, Republican Jews were almost twice as likely to believe that the Netanyahu government was "making a sincere effort to bring about a peace settlement with the Palestinians" (62 percent versus 32 percent).

50. Most Jewish Democrats (60 percent) favor the establishment of a Palestinian state, while most Jewish Republicans (76 percent) are opposed to this. Robert P. Jones and Daniel Cox, *Chosen for What? Jewish Values in 2012: Finding from the 2012 Jewish Values Survey* (Washington, DC: Public Religion Research Institute, 2012), p. 24.

51. Pew Survey, pp. 89–91. The Pew survey data also suggests that young American Jews are more likely to be alienated from Israel. Based on a cross-tabulation of this data, one in five young non-Orthodox Jews could be described as alienated

from Israel (not merely disconnected from it). These young Jews not only express little emotional attachment to Israel but also think that the United States is too supportive of Israel and that the Israeli government is not sincerely trying to make peace with the Palestinians. Overall, alienation from Israel is significantly higher among younger American Jews.

52. Pew Survey, p. 93. Among the non-Orthodox, 27 percent of young non-Orthodox American Jews thinks that the United States is too supportive of Israel, compared with 14 percent of 30- to 49-year-olds, 7 percent of 50- to 64-year-olds, and 6 percent of those over 65.

53. Daniel Cluchey, "Generation Why: Young American Jews and Israeli Exceptionalism," *Huffington Post*, June 8, 2010.

54. Peter Beinart made this claim in his much-discussed article "The Failure of the American Jewish Establishment," *New York Review of Books*, May 28, 2010.

55. Theodore Sasson, Leonard Saxe, and Michelle Shain, "How Do Young American Jews Feel about Israel?," *Tablet*, February 24, 2015.

56. Pew Research Center, "The Generation Gap and the 2012 Election," November 2011.

57. In a survey taken by Pew during the 2014 Gaza War, more Americans under the age of 30 blamed Israel for the war than Hamas. In a survey taken in December 2014, young Democrats were slightly more likely to want the United States to favor the Palestinians than Israelis, unlike any other age group; and 50 percent of young Democrats wanted the United States to enact economic sanctions in response to Israeli settlement building. Shibley Telhami and Katayoun Kishi, "Widening Democratic Party Divisions on the Israeli-Palestinian Issue," *Washington Post*, December 15, 2014.

58. In the Pew survey, 60 percent of young American Jews described themselves as liberal and only 10 percent as conservative.

59. Dana Goldstein, "Why Fewer Young American Jews Share Their Parents' View of Israel," *Time*, September 29, 2011. Research shows that American Jews who support compromise with the Palestinians and Israeli concessions are more likely to see the Israeli-Palestinian conflict at least partly through the lens of the Palestinian narrative—acknowledging the Palestinians as indigenous inhabitants of the land, and as having been dispossessed and suffering from discrimination and military rule. Ella Ben Hagai, Eileen L. Zurbriggen, Phillip L. Hammack, and Megan Ziman, "Beliefs Predicting Peace, Beliefs Predicting War: Jewish-Americans and the Israeli-Palestinian Conflict," *Analyses of Social Issues and Public Policy* vol. 13, no. 1 (2013): 286–309.

60. There is a big difference between older and younger Jews in the importance they attribute to the Holocaust in shaping their political beliefs and action. In a 2012 survey, 68 percent of American Jews aged over 60 described it as very important, compared to 41 percent of American Jews aged between 18 and 39. Robert P. Jones and Daniel Cox, *Chosen for What? Jewish Values in 2012: Finding from the 2012 Jewish Values Survey*, p. 7.

CHAPTER 5: THE FRACTURING OF THE PRO-ISRAEL LOBBY

1. George P. Shultz, "The 'Israel Lobby' Myth," *U.S. News and World Report*, September 9, 2007.

2. It is inaccurate to describe the pro-Israel lobby in the United States as the "Jewish lobby" because it is now composed not only of primarily Jewish groups, but also of Christian organizations that represent the millions of evangelical Christians in the United States who ardently support Israel. In fact, by far the largest pro-Israel organization in the United States today is Christians United for Israel (CUFI), which claims to have over two million members. Since it was founded by Texas-based Pastor John Hagee in 2006, CUFI has raised more than $43 million for Israeli causes, particularly through its "Nights to Honor Israel" held in cities across the United States. It has also established chapters on over a hundred college campuses.

3. AIPAC's very public failure in September 2015 to secure enough votes in Congress to overturn President Obama's veto of a Congressional resolution against the Iran nuclear agreement has dealt a serious blow to its fearsome reputation, which may therefore end up reducing its future influence in Congress. See Jonathan Broder, "How the Iran Nuclear Deal Weakened AIPAC, Washington's Most Powerful Interest Group," *Newsweek*, September 1, 2015; Karoun Demirjian and Carol Morello, "How AIPAC Lost the Iran Deal Fight," *Washington Post*, September 3, 2015.

4. For a detailed rebuttal of this claim, see Dov Waxman, "From Jerusalem to Baghdad? Israel and the War in Iraq," *International Studies Perspectives* vol. 10, no. 1 (2009): 1–17.

5. John J. Mearsheimer and Stephen M. Walt, *The Israel Lobby and U.S. Foreign Policy* (New York: Farrar, Straus and Giroux, 2007).

6. Christopher Hitchens, "Overstating Jewish Power," *Slate*, March 27, 2006; David Gergen, "An Unfair Attack," *U.S. News & World Report*, April 3, 2006; Max Boot, "Policy Analysis—Paranoid Style," *Los Angeles Times*, March 29, 2006.

7. Michael Massing, "The Storm over the Israel Lobby," *New York Review of Books* vol. 53, no. 10 (June 8, 2006).

8. Juan Cole, "Breaking the Silence," *Salon*, April 19, 2006; Rupert Cornwell, "At Last, a Debate on America's Support for Israel," *Independent*, April 7, 2006.

9. For this criticism, see Abraham H. Foxman, *The Deadliest Lies: The Israel Lobby and the Myth of Jewish Control* (New York: Palgrave Macmillan, 2007), pp. 41–91. See also, "Of Israel, Harvard and David Duke," *Washington Post*, March 26, 2006; Julian Borger, "US Professors Accused of Being Liars and Bigots over Essay on Pro-Israeli Lobby," *Guardian*, March 31, 2006; Eliot Cohen, "Yes, It's Anti-Semitic," *Washington Post*, April 5, 2006.

10. Mearsheimer and Walt themselves, unlike some of their supporters, did in fact acknowledge in their book that the Israel lobby is not monolithic, noting that "it would be clearly wrong to think of the lobby as a single-minded

monolith." They also wrote: "The lobby is not a single, unified movement with a central leadership, however, and individuals and groups that make up this broad coalition sometimes disagree on specific policy issues." Mearsheimer and Walt, *The Israel Lobby and U.S. Foreign Policy*, pp. 112, 114. Nevertheless, despite these qualifications, their book tends to overlook the Israel lobby's political diversity and often depicts it as a unified actor with a single political agenda.

11. Ibid., p. 112.
12. Ibid., p. 114.
13. This definition excludes individuals, typically very wealthy and politically well connected, who personally engage in pro-Israel lobbying (for example, Sheldon Adelson and Haim Saban).
14. AIPAC's educational arm is one of the biggest sponsors of congressional travel, spending about $9 million on nearly 900 lawmaker trips to Israel since 2000. Sara Sorcher and Elahi Izadi, "How a Weaker AIPAC Makes It Easier to Vote against Iran Sanctions," *National Journal*, January 22, 2014.
15. Terry Atlas, "Iran Deal Puts AIPAC at Risk of Losing Its Biggest Fight," *BloombergPolitics*, August 21, 2015.
16. AIPAC, for example, in recent years "has reached out to Hispanics, African-Americans, and evangelical Christians, in the hope that greater diversity will translate into continued support in Congress." Connie Bruck, "Friends of Israel," *New Yorker*, September 1, 2014.
17. "The Israel Project," for example, works with journalists and media outlets in an effort to positively shape media coverage of Israel, and the Committee for Accuracy in Middle East Reporting in America (CAMERA) constantly monitors the media for alleged bias against Israel.
18. College campuses have become the focus of a lot of pro-Israel advocacy in recent years. Newer "start-up" pro-Israel advocacy groups like Stand with Us and The David Project (both of which were formed during the second Intifada) have directed a lot of attention to "educating" Jewish students about Israel and training them to become effective defenders of Israel on college campuses in the face of ongoing pro-Palestinian campaigns. Carl Schrag, *Ripples from the Matzav: Grassroots Responses of American Jewry to the Situation in Israel* (New York: American Jewish Committee, 2004). The Jewish campus organization Hillel also engages in Israel advocacy, albeit less overtly—working closely with AIPAC to develop pro-Israel advocacy on campuses.
19. John Judis, *Genesis: Truman, American Jews and the Origins of the Arab-Israeli Conflict* (New York: Farrar, Straus and Giroux, 2014).
20. Interview with Malcolm Hoenlein, executive vice chairman of the Conference of Presidents, October 31, 2011.
21. J. J. Goldberg, *Jewish Power: Inside the American Jewish Establishment*, p. 199.
22. Ibid., p. 224.
23. Ibid., pp. 202–203.

24. Ibid., pp. 213–215.
25. Ibid., pp. 217–218.
26. Ibid., pp. 136–137.
27. See, for example, Paul Findley, *They Dare to Speak Out: People and Institutions Confront Israel's Lobby* (Westport, CT: Lawrence Hill, 1985); Edward Tivan, *The Lobby: Jewish Political Power and American Foreign Policy* (New York: Simon and Schuster, 1987); Richard Curtiss, *Stealth Pacs: How Israel's American Lobby Took Control of U.S. Middle East Policy* (Washington, DC: American Educational Trust, 1990).
28. Quoted in Goldberg, *Jewish Power*, pp. xv–xvi.
29. Ofira Seliktar, *Divided We Stand: American Jews, Israel, and the Peace Process* (New York: Praeger, 2002).
30. Jonathan Rynhold, "Israel's Foreign and Defence Policy and Diaspora Jewish Identity," in Danny Ben Moshe and Zohar Segev, eds., *Israel, the Diaspora and Jewish Identity*, p. 149. In the fall of 1998, Israel Policy Forum in particular played a key role in persuading President Clinton to apply more pressure on Prime Minister Netanyahu to stop settlement building and agree to a further Israeli withdrawal from the West Bank. This helped produce the Wye River Agreement of October 1998.
31. Neil Rubin, *American Jewry and the Oslo Years*, p. 56. In a 2009 newspaper interview, Morton Klein said: "I personally don't understand adopting a position of support for whatever the Israeli government wants and does. I consider that perplexing, at best. . . . I, Morton Klein, and people who think like me, recognize the right and obligation of Israel to make the final decision on every issue. But I feel I have the right—and even the obligation, as a Jew who feels deeply about Israel—to make my opinion known. The Israeli people or government can reject it. But I have the right to express my concerns." Quoted in Ruthie Blum Leibowitz, "Interview with Morton Klein: 'American Jews Grasp the Reality of the Situation Much More than They Ever Did,'" *Jerusalem Post*, February 25, 2009.
32. Ofira Seliktar, "The Changing Identity of American Jews, Israel and the Peace Process," in Danny Ben Moshe and Zohar Segev, eds., *Israel, the Diaspora and Jewish Identity*, p. 126. According to one scholar, Benjamin Netanyahu, then the leader of the opposition Likud Party in Israel, personally encouraged American Jews to lobby Congress to pass legislation that would undermine the Rabin government's effort at peacemaking with the Palestinians. Steven T. Rosenthal, *Irreconcilable Differences?*, pp. 128–129.
33. Seliktar, "The Changing Identity of American Jews, Israel and the Peace Process," p. 127.
34. Rubin, *American Jewry and the Oslo Years*, p. 2.
35. Quoted in Steven T. Rosenthal, *Irreconcilable Differences?*, p. 129.
36. Rafael Medoff, *Jewish Americans and Political Participation* (Santa Barbara, CA: ABC-CLIO, 2002), p. 250.
37. Following his 1992 election victory, Prime Minister Yitzhak Rabin publicly chastised AIPAC for supporting Yitzhak Shamir's right-wing government

and harming U.S.-Israeli relations. According to Daniel Kurtzer, then the U.S. deputy assistant secretary of state for Near Eastern affairs: "Rabin was furious with AIPAC. He felt they were allied with Likud and would undermine him in what he was trying to do." Quoted in Connie Bruck, "Friends of Israel," *New Yorker*, September 1, 2014.

38. Yossi Beilin, *His Brother's Keeper: Israel and Diaspora Jewry in the Twenty-first Century* (New York: Schocken Books, 2000), p. 78.

39. Quoted in Fleshler, *Transforming America's Israel Lobby* (Washington, DC: Potomac Books, 2009), p. 66.

40. Quoted in Connie Bruck, "Friends of Israel," *New Yorker*, September 1, 2014.

41. Donations to AIPAC also soared after the outbreak of the second Intifada. "AIPAC Doubles Earnings," *Jewish Telegraphic Agency*, February 12, 2009. During the years of the second Intifada, AIPAC's membership rose from 55,000 to 85,000. Carl Schrag, *Ripples from the Matzav: Grassroots Responses of American Jewry to the Situation in Israel*, p. 12.

42. Interview with Malcolm Hoenlein, October 31, 2011.

43. Shmuel Rosner, "U.S. Jewish Leadership Declares Support for Disengagement," *Ha'aretz*, August 17, 2005; Amiram Barkat, "U.S. Jewish Group's Stand on Pullout Attacked," *Ha'aretz*, February 17, 2005; Joseph Berger and Robin Shulman, "Pain of Israel's Withdrawal from Gaza Strip Is Felt by American Jews, Too," *New York Times*, August 14, 2005.

44. Ron Kampeas and Ami Eden, "Debate Erupts over Role of Jewish Groups," *Jewish Telegraphic Agency*, November 19, 2007.

45. Ami Eden, "Criticism of Olmert Foreshadows Jewish Showdown," *Jewish Telegraphic Agency*, November 27, 2007.

46. Ibid.

47. Ibid.

48. Mearsheimer and Walt, for instance, wrote that: "some of the most important groups in the [Israel] lobby—including AIPAC and the Conference of Presidents—have become increasingly conservative over time and are now led by hard-liners who support the positions of their hawkish counterparts in Israel." Mearsheimer and Walt, *The Israel Lobby and U.S. Foreign Policy*, p. 126. See also, J. J. Goldberg, *Jewish Power*, pp. 218–219. For a contrary view, see Mitchell G. Bard, "AIPAC and US Middle East Policy," in Eytan Gilboa and Efraim Inbar, eds., *US-Israeli Relations in a New Era* (New York: Routledge, 2009), p. 88.

49. Rabbi Eric Yoffie, then the president of the Reform movement (the largest member organization of the Conference of Presidents), publicly criticized its right-wing tilt, claiming that the organization "has been much more outspoken and forceful in supporting [Israeli] governments of the right than those of the left." Quoted in Michael Massing, "Deal Breakers," *American Prospect* vol. 13, no. 5 (March 11, 2002). Another longtime member of the Conference of Presidents, Kenneth Bob, the president of Ameinu, also believes that the organization has tilted to the right. In his words: "Its enthusiasm leans to the

right." Author interview with Kenneth Bob, November 10, 2011. Similarly, Mark Rosenblum, the founder and former head of Americans for Peace Now (APN), claims that: "Most people in the [Presidents'] Conference over all years I've represented APN, are silenced by intimidation, particularly as the Conference has moved in a particular direction." According to Rosenblum: "[Malcolm Hoenlein] tilts it any way he wants." Interview with Mark Rosenblum, October 22, 2011.

50. Rabbi Eric Yoffie publicly complained that: "I feel strongly that during the Rabin and Barak years the [Presidents] conference simply did not demonstrate the same kind of energy and aggressive support for the policies of the Israeli government that it did during the Shamir and Netanyahu years." Quoted in Michael Massing, "Deal Breakers," *American Prospect* vol. 13, no. 5 (March 11, 2002).

51. Massing, "Deal Breakers," *American Prospect* vol. 13, no. 5 (March 11, 2002). For similar claims, see Philip Weiss, "AIPAC Alternative?" *Nation*, April 23, 2007; and Gary Kamiya, "Can American Jews Unplug the Israel Lobby?" *Salon*, March 20, 2007. Ambassador Dennis Ross, a longtime U.S. diplomat closely involved in the Israeli-Palestinian peace process, has disputed this claim, writing that: "[N]ever in the time that I led the American negotiations on the Middle East peace process did we take a step because 'the lobby' wanted us to. Nor did we shy away from one because 'the lobby' opposed it." Dennis Ross, "The Mind-set Matters," *Foreign Policy* (July/August 2006).

52. John Mearsheimer and Stephen Walt, "The Israel Lobby," *London Review of Books* vol. 28, no. 6 (March 2006), and John Mearsheimer and Stephen Walt, "The Israel Lobby and U.S. Foreign Policy," KSG Working Paper No. RWP06-011, March 2006.

53. See www.JStreet.org (accessed January 19, 2015).

54. Quoted in Ruthie Blum Leibowitz, "Israel's Rights . . . and Wrongs," *Jerusalem Post*, April 29, 2009.

55. Jeremy Ben-Ami, *A New Voice for Israel*, pp. 94–95.

56. Quoted in James Traub, "The New Israel Lobby," *New York Times Magazine*, September 13, 2009.

57. See, for example, Robert Dreyfuss, "Is AIPAC Still the Chosen One?" *Mother Jones*, September 9, 2009; Adam Horowitz and Philip Weiss, "American Jews Rethink Israel," *Nation*, October 14, 2009.

58. Jeremy Ben-Ami denies having any intention to compete with AIPAC, categorically stating in one interview: "We [J Street] are not, in any way, in opposition to AIPAC. In fact, we want to work with them on much of what they do." Quoted in Ruthie Blum Leibowitz, "Israel's Rights . . . and Wrongs," *Jerusalem Post*, April 29, 2009. In an interview with the author, however, he said: "Just getting members of congress to say no when AIPAC calls is the first step." Author interview with Jeremy Ben-Ami, Washington, DC, November 1, 2011.

59. Jonathan Broder, "New Pro-Israel Lobby, New Point of View," *Congressional Quarterly*, August 15, 2009.

60. J Street took advantage of the "Netroots" Internet revolution in politics, spearheaded by MoveOn and Barack Obama's 2008 presidential campaign, to raise significant amounts of money online from many small contributions.

61. This amount was still only a fraction of the money raised by all other pro-Israel PACs. According to the Open Secrets website (www.opensecrets.org), pro-Israel PACs donated more than $2.5 million in the 2008 election, an amount that does not include the additional millions of dollars pro-Israel individuals donated and raised for candidates—according to figures compiled by the Center for Responsive Politics, total pro-Israel contributions to Congressional candidates in the 2008 election amounted to $11.5 million. Eric Fingerhut, "Will J Street Money Translate into Influence?" *Jewish Telegraphic Agency*, November 11, 2008.

62. Dan Eggen, "New Liberal Jewish Lobby Quickly Makes Its Mark," *Washington Post*, April 17, 2009.

63. James Traub, "The New Israel Lobby," *New York Times Magazine*, September 13, 2009. See also Jonathan Broder, "New Pro-Israel Lobby, New Point of View," *Congressional Quarterly*, August 15, 2009.

64. Daniel Treiman, "J Street and Main Street: The Israel Lobby We Need," *Forward*, October 14, 2009.

65. Ben-Ami, *A New Voice for Israel*, p. 108; Terry Atlas, "Iran Deal Puts AIPAC at Risk of Losing Its Biggest Fight," *BloombergPolitics*, August 21, 2015.

66. J Street's ties to the Obama administration undoubtedly boosted its prestige and significance. When the newly elected President Obama included the leader of J Street in a meeting he held with the leaders of American Jewish organizations at the start of his first term in office in 2009, this helped the young group gain prominence.

67. The same unnamed Israeli government official also described J Street as a friend, albeit one with whom the Israeli government had disagreements. Ron Kampeas, "J Street and Israel Are Still Arguing—but on Friendlier Terms," *Jewish Telegraphic Agency*, March 27, 2012.

68. J Street activists sent out 15,000 letters and made over 1,000 phone calls to senators urging them to oppose the amendment, and none of the house members and senators who had been endorsed by J Street's PAC supported the amendment. "J Street Wins as Senate Omits Statehood Slap," *Forward*, December 5, 2012.

69. Arguably, J Street has had more success in lobbying against the imposition of new U.S. sanctions on Iran. In January 2014, it lobbied against a bill in the Senate (called the Nuclear Weapon Free Iran Act) that was strongly backed by AIPAC and other major American Jewish groups. According to a report in the *National Journal*: "The rise of J Street, a younger pro-Israel lobby pushing hard against the new sanctions, is serving as a counterweight to AIPAC on this issue [Iran sanctions]. . . . By decoupling support for Israel with support for new sanctions against Iran, the group is making it easier for lawmakers inclined to support the White House." Sara Sorcher and Elahi Izadi, "How a Weaker AIPAC Makes It Easier to Vote against Iran Sanc-

tions," *National Journal*, January 23, 2014. AIPAC's inability to secure enough Senate votes to override a threatened veto of the bill by President Obama was widely attributed, at least in part, to the efforts of J Street. None of the seven Senate candidates that J Street officially endorsed in the 2012 election supported the sanctions bill, and Senator Diane Feinstein, one of the biggest recipients of JStreetPAC money, was an outspoken critic of the bill.

70. Michael Massing, "The Storm over the Israel Lobby," *New York Review of Books*.

71. Ibid.

72. William Kristol, the editor of the *Weekly Standard* magazine; Gary Bauer, a former Republican presidential candidate; and conservative writer Rachel Abrams founded the Emergency Committee for Israel (ECI). Kristol has described his group as "the pro-Israel wing of the pro-Israel community." Quoted in Ben Smith, "Group to Oppose President Obama's Mideast Policy," *Politico*, July 12, 2010. Like J Street, ECI also has its own political action committee (ECIPAC). It regularly publishes advertisements in the print media and runs attack ads on television accusing politicians of being "anti-Israel" and even "pro-Hamas."

73. Quoted in Connie Bruck, "Friends of Israel," *New Yorker*, September 1, 2014.

74. In 2010, AIPAC had a huge $140 million endowment. Alan Fram, "The Influence Game: Pro-Israel Doves Seek DC Clout," *Associated Press*, May 25, 2009.

75. AIPAC's fifty-member national board is comprised of major donors, fundraisers, and past presidents of AIPAC, many of whom are also big fundraisers and donors to U.S. politicians and political parties. Between 2000 and 2004, for instance, AIPAC board members contributed an average of $72,000 each to campaigns and political committees. In 2004, one in every five AIPAC board members was a top fundraiser for Kerry or Bush. Thomas B. Edsall and Molly Moore, "Pro-Israel Lobby Has Strong Voice," *Washington Post*, September 5, 2004.

76. Nathan Guttman, "ADL and AJC Suffer Big Drop in Donations," *Forward*, December 16, 2011; Terry Atlas, "Iran Deal Puts AIPAC at Risk of Losing Its Biggest Fight," *BloombergPolitics*, August 21, 2015.

77. In 2013, more than three-fourths of the total amount spent on pro-Israel lobbying that year was spent by AIPAC. Sara Sorcher and Elahi Izadi, "How a Weaker AIPAC Makes It Easier to Vote against Iran Sanctions," *National Journal*, January 22, 2014.

78. The information is available on its website, at https://www.opensecrets.org/ (accessed January 19, 2015).

79. Connie Bruck, "Friends of Israel," *New Yorker*.

80. J. J. Goldberg, *Jewish Power*, p. 224.

81. Dan Fleshler, *Transforming America's Israel Lobby*, p. 37.

82. Quoted in Michael Massing, "Deal Breakers," *The American Prospect*.

83. Quoted in Alan Fram, "The Influence Game: Pro-Israel Doves Seek DC Clout," *Associated Press*, May 25, 2009.

84. Ron Kampeas, "Sitting between Bibi and Obama, AIPAC Criticized by Left and Right," *Jewish Telegraphic Agency*, May 7, 2009.

85. James Besser, "AIPAC's Positioning Problem," *New York Jewish Week*, May 8, 2009.

86. Sheldon Adelson, who had been one of AIPAC's biggest donors and who gave much of the money to pay for the building of its new headquarters in Washington, DC, stopped his contributions to AIPAC after it supported a Congressional letter in November 2007 that urged the Bush administration to increase U.S. aid to the PA. Ron Kampeas, "AIPAC Stance Irks Donors," *Jewish Telegraph Agency*, November 19, 2007.

87. Paul Berger, "Levy Report Tests American Consensus," *Forward*, July 27, 2012.

88. Nathan Guttman, "At AIPAC, Mideast Peace Process Is Way Down the Agenda," *Forward*, March 5, 2014.

89. Dov Waxman, "The Israel Lobbies: A Survey of the Pro-Israel Community in the United States," *Israel Studies Forum* vol. 25, no. 1 (2010): 5–28.

90. "ZOA Blasts Disunity among Jewish-American Groups over PM's Speech," *Times of Israel*, February 9, 2015.

91. Felicia Schwartz, "Pro-Israel Groups in US Square Off over Iran Nuclear Deal," *Wall Street Journal*, July 16, 2015; Greg Sargent, "Which Side Is Really 'Pro-Israel'? Backers of the Iran Deal Ramp Up," *Washington Post*, July 29, 2015.

92. AIPAC formed a new 501(c) group, Citizens for a Nuclear Free Iran, to run a multimillion-dollar television advertising campaign against the nuclear deal. Alexander Bolton, "New Group Backed by AIPAC Targets Deal," *Hill*, July 17, 2015; Byron Tau, "AIPAC Funds Ads Opposing Iran Nuclear Deal," *Wall Street Journal*, July 17, 2015. On J Street's multimillion-dollar advertising campaign, see Jacob Kornbluh, "J Street Launches Multimillion Dollar Campaign in Support of Iran Nuclear Deal," *Ha'aretz*, July 16, 2015. See also Julie Hirschfeld Davis, "Lobbying Fight over Iran Nuclear Deal Centers on Democrats," *New York Times*, August 17, 2015.

93. "Obama to Meet with Jewish Leaders for First Time since Iran Deal," *Jewish Telegraphic Agency*, August 3, 2015.

94. Quoted in Natasha Mozgovaya, "Biden: Israel's Decisions Must Be Made in Jerusalem, Not D.C.," *Ha'aretz*, September 4, 2008.

95. Quoted in Jonathan Broder, "New Pro-Israel Lobby, New Point of View."

96. Author interview with Malcolm Hoenlein, executive vice chairman of the Conference of Presidents, October 31, 2011.

97. Ben-Ami, *A New Voice for Israel*, p. 149. J Street does not claim or aspire to represent the American Jewish community as a whole. "The goal of J Street is to be a new voice for Israel," Ben-Ami has written, "not to be 'the' voice of the American Jewish community. . . . We simply want the message that reaches Washington to reflect the true diversity of opinions in the American Jewish community." Ibid., p. 110.

98. Author interview with Jeremy Ben-Ami, Washington, DC, November 1, 2011.

99. When campaigning for the presidency in February 2008, Obama implied that there were different ways of being "pro-Israel" when he told Jewish leaders in Cleveland, Ohio: "There is a strain within the pro-Israel community that says unless you adopt an unwavering pro-Likud approach to Israel that you're anti-Israel." Ron Kampeas, "Obama: Don't Equate 'Pro-Israel' and 'Pro-Likud,'" *Jewish Telegraphic Agency*, February 24, 2008.

100. Greg Sargent, "Which Side Is Really 'Pro-Israel'? Backers of the Iran Deal Ramp Up," *Washington Post*, July 29, 2015.

101. Peter Beinart, "Collapse of the American Jewish Center," *Open Zion*, May 7, 2013; available at www.thedailybeast.com/articles/2013/05/07/collapse-of -the-american-jewish-center.html (accessed May 8, 2013).

102. Quoted in Ron Kampeas, "Will US Jewish Groups Pivot Left if Herzog Wins?" *Times of Israel*, December 17, 2014.

CHAPTER 6: THE CHALLENGE TO THE JEWISH ESTABLISHMENT

1. Peter Beinart, "The Failure of the American Jewish Establishment," *New York Review of Books*, May 28, 2010.

2. Allison Hoffman, "King without a Crown," *Tablet*, May 10, 2010.

3. Interview with Malcolm Hoenlein, executive vice chairman of the Conference of Presidents, October 31, 2011. Hoenlein has publicly opposed the division of Jerusalem in any future peace agreement with the Palestinians, but he has also expressed support for a two-state solution to the Israeli-Palestinian conflict, albeit in a highly qualified manner, telling a reporter: "I don't know any alternative to it [the two-state solution] right now, but I don't see it when you don't have a partner." Judy Maltz, "Hoenlein to Haaretz: World Jewry Must Say 'Enough' to Delegitimization of Israel," *Ha'aretz*, June 24, 2013.

4. Although Hoenlein's official role is only to act on behalf of the organizations that comprise the membership of the Conference of Presidents and he is formally subordinate to the chairman of the conference (who is elected by its members), in practice Hoenlein is able to exercise a great deal of influence due to the fact that the Conference of Presidents is made up of so many organizations and has only a very small professional staff. Hoenlein's outsize role in the organization has been criticized by some of its members. For instance, Abraham Foxman, the national director of the Anti-Defamation League, has stated that: "there needs to be greater participation in the decision-making process. It cannot be a one- or two-person show." Quoted in Rebecca Spence, "Conference of Presidents Pick Hailed by Groups Critical of Hoenlein's Role," *Forward*, April 20, 2007. Hoenlein himself adamantly rejects this criticism, insisting that: "Decisions [by the Conference of Presidents] are made on the basis of discussion and consultation." Interview

with Malcolm Hoenlein, executive vice chairman of the Conference of Presidents, October 31, 2011.

5. Interview with Malcolm Hoenlein, executive vice chairman of the Conference of Presidents, October 31, 2011.

6. Ibid.

7. J Street failed to win the support of a two-thirds majority of the entire Conference of Presidents that it needed to join the organization (it received only 17 votes in favor of its membership, with 22 votes against it, and 3 abstentions). The vote reportedly broke down largely along political and religious lines, with left-wing and non-Orthodox groups supporting J Street's membership and right-wing and Orthodox groups opposing it. Nathan Guttman, "J Street Fails Badly in Bid for Admission to Presidents Conference," *Forward*, April 30, 2014; J. J. Goldberg, "Blackballing J Street: Who Voted How," *Forward*, May 4, 2014.

8. Chemi Shalev, "J Street's Rejection Is a Milestone in the Growing Polarization of American Jews," *Ha'aretz*, May 1, 2014. For similar reactions, see Leon Wieseltier, "J Street's Rejection Is a Scandal," *New Republic*, May 7, 2014; Leonard Fein, "Those Who Reject J Street Are Blind," *Forward*, May 3, 2014.

9. Quoted in Michael Paulson, "Jewish Coalition Rejects Lobbying Group's Bid to Join," *New York Times*, April 29, 2014.

10. It was not just the Conference of Presidents's decision to reject J Street that was criticized by observers, but also the secretive manner in which the decision was made. As one commentator wrote: "Without a clear reasoning of the grounds on which J Street was rejected, without an open tally of the vote—without, that is, any measure of transparency or accountability—it is very difficult to entertain the thought that the Conference of Presidents does or ought to represent the American Jewish community at large." Liel Leibovitz, "Forget J Street; Should We Accept the Conference of Presidents?" *Tablet*, May 1, 2014.

11. Chemi Shalev, "J Street's Rejection Is a Milestone in the Growing Polarization of American Jews," *Ha'aretz*, May 1, 2014.

12. Nathan Guttman, "J Street Turns Tables on President Conference after Application Snubbed," *Forward*, May 1, 2014.

13. Large organizations like the Reform and Conservative movements are outnumbered in the Conference of Presidents by smaller, often more religiously and politically conservative ones (although there are several organizations affiliated with the Reform and Conservative movements in the Conference of Presidents). The fact that organizations representing hundreds of thousands of Jews have the same vote as ones representing just thousands of Jews has led to persistent demands for the decision-making process within the Conference of Presidents to be reformed. See, for example, Eric Yoffie, "Reform the Conference," *Forward*, August 2, 2002; Nathan Guttman, "Conference Fails to Live Up to Name," *Forward*, March 9, 2012.

14. Michael Kaplan, "Rick Jacobs Threatens to Pull URJ Out of Presidents Conference after J Street Fiasco," *Forward*, May 1, 2014. In order for his organization to remain in the Conference of Presidents, Jacobs demanded that its internal structure and voting procedures be reformed in order to make it more representative of the American Jewish community. Nathan Guttman "'Broken' Presidents Conference Faces Powerful Rebellion after J Street Debacle," *Forward*, May 7, 2014. Such reforms were later initiated in the wake of the controversy over the J Street vote. See Nathan Guttman, "Presidents Conference Takes Tentative Steps to More Democratic Structure," *Forward*, July 5, 2014.

15. In the words of Dan Fleshler, a longtime American Jewish peace activist: "Name the issue, name the moment, and chances are polls will show that AIPAC and the Presidents Conference were not in step with a large proportion of the community they purported to represent." Dan Fleshler, *Transforming America's Israel Lobby*, p. 10. See also Eric Alterman, "Bad for the Jews," *Nation*, January 7, 2008; J. J. Goldberg, "Look Who's Speaking for America's Jews," *Forward*, May 7, 2010.

16. When he founded the American Jewish Congress in 1918, for instance, Rabbi Stephen Wise declared: "The time is come for a leadership by us to be chosen, a leadership that shall democratically and wisely lead rather than autocratically command." Quoted in Melvin I. Urofsky, *A Voice That Spoke for Justice*, pp. 130–131. There has, in fact, always been a concern with the question of who represented the American Jewish community and how they should be selected, as Jonathan Woocher notes: "For almost as long as there has been an American Jewish community, there has been discussion and debate over its organization and governance." Jonathan Woocher, "The Democratization of the American Jewish Polity," *Contemporary Jewry* vol. 8, no. 1 (1987): p. 28.

17. Peter Beinart, "The Failure of the American Jewish Establishment," *New York Review of Books*, May 28, 2010.

18. Ibid.

19. Ibid.

20. Peter Beinart, *The Crisis of Zionism*.

21. Allison Hoffman, "Lightening Rod," *Tablet*, March 22, 2014.

22. Dan Klein, "Beinart, Gordis Debate in Front of Packed House," *Tablet*, May 3, 2012.

23. For instance, at the General Assembly of the Jewish Federations of North America, held in November 2011 in Denver.

24. Ronn Torossian, "Peter Beinart Represents Zionism Like a Black KKK Member Represents African-Americans," *Algemeiner*, March 18, 2012. See also Bret Stephens, "Peter Beinart's False Prophecy," *Tablet*, March 26, 2012.

25. See, for instance, Theodore Sasson and Leonard Saxe, "Wrong Numbers," *Tablet*, May 28, 2010; Gal Beckerman, "Survey Says Young Jews Do Care about Israel," *Forward*, September 1, 2010; Matthew Ackerman, "The Silent Young Jewish Majority," *Commentary*, January 10, 2012.

26. Peter Beinart, "The Failure of the American Jewish Establishment."
27. Quoted in Paul Vitello, "On Israel, Jews and Leaders Often Disagree," *New York Times*, May 6, 2010.
28. Mira Sucharov, "We Are All the American Jewish Establishment," *Ha'aretz*, May 31, 2012.
29. There are thousands of Jewish organizations in the United States. According to one count, taken in 2008, there were 9,482 Jewish nonprofit organizations. Paul Burstein, "Jewish Nonprofit Organizations in the U.S.: A Preliminary Survey," *Journal of Contemporary Jewry* vol. 21 (2011): 129–148. Collectively, the organized Jewish community—its federations, schools, health care and social service organizations, cultural and communal organizations, and advocacy groups (excluding synagogues and other religious organizations)—has a net worth of $26 billion, and an annual revenue in 2014 of between $12 billion to $14 billion, roughly the same as Starbucks's annual revenue. Josh Nathan-Kazis, "26 Billion Bucks: The Jewish Charity Industry Uncovered," *Forward*, March 28, 2014.
30. The Conference of Presidents, for example, though widely perceived by those on the left as a right-of-center organization, actually has some left-wing groups among its members, most notably Americans for Peace Now and Ameinu, and because of their membership in the Conference of Presidents, both groups also have seats on AIPAC's National Council. As such, both are clearly part of the American Jewish establishment.
31. Despite the fact that the Iranian nuclear deal was very controversial and divisive among American Jews, and some polls indicated that a majority of American Jews actually supported the agreement, the vast majority of Jewish establishment organizations, including many local Jewish Federations, came out publicly against it and tried to mobilize American Jews to lobby their representatives in Congress to vote against the deal. (The Conference of Presidents and the Federation umbrella group, the Jewish Federations of North America, avoided taking a formal position, although their leaders appeared at a public rally in New York protesting the deal.) This immediately provoked criticism that these organizations were not accurately representing American Jewish opinion on the nuclear deal, and that the local Federations in particular should not have issued public statements opposing the deal when there was no consensus within their communities on the issue. Todd Gitlin and Steven M. Cohen, "On the Iran Deal, American Jewish 'Leaders' Don't Speak for Most Jews," *Washington Post*, August 14, 2015; Ron Kampeas, "Mixed Messages as Federations across US Take Stands on Iran Deal," *Jewish Telegraphic Agency*, August 14, 2015; Rob Eshman, "Federation: Take It Back," *L.A. Jewish Journal*, July 26, 2015; Jared Sichel, "Federation's Letter against Iran Deal Brings Community's Divide to the Surface," *L.A. Jewish Journal*, July 30, 2015; Nathan Guttman, "Federations Split as Some Call for Action to Block Iran Deal," *Forward*, July 29, 2015; Uriel Heilman, "Jewish Groups Stake Out Positions on Iran Deal, but Whom Do They Represent?" *Jewish Telegraphic Agency*, July 28, 2015. On American Jewish public opinion

about the nuclear deal, see "Poll: Most of American Jews Think Congress Should Approve Iran Deal," *Ha'aretz*, July 24, 2015.

32. In my interviews with them, for example, two prominent leaders in the American Jewish establishment, John Ruskay and Barry Shrage, were both strongly critical of Israeli settlement construction in the West Bank.

33. In two surveys carried out on behalf of J Street in 2008 and 2009, 49 percent and 47 percent, respectively, of American Jews thought that "traditional Jewish organizations" did a good job of representing their views on Israel, whereas just 29 percent in both surveys thought they did a poor job. "J Street National Survey of American Jews" July 2008, and "J Street National Survey of American Jews" March 2009; both available at http://jstreet.org/policy/polling/page/8 (accessed November 10, 2015).

34. UJA-Federation of New York, "Jewish Community Study of New York: 2011 Comprehensive Report," p. 147.

35. J. J. Goldberg, *Jewish Power*, p. 76.

36. Ibid.

37. In Boston, for example, the local Jewish Community Relations Council was criticized and constantly pressured by a right-wing Jewish group called "The David Project" for not being sufficiently assertive in its pro-Israel advocacy during the second Intifada. Interview with Nancy Kaufman, CEO of the National Council of Jewish Women, January 11, 2013. Kaufman formerly served for twenty years as the executive director of Boston's JCRC.

38. Jonathan Woocher, "The Democratization of the American Jewish Polity," *Contemporary Jewry* vol. 8, no. 1 (1987): p. 31.

39. Daniel J. Elazar, *Community and Polity: The Organizational Dynamics of American Jewry*, p. 426; Hal M. Lewis, *Models and Meanings in the History of Jewish Leadership* (Lewiston, NY: Edward Mellen Press, 2004), p. 279.

40. Two observers note that "the central role played by philanthropy in Jewish community life means that money is a central determinant of who gets to make use of the institutional prestige of venerable organizational names in order to obtain a platform for his views." Yossi Shain and Steven Lenzner, "Jewish Voices, Jewish Influence, and Neoconservatism," *Occasional Papers on Jewish Civilization, Jewish Thought and Philosophy* (Summer 2005): 23. Thus, the billionaires Ronald Lauder, Mortimer Zuckerman, and James S. Tisch have all been chairmen of the Conference of Presidents.

41. Daniel J. Elazar, *Community and Polity: The Organizational Dynamics of American Jewry*, p. 429.

42. Interview with John Ruskay, former executive vice president and CEO of the UJA-Federation of New York, May 14, 2015.

43. Quoted in Chemi Shalev, "Hoenlein: The Iranians Have Been Bazaaris for 2000 Years; They Can Run Rings around Us," *Ha'aretz*, January 31, 2014.

44. Steven Bayme, "On Gabriel Sheffer's 'Loyalty and Criticism in the Relations between World Jewry and Israel,'" *Israel Studies* vol. 17, no. 2 (2012): p. 116.

45. Quoted in Josh Nathan-Kazis, "Jews Express Wide Criticism of Israel in Pew Survey but Leaders Dismiss Findings," *Forward*, October 2, 2013.
46. Interview with John Ruskay, May 14, 2015.
47. According to John Ruskay: "Every poll shows us that sixty to seventy percent of American Jews voted for President Obama. . . . Yet it is also clear that among those most involved in what is called the Jewish establishment that vote is probably reversed, if not more." Interview with John Ruskay, May 14, 2015.
48. In the 2013 Pew survey of American Jews, Orthodox Jews and politically conservative Jews were much more likely than other Jews to belong to Jewish organizations. Pew Survey, p. 61.
49. J. J. Goldberg, *Jewish Power*, p. 76.
50. Interview with John Ruskay, May 14, 2015.
51. There has been a significant increase of Orthodox involvement in pro-Israel activism in recent years. This has been evident at AIPAC's annual policy conferences, which now only serve glatt kosher food (the highest level of kashrut). AIPAC has also formed close ties with the Orthodox Union.
52. Steven Bayme, "On Gabriel Sheffer's "Loyalty and Criticism in the Relations between World Jewry and Israel," *Israel Studies* vol. 17, no. 2 (2012): p. 113.
53. Conversely, when the center-left does show up, it often wins because they tend to outnumber the right. For example, when a special meeting of the Jewish Community Relations Council of Greater Boston was held in May 2011 to take a vote on whether J Street should be allowed to retain its membership on the council or be expelled from it, the outcome of the vote was decisively in J Street's favor (57 to 9). Leonard Fein, "Treating J Street with a Little Respect," *Forward*, June 10, 2011.
54. Todd Gitlin and Steven M. Cohen have pointed out that the Pew Research Center's 2013 survey of Jewish Americans shows that "those who belong to Jewish organizations (18 percent of all Jews) differ in many ways from those who do not. The affiliated are more affluent (31 percent have incomes of at least $150,000, as opposed to 24 percent among the unaffiliated), more Republican (18 percent vs. 12 percent) and less likely to identify as liberal (46 percent vs. 53 percent)." Todd Gitlin and Steven M. Cohen, "On the Iran Deal, American Jewish 'Leaders' Don't Speak for Most Jews," *Washington Post*, August 14, 2015.
55. Membership in Jewish organizations is linked to age, so that the older you are the more likely you are to belong to a Jewish organization. Uzi Rebhun, "Recent Developments in Jewish Identification in the United States: A Cohort Follow-up and Facet Analysis," in Sergio DellaPergola and Judith Even, eds., *Papers in Jewish Demography 1997* (Jerusalem: Avraham Harman Institute of Contemporary Jewry, Hebrew University of Jerusalem, 2001), pp. 266–267.
56. The declining membership of Jewish establishment organizations is partly due to the fact that most Jews have much less need for such organizations

today. Jewish acceptance into mainstream American society and the rise of Jewish individualism have reduced the need for Jewish organizations. They have simply become irrelevant to the daily lives of most Jews. Steven M. Cohen, "Jewish Identity Research in the United States: Ruminations on Concepts and Findings," in Sol Encel and Leslie Stein, *Continuity, Commitment and Survival: Jewish Communities in the Diaspora* (Westport, CT: Praeger, 2003), p. 8. Another part of the reason for the declining membership of Jewish establishment organizations is the general decline in organizational membership in the United States, a trend highlighted by Robert D. Putnam in his book *Bowling Alone: The Collapse and Revival of American Community* (New York: Simon & Schuster, 2000). Putnam showed that large, mass membership organizations in the United States such as trade unions and fraternal associations have been in decline for decades. See also, Theda Skocpol, *Diminished Democracy: From Membership to Management in American Civic Life* (Norman: University of Oklahoma Press, 2003). There has also been a decline in membership in political parties in Western democracies. Paul F. Whiteley, "Is the Party Over? The Decline of Party Activism and Membership across the Democratic World," *Party Politics* vol. 17, no. 1 (January 2011): 21–44.

57. Elazar, *Community and Polity*, p. 265.

58. Rebhun, "Recent Developments in Jewish Identification in the United States," p. 267. There was also a decline in synagogue membership from 1970 to 1990, even though synagogue attendance remained about the same. Even among those American Jews aged between 38 and 57 (the age in which people are most likely to join a synagogue because of their children), the percentage that belonged to a synagogue dropped from 56.5 percent in 1970 to 39.2 percent in 1990, but the percentage of American Jews aged between 38 and 57 who attended synagogue remained roughly the same (77 percent in 1970 and 78.6 percent in 1990). Thus, American Jews were going to synagogue just as much as in the past, but joining synagogues much less. Ibid., pp. 267–269.

59. The survey also found that 44 percent of American Jews were completely "unaffiliated"—they did not belong to a synagogue, JCC, or any other Jewish organization. "The National Jewish Population Survey 2000–2001," United Jewish Communities Report, September 2003, p.10.

60. Pew Research Center, "A Portrait of Jewish Americans," p. 60. In the Pew survey, just 4 percent of secular Jews (those termed "Jews of no religion") belonged to Jewish organizations, although they make up almost a quarter—22 percent—of the overall Jewish population in the United States. Pew Survey, p. 61.

61. Steven M. Cohen, "From Jewish People to Jewish Purpose: Establishment Leaders and Their Nonestablishment Successors," in Jack Wertheimer, ed., *The New Jewish Leaders: Reshaping the American Jewish Landscape*, p. 47.

62. Cohen, "From Jewish People to Jewish Purpose," p. 45. Not all establishment organizations are struggling. The AJC is thriving, according to its executive director David Harris. "The AJC has never been stronger than it is today," he claims. In 2014, it had more than 175,000 supporters (people who had

donated money in the previous three years), and this figure remained stable. The number of major donors (those giving above $50,000) to the AJC has actually significantly increased in the past fifteen years. AJC has also engaged approximately 12,000 young Jews in the United States and in Israel through its young leadership program, ACCESS, which it started in 2005. Interview with David Harris, executive director of the American Jewish Committee, January 23, 2014.

63. Jack Wertheimer, "Current Trends in American Jewish Philanthropy," *American Jewish Yearbook* 1997: 81.

64. One of the reasons why Jewish organizations have become increasingly financially dependent on a few big donors is because they have found it more efficient to focus their fundraising efforts on soliciting major donations from a small number of people than trying to encourage small donations from lots of people. J. J. Goldberg, *Jewish Power*, p. 363. According to John Ruskay, the decline in the number of small donors to Jewish Federations (that is, those who give less than $1,000) is due to the failure of direct marketing campaigns (for example, telemarketing and mass mailing). He claims that the number of donors to Federations of $10,000 and above is actually growing nationally. Interview with John Ruskay, May 14, 2015.

65. On changes in the patterns of American Jewish philanthropy, see Chaim I. Waxman, "American Jewish Philanthropy, Direct Giving, and the Unity of the Jewish Community," in Yossi Prager, ed., *Toward a Renewed Ethic of Jewish Philanthropy* (New York: Yeshiva University Press, 2009).

66. Klarman also funds the Boston-based David Project, and he allegedly pressured the head of the local JCRC to work with the David Project and support its campaign against the construction of a local mosque (which ultimately failed). Interview with Nancy Kaufman. Klarman is also the owner of the web-only English-language newspaper *Times of Israel*. Josh Nathan-Kazis, "The Soft-Spoken Man behind Times of Israel," *Forward*, February 29, 2012.

67. Adelson is one of the main funders of Taglit-Birthright (providing it with nearly $100 million), and is also a major donor to the right-wing Zionist Organization of America. He used to be a major supporter of AIPAC, but stopped supporting it in 2007 after AIPAC lobbied in favor of a large increase in U.S. government funding to the Palestinian Authority. Ron Kampeas, "For Sheldon Adelson, Political and Jewish Giving Are All of a Piece," *Jewish Telegraphic Agency*, August 7, 2012.

68. Back in the nineteenth century, for example, the philanthropist Sir Moses Montefiore had a major role in the British Jewish community, while Baron Gustave de Rothschild had a similar role in the French Jewish community, as did Jacob Schiff in the American Jewish community in the late nineteenth and early twentieth century.

69. Daniel J. Elazar, *Community and Polity: The Organizational Dynamics of American Jewry*, pp. 444–445.

70. J. J. Goldberg, *Jewish Power*, p. 363.

71. Isi Leibler, "A Looming Jewish Leadership Crisis," *Israel Hayom*, August 16, 2012.

72. The Jewish Federation of New York even established a "Gen i" task force, with a half million dollar budget, to support outreach initiatives to unaffiliated Jews in their twenties and thirties.

73. Jack Wertheimer, "Mapping the Scene: How Younger American Jewish Adults Engage with Jewish Community," in Jack Wertheimer, ed., *The New Jewish Leaders: Reshaping the American Jewish Landscape*, p. 11.

74. In one study of young American Jews, the majority of those surveyed did not know what the acronyms AIPAC or AJC stood for or what these organizations did. Reboot, *"Grande Soy Vanilla Latte with Cinnamon, No Foam . . .": Jewish Identity and Community in a Time of Unlimited Choices.*

75. Ibid., p. 32. For more information on the beliefs and attitudes of young American Jews, see Jack Wertheimer, "Generation of Change: How Leaders in Their Twenties and Thirties Are Reshaping American Jewish Life," Avi Chai Foundation (2010); Jacob B. Ukeles, Ron Miller, and Pearl Beck, "Young Jewish Adults in the United States Today," American Jewish Committee (2006); Fern Chertok, Jim Gerstein, Joshua Tobias, Shirah Rosin, and Matthew Boxer, *Volunteering + Values: A Repair the World Report on Jewish Young Adults* (New York: Repair the World, 2011).

76. Steven M. Cohen and Ari Y. Kelman, *The Continuity of Discontinuity: How Young Jews Are Connecting, Creating, and Organizing Their Own Jewish Lives*, 2007.

77. UJA-Federation of New York, "Jewish Community Study of New York: 2011 Comprehensive Report," pp. 153–154. Similarly, a study of the Baltimore Jewish community conducted in 2010 showed that while just 14 percent of young non-Orthodox Jews said they wanted to be part of the Jewish community, 55 percent said that being Jewish was important to them. Sue Fishkoff, "With Flurry of New Local Studies, Jewish Communities Seeing Trends and Making Changes," *Jewish Telegraphic Agency*, July 10, 2011.

78. This was not always the case. The agenda of Jewish establishment organizations is narrower now than it was in the past (in the 1950s, 1960s, and 1970s). In an earlier era, Jewish organizations (with the exception of AIPAC, which was always solely concerned with the issue of Israel) were focused on a wide range of domestic issues. The best example of this was the now defunct American Jewish Congress, which was very active in championing liberal causes, particularly the separation of church and state.

79. For example, the AJC was at the forefront of international human rights and domestic civil rights activism in the 1950s and 1960s. In recent decades, however, the AJC's focus has gradually shifted from human rights and civil rights activism mainly toward supporting Israel. Michael Galchinsky, *Jews and Human Rights: Dancing at Three Weddings* (Lanham, MD: Rowman & Littlefield, 2008), p. 49.

80. In a 2011 survey of young American Jews, when asked to list which causes they care about most and for which they would be willing to volunteer,

"Israel/Middle East peace" appeared tenth on the list, behind social justice issues, the environment, human rights, and animal rights. In other words, these young American Jews cared more about saving the environment and protecting animals than Israel. Fern Chertok et al., *Volunteering + Values: A Repair the World Report on Jewish Young Adults*, p. 26.

81. Interview with Stosh Cotler, chief executive officer of Bend the Arc: Jewish Alliance for Justice, November 10, 2011. Interview with Rabbi Jill Jacobs, executive director of T'ruah: The Rabbinical Call for Human Rights, October 31, 2011. Part of the appeal to young American Jews of Jewish social justice activism, according to Jacobs, is that they "can focus on food justice in America, worker's issues, . . . be proud of Judaism, and . . . don't have to deal with Israel."

82. Shifra Bronznick, and Didi Goldenhar, *Visioning Justice and the American Jewish Community* (New York: Nathan Cummings Foundation, 2008), p. 57.

83. Ibid., pp. 20–26. Some Jewish establishment organizations, particularly Jewish federations, have actually played a key role in nurturing the development of new Jewish social justice and environmental organizations, providing them with seed money, office space, and networking opportunities. Jewish family foundations, like the Nathan Cummings Foundation, the Schusterman Foundation, and the Bronfman Foundation have also funded and facilitated the development of new Jewish social justice and environmental organizations.

84. Ibid., p. 20. Ruth Messinger, the president of AJWS, argues that: "We live in a world in which Jews should be able to acknowledge the real problems in their individual Jewish communities, and the real problems in the Jewish community writ large around the world, and still have energy and resources left to respond to what is by any standard more pervasive and dramatic need in some other parts of the world." Interview with Ruth Messinger, president of the American Jewish World Service, October 13, 2011.

85. Steven M. Cohen, "The New Jewish Organizing," *Sh'ma* vol. 40 (2010).

86. Steven Windmueller, "The Second American Jewish Revolution," *Journal of Jewish Communal Service* vol. 82, no. 3 (2007): 254. See also Steven M. Cohen, "From Jewish People to Jewish Purpose: Establishment Leaders and Their Nonestablishment Successors," in Jack Wertheimer, ed., *The New Jewish Leaders: Reshaping the American Jewish Landscape*, pp. 47–48.

87. Tamar Snyder, "Philanthropy Watch: Jewish Start-ups Continue to Grow," *Jewish Week*, April 12, 2011.

88. Interview with Lisa Colton, founder and president of Darim Online, November 8, 2011.

89. Jack Wertheimer, "Mapping the Scene: How Younger American Jewish Adults Engage with Jewish Community," p. 37. David Harris, executive director of the AJC, welcomes this development, declaring: "Let a hundred new [Jewish] organizations bloom, be they religious, be they spiritual, be they cultural, be they historical, be they musical, be they ethnological, be they political, let them bloom." Interview with David Harris, executive director of the American Jewish Committee, January 23, 2014.

90. Joshua Avedon, "Where Would Darwin Daven?" *Forward*, December 4, 2008. In the same vein, a report on the new Jewish "start-ups" declared that: "In and beyond the Jewish community, a new generation of organic, decentralized, and flexible structures is replacing the twentieth century's mechanical, centralized, and top-down organizations." Jumpstart, the Natan Fund and the Samuel Bronfman Foundation, *The Innovation Ecosystem: Emergence of a New Jewish Landscape* (Los Angeles and New York: Jumpstart, the Natan Fund and the Samuel Bronfman Foundation, 2009), p. 1.

91. Steven M. Cohen, "From Jewish People to Jewish Purpose: Establishment Leaders and Their Nonestablishment Successors," in Jack Wertheimer, ed., *The New Jewish Leaders: Reshaping the American Jewish Landscape*, pp. 45–83.

92. Cohen, "From Jewish People to Jewish Purpose," p. 66.

93. Steven M. Cohen, "Expressive, Progressive and Protective: Three Impulses for Nonestablishment Organizing among Young Jews Today," in Jack Wertheimer, ed., *The New Jewish Leaders: Reshaping the American Jewish Landscape*, p. 84.

94. In Cohen's survey, "the percentage of those who are very worried about threats to Israel's security is almost three times as great among older establishment leaders as among young nonestablishment leaders." Cohen, "From Jewish People to Jewish Purpose," pp. 68–69.

95. Cohen, "From Jewish People to Jewish Purpose," p. 76.

96. Leaders of nonestablishment organizations were also more critical of pro-Israel advocacy groups such as AIPAC and more positive about "pro-Israel/pro-peace groups" like J Street than leaders of establishment organizations. Ibid., p. 76.

97. The journalist and historian Eric Alterman, for instance, states that: "The Jewish establishment is a dying establishment in American Jewish life." Interview with Eric Alterman, October 21, 2011.

98. Steven M. Cohen, "From Jewish People to Jewish Purpose," p. 47. Somewhat less judiciously Cohen also writes that: "the vast institutional infrastructure of American Jewry is in decline." Ibid., p. 80.

99. Although the organization still officially exists, it is little more than a website.

100. Interview with Malcolm Hoenlein, executive vice chairman of the Conference of Presidents, October 31, 2011. Barry Shrage, who runs Greater Boston's Jewish Federation, put it even more succinctly, telling me: "Those [Jewish organizations] that deserve to die will die." Interview with Barry Shrage, president of Combined Jewish Philanthropies, May 15, 2015.

101. Steven Windmueller claims that: "a fundamental reconfiguration of institutional life is taking place in American Jewish life." He argues that since the mid-1980s, the American Jewish community has been undergoing the "second American Jewish revolution" (the first revolution occurred in the late nineteenth century and early twentieth century), driven by changes in philanthropy, new technologies, and new models of organizing. According to Windmueller: "This revolution involves a shift from a centralized system of giving and a shared communal agenda to a competitive and individualized

marketplace." Steven Windmueller, "The Second American Jewish Revolution," *Journal of Jewish Communal Service* vol. 82, no. 3 (2007): 259.

CHAPTER 7: THE POLARIZATION OF AMERICAN JEWRY

1. Dana Evan Kaplan, "Introduction," in Dana Evan Kaplan, ed., *The Cambridge Companion to American Judaism*, p. 17.

2. "One Jewish People, One Jewish Reality," Ambassador Michael Oren—Israeli Ambassador to the United States, May 4, 2012, Address to AJC ACCESS 20/20, Washington, DC; available at http://www.ajc.org/site/apps/nlnet/content2.aspx?c=ijITI2PHKoG&b=8079159&ct=11744505 (accessed November 10, 2015).

3. The divide between American Jews and Israeli Jews has been undeniable in recent years, especially as a result of the constant tensions and disagreements between President Obama and Prime Minister Netanyahu. One indication of this was President Obama's enduring popularity with a majority of American Jews (he received about 74 percent of the "Jewish vote" in the 2008 and 70 percent in the 2012 presidential elections) and his unpopularity with Israelis (59 percent of whom gave him an unfavorable rating in a poll taken in 2015 and 50 percent in a similar poll in 2014). Another indication was the starkly different opinions that most American Jews and Israeli Jews held regarding the Obama administration's effort to reach an agreement with Iran to restrict its nuclear program. Stephan Miller, "3 in 4 Israelis Don't Trust Obama to Keep Iran from Nukes," *Times of Israel*, February 11, 2015.

4. For a detailed analysis of the division between Israeli Jews and its impact on Israeli politics and foreign policy in the 1990s, see Dov Waxman, *The Pursuit of Peace and the Crisis of Israeli Identity*, pp. 114–140.

5. Peter Beinart, "Establishment's Rebuff Highlights J Street's Success in Changing Jewish America," *Ha'aretz*, May 7, 2014.

6. Pew Research Center, "A Portrait of Jewish Americans," p. 48.

7. This is also true of Americans in general. The common claim of a "culture war" pitting "red state" America against "blue state" America is grossly exaggerated; see Morris P. Fiorina, Samuel J. Abrams, and Jeremy C. Pope, *Culture War: The Myth of a Polarized America* (New York: Pearson Longman, 2005).

8. Jonathan Sarna, "The Relationship of Orthodox Jews with Believing Jews of Other Religious Ideologies and Non-believing Jews: The American Situation in Historical Perspective," *Orthodox Forum* vol. 20 (August 2010): 1–26.

9. Samuel G. Freedman, *Jew vs. Jew: The Struggle for the Soul of American Jewry* (New York: Simon and Schuster, 2000).

10. Jack Wertheimer, *A People Divided: Judaism in Contemporary America* (Hanover, MA: University Press of New England, 1997).

11. When Israel is at war, American Jewish solidarity with Israel surges and criticism largely subsides. This was evident in the American Jewish community's reaction to the second Intifada, the second Lebanon war against Hezbollah,

and its wars against Hamas in the Gaza Strip in 2008/9, 2012, and 2014. When the level of perceived threat to Israel increases, American Jewish political divisions over Israel decrease. This reaction is typical of groups facing external threat, as social psychologists have long documented how the cohesion of a group increases in response to external threats.

12. Jack Wertheimer, "American Jews and Israel: A 60-Year Retrospective," in *American Jewish Yearbook 2008*, p. 75.

13. See, for instance, Robert D. Putnam and David E. Campbell, *How Religion Divides and Unites Us* (New York: Simon and Schuster, 2010).

14. James Davison Hunter, *Culture Wars: The Struggle to Define America* (New York: Basic Books, 1991).

15. Jonathan Haidt, *The Righteous Mind: Why Good People Are Divided by Religion and Politics* (New York: Vintage Books, 2012).

16. Despite their theological objections to the State of Israel, most ultra-Orthodox American Jews (*haredim*) hold hawkish positions on issues related to Israel's relations with the Palestinians, and especially on the issue of the Occupied Territories. Eliezer Don-Yehiya, "Orthodox Jewry in Israel and America," *Israel Studies* vol. 10, no. 1 (2005): 175.

17. Laurence Kotler-Berkowitz, "The Structure of Political Divisions among American Jews," paper presented at the annual meeting of the Association for Jewish Studies, Baltimore, December 14, 2014.

18. Laurence Kotler-Berkowitz, "Political Diversification and Division in the American Jewish Community: The Effect on Consensus Building and Jewish Advocacy," *Journal of Jewish Communal Service* vol. 71 (Summer 1995): pp. 270–271.

19. Ibid., p. 272.

20. Although ultra-Orthodox Jews in the United States are not Zionists ideologically, they are not anti-Israel. On the contrary, they are very attached to Israel, regularly visiting the country, studying there (in Israeli *Yeshivot*) and closely following Israeli current affairs. Eliezer Don-Yehiya, "Modern and Haredi Orthodox American Jews and Their Attitude to the State of Israel," in Danny Ben Moshe and Zohar Segev, eds., *Israel, the Diaspora and Jewish Identity*, pp. 62–66.

21. Jay Michaelson, "How I Am Losing My Love for Israel," *Forward*, September 25, 2009.

22. Pew Research Center, "A Portrait of Orthodox American Jews."

23. Pew Research Center, "A Portrait of Jewish Americans," p. 98.

24. Orthodox American Jews are similar to white evangelical Christians in a number of other respects. As a 2015 study by the Pew Research Center noted: "Indeed, in a few ways, Orthodox Jews more closely resemble white evangelical Protestants than they resemble other U.S. Jews. For example, similarly large majorities of Orthodox Jews (83%) and white evangelicals (86%) say that religion is very important in their lives, while only about one-fifth of other Jewish Americans (20%) say the same. Roughly three-quarters of both

Orthodox Jews (74%) and white evangelicals (75%) report that they attend religious services at least once a month. And eight-in-ten or more Orthodox Jews (84%) and white evangelicals (82%) say that Israel was given to the Jewish people by God—more than twice the share of other American Jews (35%) who express this belief." Pew Research Center, "A Portrait of Orthodox American Jews." See also Nathan Guttman, "Pew Study Finds Orthodox Similar to Evangelical Christians—Not Other Jews," *Forward*, August 26, 2015.

25. In the 2013 Pew Survey, most non-Orthodox Jews (62 percent) approved of President Obama's handling of U.S.-Israel relations, compared to only 36 percent of Orthodox Jews who approved of Obama's policy toward Israel. Pew Research Center, "A Portrait of Jewish Americans," p. 100.

26. In a survey before the 2008 U.S. election, a quarter of Orthodox Jews said that support for Israel was the single most important factor determining how they would vote. By contrast, this was the most important issue to only 6 percent of Conservative Jews, 3 percent of Reform Jews, and 4 percent of respondents who characterized themselves as "just Jewish." Gary Rosenblatt, "Why the American Jewish Divide Is Growing," *Jewish Week*, February 28, 2008. Similarly, in a post-election survey in 2012, a quarter of Orthodox Jews said that Israel was one of the top two issues that decided their vote in the presidential election between Barack Obama and Mitt Romney, compared to only 8 percent of non-Orthodox American Jews for whom Israel was a top issue. Post-election survey of 800 American Jewish voters conducted on behalf of J Street on November 6, 2012.

27. For a statistical snapshot of many of the differences between Orthodox and non-Orthodox Jews, see Pew Research Center, "A Portrait of Orthodox American Jews."

28. Jack Wertheimer, "All Quiet on the Religious Front: Jewish Unity, Denom-inationalism, and Postdenominationalism in the United States" (New York: American Jewish Committee, 2005), p. 18.

29. Ibid., p. 18.

30. Pew Research Center, "A Portrait of Jewish Americans," p. 51.

31. Ibid., p. 52.

32. Chaim Waxman notes that: "Like many of their non-Jewish countrymen, young American Jews increasingly shun organized public religion and are now turned inward. Their religious and/or spiritual quest and activity takes place in the private sphere, as they search for that which is meaningful to them." Chaim Waxman, "Beyond Distancing: Jewish Identity, Identification, and America's Young Jews," *Contemporary Jewry* vol. 30 (2010): 229.

33. Dana Evan Kaplan, "Introduction," in Dana Evan Kaplan, ed., *The Cambridge Companion to American Judaism*, p. 9.

34. Steven M. Cohen and Arnold M. Eisen, *The Jew Within: Self, Family, and Community in America* (Bloomington: Indiana University Press, 2000).

35. A small minority of Modern Orthodox Jews in the United States, mostly younger ones, belongs to what is known as the "Open Orthodoxy" move-ment, which promotes a more egalitarian and liberal approach to Orthodox

Judaism. The movement has its own institution for ordaining rabbis (Yeshiva Chovevei Torah), founded by Rabbi Avi Weiss. See Yair Ettinger, "Is Modern Orthodoxy Reaching Its Breaking Point?," *Ha'aretz*, August 31, 2015.

36. Steven M. Cohen and Jack Wertheimer, "Whatever Happened to the Jewish People," *Commentary* vol. 121, no. 6 (2006): 33–37. See also Steven M. Cohen, "Jewish Identity Research in the United States: Ruminations on Concepts and Findings," in Sol Encel and Leslie Stein, *Continuity, Commitment and Survival: Jewish Communities in the Diaspora*, p. 8.

37. Pew Research Center, "A Portrait of Jewish Americans," p. 52.

38. Ibid., p. 61.

39. Back in the mid-1990s, the sociologists Seymour Lipset and Earl Rabb argued that tribalism is gradually weakened in the melting pot of the United States. In what they described as the "almost inexorable American pattern of decline in tribal cohesion," a number of earlier ethnic immigrant groups (such as Italian-Americans and Irish-Americans) have already assimilated into white American society and lost their sense of ethnic cohesion. American Jews are bound to undergo the same process, they argued. Seymour M. Lipset and Earl Rabb, *Jews and the New American Scene* (Boston: Harvard University Press, 1995), p. 53. For a similar argument about the inevitable decline of Jewish ethnicity and the likelihood of Jewish assimilation into the American melting pot, see Zvi Gitelman, "The Decline of the Diaspora Jewish Nation: Boundaries, Content, and Jewish Identity," *Jewish Social Studies* vol. 4, no. 2 (1998): 112–127.

40. Shaul Magid, *American Post-Judaism: Identity and Renewal in a Postethnic Society* (Bloomington: Indiana University Press 2013).

41. For example, in the 2000/2001 National Jewish Population Study, 75 percent of American Jews aged over 65 strongly agreed to the statement "I have a strong sense of belonging to the Jewish people," compared to 47 percent of those aged under 35. Cohen and Wertheimer, "Whatever Happened to the Jewish People," p. 34.

42. Reboot, *"Grande Soy Vanilla Latte with Cinnamon, No Foam . . .": Jewish Identity and Community in a Time of Unlimited Choices.*

43. See, for example, Cohen and Wertheimer, "Whatever Happened to the Jewish People."

44. In the Pew Survey, 60 percent of American Jews (including Orthodox Jews) aged 18–29 said they felt a special responsibility to care for Jews in need, compared with 67 percent of those aged over 65. Pew Research Center, "A Portrait of Jewish Americans," p. 52.

45. Sylvia Barack Fishman, with Rachel S. Bernstein and Emily Sigalow, "Reimagining Jewishness: Younger American Jewish Leaders, Entrepreneurs, and Artists in Cultural Context," in Jack Wertheimer, ed., *The New Jewish Leaders: Reshaping the American Jewish Landscape*, p. 174.

46. Daniel Gordis, "From a Jewish People to a Jewish Religion: A Shifting American Jewish Weltanschauung and Its Implications for Israel," *Israel Studies* vol. 17, no. 2 (2012): 104–105.

47. Pew Research Center, "A Portrait of Jewish Americans," pp. 35–37.

48. Theodore Sasson, "New Analysis of Pew Data: Children of Intermarriage Increasingly Identify as Jews," *Tablet*, November 11, 2013.
49. Steven M. Cohen, "Jewish Identity Research in the United States: Ruminations on Concepts and Findings," in Sol Encel and Leslie Stein, eds., *Continuity, Commitment and Survival: Jewish Communities in the Diaspora*, p. 9.
50. Steven M. Cohen and Ari Kelman, *Beyond Distancing: Young Adult American Jews and Their Alienation from Israel*, p. 21.
51. Cohen and Kelman, "Beyond Distancing," pp. 14–15. See also, Steven M. Cohen and Ari Y. Kelman, "Distancing Is Closer than Ever," *Contemporary Jewry* vol. 30 (2010): 145–148.
52. Steven M. Cohen and Ari Y. Kelman, "Thinking about Distancing from Israel," *Contemporary Jewry* vol. 30 (2010): 295.
53. Numerous studies have now been conducted on the impact of Birthright tours on participants' Jewish identities and attachment to Israel. These studies indicate that the trips have succeeded, at least in the short term, in strengthening attachment to Israel and Jewish identity. See Leonard Saxe, Charles Kadushin, Shahar Hecht, Benjamin Phillips, Mark I. Rosen, and Shaul Kelner, *Evaluating Birthright Israel: Long Term Impact and Recent Findings* (Waltham, MA: Cohen Center for Modern Jewish Studies, Brandeis University, 2004); Leonard Saxe, Benjamin Phillips, Graham Wright, Mathew Boxer, Shahar Hecht, and Theodore Sasson, *Taglit-Birthright Israel: 2007–2008 North American Cohorts* (Waltham, MA: Cohen Center for Modern Jewish Studies, Brandeis University, 2008); Leonard Saxe, Benjamin Phillips, Theodore Sasson, Shahar Hecht, Michelle Shain, Graham Wright, and Charles Kadushin, *Generation Birthright Israel: The Impact of an Israel Experience on Jewish Identity and Choices* (Waltham, MA: Cohen Center for Modern Jewish Studies, Brandeis University, 2009); Leonard Saxe, Theodore Sasson, Shahar Hecht, Benjamin Phillips, Michelle Shain, Graham Wright, and Charles Kadushin, *Jewish Futures Project: The Impact of Taglit-Birthright Israel: 2010 Update* (Waltham: Cohen Center for Modern Jewish Studies, 2011).
54. Steven M. Cohen and Ari Kelman, *Beyond Distancing: Young Adult American Jews and Their Alienation from Israel*, p. 11.
55. See Theodore Sasson, Charles Kadushin, and Leonard Saxe, "Trends in American Jewish Attachment to Israel: An Assessment of the "Distancing" Hypothesis," *Contemporary Jewry* vol. 30, nos. 2–3 (2010): 297–319.
56. Cohen and Kelman, "Distancing Is Closer than Ever," pp. 145–148.
57. In the Pew survey, a majority (55 percent) of completely secular Jews (those who describe themselves as "Jews of no religion") reported that they have little, if any, emotional attachment to Israel. Pew Research Center, "A Portrait of Jewish Americans," p. 13. These Jews now make up almost a quarter (22 percent) of the overall Jewish population in the United States, a percentage that has been steadily increasing over time—paralleling the increase among Americans in general who do not claim any religious identity (the so-called

nones). See, Ariela Keysar, "Distancing from Israel: Evidence on Jews of No Religion," *Contemporary Jewry* vol. 30 (2010): 199–204.

58. Pew Research Center, "A Portrait of Jewish Americans," p. 82.

59. Steven Bayme, "On Gabriel Sheffer's 'Loyalty and Criticism in the Relations between World Jewry and Israel,'" *Israel Studies* vol. 17, no. 2 (2012): 113.

60. Kenneth Wald and Bryan D. Williams. "American Jews and Israel: The Sources of Politicized Ethnic Identities," *Nationalism and Ethnic Politics* vol. 12 (2006): 205–237.

61. Ephraim Tabory, "Attachment to Israel and Jewish Identity: An Assessment of an Assessment," *Contemporary Jewry* vol. 30 (2010): 195.

62. Gary Rosenblatt, "Mind the Gap between Orthodox and Other Jews," *Jewish Week*, November 29, 2011.

63. Ephraim Tabory, "Attachment to Israel and Jewish Identity: An Assessment of an Assessment," *Contemporary Jewry* vol. 30 (2010): 196.

64. Dana Evan Kaplan, "Introduction," in Dana Evan Kaplan, ed., *The Cambridge Companion to American Judaism.*

65. Steven M. Cohen, "A Tale of Two Jewries: The 'Inconvenient Truth' for American Jews," Jewish Life Network/Steinhardt Foundation, November 2006, p. 8.

66. The growing polarization between non-Orthodox and Orthodox American Jews mirrors that occurring among Christians in the United States with an increase in the number of Evangelicals and decrease in the number of mainline Protestants.

67. In the Pew survey, only 7 percent of Jews born between 1914 and 1927 say they have no religion, compared with 32 percent of Jews born since 1980.

68. According to Laurence Kotler-Berkowitz, senior director of research and analysis at the Jewish Federations of North America, the Pew survey portends "growing polarization" between religious and nonreligious Jews. Quoted in Laurie Goodstein, "Poll Shows Major Shift in Identity of U.S. Jews," *New York Times*, October 1, 2013. On a smaller scale, a 2011 study of New York's Jewish community, conducted by UJA-Federation of New York, showed that it is becoming increasingly polarized, as Jews become more secular and more Orthodox. While the Orthodox Jewish population rapidly increased, growing by more than 100,000 people in a decade, the proportion of nondenominational and no-religion Jewish households also greatly increased between 1991 and 2011 (from 15 percent to 37 percent of all Jewish households). UJA-Federation of New York, "Jewish Community Study of New York: 2011 Comprehensive Report." One of the main authors of the report commented: "There are more deeply engaged Jews and there are more unengaged Jews. These two wings are growing at the expense of the middle." Quoted in Joseph Berger, "Aided by Orthodox, City's Jewish Population Is Growing Again," *New York Times*, June 11, 2012.

69. The Conservative movement, once the largest Jewish religious denomination in the United States, is actually declining: in 1971, 41 percent of American

Jews were affiliated with it, while it now claims the allegiance of only 18 percent of American Jews, and just 11 percent of those under the age of 30. Daniel Gordis, "Conservative Judaism: A Requiem," *Jewish Review of Books*, Winter 2014.

70. Gary Rosenblatt, "Why the American Jewish Divide Is Growing," *Jewish Week*, February 28, 2008; see also David Berkman, "Gap Grows between Orthodox and Others," *Los Angeles Jewish Journal*, February 7, 2008.

71. Sandy Goodman, "Bad for the Jews, Bad for America," *Huffington Post*, May 26, 2015.

72. Pew Research Center, "A Portrait of Orthodox American Jews."

73. Laurie Goodstein, "Poll Shows Major Shift in Identity of U.S. Jews," *New York Times*, October 1, 2013.

74. Jack Wertheimer and Steven M. Cohen, "The Pew Survey Reanalyzed: More Bad News, but a Glimmer of Hope," *Mosaic*, November 2, 2014. It must be noted, however, that there is bound to be some attrition within the population of ultra-Orthodox Jews, and that some Orthodox Jews are bound to become secular Jews.

75. These were the main findings of a landmark study of New York's Jewish community conducted by the UJA-Federation of New York in 2011. Although New York has an unusually large concentration of ultra-Orthodox Jews, so the growth of that population, which has a very high fertility rate, is much faster there than in other parts of the United States, the general demographic trends in New York's Jewish population are true of the American Jewish population as a whole. In fact, the gradual demographic transformation of New York's Jewish community is a microcosm of what is happening across the Jewish world, in the Diaspora and in Israel. The Orthodox proportion of the European Jewish population is also growing, especially since the fertility rate among non-Orthodox European Jews has been below the replacement level for a long time. The number of *haredim* in the United Kingdom, for instance, has rapidly increased in recent years. They now make up an estimated 17 percent of Britain's Jewish population, and account for three-quarters of all British Jewish births. Thus, it has been predicted that half of all British Jews will be *haredi* by 2050. The same demographic trend is occurring in Israel, where the ultra-Orthodox population is expected to rise to over 30 percent of the population in the next fifty years (from 10 percent at present).

76. Dov Waxman, "There Goes the Neighborhood," *Ha'aretz*, June 22, 2012.

77. See, for example, Nathan Guttman, "How Orthodox Money Is Reshaping Republican Politics," *Forward*, May 4, 2015.

78. Samuel C. Heilman, *Sliding to the Right: The Contest for the Future of American Jewish Orthodoxy* (University of California Press: Berkeley, 2006), pp. 6–12.

79. Chaim Waxman, "From Institutional Decay to Primary Day: American Orthodox Jewry since World War II, *American Jewish History* vol. 91, nos. 3–4 (2003): 405–421.

80. David Brooks, "The Orthodox Surge," *New York Times*, March 7, 2013.

CONCLUSION

1. Leon Wieseltier, "J Street's Rejection Is a Scandal," *New Republic*, May 7, 2014.
2. Gary Rosenblatt, "I Love Israel, but Does Israel Love Me?" *Jewish Week*, May 27, 2015.
3. Quoted in Philip Weiss, "Foxman Bashes Israel for Taking US and Jewish Support for Granted and Not Coming Up with a Peace Plan," *Mondoweiss*, June 11, 2015.
4. In a 2015 survey of 1,000 Jewish adults conducted on behalf of J Street, 84 percent of respondents said they supported "the United States playing an active role in helping the parties to resolve the Arab-Israeli conflict," and 69 percent said they would also support this "if it meant the United States exerting pressure on both the Israelis and Arabs to make the compromises necessary to achieve peace." "J Street National Survey," May 31–June 3, 2015, conducted by Gerstein Bocian Agne.
5. Jeffrey Goldberg interview with President Obama, "The Middle East Interview: President Obama on ISIS, Iran, and Israel," *Atlantic*, May 21, 2015.
6. In the 2015 J Street survey, 56 percent of American Jews thought that it was acceptable for President Obama to publicly criticize Prime Minister Netanyahu's policies. "J Street National Survey," May 31–June 3, 2015, conducted by Gerstein Bocian Agne.

BIBLIOGRAPHY

Alexander, E., and P. Bogdanor, eds. *The Jewish Divide over Israel*. New Brunswick, NJ: Transaction Press, 2006.

Arkush, Allan. "From Diaspora Nationalism to Radical Diasporism." *Modern Judaism* vol. 29, no. 3 (2009): 326–350.

Aslan, Reza, and Aaron J. Hahn Tapper, eds. *Muslims and Jews in America: Commonalities, Contentions, and Complexities*. New York: Palgrave Macmillan, 2011.

Auerbach, J. S. *Are We One? Jewish Identity in the United States and Israel*. New Brunswick, NJ: Rutgers University Press, 2001.

Aviv, Caryn, and David Shneer. *New Jews: The End of the Jewish Diaspora*. New York: New York University Press, 2005.

Bard, Mitchell G. "AIPAC and US Middle East Policy." In *US-Israeli Relations in a New Era*, edited by Eytan Gilboa and Efraim Inbar. New York: Routledge, 2009. pp. 76–90.

Bayme, Steven. "American Jewry and the State of Israel: How Intense the Bonds of Peoplehood?" *Jewish Political Studies Review* vol. 20, nos. 1–2 (Spring 2008).

———. "American Jewry Confronts the Twenty-first Century." In *American Jewry's Comfort Level: Present and Future*, edited by Manfred Gerstenfeld and Steven Bayme. Jerusalem: Jerusalem Center for Public Affairs, 2010, pp. 15–54.

———. "On Gabriel Sheffer's 'Loyalty and Criticism in the Relations between World Jewry and Israel.'" *Israel Studies* vol. 17, no. 2 (Summer 2012): 111–119.

Becker, Aliza. "The American Jewish Peace Movement for a Two-State Solution to the Israeli-Palestinian Conflict: An Overview of National Initiatives, 1969–2012." Washington, DC: Brit Tzedek v'Shalom, 2013.

Beilin, Yossi. *His Brother's Keeper: Israel and Diaspora Jewry in the Twenty-First Century*. New York: Schocken Books, 2000.

Beinart, Peter. *The Crisis of Zionism*. New York: Times Books, 2012.

———. "The Failure of the American Jewish Establishment." *New York Review of Books*, June 10, 2010.

Bellah, R., Richard Madsen, William M. Sullivan, and Steven M. Tipton. *Habits of the Heart: Individualism and Commitment in American Life*. Berkeley: University of California Press, 1996.

Ben-Ami, Jeremy. *A New Voice for Israel: Fighting for the Survival of the Jewish Nation.* New York: Palgrave Macmillan, 2011.

Ben Hagai, Ella, Eileen L. Zurbriggen, Phillip L. Hammack, and Megan Ziman. "Beliefs Predicting Peace, Beliefs Predicting War: Jewish-Americans and the Israeli-Palestinian Conflict." *Analyses of Social Issues and Public Policy* vol. 13, no. 1 (2013): 286–309.

Ben Moshe, Danny, and Zohar Segev, eds. *Israel, the Diaspora and Jewish Identity.* Brighton, UK: Sussex Academic Press, 2007.

Benor, Sarah Bunin. "Young Jewish Leaders in Los Angeles: Strengthening the Jewish People in Conventional and Unconventional Ways." In *The New Jewish Leaders: Reshaping the American Jewish Landscape,* edited by Jack Wertheimer. Waltham, MA: Brandeis University Press, 2011, pp. 112–158.

Biale, David. *Power and Powerlessness in Jewish History.* New York: Schocken Books, 1986.

Boyarin, Daniel, and Jonathan Boyarin. "Diaspora: Generation and the Ground of Jewish Identity," *Critical Inquiry* vol. 19, no. 4 (1993): 693–725.

Brackman, Nicole. "Who Is a Jew? The American Jewish Community in Conflict with Israel." *Journal of Church and State* vol. 4, no. 4 (1999): 795–822.

Brettschneider, Marla. *Cornerstones of Peace: Jewish Identity Politics and Democratic Theory.* New Brunswick, NJ: Rutgers University Press, 1996.

Bronznick, Shifra, and Didi Goldenhar. *Visioning Justice and the American Jewish Community.* New York: Nathan Cummings Foundation, 2008.

Burstein, Paul. "Jewish Nonprofit Organizations in the U.S.: A Preliminary Survey." *Journal of Contemporary Jewry* vol. 31, no. 2 (2011): 129–148.

Butler, Judith. "The Charge of Anti-Semitism: Jews, Israel, and the Risks of Public Critique." In *Wrestling with Zion: Progressive Jewish-American Responses to the Israeli-Palestinian Conflict,* edited by Tony Kushner and Alisa Solomon. New York: Grove Press, 2003, pp. 249–268.

———. "Jews and the Bi-National Vision." *Logos* vol. 3, no. 1 (Winter 2004).

———. *Parting Ways: Jewishness and the Critique of Zionism.* New York: Columbia University Press, 2012.

Carter, Jimmy. *Palestine: Peace, Not Apartheid.* New York: Simon & Schuster, 2006.

Cavari, Amnon. "Religious Beliefs, Elite Polarization, and Public Opinion on Foreign Policy: The Partisan Gap in American Public Opinion toward Israel." *International Journal of Public Opinion Research* vol. 25, no. 1 (Spring 2013): 1–22.

Chanes, Jerome A. *A Primer on the American Jewish Community.* New York: The American Jewish Committee, 2002.

Chanin, Mitch, and Rebecca Ennen. *Guidebook for Deliberation about the Israeli-Palestinian Conflict.* Philadelphia: Jewish Dialogue Group, 2013.

Chertok, Fern, Joshua Tobias, Sarah Rosin, and Mathew Boxer. "Volunteering + Values: A Repair the World Report on Jewish Young Adults." Cohen Center for Modern Jewish Studies, Waltham, MA: Brandeis University Press, 2011.

Chesler, Phyllis. *The New Anti-Semitism: The Current Crisis and What We Must Do about It*. San Francisco: Jossey-Bass, 2003.

Cockburn, Alexander, and Jeffrey St. Clair, eds. *The Politics of Anti-Semitism*. Petrolia, CA: CounterPunch/AK Press, 2003.

Cohen, Anthony P. *The Symbolic Construction of Community*. London: Tavistock, 1985.

Cohen, Mark P. "American Jewish Response to the Palestinian Uprising," *Journal of Palestine Studies* vol. 17, no. 4 (Summer 1988): 97–104.

Cohen, Naomi W. *The Americanization of Zionism, 1897–1948*. Lebanon, NH: Brandeis University Press and University Press of New England, 2003.

———. *American Jews and the Zionist Idea*. New York: Ktav Publishing House, 1975.

Cohen, Steven M. *Are American and Israeli Jews Drifting Apart?* New York: American Jewish Committee, 1989.

———. "Did American Jews Really Grow More Distant from Israel, 1983–1993? A Reconsideration." In *Envisioning Israel: The Changing Ideals and Images of North American Jews*, edited by Allon Gal. Jerusalem and Detroit: Magnes Press and Wayne State University Press, 1996, pp. 352–373.

———. "From Jewish People to Jewish Purpose: Establishment Leaders and Their Nonestablishment Successors." In *The New Jewish Leaders: Reshaping the American Jewish Landscape*, edited by Jack Wertheimer. Waltham, MA: Brandeis University Press, 2011, pp. 45–83.

———. "Highly Engaged Young American Jews: Contrasts in Generational Ethos," September 15, 2010. Available at http://jcpa.org/article/highly-engaged-young -american-jews-contrasts-in-generational-ethos/(accessed November 11, 2015).

———. "Israel in the Jewish Identity of American Jews: A Study in Dualities and Contrasts." In *Jewish Identity in America*, edited by David Gordis and Yoav Ben Horin. Los Angeles: Wilstein Institute, 1991, pp. 119–136.

———. "JTS Rabbis and Israel, Then and Now: The 2011 Survey of JTS Ordained Rabbis and Current Students." *Jewish Political Studies Review* vol. 24 (2012): 59–98.

———. "The New Jewish Organizing." *Sh'ma, A Journal of Jewish Ideas* vol. 40, no. 666 (2010). Available at http://www.bjpa.org/Publications/details.cfm?Publica tionID=5067 (accessed November 11, 2015).

———. "Relationships of American Jews with Israel: What We Know and What We Need to Know." *Contemporary Jewry* vol. 23, no. 1 (2002): 132–155.

———. "Ties and Tensions: The 1986 Survey of American Jewish Attitudes toward Israel and Israelis." New York: American Jewish Committee, 1987.

Cohen, Steven M., and Sam Abrams. "Israel off Their Minds: The Diminished Place of Israel in the Political Thinking of Young Jews." New York: Berman Jewish Policy Archive, 2008.

Cohen, Steven M., and Arnold M. Eisen. *The Jew Within: Self, Family, and Community in America*. Bloomington: Indiana University Press, 2000.

Cohen, Steven M., and Leonard Fein. *American Jews and Their Social Justice Involvement: Evidence from a National Survey.* Amos – The National Jewish Partnership for Social Justice, 2001. Available at http://www.bjpa.org/Publications/details .cfm?PublicationID=4692 (accessed November 11, 2015).

Cohen, Steven M., and Jason Gitlin. "Reluctant or Repressed? Aversion to Expressing Views on Israel among American Rabbis." New York: Jewish Council for Public Affairs, 2013.

Cohen, Steven M., and Ari Y. Kelman. "Beyond Distancing: Young Adult American Jews and Their Alienation from Israel." New York: Andrea and Charles Bronfman Philanthropies, 2007.

———. *The Continuity of Discontinuity: How Young Jews Are Connecting, Creating, and Organizing Their Own Jewish Lives.* New York: Andrea and Charles Bronfman Philanthropies, May 2007.

———. "Distancing Is Closer than Ever." *Contemporary Jewry* vol. 30 (2010): 145–148.

———. "Thinking about Distancing from Israel." *Contemporary Jewry* vol. 30 (2010): 287–296.

Cohen, Steven M., and Charles S. Liebman, "American Jewish Liberalism: Unravelling the Strands." *Public Opinion Quarterly* vol. 61 (1997): 405–430.

———. "Israel and American Jewry in the Twenty-First Century." In *Beyond Survival and Philanthropy: American Jewry and Israel*, edited by Allon Gal and Alfred Gottschalk. Cincinnati: Hebrew Union College Press, 2000.

Cohen, Steven M., Jack B. Ukeles, and Ron Miller. *Jewish Community Study of New York: 2011.* New York: UJA Federation, 2012. Available at http://www.jewish databank.org/studies/details.cfm?StudyID=597 (accessed November 11, 2015).

Cohen, Steven M., and Jack Wertheimer. "Whatever Happened to the Jewish People?" *Commentary* vol. 121, no. 6 (June 2006): 33–37.

Curtiss, Richard. "Stealth Pacs: How Israel's American Lobby Took Control of U.S. Middle East Policy." Washington, DC: American Educational Trust, 1990.

Dawidowicz, Lucy. "American Public Opinion." In *American Jewish Year Book 1968*, edited by Morris Fine and Milton Himmelfarb. New York: American Jewish Committee, 1968, p. 198.

DellaPergola, Sergio. *World Jewish Population 2010.* Association for the Social Scientific Study of Jewry, North American Jewish Data Bank, Jewish Federations of North America, 2010. Available at http://www.bjpa.org/Publications/details .cfm?PublicationID=8075 (accessed November 11, 2015).

Dershowitz, Alan M. *The Case for Israel.* Hoboken, NJ: John Wiley & Sons, 2003.

———. *The Vanishing American Jew: In Search of Jewish Identity for the Next Century.* Boston: Little, Brown and Company, 1997.

Dollinger, Marc. "Jewish Identities in 20th-Century America." *Contemporary Jewry* vol. 24 (2003–2004): 9–28.

———. *Quest for Inclusion: Jews and Liberalism in Modern America.* Princeton, NJ: Princeton University Press, 2000.

Don-Yehiya, Eliezer. "Modern and Haredi Orthodox American Jews and Their Attitude to the State of Israel." In *Israel, the Diaspora and Jewish Identity*, edited by Danny Ben Moshe and Zohar Segev. Brighton, UK: Sussex Academic Press, 2007, pp. 62–66.

———. "Orthodox and Other American Jews and Their Attitude to the State of Israel," *Israel Studies* vol. 17, no. 2 (2012):120–128.

Elazar, Daniel J. "Changing Places, Changing Cultures: Divergent Jewish Political Cultures." In *Divergent Jewish Cultures: Israel and America*, edited by Deborah Dash Moore and S. Ilan Troen. New Haven, CT: Yale University Press, 2001, pp. 319–330.

———. *Community and Polity: The Organizational Dynamics of American Jewry*. Philadelphia: Jewish Publication Society, 1995.

———. "Jewish Political Studies." *Modern Judaism* vol. 11 (1991): 67–90.

———. *Kinship and Consent: The Jewish Political Tradition and Its Contemporary Uses*. Philadelphia: Turtledove Press, 1981.

———. "The New Jewish Politics." In *The New Jewish Politics*, edited by Daniel J. Elazar. Jerusalem: Jerusalem Center for Public Affairs, 1988.

Elazar, Daniel J., and Stuart A. Cohen. *The Jewish Polity: Jewish Political Organization from Biblical Times to the Present*. Bloomington: Indiana University Press, 1985.

Ellis, Mark H. *Israel and Palestine—Out of the Ashes: The Search for Jewish Identity in the Twenty-First Century*. London: Pluto Press, 2002.

Farber, Seth, ed. *Rabbis, Prophets, and Peacemakers: Conversations with Jewish Critics of Israel*. Monroe, ME: Common Courage Press, 2005.

Findley, Paul. *They Dare to Speak Out: People and Institutions Confront Israel's Lobby*. Westport, CT: Lawrence Hill, 1985.

Finkelstein, Norman. *Knowing Too Much: Why the American Jewish Romance with Israel Is Coming to an End*. New York: OR Books, 2012.

Fiorina, Morris P., Samuel J. Abrams, and Jeremy C. Pope. *Culture War: The Myth of a Polarized America*. New York: Pearson Longman, 2005.

Fishman, Sylvia Barack, Rachel S. Bernstein, and Emily Sigalow. "Reimagining Jewishness: Younger American Jewish Leaders, Entrepreneurs, and Artists in Cultural Context." In *The New Jewish Leaders: Reshaping the American Jewish Landscape*, edited by Jack Wertheimer. Waltham, MA: Brandeis University Press, 2011, pp. 159–213.

Fleisch, Eric, and Theodore Sasson. *The New Philanthropy: American Jewish Giving to Israeli Organizations*. Waltham, MA: Cohen Center for Modern Jewish Studies, 2012.

Fleshler, Dan. *Transforming America's Israel Lobby*. Washington, DC: Potomac Books, 2009.

Frankel, Glen. *Beyond the Promised Land: Jews and Arabs on a Hard Road to a New Israel*. New York: Simon & Schuster, 1994.

Freedman, Samuel. *Jew vs. Jew: The Struggle for the Soul of American Jewry.* New York: Touchstone, 2000.

Gal, Allon, ed. *Envisioning Israel: The Changing Images and Ideals of North American Jews.* Jerusalem and Detroit: Magnes Press and Wayne State University Press, 1996.

Gal, Allon, and Alfred Gottschalk, eds. *Beyond Survival and Philanthropy: American Jewry and Israel.* Cincinnati: Hebrew Union College Press, 2000.

Galchinsky, Michael. *Jews and Human Rights: Dancing at Three Weddings.* Lanham, MD: Rowman & Littlefield, 2008.

———. "Scattered Seeds: A Dialogue of Diasporas." In *Insider/Outsider: American Jews and Multiculturalism,* edited by David Biale, Michael Galchinsky, and Susannah Heschel. Berkeley: University of California Press, 1998, pp. 185–211.

Ganin, Zvi. *An Uneasy Relationship: American Jewish Leadership and Israel, 1948–1957.* Syracuse, NY: Syracuse University Press, 2005.

Gerstein, Jim. "J Street: National Survey of American Jews." Washington, DC: J Street, 2008.

Gerstenfeld, Manfred, ed. *American Jewry's Challenge: Conversations Confronting the Twentieth Century.* Lanham, MD: Rowman & Littlefield, 2005.

Gerstenfeld, Manfred, and Steven Bayme, eds. *American Jewry's Comfort Level: Present and Future.* Jerusalem: Jerusalem Center for Public Affairs, 2010.

Gingras, Robbie. "Hugging and Wrestling: Alternative Paradigms for the Diaspora -Israel Relationship." Available at http://makomisrael.org/blog/hugging-and -wrestling-2/ (accessed November 11, 2015).

Gitelman, Zvi. "The Decline of the Diaspora Jewish Nation: Boundaries, Content, and Jewish Identity." *Jewish Social Studies* vol. 4, no. 2 (1998): 112–127.

Glazer, Nathan. *American Judaism.* Chicago: University of Chicago Press, 1957.

Goldberg, J. J. *Jewish Power: Inside the American Jewish Establishment.* Reading, MA: Addison-Wesley, 1996.

Gordis, Daniel. "Are Young Rabbis Turning on Israel?" *Commentary* (June 2011): 18–24.

———. "From a Jewish People to a Jewish Religion: A Shifting American Jewish Weltanschauung and Its Implications for Israel." *Israel Studies,* vol. 17, no. 2 (2012): 102–110.

Gorny, Yosef. "Shlilat Ha-Galut: Past and Present." In *Beyond Survival and Philanthropy: American Jewry and Israel,* edited by Allon Gal and Alfred Gottschalk. Cincinnati: Hebrew Union College Press, 2000, pp. 41–58.

———. *The State of Israel in Jewish Public Thought: The Quest for Collective Identity.* New York: New York University Press, 1994.

Greenberg, Anna. *OMG! How Generation Y is Redefining Faith in the iPod Era.* Reboot, 2005. Available at http://www.bjpa.org/Publications/details.cfm?Publication ID=331 (accessed November 11, 2015).

Habib, Jasmin. *Israel, Diaspora and the Routes of National Belonging.* Toronto: University of Toronto Press, 2004.

Haidt, Jonathan. *The Righteous Mind: Why Good People Are Divided by Politics and Religion.* New York: Knopf, 2013.

Halkin, Hillel. "The Jewish State and the Jewish People(s)." *Commentary*, vol. 105, no. 5 (1998): 50–55.

Halpern, Ben. *The American Jew.* New York: Theodor Herzl Foundation, 1956.

———. "The Impact of Israel on American Jewish Ideologies." *Jewish Social Studies* vol. 21 (January 1959): 62–81.

Hartman, Donniel. "Jewish Peoplehood and the Toxic Discourse around Israel." *Havruta* no. 8 (February 2012): 22–31.

Heilman, Samuel. *Sliding to the Right: The Contest for the Future of American Jewish Orthodoxy.* Berkeley: University of California Press, 2006.

Hertzberg, Arthur. "Afterword." In *The Zionist Idea: A Historical Analysis and Reader*, edited by Arthur Hertzberg. Philadelphia: Jewish Publication Society, 1997, pp. 621–630.

Hertzberg, Arthur, ed. *The Zionist Idea: A Historical Analysis and Reader.* Philadelphia: Jewish Publication Society, 1997.

Jacobs, Jill. *Where Justice Dwells: A Hands-on Guide to Doing Social Justice in Your Jewish Community.* Woodstock, VT: Jewish Lights, 2011.

Jones, Robert P., and Daniel Cox. *Chosen for What? Jewish Values in 2012: Finding from the 2012 Jewish Values Survey.* Washington, DC: Public Religion Research Institute, March 2012. Available at http://publicreligion.org/site/wp-content/uploads/2012/04/Jewish-Values-Survey-2012-Presentation.pdf (accessed November 11, 2015).

Judis, John. *Genesis: Truman, American Jews and the Origins of the Arab-Israeli Conflict.* New York: Farrar, Straus and Giroux, 2014.

Judt, Tony. "Israel: The Alternative." *New York Review of Books*, October 23, 2003. Available at http://www.nybooks.com/articles/archives/2003/oct/23/israel-the-alternative/ (accessed November 11, 2015).

Jumpstart, the Natan Fund, and the Samuel Bronfman Foundation. *The Innovation Ecosystem: Emergence of a New Jewish Landscape.* Los Angeles and New York: Jumpstart, the Natan Fund, and the Samuel Bronfman Foundation, 2009.

Kahn-Harris, Keith. *Uncivil War: The Israel Conflict in the Jewish Community.* London: David Paul, 2014.

Kahn-Harris, Keith, and Ben Gidley. *Turbulent Times: The British Jewish Community Today.* London: Continuum, 2010.

Kamiya, Gary. "Can American Jews Unplug the Israel Lobby?" *Salon*, March 20, 2007. Available at http://www.salon.com/2007/03/20/aipac_2/ (accessed November 11, 2015).

Kaplan, Dana Evan. "Introduction." In *The Cambridge Companion to American Judaism*, edited by Dana Evan Kaplan. New York: Cambridge University Press, 2005, pp. 1–19.

Kaplan, Dana Evan, ed. *The Cambridge Companion to American Judaism*. New York: Cambridge University Press, 2005.

Kaplan, Esther. "The Jewish Divide over Israel." *Nation*, July 12, 2004. Available at http://www.thenation.com/article/jewish-divide-israel/ (accessed November 11, 2015).

Karpf, Anne, Brian Klug, Jacqueline Rose, and Barbara Rosenbaum, eds. *A Time to Speak Out: Independent Jewish Voices on Israel, Zionism and Jewish Identity*. London: Verso, 2008.

Katz, Steven T., ed. *Why Is America Different: American Jewry on Its 350ᵗʰ Anniversary*. Lanham, MD: University Press of America, 2010.

Kaunfer, Elie. *Empowered Judaism: What Independent Minyanim Can Teach Us about Building Vibrant Jewish Communities*. Woodstock, VT: Jewish Lights, 2010.

Kaye/Kantrowitz Melanie. *The Colors of Jews: Racial Politics and Radical Diasporism*. Bloomington: Indiana University Press, 2007.

Kelman, Ari Y. "The Reality of the Virtual: Looking for Jewish Leadership Online." In *The New Jewish Leaders: Reshaping the American Jewish Landscape*, edited by Jack Wertheimer. Waltham, MA: Brandeis University Press, 2011, pp. 214–260.

Kelner, Shaul. "In Its Own Image: Independent Jewish Philanthropy and the Cultivation of Young Jewish Leadership." In *The New Jewish Leaders: Reshaping the American Jewish Landscape*, edited by Jack Wertheimer. Waltham, MA: Brandeis University Press, 2011, pp. 261–321.

———. "Ritualized Protest and Redemptive Politics: Cultural Consequences of the American Mobilization to Free Soviet Jewry." *Jewish Social Studies: History, Culture, Society* vol. 14, no. 3 (Spring/Summer 2008): 1–37.

———. *Tours That Bind: Diaspora, Pilgrimage, and Israeli Birthright Tourism*. New York: New York University Press, 2010.

Kosmin, Barry A., Antony Lerman, and Jacqueline Goldberg. *The Attachment of British Jews to Israel*. London: Institute for Jewish Policy Research, 1997.

Kotler-Berkowitz, Laurence A. "Ethnic Cohesion and Division among American Jews: The Role of Mass-level and Organizational Politics." *Ethnic and Racial Studies* vol. 20, no. 4 (1997): 797–829.

———. "Political Diversification and Division in the American Jewish Community: The Effect on Consensus Building and Jewish Advocacy." *Journal of Jewish Communal Service* vol. 71, no. 4 (1995): 266–274.

———. "Social Cleavages and Political Divisions: A Comparative Analysis of British, American, and South African Jews in the 1990s." *Journal of Modern Jewish Studies* vol. 1 (2002): 204–233.

Kotler-Berkowitz, Laurence A., and Lawrence Sternberg. "The Politics of American Jews: Cohesion, Division, and Representation at the Institutional Level." *Jewish Political Studies Review* vol. 12, nos. 1–2 (Spring 2000). Available at http://bjpa.org/Publications/details.cfm?PublicationID=2364 (accessed November 11, 2015).

Kovel, Joel. *Overcoming Zionism: Creating a Single Democratic State in Israel/Palestine.* London: Pluto, 2007.

Kushner, Tony, and Alisa Solomon, eds. *Wrestling with Zion: Progressive Jewish-American Responses to the Israeli-Palestinian Conflict.* New York: Grove Press, 2003.

Landy, David. *Jewish Identity and Palestinian Rights: Diaspora Jewish Opposition to Israel.* London: Zed Books, 2011.

Lappin, Shalom. "The Need for a New Jewish Politics." *Dissent* vol. 51, no. 3 (2004): 34–38.

Lasensky, Scott. "Israeli Politics in the Diaspora and Jewish Identity." In *Israel, the Diaspora and Jewish Identity,* edited by Danny Ben Moshe and Zohar Segev. Brighton, UK: Sussex Academic Press, 2007, pp. 140–143.

Lewis, Hal. M. *Models and Meanings in the History of Jewish Leadership.* Lewiston, NY: Edward Mellen Press, 2004.

Liebman, Charles S. *Pressure without Sanctions: The Influence of World Jewry on Israeli Policy.* Cranbury, NJ: Associated University Presses, 1977.

———. "Religious Trends among American and Israeli Jews." In *Terms of Survival: The Jewish World since 1945,* edited by Robert S. Wistrich. New York: Routledge, 1995, pp. 299–319.

———. "Restructuring Israel-Diaspora Relations." *Israel Studies* vol. 1, no. 1 (1996): 315–322.

Liebman, Charles S., and Steven M. Cohen. *Two Worlds of Judaism: The Israeli and American Experiences.* New Haven, CT: Yale University Press, 1990.

Lipset, Seymour M. "The Political Profile of American Jewry." In *Terms of Survival: The Jewish World Since 1945,* edited by Robert S. Wistrich. New York: Routledge, 1995, pp. 142–162.

Lipset, Seymour M., and Earl Rabb. *Jews and the New American Scene.* Boston: Harvard University Press, 1995.

Lipstadt, Deborah E., Samuel G. Freedman, and Chaim Seidler-Feller. *American Jewry and the College Campus: Best of Times or Worst of Times?* New York: American Jewish Committee, 2005.

Luntz, Frank. "Israel and American Jews in the Age of Eminem." New York: Andrea and Charles Bronfman Philanthropies, 2003.

Lyons, Terrence. "Engaging Diasporas to Promote Conflict Resolution: Transforming Hawks into Doves." George Mason University, Institute for Conflict Analysis and Resolution, 2004. Available at http://www.tamilnation.co/conflict resolution/lyons.pdf (accessed November 11, 2015).

Magid, Shaul. *American Post-Judaism: Identity and Renewal in a Postethnic Society.* Bloomington: Indiana University Press, 2013.

———. "Butler Trouble: Zionism, Excommunication, and the Reception of Judith Butler's Work on Israel/Palestine." *Studies in American Jewish Literature* vol. 33, no. 2 (2014): 237–259.

————. "Dogmas and Allegiances in Contemporary Judaism." *Sh'ma*, vol. 40, no. 669 (April 2010): 3–4.

————. "Who Is Boycotting Whom: National Hillel Guidelines, Dissent, and Legitimate Protest." *Zeek*, January 10, 2014. Available at http://zeek.forward.com/articles/117993/ (accessed November 11, 2015).

Mannheim, Karl. "The Problem of Generations," In *Essays on the Sociology of Knowledge*, edited by P. Kecskemeti. London: Routledge and Kegan Paul, 1952, pp. 276–322.

Massing, Michael. "Deal Breakers." *American Prospect* vol. 13, no. 5 (March 11, 2002). Available at http://prospect.org/article/deal-breakers (accessed November 11, 2015).

————. "The Storm over the Israel Lobby." *New York Review of Books* vol. 53, no. 10 (June 8, 2006). Available at http://www.nybooks.com/articles/archives/2006/jun/08/the-storm-over-the-israel-lobby/ (accessed November 11, 2015).

Mearsheimer, John J., and Stephen M. Walt. *The Israel Lobby*. New York: Farrar, Straus and Giroux, 2008.

Medding, Peter Y. "The New Jewish Politics in America." In *Terms of Survival: The Jewish World Since 1945*, edited by Robert S. Wistrich. New York: Routledge, 1995, pp. 86–114.

————. "Towards a General Theory of Jewish Political Interests and Behavior." *Jewish Journal of Sociology* vol. 19 (1977): 115–144.

————. *The Transformation of American Jewish Politics*. New York: American Jewish Committee, 1989.

Medoff, Raphael. *Jewish Americans and Political Participation*. Santa Barbara, CA: ABC-CLIO, 2002.

Mellman, Mark S., Aaron Strauss, and Kenneth D. Wald. *Jewish American Voting Behavior 1972–2008: Just the Facts*. Washington, DC: Solomon Project, 2012.

Mendelsohn, Ezra. *On Modern Jewish Politics*. New York: Oxford University Press 1993.

Michels, Tony. "Is America 'Different'? A Critique of American Jewish Exceptionalism." *American Jewish History* vol. 96, no. 3 (2010): 201–224.

Miller, Ron, and Arnold Dashefsky. "Brandeis v. Cohen et al.: The Distancing from Israel Debate." *Contemporary Jewry* vol. 30 (2009): 155–164.

Moore, Deborah D. "Introduction." In *American Jewish Identity Politics*, edited by Deborah Dash Moore. Ann Arbor: University of Michigan Press, 2009, pp. 10–29.

National Jewish Population Survey (NJPS). *The National Jewish Population Survey 2000–1: Strength, Challenge and Diversity in the American Jewish Population*. New York: United Jewish Communities, 2003.

Nepon, Ezra Berkley. *Justice, Justice Shall You Pursue: A History of New Jewish Agenda*. Philadelphia: Thread Makes Blanket Press, 2012.

Novick, Peter. *The Holocaust in American Life*. Boston: Houghton Mifflin, 1999.

Packer, Dominic J. "On Being Both with Us and against Us: A Normative Conflict Model of Dissent in Social Groups." *Personality and Social Psychology Review* vol. 12, no. 1 (2008): 50–72.

Perlmann, Joel. "American Jewish Opinion about the Future of the West Bank: A Reanalysis of American Jewish Committee Surveys." Working Paper No. 526. Annandale-on-Hudson, NY: Levy Economics Institute, Bard College, December 2007.

Pew Research Center. "A Portrait of Jewish Americans: Findings from a Pew Research Center Survey of U.S. Jews," October 2013. Available at http://www .pewforum.org/2013/10/01/jewish-american-beliefs-attitudes-culture-survey/ (accessed November 11, 2015).

Phillips, Bruce. "American Judaism in the Twenty-First Century." In *The Cambridge Companion to American Judaism*, edited by Dana Evan Kaplan. New York: Cambridge University Press, 2005, pp. 397–415.

Podhoretz, Norman. *The Long Struggle against Islamofascism*. New York: Doubleday, 2007.

Potts, Erin, Roger Bennett, Rachel Levin, and Stacy Abramson. *Grand Soy Vanilla Latte with Cinnamon, No Foam: Jewish Identity and Community in a Time of Unlimited Choices*. 2006. Available at. http://www.acbp.net/pdf/pdfs-research-and -publications/Latte%20Report%202006.pdf (accessed November 11, 2015).

Putnam, Robert D. *Bowling Alone: The Collapse and Revival of American Community*. New York: Simon & Schuster, 2011.

Raab, Earl, and Larry Sternberg. *The Silent, Ambivalent Majority of Affiliated American Jews and the Pro-Israel Advocacy Agencies*. Waltham, MA: Perlmutter Institute for Jewish Advocacy, Brandeis University, June, 1998.

Rabkin, Yakov. *A Threat from Within: A History of Jewish Opposition to Zionism*. London: Zed Books, 2006.

Raffel, Martin J. "History of Israel Advocacy." In *Jewish Polity and American Civil Society: Communal Agencies and Religious Movements in the American Public Square*, edited by A. Mittleman, J. Sarna, and R. Licht. Lanham, MD: Rowan & Littlefield Publishers, pp. 103–179.

Raider, Mark. *The Emergence of American Zionism*. New York: New York University Press, 1998.

Rapaport, Lynn. "The Holocaust in American Jewish Life." In *The Cambridge Companion to American Judaism*, edited by Dana Evan Kaplan. New York: Cambridge University Press, pp. 187–208.

Rebhun, Uzi. "Recent Developments in Jewish Identification in the United States: A Cohort Follow-Up and Facet Analysis." In *Papers in Jewish Demography 1997*, edited by Sergio DellaPergola and Judith Even. Jerusalem: Avraham Harman Institute of Contemporary Jewry, Hebrew University of Jerusalem, 2001, pp. 261–279.

Roberts, Helen. "American Jewish Donations to Israel." *Contemporary Jewry* vol. 20, no. 1 (1999): 201–213.

Rose, Or, Jo Ellen Green Kaiser, and Margie Klein, eds. *Righteous Indignation: A Jewish Call for Justice*. Woodstock, VT: Jewish Lights, 2007.

Rosenthal, Steven T. *Irreconcilable Differences? The Waning of the American Jewish Love Affair with Israel*. Lebanon, NH: Brandeis University Press, 2001.

———. "Long-distance Nationalism: American Jews, Zionism, and Israel." In *The Cambridge Companion to American Judaism*, edited by Dana Evan Kaplan. New York: Cambridge University Press, 2005, pp. 209–224.

Rosner, Shmuel, and Inbal Hakman. *The Challenge of Peoplehood: Strengthening the Attachment of Young American Jews to Israel in the Time of the Distancing Discourse*. Jerusalem: Jewish People Policy Institute, 2011.

Rosner, Shmuel, and Michael Herzog. *Jewish Values and Israel's Use of Force in Armed Conflict: Perspectives from World Jewry*. Jerusalem: Jewish People Policy Institute, 2015.

Rubin, Neil. *American Jewry and the Oslo Years*. New York: Palgrave Macmillan, 2012.

Rushdie, Salman. *Imaginary Homelands: Essays and Criticism, 1981–1991*. London: Granta Books, 1991.

Rutland, Suzanne D. "Identity with Israel from Afar: The Australian Story." In *Israel, the Diaspora and Jewish Identity*, edited by Danny Ben Moshe and Zohar Segev. Brighton, UK: Sussex Academic Press, 2007, pp. 254–267.

Rynhold, Jonathan. "Israel's Foreign and Defence Policy and Diaspora Jewish Identity." In *Israel, the Diaspora and Jewish Identity*, edited by Danny Ben Moshe and Zohar Segev. Brighton, UK: Sussex Academic Press, 2007, pp. 144–157.

Sarna, Jonathan. *The American Jewish Experience*. New York: Holmes and Meier, 1986.

———. "A Projection of America as It Ought to Be: Zion in the Mind's Eye of American Jews." In *Envisioning Israel: The Changing Images and Ideals of North American Jews*, edited by Allon Gal. Jerusalem and Detroit: Magnes Press and Wayne State University Press, 1996, pp. 41–59.

———. "The Question of Shlilat Ha-Galut in American Zionism." In *Beyond Survival and Philanthropy: American Jewry and Israel*, edited by Allon Gal and Alfred Gottschalk. Cincinnati: Hebrew Union College Press, 2000, pp. 59–63.

Sartre, Jean Paul. *Anti-Semite and Jew*. New York: Schocken Books, 1948.

Sasson, Theodore. "Mass Mobilization to Direct Engagement: American Jews' Changing Relationship to Israel." *Israel Studies* vol. 15, no. 2 (2010): 173–195.

———. *The New American Zionism*. New York: New York University Press, 2013.

———. "The New Realism: American Jewish Views about Israel." New York: American Jewish Committee, 2009.

Sasson, Theodore, Charles Kadushin, and Leonard Saxe. "On Sampling, Evidence and Theory: Concluding Remarks on the Distancing Debate." *Contemporary Jewry* vol. 30, nos. 2/3 (2010): 149–153.

———. "Trends in American Jewish Attachment to Israel: An Assessment of the 'Distancing' Hypothesis." *Contemporary Jewry* vol. 30, nos. 2/3 (2010): 297–319.

Sasson, Theodore, Benjamin Phillips, Charles Kadushin, and Leonard Saxe. *Still Connected: American Jewish Attitudes about Israel.* Waltham, MA: Cohen Center for Modern Jewish Studies, Brandeis University, 2010.

Sasson, Theodore, Benjamin Phillips, Graham Wright, Charles Kadushin, and Leonard Saxe. "Understanding Young Adult Attachment to Israel: Period, Life-cycle, and Generational Dynamics." *Contemporary Jewry* vol. 32, no. 1 (2012): 67–84.

Saxe, Leonard, and Matthew Boxer. "Loyalty and Love of Israel by Diasporan Jews." *Israel Studies* vol. 17, no. 2 (2012): 92–101.

Saxe, Leonard, and Barry Chazan. *Ten Days of Birthright Israel: A Journey in Young Adult Identity.* Lebanon, NH: Brandeis University Press, 2008.

Saxe, Leonard, Charles Kadushin, Shahar Hecht, Benjamin Phillips, Mark I. Rosen, and Shaul Kelner. *Evaluating Birthright Israel: Long-Term Impact and Recent Findings.* Waltham, MA: Cohen Center for Modern Jewish Studies, Brandeis University, 2004.

Saxe, Leonard Benjamin Phillips, Theodore Sasson, Shahar Hecht, Michelle Shain, Graham Wright, and Charles Kadushin. *Generation Birthright Israel: The Impact of an Israel Experience on Jewish Identity and Choices.* Waltham, MA: Cohen Center for Modern Jewish Studies, Brandeis University, 2009.

Saxe, Leonard, Benjamin Phillips, Graham Wright, Matthew Boxer, Shahar Hecht, and Theodore Sasson. *Taglit-Birthright Israel: 2007–2008 North American Cohorts.* Waltham, MA: Cohen Center for Modern Jewish Studies, Brandeis University, 2008.

Schrag, Carl. *Ripples from the Matzav: Grassroots Responses of American Jewry to the Situation in Israel.* New York: American Jewish Committee, 2004.

Schuman, Howard, and Amy Corning. "Generational Memory and the Critical Period: Evidence for National and World Events." *Public Opinion Quarterly* vol. 76, no. 1 (2012): 1–31.

Schwarz, Sidney. *Judaism and Justice: The Jewish Passion to Repair the World.* Woodstock, VT: Jewish Lights, 2006.

Segev, Zohar. "American Zionists' Place in Israel after Statehood: From Involved Partners to Outside Supporters." *American Jewish History* vol. 93, no. 3 (2007): 277–302.

Seliktar, Ofira. "The Changing Identity of American Jews, Israel, and the Peace Process." In *Israel, Diaspora, and Jewish Identity*, edited by D. Ben-Moshe and Z. Segev. Brighton and Portland, UK: Sussex Academic Press, 2007, pp. 124–137.

———. *Divided We Stand: American Jews, Israel, and the Peace Process.* Westport, CT: Praeger, 2002.

Shain, Yossi, and Barry Bristman. "Diaspora Kinship and Loyalty: The Renewal of Jewish National Security." *International Affairs* vol. 78, no. 1 (2002): 69–96.

Shain, Yossi, and Tamara Cofman Wittes. "Jewish Kinship at the Crossroads: Lessons for Homelands and Diasporas." *Political Science Quarterly* vol. 117, no. 2 (2002): 279–309.

———. *Kinship and Diasporas in International Affairs*. Ann Arbor: University of Michigan Press, 2008.

———. *Marketing the American Creed Abroad: Diasporas in the U.S. and Their Homelands*. Cambridge, UK: Cambridge University Press, 1999.

———. "Peace as a Three-Level Game: The Role of Diasporas in Conflict Resolution." In *Ethnic Identity Groups and U.S. Foreign Policy*, edited by Thomas Ambrosio. Praeger: Westport, 2002, pp. 169–197.

Shain, Yossi, and Steven Lenzner. "Jewish Voices, Jewish Influence, and Neoconservatism." *Occasional Papers on Jewish Civilization, Jewish Thought and Philosophy*, (Summer 2005): 18–36.

Shatz, Adam, ed. *Prophets Outcast: A Century of Dissident Jewish Writing about Zionism and Israel*. New York: Nation Books, 2004.

Sheffer, Gabriel. *Diaspora Politics: At Home Abroad*. Cambridge, UK: Cambridge University Press, 2003.

———. "Israel-Diaspora Relations in Comparative Perspective." In *Israel in Comparative Perspective: Challenging the Conventional Wisdom*, edited by Michael N. Barnett. Albany: SUNY Press, 1996, pp. 53–83.

———. "Is the Jewish Diaspora Unique? Reflections on the Diaspora's Current Situation." *Israel Studies* vol. 10, no. 1 (2005): 1–35.

———. "Loyalty and Criticism in the Relations between World Jewry and Israel." *Israel Studies* vol. 17, no. 2 (2012): 77–85.

———. "A Nation and Its Diaspora: A Re-examination of Israeli-Jewish Diaspora Relations." *Diasporas* vol. 11, no. 3 (2002): 351–358.

Sheffer, Gabriel, ed. *Modern Diasporas in International Politics*. New York: St. Martin's Press, 1986.

Shimoni, Gideon. "Reformulations of Zionist Ideology since the Establishment of the State of Israel." In *Values, Interests, and Identity: Jews and Politics in a Changing World*, edited by Peter Medding. New York: Oxford University Press, 1995, pp. 11–36.

Silberstein, Laurence J. "American Jewry's Identification with Israel Problems and Prospects." In *The Wiley-Blackwell History of Jews and Judaism*, edited by Alan T. Levenson. Oxford, UK: Wiley-Blackwell, 2012, pp. 619–642.

———. *The Post-Zionism Debates: Knowledge and Power in Israeli Culture*. New York and London: Routledge, 1999.

Silberstein, Laurence J., ed. *Mapping Jewish Identities*. New York: New York University Press, 2000.

Silver, M. M. *Our Exodus: Leon Uris and the Americanization of Israel's Founding Story*. Detroit: Wayne State University Press, 2010.

Sklare, Marshall, and Joseph Greenblum. *Jewish Identity on the Suburban Frontier: A Study of Group Survival in the Open Society.* New York: Basic Books, 1967.

Skocpol, Theda. *Diminished Democracy: From Membership to Management in American Civic Life.* Norman: University of Oklahoma Press, 2003.

Smith, Hazel. "Diasporas in International Conflict." In *Diasporas in Conflict: Peace-Makers or Peace-Wreckers?*, edited by Hazel Smith and Paul Stares. New York: United Nations University Press, 2007, pp. 218–238.

Smith, Tom, W. *Jewish Distinctiveness in America: A Statistical Portrait.* New York: American Jewish Committee, 2005.

Smith, Tony. *Foreign Attachments: The Power of Ethnic Groups in the Making of American Foreign Policy.* Cambridge, MA: Harvard University Press, 2001.

Spiegel, Steven L. "American Jews and United States Foreign Policy (1945–90)." In *Terms of Survival: The Jewish World since 1945*, edited by Robert S. Wistrich. New York: Routledge, 1995, pp. 168–194.

Staub, Michael E. *Torn at the Roots: The Crisis of Jewish Liberalism in Postwar America.* New York: Columbia University Press: 2002.

Staub, Michael E. "Holocaust Consciousness and American Jewish Politics." In *The Columbia History of Jews and Judaism in America*, edited by Marc Lee Raphael. New York: Columbia University Press, 2008, pp. 313–336.

Strachan, J. Cherie, and Michael R. Wolf. "Political Civility." *PS: Political Science & Politics* vol. 45 (July 2012): 401–404.

Sucharov, Mira. "Values, Identity, and Israel Advocacy." *Foreign Policy Analysis* vol. 7, no. 4 (October 2011): 361–380.

Svonkin, Stuart. *Jews against Prejudice: American Jews and the Fight for Civil Liberties.* New York: Columbia University Press, 1999.

Tabory, Ephraim. "Attachment to Israel and Jewish Identity: An Assessment of an Assessment." *Contemporary Jewry* vol. 30, no. 2 (2010): 191–197.

Tapper, Aaron J. "The War of Words: Jews, Muslims, and the Israeli-Palestinian Conflict on American University Campuses." In *Muslims and Jews in America: Commonalities, Contentions, and Complexities*, edited by Reza Aslan and Aaron J. Hahn Tapper. New York: Palgrave Macmillan, 2011.

Tivnan, Edward. *The Lobby: Jewish Political Power and American Foreign Policy.* New York: Simon and Schuster, 1987.

Tobin, Gary A., with Sharon L. Sassler. *Jewish Perceptions of Anti-Semitism.* New York: Plenum Press, 1988.

Tobin, Jonathan. "Anti-Zionists Must Not Be Allowed to Hijack the Jewish Community." *Commentary*, February 21, 2014. Available at https://www.commentary magazine.com/culture-civilization/religion/judaism/anti-zionists-must-not-be -allowed-to-hijack-the-jewish-community/ (accessed November 11, 2015).

Traub, James. "The New Israel Lobby." *New York Times Magazine*, September 13, 2009, pp. MM36.

Troen, Ilan S., "Beyond Zionist Theory: Coming to Terms with the American Jewish Experience." In *Beyond Survival and Philanthropy: American Jewry and Israel*, edited by Allon Gal and Alfred Gottschalk. Cincinnati: Hebrew Union College Press, 2000, pp. 64–71.

Ukeles, Jacob B., Ron Miller, and Pearl Beck. *Young Jewish Adults in the United States Today*. New York: American Jewish Committee, 2006.

Urofsky, Melvin I. *American Zionism from Herzl to the Holocaust*. Garden City, NY: Anchor Press, 1975.

Verbit, Mervin F. "American Jews—More Right than Left on the Peace Process." *Jewish Political Studies Review* vol. 24, nos. 1/2 (2012): 45–58.

Vital, David. *The Future of the Jews: A People at the Crossroads?* Cambridge, MA: Harvard University Press, 1990.

Vorspan, Albert, and David Saperstein. *Jewish Dimensions of Social Justice: Tough Moral Choices of Our Time*. New York: Union of American Hebrew Congregations Press, 1998.

Wald, Kenneth D., and Williams, Bryan. "Diaspora Political Consciousness: Variation in the Transnational Ethnic Alliance of American Jews." Paper presented at the annual meeting of the American Political Science Association, Washington, DC, September 2005.

Walt, Stephen, and John Mearsheimer. *The Israel Lobby and U.S. Foreign Policy*. New York: Farrar, Straus and Giroux, 2007.

Waxman, Chaim I. "American Jewish Philanthropy, Direct Giving, and the Unity of the Jewish Community," In *Toward a Renewed Ethic of Jewish Philanthropy*, edited by Yossi Prager. New York and Jersey City: Yeshiva University Press and Ktav, 2010, pp. 53–77.

Waxman, Dov. "The Israel Lobbies: A Survey of the Pro-Israel Community in the United States." *Israel Studies Forum* vol. 25, no. 1 (Summer 2010): 1–28.

———. "The Pro-Israel Lobby in the United States: Past, Present, and Future." In *Israel and the United States: Six Decades of US–Israeli Relations*, edited by Robert O. Freedman. Boulder, CO: Westview Press, 2012, pp. 79–99.

Weiss, Phillip, and Adam Horowitz. "American Jews Rethink Israel." *Nation*, November 2, 2009. Available at http://www.thenation.com/article/american-jews -rethink-israel/ (accessed November 11, 2015).

Wertheimer, Jack. "American Jews and Israel: A 60-Year Retrospective." In *American Jewish Yearbook 2008*, edited by David Singer and Lawrence Grossman. New York: American Jewish Committee, 2008, pp. 3–79.

———. "Breaking the Taboo: Critics of Israel and the American Jewish Establishment." In *Envisioning Israel: The Changing Ideals and Images of North American Jews*, edited by Allon Gal. Jerusalem and Detroit: Magnes Press and Wayne State University Press, 1996, pp. 397–419.

———. *Generation of Change: How Leaders in Their Twenties and Thirties Are Reshaping American Jewish Life*. New York: Avi Chai Foundation, 2010.

————. "Jewish Organizational Life in the United States since 1945." *American Jewish Year Book* vol. 95 (1995): 3–98.

————. "Jewish Security and Jewish Interests." *Commentary*, October 1, 2004: 54–59.

————. "Mapping the Scene: How Younger American Jewish Adults Engage with Jewish Community." In *The New Jewish Leaders: Reshaping the American Jewish Landscape*, edited by Jack Wertheimer. Waltham, MA: Brandeis University Press, 2011, pp. 1–44.

————. *The New Jewish Leaders: Reshaping the American Jewish Landscape*. Waltham, MA: Brandeis University Press, 2011.

————. *A People Divided: Judaism in Contemporary America*. Waltham, MA: Brandeis University Press, 1997.

Wertheimer, Jack, and Steven Cohen. "Whatever Happened to the Jewish People?" *Commentary*, June 1, 2006: 33–37.

Whiteley, Paul F. "Is the Party Over? The Decline of Party Activism and Membership across the Democratic World," *Party Politics* vol. 17, no. 1 (January 2011): 21–44.

Windmueller, Steven. "The Second American Jewish Revolution," *Journal of Jewish Communal Service* vol. 82, no. 3 (2007), pp. 252–260.

Wisse, Ruth R. *Jews and Power*. New York: Schocken, 2007.

Wistrich, Robert S., ed. *Terms of Survival: The Jewish World since 1945*. New York: Routledge, 1995.

Woocher, Jonathan. "The Democratization of the American Jewish Polity." *Contemporary Jewry* vol. 8, no. 1 (1987): 27–46.

————. *Sacred Survival: The Civil Religion of American Jews*. Bloomington: Indiana University Press, 1986.

————. "'Sacred Survival' Revisited: American Jewish Civil Religion in the New Millennium." In *The Cambridge Companion to American Judaism*, edited by Dana Evan Kaplan. New York: Cambridge University Press, 2005, pp. 283–297.

Zeitz, Joshua Michael. "'If I Am Not for Myself . . .': The American Jewish Establishment in the Aftermath of the Six Day War." *American Jewish History* vol. 88, no. 2 (2000): 253–286.

INDEX

Note: Page numbers in *italics* indicate figures; those with a *t* indicate tables.

Abbas, Mahmoud, 124; Olmert's talks with, 162, 240n72, 249n8
Abraham, Daniel, 59, 235n14
Abrams, Elliot, 100
Abrams, Rachel, 269n72
Adelson, Sheldon, 59–60, 97, 168, 264n13, 278n67; Republican Party contributions of, 186; think tanks funded by, 100
ADL. *See* Anti-Defamation League
AIPAC. *See* American Israel Public Affairs Committee
AJC. *See* American Jewish Committee
All That's Left (organization), 55
Al Qaeda, 100, 258n18
Ameinu (organization), 238n50
American Emergency Committee for Zionist Affairs (AECZA), 153
American Friends for a Safe Israel, 75–76
American Friends of Likud, 59
American Friends of Peace Now, 42
American Israel Public Affairs Committee (AIPAC), 4, 14, 35, *145*, 176; battle over U.S. loan guarantees, 157–58; board members of, 269n75; centrist politics of, 95, 163, 168; Citizens for a Nuclear Free Iran of, 270n92; diversity initiative of, 264n16; Gaza disengagement and, 162; history of, 154–57; J Street and, 5, 79, 148, 163; lawmakers' trips to Israel paid by, 264n14; Olmert and, 162–63; Oslo peace process and, 160–61; political influence of, 147, 148, 165–73; predecessor of, 30; Rabin and, 160, 265n37; second Intifada and, 161; Shamir and, 157; ZOA and, 159, 168

American Jewish Committee (AJC), 30, 123–38, 180, 256n2; criticism of Israel by, 72; on civil discourse, 119; J Street and, 79
American Jewish Congress, 273n16
American Jewish Joint Distribution Committee, 180
American Jewish World Service (AJWS), 188–89
Americans for a Safe Israel, *140*, 159
Americans for Peace and Tolerance, 79
Americans for Peace Now (APN), 59, 77–79, *140*, 248n159; predecessor of, 42; Bush and, 158; Clinton and, 159; Obama and, 170–71
American Zionist Committee for Public Affairs, 155
American Zionist Council of Public Affairs, 30
American Zionist Emergency Council (AZEC), 153–55
Anti-Defamation League (ADL), 180; criticism of Israel by, 72, 239n65; on civil discourse, 119; J Street and, 79, 82
anti-Semitism, 11, 24–25, 112; anti-Zionism as, 89, 95; assimilation and, 25; BDS campaign as, 97; philo-Semitism and, 7; Jewish criticism of Israel and, 69
antiwar movement, 105
apartheid, 94, 106, 199, 245n131
Arab American organizations, 84
Arafat, Yasser, 95, 160, 249n8, 258n18
Ashley, Sharon, 247n153
Avedon, Joshua, 189
Avodah (organization), 188–89

Kelner, Shaul, 25
Kenen, Isaiah, 155
Khalidi, Rashid, 85
Kissinger, Henry, 156
Klarman, Seth, 186, 278n66
Klein, Morton, 100, *145*, 159, 173, 265n31
Klug, Brian, 252n49
Klutznick, Philip, 155
Kotler-Berkowitz, Laurence, 198, 287n68
Krauthammer, Charles, 100
Kristol, William, 100, 249n13, 269n72
Kurtzer, Daniel, 266n37

"land for peace," 98, 125
Labor Party, 40, 41, 240n77, 250n18; AIPAC
    and, 160
Land of Israel (*Eretz Yisrael*), 27, 29, 99,
    249n12
Lebanon War, First (1982), 42, 45, 52, 78,
    229n118, 251n30
Lebanon War, Second (2006), 45, 122,
    282n11
Lerman, Antony, 237n48
Lerner, Motti, 67
Lerner, Rachel, 81
Lewis, Sheldon, 117
liberalism, 132, 178, 208, 260n37
Lieberman, Avigdor, 59
Liebman, Charles, 23, 25, 90; on Land of
    Israel, 249n12; on American Jews' view
    of Israel, 28–29, 47
Likud Party, 33, 51, 52, 228n105; AIPAC
    and, 157; rise of, 41–42
Likud USA, 59
Lipset, Seymour M., 285n39
Livni, Tzipi, 165

Madrid peace conference (1991), 125
Magid, Shaul, 30, 64, 89
marriage: interfaith, 52, 137, 196, 202–4;
    same-sex, 197, 199
Masa Israel Journey program, 55–56
Mearsheimer, John, 148, 149, 163, 263n10,
    266n48
memory, collective, 21, 37–40, 49, 114, 137
Messinger, Ruth, 280n84
Michaelson, Jay, 199
"millennials," 187–88, 203. *See also* genera-
    tional divide
Misgav, Uri, 59

Montefiore, Moses, 278n68
Mormons, 199
Morris, Benny, 46
Morse, Arthur D., 38
MoveOn (organization), 268n60
Munich Olympic games (1972), 37
Muslim American organizations, 84

National Community Relations Advisory
    Council (NCRAC), 156, 157
National Jewish Population Survey, 25, 185,
    222n16, 277n59
National Rifle Association, 147
neo-conservatives, 99–100, 150, 166, 249n13
Netanyahu, Benjamin, 59–60, 80, 133–134,
    214, 221n10, 230n125, 243n111,
    259n28, 261n46, 261n49; Clinton and,
    265n30; on Iran nuclear deal, 16–17,
    219n29; at Jewish Federations of North
    America General Assembly, 1–2, 87;
    Obama and, 16–17, 166, 169–70, 282n3;
    289n6; Oslo peace process and, 159,
    265n32; on Palestinian statehood, 96, 214
New Historians, 48
New Israel Fund (NIF), 59, 66, *140*, 220n4,
    234n13, 235n27
New Jewish Agenda, 77–79
Nixon, Richard, 156
"Not in My Name" placards, 107, *141*

Obama, Barack, 10, 276n47; American Jews'
    support for, 200, 282n3; Iran nuclear pro-
    gram and, 16–17, 170–71, 219n32; J Street
    and, 164, 169–71, 268n66; Netanyahu
    and, 16–17, 166, 169–70, 282n3, 289n6;
    Orthodox Jews and, 200, 284n25, 284n26;
    policy toward Israel of, 133, 166, 169–70,
    200, 215, 271n99, 284n26; presidential
    campaign of (2008), 268n60, 271n99
Olmert, Ehud, 61, 173; Abbas' talks with,
    162–63, 240n72, 249n8
One Israel Fund, 59
one-state solution, 74, 83, 89, 94, 108
Open Hillel campaign, 85, 136, *143*,
    246n139
Open Orthodoxy movement, 284–85n35
Open Secrets (organization), 268n61
"Operation Cast Lead" (2008–9), 45, 79, 88,
    112, 122, 247n156; effectiveness of, 125;
    American Jewish support for, 257n11

313

Zionism (*continued*)
32, 64, 89, 106; Ben-Gurion on, 225n57;
Brandeis and, 32, 151–52; "classical,"
31, 223n28; "cultural," 226n67; "European," 32; "liberal," 101–3, 178, 238n50,
250n18; "messianic religious," 27,
260n36; "philanthropic," 32; "post-Zionists," 106; "pro-Israelism" versus, 29–30;
"Revisionist," 99, 249n11

Zionist Organization of America (ZOA),
30, 73, *145*; Adelson as major donor
to, 97, 278n67; AIPAC and, 159, 168;
on Breira, 75; on global terrorism, 100;
on J Street, 79; lobbying by, 152–53,
159–60, 162, 170, 173; membership in,
226n66, 226n71; Oslo Accords and, 159,
160; Rabin on, 159
Zochrot (organization), 235n27